INDUSTRIAL RELATIONS IN IRELAND

THEORY AND PRACTICE

Patrick Gunnigle, Gerard McMahon
and
Gerard Fitzgerald

GILL & MACMILLAN

Gill & Macmillan Ltd
Goldenbridge
Dublin 8
with associated companies throughout the world
© Patrick Gunnigle, Gerard McMahon and Gerard Fitzgerald 1995

0 7171 2257 3

Index compiled by Julitta Clancy

Design and print origination in Ireland by
O'K Graphic Design, Dublin

Contents

List of Abbreviations   xi

List of Figures and Tables   xiv

1. INDUSTRIAL RELATIONS: A CONTEXTUAL AND THEORETICAL OVERVIEW   1

1.1. Introduction: What Do We Mean by Industrial Relations?   1
1.2. The Contextual Setting of Industrial Relations   6
    1.2.1. History and Industrial Relations   7
    1.2.2. Economics and Industrial Relations   10
    1.2.3. The Labour Market and Industrial Relations   14
    1.2.4. Politics and Industrial Relations   18
1.3. The Role of Theory in Industrial Relations   22
    1.3.1. Pluralist Analysis   23
    1.3.2. Unitary Analysis   24
    1.3.3. Marxist Analysis   26
    1.3.4. Social Action Analysis   27
    1.3.5. Systems Analysis   28
    1.3.6. Conclusion and Critique of Models   29

2. THE ROLE OF THE LAW   31

2.1. Individual Employment Law   31
    2.1.1. The Contract of Employment   32
    2.1.2. Dismissal and the Law   33
    2.1.3. Employment Equality and the Law   38
    2.1.4. Health, Safety and Welfare at Work   42
    2.1.5. Other Employment Legislation   45
2.2. Collective Labour Law   49
    2.2.1. The Evolution of Irish Collective Labour Law   50
    2.2.2. The Reform of Collective Labour Law—The Debate   55
    2.2.3. The Industrial Relations Act 1990   58

3. THE ROLE OF THE STATE   63

3.1. Introduction   63
3.2. State Approaches to Industrial Relations   65
    3.2.1. Market Individualism   65
    3.2.2. Liberal Collectivism   66

3.2.3. Corporatism 66
3.2.4. Bargained Corporatism 68
3.3. The Changing Nature of Irish State Strategies 69
3.4. The State as a Provider of Dispute Resolution Facilities 69
3.4.1. The Labour Court 71
3.4.2. The Employment Appeals Tribunal 76
3.4.3. The Labour Relations Commission 80
3.4.4. Rights Commissioners 87
3.4.5. Equality Officers 89
3.5. The State as Legislator 91
3.6. The State as an Employer—Industrial Relations in the Public
Sector 92

4. TRADE UNIONS 95

4.1. Introduction 95
4.2 The Historical Development of Trade Unions 95
4.3. The Nature and Role of Trade Unions 99
4.3.1. Alternatives to Trade Union Organisation 99
4.3.2. The Role and Objectives of Trade Unions 100
4.3.3. Legal Position 101
4.4. Types of Trade Union 102
4.4.1. Craft Unions 103
4.4.2. General Unions 104
4.4.3. White-Collar Unions 105
4.5. Trade Union Structure and Government 106
4.5.1. Irish Congress of Trade Unions (ICTU) 110
4.5.2. Trades Councils 111
4.6. Trade Union Membership 111
4.7. Trade Union Density 113
4.7.1. Trade Union Membership at Organisation Level 114
4.7.2. Factors Affecting Union Density 115
4.8. Trade Union Recognition 117
4.8.1. Trade Union Recognition at Organisation Level 118
4.8.2. Factors Affecting Union Recognition 120
4.9. Trade Union Influence 122
4.10. Current Issues Facing Irish Trade Unions 123
4.10.1. Declining Membership 123
4.10.2. Trade Union Rationalisation 123
4.10.3. British and Irish Unions 124
4.10.4. Trade Union Democracy 125
4.10.5. Trade Unions and Human Resource Management
(HRM) Practices 125
4.11. Conclusion 132

5. EMPLOYER ASSOCIATIONS   133

5.1. Introduction   133
5.2. Employer Objectives in Industrial Relations   133
5.3. The Historical Development of Employer Organisation   135
5.4. Employer Associations in Ireland   135
    5.4.1. The Irish Business and Employers' Confederation (IBEC)   136
    5.4.2. Construction Industry Federation (CIF)   138
    5.4.3. Other Employer Associations in Ireland   138
    5.4.4. The Irish Employers' Confederation   139
    5.4.5. Other Employer Groupings   139
5.5. Objectives of Employer Associations   140
5.6. Membership of Employer Organisations   143
5.7. Advantages and Disadvantages of Employer Association
    Membership   145
5.8. The Governing Structure of Employer Associations   148
    5.8.1. The Governing Structure of the Irish Business and
        Employers' Confederation   151
5.9. Employer Association Membership and Managerial
    Approaches in Industrial Relations   152
5.10.Employer Association Services   153
    5.10.1. Disputes Procedures and Adjustment   159
5.11.Summary   159

6. COLLECTIVE BARGAINING   161

6.1. What Is Collective Bargaining?   161
6.2. The Nature of Collective Bargaining   162
    6.2.1. Three Theories of Collective Bargaining   165
6.3. The Structure of Collective Bargaining   167
    6.3.1. Bargaining Levels   167
    6.3.2. Bargaining Units, Forms and Scope   169
6.4. Collective Bargaining—An Appraisal   170
6.5. Collective Bargaining in Ireland   172
6.6. The Development of Collective Bargaining and
    Pay Determination in Ireland   173
    6.6.1. The Beginnings   174
    6.6.2. The Wage Rounds   175
    6.6.3. The Evolution of the Wage Rounds   177
    6.6.4. The Emergence of National Wage Agreements   179
    6.6.5. The National Wage Agreements   180
    6.6.6. The Evolution of the National Wage Agreements   181
    6.6.7. The National Understandings   184

6.6.8. The Performance of Centralised Bargaining, 1970–81   186
6.6.9. The Experience of Decentralised Bargaining, 1982–87   187
6.6.10. The Programme for National Recovery (PNR)   189
6.6.11. The Programme for Economic and Social Progress (PESP)   193
6.6.12. The Programme for Competitiveness and Work (PCW)   195
6.6.13. A Note on the Future   197

7. COLLECTIVE BARGAINING PRACTICE   199

7.1. Introduction   199
7.2. Industrial Relations Negotiations   200
     7.2.1. The Negotiating Process   201
     7.2.2. Stages in Bargaining   208
7.3. Towards Effective Negotiation   211
     7.3.1. Industrial Conflict   212
     7.3.2. Forms of Industrial Conflict   213
     7.3.3. An Overview of Irish Strike Patterns   214
     7.3.4. Other Forms of Industrial Action   219
     7.3.5. Conflict Resolution   220
7.4. The Handling of Grievances and Disputes   221
     7.4.1. Grievance and Disputes Procedures   222
     7.4.2. The Grievance Interview   225
     7.4.3. External Referral   226
7.5. Discipline Administration   227
     7.5.1. Legal Context for Discipline Administration   228
     7.5.2. Disciplinary Procedures   229

8. HUMAN RESOURCE MANAGEMENT AND INDUSTRIAL RELATIONS:
THE CURRENT DEBATE AND IRISH CONTEXT   237

8.1. Introduction   237
8.2. Human Resource Management   238
     8.2.1. The Emergence of Human Resource Management in Ireland   240
     8.2.2. HRM and the Non-Union Phenomenon   240
     8.2.3. The Nature of Human Resource Management   241
     8.2.4. HRM versus Traditional Personnel Management   244
     8.2.5. Contradictions and Inconsistencies in HRM   245
8.3. Business Strategy and Personnel Policy Choice   248
     8.3.1. Levels of Strategic Decision Making   249
     8.3.2. The Importance of Competitive Strategy   252
     8.3.3. Linking Business/Competitive Strategy and
            Personnel/Industrial Relations Policy Choice   253
     8.3.4. Models of Business Strategy—Personnel Policy Linkages   255
8.4. The Influence of the Product Market   262
8.5. Summary and Conclusions   263

9. CHANGING PATTERNS OF INDUSTRIAL RELATIONS: THE SIGNIFICANCE
   OF MANAGEMENT STYLES IN INDUSTRIAL RELATIONS   266

9.1. Introduction   266
9.2. Management Styles in Industrial Relations   267
   9.2.1. The Meaning of Management Style   267
   9.2.2. Strategic Decision Making and Industrial Relations   268
   9.2.3. The Impact of Strategic Choice on Industrial Relations
          Style   270
9.3. The Context for Choice: Influences on Industrial Relations
     Style   271
   9.3.1. The External Environment   272
   9.3.2. The Internal Environment   275
   9.3.3. Managerial Values and Ideology   276
9.4. The Nature of Choice: Dimensions of Industrial Relations
     Style   279
   9.4.1. Strategic Integration   279
   9.4.2. Individualism   280
   9.4.3. Collectivism   281
9.5. Personnel Policy Choice and Industrial Relations Style   283
   9.5.1. Key Areas of Personnel Policy Choice   283
9.6. The Outcome of Choice: Categorising Management Styles
     in Industrial Relations   289
   9.6.1. Frames of Reference   289
   9.6.2. 'Ideal-typical' Style Typologies   291
9.7. Changing Patterns of Industrial Relations: Explaining Develop-
     ments in Management Styles in the Republic of Ireland   293
   9.7.1. Industrial Relations in Ireland: Towards a Typology of
          Management Styles   294
   9.7.2. Analysing Management Styles   298
   9.7.3. Emergent Management Styles in Ireland   298
9.8. Conclusions   299

10.   CONTEMPORARY DEVELOPMENTS IN INDUSTRIAL RELATIONS   301

10.1. Introduction   301
10.2. The Context for Developments in Irish Industrial Relations   301
   10.2.1. Public Policy   302
10.3. Change in Industrial Relations   304
   10.3.1. Labour Market Developments   304
   10.3.2. The Growth of 'Atypical' Employment   306
   10.3.3. The Flexibility Debate   308
10.4. Employee Participation   310
   10.4.1. Options in Participation   312

10.4.2. Trade Unions and Employee Participation   315
10.4.3. Achieving Participation   317
10.5. Management–Employee Communications   318
10.6. Technological Change   320
10.6.1. The Labour Market Impact   321
10.6.2. Employer and Trade Union Perspectives   322
10.6.3. Implementing Technological Change   323
10.6.4. Technology Agreements   324
10.7. New Work Organisation and Quality Initiatives   326
10.7.1. Why Does TQM Fail?   328
10.8. The European Union and Developments in Industrial
Relations   331
10.9. Conclusions   334

Bibliography   336
Index   355

List of Abbreviations

ACAS	Advisory Conciliation and Arbitration Service
ADC	Annual Delegates Conference
AEEU	Amalgamated Engineering and Electrical Union
AGM	Annual General Meeting
ASTI	Association of Secondary Teachers of Ireland
ASTMS	Association of Scientific Technical and Managerial Staffs
ATGWU	Amalgamated Transport and General Workers' Union
BATU	Building and Allied Trades' Unions
C&A	Conciliation and Arbitration
CIF	Construction Industry Federation
CII	Confederation of Irish Industry
CPI	Consumer Price Index
CPSU	Civil and Public Services' Union
CWU	Communications Workers' Union
DEA	Dairy Executives' Association
DUES	The Development of Trade Union Systems in Western European Societies after World War II
EAT	Employment Appeals Tribunal
EC	European Commission/European Community
EEA	Employment Equality Agency
EEC	European Economic Community
ELC	Employer Labour Conference
ER	Employee Relations
ERO	Employment Regulation Order
ERS	Employee Relations Services
ESB	Electricity Supply Board
ESBOA	ESB Officers' Association
ESRI	Economic and Social Research Institute
EU	European Union
FAS	Foras Aiseanna Saothair; Training and Employment Authority
FIE	Federation of Irish Employers
FUE	Federated Union of Employers
FWUI	Federated Workers' Union of Ireland
GDP	Gross Domestic Product

GNP	Gross National Product
HBS	Harvard Business School
HR	Human Resources
HRM	Human Resource Management
HSA	Health and Safety Authority
IBEC	Irish Business and Employers' Confederation
IBOA	Irish Bank Officials' Association
ICTU	Irish Congress of Trade Unions
IDATU	Irish Distributive and Administrative Trade Union
IEC	Irish Employers' Confederation
ILO	International Labour Organisation/Office
IMI	Irish Management Institute
IMPACT	Irish Municipal, Public and Civil Trade Union
INO	Irish Nurses' Organisation
INTO	Irish National Teachers' Association
INUVGATA	Irish National Union of Vintners, Grocers and Allied Trades Assistants
IOE	International Organisation of Employers
IPA	Institute of Public Administration
IPC	Irish Productivity Centre
IPM	Institute of Personnel Management
IQA	Irish Quality Association
IR	Industrial Relations
IRN	*Industrial Relations News*
IRO	Industrial Relations Officer
ISO	International Standards Organisation
ITGWU	Irish Transport and General Workers' Union
ITUC	Irish Trades Union Congress
JIC	Joint Industrial Council
JIT	just-in-time (system)
JLC	Joint Labour Committee
LGNSB	Local Government Staff Negotiations Board
LRC	Labour Relations Commission
MBO	Management by Objectives
MNC	Multinational Company
MPGWU	Marine Port and General Workers' Union
MSF	Manufacturing Services and Finance Union
NBRWU	National Bus and Rail Workers' Union

NESC	National Economic and Social Council
NEETU	National Engineering and Electrical Trade Union
NIEC	National Industrial and Economic Council
NU	National Understanding
NUDL	National Union of Dock Labourers
NUR	National Union of Railwaymen
NUSMWI	National Union of Sheet Metal Workers of Ireland
NWA	National Wage Agreement
OECD	Organisation for Economic Co-operation and Development
OPATSI	Operative Plasterers' and Allied Trades' Society of Ireland
PAYE	Pay As You Earn
PCW	Programme for Competitiveness and Work
PESP	Programme for Economic and Social Progress
PNR	Programme for National Recovery
PRP	Performance-related Pay
PSA	Psychiatric Nurses' Association
PSEU	Public Services Executive Union
PWC	Price Waterhouse Cranfield
QC	Quality Circle
quango	quasi-autonomous non-governmental organisation
QWL	Quality of Working Life
RC	Rights Commissioner(s)
RTC	Regional Technical College
SIPTU	Services Industrial Professional and Technical Union
TD	Teachta Dála
TEEU	Technical, Electrical and Engineering Union
TQM	Total Quality Management
TUI	Teachers' Union of Ireland
UCATT	Union of Construction and Allied Trades and Technicians
UCD	University College, Dublin
UNICE	Union of Industrial and Employers Confederations in Europe
VEC	Vocational Education Committee
WCM	World-Class Manufacturing
WIRS	Workplace Industrial Relations Survey

List of Figures and Tables

FIGURES

1.1	Model of the Irish system of industrial relations	5
3.1	State institutions for dispute resolution	70
3.2	Labour Court referral procedure	72
4.1	Model workplace trade union structure	107
5.1	Organisation structure of IBEC	151
6.1	Levels of collective bargaining	167
7.1	Adversarial and co-operative model of negotiation	201
7.2	The negotiating process	202
7.3	Management–trade union bargaining range	205
7.4	Stages in bargaining	209
7.5	Strike activities in Ireland, 1922–91	215–6
7.6	Grievance procedure	223
8.1	HBS model of Human Resource Management	241
8.2	Definitions of Human Resource Management	242
8.3	A theory of Human Resource Management	243
8.4	Levels of strategic decision making	249
8.5	Upstream and downstream strategic decisions	250
8.6	Product market change, business strategy and industrial relations	262
9.1	Management style in industrial relations	268
9.2	Continuum of strategic decision making in industrial relations	269
9.3	Product market conditions and industrial relations style	274
9.4	Dimension 1: strategic integration	280
9.5	Dimension 2: individualism	281
9.6	Dimension 3: collectivism	282
9.7	Management style and personnel policy choice in industrial relations	284
9.8	Management styles in industrial relations	292

TABLES

1.1 Labour force classification by males, females and married females, 1977–92   16

1.2 Employment changes by sector, 1961–92   16

2.1 Key differences between contracts of service and contracts for service   32

2.2 Summary of other employment legislation in Ireland   45

2.3 Collective labour legislation enacted by the Oireachtas   54

3.1 State approaches to industrial relations   65

3.2 Labour Court recommendations   74

3.3 Labour Court determinations, 1978–92   76

3.4 Summary of appeals referred in 1993 and the outcome of the appeals disposed of in 1993   77

3.5 Number of EAT referrals, 1978–93   79

3.6 Conciliation service referrals, 1971–92   83

3.7 Rights Commissioner activity, 1979–91   89

3.8 Number of Equality Officer recommendations, 1978–92   90

3.9 Access to adjudication bodies in the public sector   93

4.1 Trade unions and staff associations: contrasts   100

4.2 Trade union membership, 1945–90   111

4.3 Trade union membership by size of union, 1991   113

4.4 Large trade unions in Ireland   113

4.5 International employment union density   114

4.6 Trade union density   114

4.7 Level of union membership by sector   115

4.8 Union membership by size   115

4.9 Trade union recognition   118

4.10 Union status by industry   119

4.11 Union recognition by origin of company   120

4.12 Union recognition in established and greenfield companies   120

4.13 Change in trade union influence: organisational level   122

4.14 Numbers of trade unions in Ireland, 1980–90   124

4.15 Union status and utilisation of merit pay and profit-sharing schemes   128

4.16 Union status and numerical flexibility   129

4.17 Union status and flexible employment practices   130

4.18 Union status and provision of financial information/business strategy information to employees   131

4.19 Union status and trends in communication   131

5.1 Employer associations in Ireland, 1993   136

5.2 Advantages and disadvantages of employer association membership   146

5.3 Per capita subscription rates IBEC, 1994   148

5.4 Employer association membership and utilisation by country of ownership in greenfield companies   153

5.5 Employer association membership and utilisation by trade union recognition in greenfield companies   153

5.6 Utilisation of the advisory and consultancy services   155

5.7 FIE/IBEC involvement in mediation, arbitration and negotiations   156

6.1 The bargaining level for wage rounds, 1946–70   176

6.2 The terms and conditions of the National Wage Agreements   181

6.3 The terms and conditions of the National Understandings   185

6.4 Private sector pay increases, 1981–87   188

6.5 Pay terms of the Programme for Competitiveness and Work   197

7.1 Public and private sector strike activity, 1960–92   217

7.2 Working days lost — strikes, 1946–92   217

7.3 Official and unofficial strikes: frequency and working days lost, 1980–91   218

8.1 Personnel management and Human Resource Management compared   245

8.2 Linking business strategy and personnel/IR policy   256

8.3 Linking business strategy, employee characteristics and personnel/IR policy choice   257

8.4 Personnel policy menus   259

9.1 Indicative strategic decisions impacting on industrial relations   270

9.2 Role models of the specialist personnel function   287

10.1 Employment changes by sector, 1961–89   304

10.2 Ireland, some basic facts (1991)   305

10.3 Part-time employment, 1979–89   306

10.4 Temporary employment, 1983–89   306

10.5 Self-employment, 1979–89   307

10.6 Atypical/typical employment, 1983–89   307

10.7 Change in reward systems   310

10.8 Utilisation of merit-/performance-related pay   310

10.9 Communications with employees   318

10.10 Management communications on strategy and financial performance   319

CHAPTER ONE

Industrial Relations: A Contextual and Theoretical Overview

1.1. INTRODUCTION: WHAT DO WE MEAN BY INDUSTRIAL RELATIONS?

The subject area of industrial relations is one of the most discussed specialist areas of organisational management. The public prominence of the topic is primarily attributable to its headline-making capacity when in the throes of such activitities as strike action, mass redundancy and wage bargaining. These events materialise at plant, industry and national level, commanding extensive media coverage and widespread public interest and concern. However, the topic is often shrouded in confusion and anxiety, at the expense of insightful analysis. This factor undoubtedly contributes to the ongoing public pronouncements which urge dramatic (and often ill-conceived) policy changes in the area. Frequently, in the heat of strike or closure situations, states of 'moral panic' consume the nation. Yet, it can be argued that there are other, more pervasive, persistent, injurious and controllable work-related phenomena, like health and safety statistics or absenteeism levels, which might be adjudged to be more newsworthy and deserving of our attention.

The term 'industrial relations' does not easily lend itself to definition. The primary focus of the subject, however, is with the employment relationship of over one million employees in the Republic of Ireland, working across all employment sectors and entity types. These include national or local government, in private companies extending from multinational subsidiaries to local corner shops, in semi-state companies and single domestic employers and co-operatives. Even the term 'industrial relations' itself has connotations of the traditional unionised blue-collar environment in the manufacturing sector, whilst the term 'employee relations' conjures up images of the non- or less unionised white-collar services sector. In this text, for ease of classification, the terms are assumed by the authors to be synonymous.

Like most subjects, a narrow conception does not facilitate genuine understanding. Therefore the subject of industrial relations can best be interpreted in the wider context of the historic, political, social and economic processes which underly the regulation of working-life relationships. The broad base of the subject, therefore, draws upon a range of disciplines to facilitate the development of an understanding of both individual and collective relationships, in white- and blue-collar work environments, and at plant, sector, national and international levels. The complexity of the topic has necessitated the adaptation of a vast array of other specialist subject areas (e.g. labour law, labour market economics) to accommodate a comprehensive analysis of all the issues which affect people at work.

Traditionally the subject matter has been concerned with considerations about trade unions. This emphasis, whilst understandable, fails to acknowledge the importance of contextual matters and contrasting perspectives on the same phenomena. These aspects are addressed in this opening chapter, whilst the centrality of the other institutions and entity types, role players, procedures, processes and products of the subject matter are reviewed in subsequent chapters. Accordingly, in addition to developing an appreciation of the main contextual influences and theoretical perspectives, familiarity with the following range of institutions and issues is warranted to enable the student to gain an informed view on the nature of and scope for development of our industrial relations system:

Institutions: trade unions, trade union section and branch committees, union confederations/national affiliations, the Irish Congress of Trade Unions (ICTU), employer organisations, the Irish Business and Employers' Confederation (IBEC), trades councils, the Labour Relations Commission (LRC) , the Labour Court, the Employer Labour Conference (ELC), the Employment Appeals Tribunal (EAT), the law courts, the European Commission and Parliament, Joint Labour Committees (JLCs), Joint Industrial Councils (JICs), Government departments, the Employment Equality Agency (EEA), Health and Safety Authority (HSA), specially appointed commissions (e.g. on industrial relations, health and safety) and relevant educational and research institutes.

Role players: shop stewards and shop-steward organisation, full-time trade union and employer organisation officials, personnel or human resource specialists, arbitrators, conciliators, adjudicators, Equality Officers, other third-party actors and Government Ministers.

Processes/Procedures: third-party referrals, strike and other industrial actions, union recognition attainment, establishing and maintaining closed shops and non-union entities, disciplinary, grievance and dispute handling procedures, consultation, involvement, participation and negotiation processes and skills.

Issues: the role of the State, the European Commission and the European

2

Parliament; the role of collective and individual labour law, the future role of trade unions and employer organisations, political decision making and national-level economic and social bargaining; economic (including industrial and employment) policy, strikes, lock-outs, picketing, pay levels and payment systems, terms and conditions of employment, union recognition and avoidance phenomena, health and safety, new technology, employee flexibility, total quality management and world-class manufacturing, employee involvement/participation, human resource management and related management styles or approaches to employee relations.

In so far as is possible this text, whilst outlining and analysing the various dimensions of the subject listed above, attempts to adopt a factual and unbiased approach to the study of industrial relations. The very nature of the subject matter inevitably means, however, that many aspects of the topic are contentious. Accordingly, an effort is made to steer a middle line, whilst outlining the central strands to the main differing viewpoints that have been expressed on the various aspects of the subject. Of course, an attractive aspect of the topic is that it allows students to develop their own opinions and to make up their own minds as to the merits of the contrasting perspectives outlined. The text therefore endeavours to facilitate this process by producing a general overview and analysis of the more significant contextual, theoretical, institutional, substantive and procedural aspects, whilst reviewing what are generally adjudged in the literature to be the more salient trends in the labour relations arena. The more contentious or debatable dimensions of the subject, including the range of political arguments and the plethora of factual data which lends itself to a multitude of interpretations, are reviewed in as objective a manner as is possible. Hopefully, then, the student will develop his/her own views and position on the issues in question.

However, it is important that the development of particular viewpoints and perspectives be embedded in an appreciation of the many central features of the system of industrial relations and the facts in and around which it operates. Accordingly then, this text endeavours to provide a balanced and comprehensive treatment of the topic, without undue emphasis on any specific area. By maximising the descriptive and minimising the analytical or academic orientation, the text opts for a practical approach to the subject matter. Where students wish to further explore particular aspects of a theme, an extensive referencing system has been adopted by the authors to facilitate same.

The structure of the text was designed to address the subject in an orderly fashion, by linking each chapter to its successor and proceeding, where possible, on a block-building process. By dividing all of the chapters into a series of sections and subsections it is intended to make the material more manageable, and to appropriately differentiate the various topics, rather than allow one topic merge into the next without any indication of a change.

In figure 1.1 an attempt is made to present a working model or overview of the Irish industrial relations system. This spans the co-operative and conflictual relationships at the heart of the system and the bargaining processes and products, or outcomes, as negotiated at organisational, industry and national levels. Where such processes fail to produce consensus the third parties are in place to assist the players in reaching agreement. Each component of the model is outlined and critically evaluated at an appropriate point in the text. For example, in this opening chapter the main contrasting theoretical perspectives and contextual factors which have determined the current—and will influence the future—shape of the industrial relations system are reviewed. The system itself can be viewed from many different angles or perspectives. However, though no one view yields a perfect understanding, each adds to our insight. The location of five theoretical perspectives on the outer perimeter of figure 1.1 is designed to convey the potential of each and all of these theories to provide their own insights, or of elements of more than one of these theoretical perspectives, or frames of reference, to explain the same phenomena or even different parts of the same system. In addition, the relevance of the perspective adopted by any individual or interest group should not, as we shall see, be underestimated. It may well be reflected in, for example:
– the nature of legislation introduced by the politician or his/her party;
– the approach to union recognition adopted by the General Manager or his/her Board of Directors;
– the intransigence cum preparedness to recommend industrial action by the worker representative and his/her union.

The prevalence of dual direction arrows attempts to convey the inextricable interrelatedness of the various components of the system. This may be reflected in a vast array of exchanges such as trade union opposition to legal intervention on grounds of history or tradition, the reform of third-party dispute-settling agencies owing to the nature and volume of (conflict) cases coming before them, the impact of the terms of a collective agreement reached at national, industrial or organisational level by employees and employer(s) (or their representative organisations) on the state of the economy, or even the content of a plant-level procedural agreement relating to disciplinary action as a result of international and national political influences culminating in legislative decisions as to what constitutes an unfair dismissal. Figure 1.1 also highlights the significant influence of such contextual factors as history, economics, technology and politics (amongst others) on the current shape of our system. These are dealt with in this chapter.

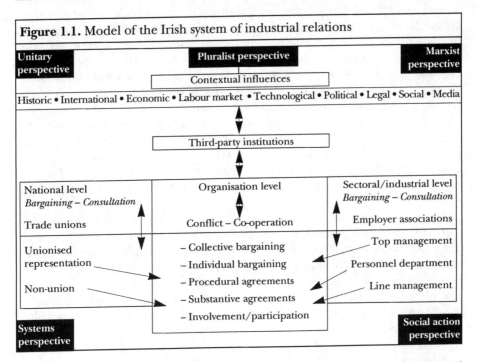

Figure 1.1. Model of the Irish system of industrial relations

Chapter 2 exposes the reader to the most significant society regulator of trade union, employer and employee relationships—the law. This chapter is divided into two main sections to accommodate the contrasting objectives of collective labour law and its preoccupation with trade unions and their operations, and individual labour law—which is primarily concerned with the rights of workers *vis-à-vis* their employers.

Chapters 3, 4 and 5 examine the main components of the system's institutional framework, i.e. the State, trade unions and employer organisations. Industrial relations has evolved many different organisations and institutions to act as the machinery or vehicle for the regulation of the employment relationship at plant, industry and national levels. The State's role has always been significant—particularly in the context of its legislative role—and in recent decades as a provider of fora for the resolution of issues which employees and employers (or their respective representative organisations) fail to agree amongst themselves. Indeed, given that about one in three of all persons engaged in non-agricultural employment operates in the public sector, it would be remiss not to also review the State's own internal industrial relations mechanisms. The main parties to the institutionalised relationship are, of course, the trade unions and employer organisations. The formation of these groups, their relative power and respective values and interests, exert a fundamental impact on the way employment relationships are managed and develop.

In chapter 6 the collective bargaining process, which is so central to industrial relations, is examined. For the student of industrial relations an understanding of the nature, development and skills associated with the collective bargaining and negotiation processes is crucial. It is through the practice of negotiation that those economic, social and political issues which structure, and are inherent to the employment relationship, are resolved. In this chapter the commonplace differentiation between the substantive and procedural products of the bargaining process is recognised. The substantive products span the various details of the effort–reward relationship (e.g. remuneration and conditions), whilst the procedural dimensions are concerned with how the substantive issues are addressed (i.e. who has the right or power to negotiate via what administrative or bargaining arrangements).

Given the extensive scope provided by the employment relationship for conflict over both substantive and procedural issues, chapter 7 provides a descriptive and analytical overview of the nature of conflict, with particular emphasis on strikes. In the face of the public's preoccupation with industrial action, together with the trade union movement's insistence upon the retention of the 'fundamental right' to withdraw labour in the event of total disagreement with their negotiating counterparts, this topic warrants detailed consideration.

Having examined the nature and relevance of 'human resource management' policies and practices in industrial relations in chapter 8, an attempt is made to broadly distinguish between the varying organisational approaches to the management of the labour relations function in the following chapter. In particular, given the influx of multinational subsidiaries to the Republic of Ireland over the past thirty years, one can distinguish significant differences in the style of employee or human resource management policies being pursued, e.g. single or dual union pre-production agreements, non-union policies.

In chapter 10 emerging trends and likely developments or influences on the future shape and nature of the system are considered. These include the extent and impact of flexibility initiatives (e.g. part-time work, multi-skilling), technological developments, total quality and world-class manufacturing initiatives, employee involvement and participation practices and international (including the European Commission — EC) influences, trends and developments.

1.2. THE CONTEXTUAL SETTING OF INDUSTRIAL RELATIONS

Any initiative designed to analyse and prescribe in the area of Irish industrial relations requires some familiarity with those influences which have helped, or forced, the system to adopt its present shape and character. The nature and structure of trade unions, employer organisations, specialist Government-funded institutions in the area, workplace practices and managerial styles, legislative initiatives and the plethora of voluntary arrangements in place can be more gainfully assessed from a knowledge base drawing on more than two centuries of change. This time span has thrown up a vast range of economic, political and social changes with major implications for the subject matter. Whilst there has been an astonishing array of such interrelated influences, in this section of the opening chapter an attempt will be made to accommodate the more salient of such influences under the interrelated headings of history, economics, the labour market and politics. Of course such coverage does not purport to be comprehensive, but it does provide some insight into the more salient influences shaping the nature and development of the Irish system of industrial relations.

1.2.1. HISTORY AND INDUSTRIAL RELATIONS

Historical factors are of particular relevance to the development of an understanding of industrial relations, and particularly trade-unionism, in Ireland today. The Industrial Revolution swept Britain during the eighteenth and nineteenth centuries, bringing with it factory-cum-machine type production and the further concentration of people in the large industrial towns and cities. Trade unions emerged at this time, and grew in an attempt to give redress to the perceived imbalance wrought by private enterprise capitalism and the prevalent *laissez-faire* economic orthodoxy. This economic system was underpinned by the belief that the market was the only means by which all prices, including wages (i.e. the price of labour), profits and economic priorities should be determined. Accordingly, as trade unions served to contest this perspective and practice, through efforts to improve and protect the interests of their members' terms and conditions of employment, they were identified as a real threat to the prevalent economic, social and political order.

The unions of Britain and Ireland are among the oldest institutions of the modern world. Defining a trade union as a 'continuous association of wage earners for the purpose of maintaining and improving the conditions of their working lives', Sidney and Beatrice Webb have identified the earliest such union as an association of London hatters in the reign of Charles II in the seventeenth century. In the opinion of the Webbs—among the very first writers on the subject—the Journeymen Hatters' Trade Union of Great Britain and Ireland could trace its origins back to that early association of London hatters (Boyd, 1984). The very first Irish trade union to be identified by name was the 'Regular Carpenters of Dublin', which was founded in 1764. There is also evidence that there were several unions or 'combinations' active in the Cork area in the middle of the eighteenth century. Their activities included organising strikes, picketing, destroying tools, materials and machinery, and of ostracising employers who would not give in to their demands. Eventually Parliament declared that anyone in Cork city found guilty of being a member of an unlawful trade union should be 'imprisoned not above six months, whipped in public and released only on giving recognisance of good behaviour for seven years' (Boyd, 1972). From 1770 there is an account of two weavers who were found guilty of 'combination', and were whipped through the streets of Dublin, from Newgate Prison to College Green. In 1780 the Irish Parliament passed further legislation for the suppression of all trade unions, an initiative which predated similar legislation in Britain by twenty years. The debate in Parliament was marked by a demonstration of 20,000 trade-unionists in Dublin city. Even members of the Irish clergy had condemned unions as 'iniquitous extortions' (Boyd, 1972). However, despite the legal and social pressures, unions maintained their influence, as individual employers disregarded the legal scenario and negotiated with them.

The State's role at this time was deemed to be one of facilitating the unfettered operations of the free market, and to confront and control any challenge which was adjudged to be in 'restraint of trade', e.g. trade unions. Consequently, as trade unions continued to emerge and grow, by the beginning of the nineteenth century there were a series of statutory and judicial decisions (dating back to 1729) which had served to make them illegal under a variety of headings. The official hostility toward unions may be primarily attributed to the *laissez-faire* economic 'religion' of the time, which debarred any interference with the laws of supply and demand. Furthermore, the minority ruling class feared the onset of civil disturbance—which had already been witnessed in the Irish rural context, with such secret societies as the Whiteboys and the Ribbonmen—and had been central to the outbreak of the French Revolution of 1789 and the ideas of democracy and republicanism which subsequently spread throughout Europe.

Nevertheless, Irish craft workers' trade unions continued to surface on a local basis during the nineteenth century. By the second half of the century numerous British craft unions had set up in Ireland and proceeded to absorb many of the small local associations. In a society plagued by unemployment, destitution and illness, skilled tradesmen enjoyed a relatively privileged place in society by virtue of their relatively high wages and permanent employment. For the purpose of maintaining that position they sought to increase the value of their trade by restricting access to same via an apprenticeship system. Such apprenticeships were generally confined to relatives. In addition, the craft unions endeavoured to increase the security of their members by providing mutual unemployment and sick benefits.

The increasing emergence and influence of trade-unionism in the British Isles at the time is reflected in the fact that, over the 1871–1906 period, a series of relevant enactments had been passed by Parliament which:
– granted legality to trade unions;
– protected union funds from court action;
– recognised collective bargaining; and
– legalised peaceful picketing.

Inter-union co-operation in Ireland formally emerged for the first time in the shape of Trades Councils, i.e. organisations representing trade-unionists in individual cities. Trades Councils were founded in Belfast in 1881 and in Dublin in 1884, and though primarily concerned with the interests of craft workers, their unification was a significant step in the overall development of the Irish trade union movement. With the growing disenchantment of Irish representatives at the lack of priority accorded their matters by the British Trades Union Congress, the Irish Trades Union Congress (ITUC) was established in 1894. By 1900 a total of 60,000 workers were in membership of the ITUC.

However, toward the end of the century the first efforts to organise unskilled workers in the country had begun. At this time Ireland was in the throes of the Land League disturbances. This was a mass movement designed to elevate tenants to landowners. Together with the lessons learned from the experiences of their British general worker counterparts, and from their rural counterparts via the Land League, mass organisation, solidarity and organised struggle surfaced in the trade union armoury by and on behalf of unskilled general workers. Unlike the craft unions, the general workers' unions were open to all, charged low subscription rates, provided no mutual benefits, had no control over access to work, were more inclined toward frequent and aggressive industrial action and retained quite explicit and radical political links.

However, the struggle to extend union membership and recognition beyond relatively privileged craft workers was a bitter and often bloody affair, on occasion involving the police and army in a series of repressive measures taken on behalf of the employers. Major confrontations occurred, for example, in Belfast 1907, Dublin 1908, Cork 1909 and Wexford 1911. Directly related to these events was the establishment of the Irish Transport and General Workers' Union (ITGWU) in 1909 by James Larkin. Probably the most renowned confrontation which this union became involved in was the 1913 Dublin lock-out. On 21 August 1913 200 tramway workers who had refused to leave the union were sacked. This was the first significant event in a bitter five-month conflict between the ITGWU, led by Larkin, and the Dublin Employers' Federation, established by the prominent businessman William Martin Murphy. This federation had actually been established in 1911, two years after its Cork counterpart on which it was modelled. It subsequently played a major role in the 1942 founding of the Federated Union of Employers (FUE)—later to merge with the Confederation of Irish Industry (CII) to become the foremost Irish employers' representative organisation, the Irish Business and Employers' Confederation (IBEC).

Such was the watershed effect of general or unskilled worker unionisation in Ireland that, within a month of the 1913 lock-out or strike starting, over 400 employers and 25,000 workers were in the throes of a violent confrontation. In the face of police assaults, the workers established a self-defence group

9

called the Irish Citizens' Army. A key tactic of the employer grouping was, effectively, to starve the strikers and their 80,000 dependants into submission —a tactic which was eventually to prove successful. In the immediate aftermath, however, the union was reorganised and eventually grew to become the largest trade union in the country (Larkin, 1965). Nevertheless, this was a slow process. The lack of extensive secondary industry in rural Ireland discouraged the formation of large groups of organised workers in the towns, and those that existed seldom extended beyond a single town. Yet by 1920 the ITGWU could boast a membership of 130,000 members, of whom nearly 50,000 were newly recruited farm labourers. Furthermore, affiliation levels to the ITUC had jumped from 110,000 in 1914 to 300,000 by 1921.

By this time the central objectives of trade-unionism were clearly established: firstly to secure recognition, secondly to procure collective agreements covering the terms and conditions of employment of their members, and thirdly to influence the State's legislative and policy-making processes in such areas as employment conditions, housing, health care, social welfare and education. These developments were inevitably accompanied by a significant change in the State's attitude to trade-unionism. The former hostility, intransigence and legal suppression was now replaced by recognition and accommodation—subject to the trade unions showing deference to the major economic, political and social structures or order of society.

1.2.2. ECONOMICS AND INDUSTRIAL RELATIONS

The policies and practices adopted by Irish trade unions over time are characterised by constant adaptations to the reality of political, economic and industrial life. Unlike many of their European counterparts—with strong linkages to those left-wing political parties that have experienced periods in Government—Irish unions have primarily adopted a reactive and pragmatic posture. This has entailed the adjustment of their priorities, principles and positions in what is perceived to be the best interests of their membership at any given time. This adaptability, however, also reflects an inability on the movement's part to significantly influence or determine the nature and consequent shape of the Irish economy, as it resigns itself to a practical role of persuasion within the accepted economic system or framework. Whilst such persuasion may take various guises, the more significant stakes are primarily pursued through ICTU's influence on Government, e.g. for job-creation measures and labour law revisions.

Though individual trade unions may participate in this process, either through the ICTU or in an independent capacity, their primary concern is to protect and improve the pay and conditions of their membership at plant level via collective bargaining. Similarly, they seek to secure the best deal for their clientele in the face of the employer's efficiency drive in the form of productivity-, technology- or flexibility-type initiatives. Nevertheless, it is worth noting that many pressure groups to the right of the political spectrum have little hesitancy in ascribing the rampant inflation of the 1960s and 1970s, together with current unemployment levels, to allegedly unreasonable pay demands and labour market rigidities respectively sought and (at least partially) secured by trade unions.

The relatively slow growth of Irish trade-unionism in the nineteenth and earlier part of the twentieth centuries may be attributed to the somewhat belated onset of the Industrial Revolution. The absence of high-grade coal and iron ore, at least in comparison with Great Britain, was a contributory factor to this tardy development. However, one cannot disregard the historical determinants, such as the colonisation of Ireland by England, which proceeded from the middle of the sixteenth century onwards, and undoubtedly prevented the growth of industry well before the Industrial Revolution. Such restrictions, which included a spell of tariff impositions and export restrictions, prevailed up to 1922 as Ireland was perceived as not just a political, but also an economic threat. By the time British policy had adjusted to one of free trade, in the earlier part of the nineteenth century, years of colonial exploitation had so severely weakened Irish industry that it was generally incapable of competing internationally. Consequently, throughout the nineteenth and early twentieth centuries Ireland remained primarily an agricultural economy.

Over the 1914–20 period trade union membership increased from 110,000 to 250,000 (Roche and Larragy, 1989a). However, it subsequently declined as a result of the depression in agriculture and trade during the 1920s. This decrease was inevitably accompanied by falling money wages and rising unemployment. Yet, on the strength of the legal tolerance or framework secured by their British counterparts (which had now been adopted by the new State), trade unions surfaced hesitantly, addressing themselves to issues of growth, consolidation and adaptation to the prevalent and primarily hostile economic order. Such was the stagnant nature of society, and a related lack of vision amongst the nation's leadership at this time, that considerable trade union energy was devoted to the establishment and maintenance of differentials—rather than the attainment of any wider economic and social goals. That is, a status rather than a class consciousness prevailed amongst trade union members.

Throughout the 1930s significant moves toward economic development were taken inside protectionist economic policies. These proved effective in securing the development of new industries and the expansion of older ones. However, the onset of the Second World War and the consequent shortage of material supplies, contributed to a decline of over a quarter of industrial output during this period. In fact, as late as 1946 agriculture accounted for 47 per cent of total employment, services for 36 per cent and manufacturing industry for just 17 per cent. Even that 17 per cent was predominantly characterised by small establishments—so that by 1958 only forty concerns outside the public service employed more than 500 workers (Lee, 1980). Over the 1945–50 period a short post-war recovery was experienced, which was accompanied by an increase of about 70 per cent in both strike frequency and union membership levels. Unlike the remainder of Europe, however, Ireland's economic performance in the 1950s was dissappointing—marked by emigration, balance of payments difficulties and virtual stagnation—with an actual decline in national output in the latter half of the decade. In O'Hagan's (1987) assessment:

> . . . at Government level and at civil service level, there were serious deficiencies in the quality of economic policy making, and a lack of purpose, of energy and of leadership, which was all too readily reflected at other levels of society. . . . There was in fact a policy vacuum, which was all too readily filled by short-term and short-sighted measures to preserve or bolster up uneconomic employment.

Whilst the level of trade union membership increased by over 7 per cent during the 1950s, as it undoubtedly benefited from State intervention in the economy, the level of strike frequency dropped significantly from its post-war heights as trade unions resigned themselves to the stagnation or lack of growth in the economy. The fact that by 1960 there were 123 operative trade unions—of which 84 had an enrolled membership of less than 1,000—provides some insight into the priority still being accorded status and relativity factors in the mind of the Irish worker, in preference to class consciousness or solidarity considerations (Lee, 1980). In contrast with this trend, however, was the progressive creation of a welfare state in the decades succeeding the Second World War. This reflected another view within society, whereby the State should accept responsibility for the provision of education, health and related social services—as effectively the 'haves' supported the weak or 'have-nots'—with equality of, rather than ability to, access dominating public policy. This perspective also dominated the economic arena as the Government persisted with the nationalisation of essential industries.

The 1960s and 1970s were periods of sustained improvements in living standards, and of considerable growth in the Irish economy. Economic development was reflected in the fact that, for example, by 1978 total output had reached two and a half times its 1926 level. This was a period of unprecedented rapid wage increases and an approximation to nearly full employment for craftsmen. Consequently, trade union membership levels rose by nearly 70 per cent (over the 1960–80 period), whilst strike frequency more than doubled. The barriers of relativity that had been established were now under pressure. Both white- and blue-collar workers engaged in some of the most ill-renowned industrial actions in the history of industrial relations, as they clamoured to preserve their differentials and position on the social ladder (McCarthy, 1973; McCarthy et al., 1975). Two of the main influences on this dramatic economic turnaround were the level of Government expenditure and the change in industrial policy. For example, Government expenditure jumped by about 20 per cent of the National Product over the 1962–76 period, whilst a revised industrial policy involved the relegation of protectionism and the encouragement of nearly 1,000 overseas companies, employing some 80,000 workers, to Ireland since the mid-1960s.

Commenting upon the changing social climate of the 1960s McCarthy (1973) suggested that it was:

> . . . a decade of upheaval. We are probably as yet too close to it to recognise its uniqueness. It was a period of national adolescence. The old structures of society were breaking down, the Second Vatican Council had shattered the timeless authoritarian image of the Roman Catholic Church. New attitudes were being painfully developed and new structures and institutions to reflect them. Television mirrored and magnified all that we did.

Indeed this period witnessed the demise of 'the deferential worker' as previously accepted values, attitudes and institutions came under challenge. The increasing media influence helped to develop a wider awareness of the outside world and facilitated a greater preparedness to question previously sacrosanct issues. Allied to this awakening was an opening-up of educational and social possibilities which had been previously denied or non-existent.

Over this period, following in the footsteps of our main trading partners, the Irish Government opted to further modify the pure *laissez-faire* approach to economic affairs and adopt a Keynesian approach to economic growth management and planning. This involved the Government in the stimulation of demand through budgetary deficits and increased expenditure, which were designed to increase levels of economic activity (via the multiplier effect) and reduce levels of unemployment. Successive Governments over this period pursued this strategy of manipulating aggregate demand, public spending and budget deficits for the attainment of full employment levels. However, this economic route brought with it a new set of ills. Chief amongst these was a spiralling level of inflation, which the Government, employers and trade unions attempted to halt via a series of national pay agreements, which came into effect from the beginning of 1971. In addition, the surge in economic confidence brought with it a drift of power to the workplace. This gave rise to the emergence of shop stewards playing a significant role in the collective bargaining process and an upsurge in unofficial industrial action, as workers seized upon the boom climate created by economic expansion, demand buoyancy and high employment levels.

By the 1980s, however, two additional problems of significance had emerged. Firstly, the accumulated foreign debt had grown from £126 million in 1972, to £7,900 million by 1985—bringing with it an increase of over £730 million in annual debt interest payments. Secondly, unemployment levels had escalated from about 6 per cent to 17 per cent over the 1971–86 period—with worse to follow. Once again, following on international trends, the Government opted for 'fiscal rectitude' through monetarist policies, primarily designed to tackle the balance of payments deficit and the attainment of international competitiveness.

Such policies, of particular relevance in the context of industrial relations, included moderate pay rises and reduced Government spending—with consequences for welfare benefit levels, Government subsidisations and public sector employment. In effect, this constituted a *'neo-laissez-faire'* economic route, involving reduced State intervention in an economy left largely to the devices of the market-place.

The advent of this 'new realism' in the 1980s and 1990s, however, has been accompanied by reduced trade union bargaining power and membership levels, spiralling unemployment and an upsurge in managerial confidence—together with instances of 'macho management' practices. As the international recession heightened coming into the 1990s, a persistent balance of payments problem, further increased unemployment and rising interest rates all combined to create real constraints and tensions between the requirements of stimulating non-inflationary recovery on the one hand, and equity and the improvement of living standards on the other. A consequence of this downturn in economic prosperity has been the intensification of divisions within society, as unemployment spirals and public expenditure on welfare benefits and services declines—just at the time when the need for them is greatest. Nevertheless, the various indices used to measure industrial action or strike levels reveal a general downward trend. This apparent decrease in trade union confidence or militancy is inevitably accompanied by a decline of nearly 13 per cent in membership levels over the 1980–89 period. Reflecting on the social and political impact of the crisis which liberal capitalism has found itself in for up to two decades, Bew et al. (1989) note:

> . . . the relative lack of class conflict. The profound changes in social and economic life . . . were not reflected in the emergence of radical politics, industrial militancy or in any fundamental change in the nature of Irish society. Ireland remained a conservative society imbued with the values of Catholicism, nationalism and ruralism, although less stridently so than in earlier periods.

1.2.3. THE LABOUR MARKET AND INDUSTRIAL RELATIONS

Though a central component of the economic framework, such is the relevance of the labour market to the evolution and operation of the Irish industrial relations system that it warrants separate consideration. In 1993, out of a population of about 3.5 million, there were approximately 1.4 million people available for work. Despite the proliferation of Government-sponsored training and education schemes, together with constraining amendments to the methodology employed for the calculation of unemployment numbers, the out-of-work figure has been escalating since the beginning of the last decade. In fact, over the 1979–93 period, unemployment jumped by about 230 per cent. By early 1993 over 300,000 people—or over 20 per cent of the labour force—were classified as unemployed. Beyond the impact of the long-running international (and consequently national) economic recession, the main causal factor giving rise to this scenario is the size of the labour force.

The three key influences on the size of the labour force are the numbers in the population in each age group, the percentages in each age (and sex) group that are active in the labour market and levels of emigration or immigration. Arising from these pressures or influences over the past twenty-five years has been a constantly increasing labour force size. Despite the declining birth-rate since 1980 this trend is set to continue into the early years of the next century, albeit at a decelerating rate. On the matter of activity rates there is evidence that the youth (i.e. fifteen to twenty-four-year olds) are increasingly opting to remain inside the educational system, males over fifty-five years are opting for early retirement, and that there is a significant increase in the participation rate of (mainly married) females in the twenty-five to forty-four years of age bracket (see table 1.1). Leddin and Walsh (1990) attempt to explain these phenomena which:

> . . . can be understood as responses to economic factors. High unemployment undoubtedly encouraged young people to postpone entry into the labour force, while many older people were offered early retirement by firms that were anxious to reduce their labour force. The increasing participation of married women in the paid labour force reflects more complex factors including the fall in the birth rate and higher levels of educational attainment among women. It also seems that more job opportunities have been available in the occupations where women are traditionally employed. There have also been changes in legislation making it harder to exclude women from employment.

The relative decline in male employment levels, together with the associated expansion in female employment (see table 1.1)—which is mainly evident in retail distribution, insurance, financial/business, professional and personal services—has a significant bearing on the nature of the industrial relations system. For example, the growth of part-time, temporary and seasonal work opportunities is primarily a female phenomenon, with implications for the rising incidence and extent of low pay, minimal job security and decreasing union membership cum collective bargaining strength. These consequences may be attributed to a traditionally lower trade union density level amongst part-time (women) workers employed in sectors of the economy which trade unions have traditionally found difficult to penetrate.

15

Table 1.1. Labour force classification by males, females and married females, 1977–92 (in thousands, % in parentheses)

Year	Males (as a % of total employed)	Females (as a % of total employed)	Married females (as a % of total females)
1977	755 (72)	288 (28)	84 (29)
1981	816 (71)	335 (29)	113 (34)
1985	743 (69)	331 (31)	135 (41)
1989	738 (68)	352 (32)	156 (44)
1992	740 (65)	399 (35)	200 (50)

Source: Labour Force Surveys, Central Statistics Office.

Related to this trend is the substantial shift in employment levels from the agricultural to the services sector (see table 1.2). According to Gunnigle and Morley (1993): '. . . the most notable changes in the Irish labour market over the past twenty years have been the dramatic fall in numbers employed in agriculture and the consistent growth in employment in the services sector which now accounts for almost 60 per cent of all employees.'

Table 1.2. Employment changes by sector, 1961–92 (in thousands, % in parentheses)

Year	Agriculture	Industry	Services
1961	380 (36)	257 (25)	415 (39)
1975	238 (22)	337 (31)	498 (47)
1979	221 (19)	365 (32)	559 (49)
1985	171 (16)	306 (28)	602 (56)
1989	163 (15)	306 (28)	621 (57)
1992	153 (13)	318 (28)	668 (59)

Source: Census of Population and Labour Force Surveys, Central Statistics Office.

The beneficiaries in this sector, however, are not the public services, as they have been the subject of successive Governments' fiscal rectitude initiatives during the 1980s. The private services employment expansion, however, can be mainly attributed to the financial and business services (42 per cent), professional services (21 per cent) and personal services (16 per cent) (Dineen, 1992). Though industrial employment levels have increased significantly over the past thirty years or so, the same cannot be said when examined over the last twenty-year span. In fact, since 1979 industrial employment levels have decreased by nearly 50,000 (see table 1.2). In addition, the composition of industrial employment has altered significantly, with contractions in many of the older labour-intensive indigenous subsectors—such as construction, textiles, clothing and footwear—and expansions in the more technology-related, export-oriented and foreign-owned employments (e.g. chemicals and engineering).

As a result the occupational structure of those at work is also altering, with the demise of traditional industry and its associated skills, and their replacement through the emergence and growth of newer ones. Most striking in this context is the overall decline of male-dominated manual jobs in the manufacturing and construction sectors—job types and sectors which have traditionally provided rich pickings for trade union organisers.

The effect of technology on such variables as the size, spread, location and duration of employment has frequently been acknowledged. The quickening pace of technological change is, however, also having a dramatic impact on the structure and nature of the labour market and all job types therein. A key dimension of this trend is the move away from manual work. Yet, the creation of replacement job opportunities resulting from the 'electronics' revolution of microchips, computers and new technical systems is too low, volatile and of the wrong sort to compensate for the attrition rate in other industries. The necessity to adapt to these changes for survival purposes has brought with it—in addition to job losses—revised working methods, job content and wage-differential and skill protection practices. Opposition to developments in this area are often prompted by losses under such headings as jobs, occupational status, skills, and employment terms and conditions. However, trade unions generally favour and co-operate with technological change—where it is undertaken jointly as opposed to imposed unilaterally by management (Daniel, 1987). This issue is considered in greater detail in chapter 10.

In brief then, the more significant implications to emerge from this overview of labour market trends are rising unemployment levels which are expected to persist—with their dampening effect on trade union confidence and militancy—together with hesitantly modest increases in the size and composition of the active labour force. The prime beneficiaries of these changes are (mainly married) female part-time workers in the services sector of the economy. The decline in male manual full-time employment in recent years is also expected to persist. In effect, one might anticipate further declining levels of unionisation, as the expanding services sector, with its predominance of part-time female workers, fails to compensate for the decline in employment levels in industry and the increasing size of the labour force. In chapter 10 the related phenomenon of increased 'atypical'

17

employment patterns (e.g. part-time, temporary and self-employment) are examined in some detail. It would be surprising if this trend did not weaken the pervasiveness and impact of collective bargaining—which may already be evident from the 70,000 decline in trade union membership over the 1980–87 period (Roche, 1992a). Indeed, it may be argued that this inevitability has been recognised by a trade union movement prepared to repeatedly commit itself to relatively modest pay increases, agreed at national level, in anticipation of a beneficial return in the form of greater employment generation efforts. Since the late 1980s pay settlements (and, many would contend, as a consequence, inflation levels) have been at appreciably lower levels than during the 1960s or 1970s, when unemployment figures were significantly lower and trade union density and negotiating strength greater. These developments also raise issues for trade unions, given the increased prominence of non-union policies, particularly amongst the newer industrial 'high-tech' and services-sector employments. Many of these employments use sophisticated human resource management practices which may pre-empt the need for a trade union among employees (McGovern, 1989b). Furthermore, the reality of these changes is forcing unions to expand their range of services and to focus more upon the needs of part-time and female workers (in negotiations with management and Government), for the purpose of maintaining their own authority, influence and membership levels.

1.2.4. POLITICS AND INDUSTRIAL RELATIONS

The role of the State in the industrial relations arena is very important. Over a century it has adjusted from casting trade unions as illegal entities, to their accommodation in a social partnership or neo-corporatist model. This revision now entails union involvement in the national-level decision-making processes, covering the whole gamut of economic and social affairs. In addition to its efforts to address the worst excesses of liberal capitalism, the State aspires to the role of independent referee and regulator of labour relations matters. However, it would be inappropriate to assign it the role of impartial facilitator. In any democratic society the State reflects the differences in power between capital and labour. It endeavours to side with whomever yields the greatest political influence. In effect then, through its various powers and agencies, successive Irish Governments have upheld the established norms, values and culture of liberal capitalism.

Nevertheless, over time the State has been cautious to refine the extremes of the *laissez-faire* ideology and to concede the more modest demands of trade unions—so long as they are peacefully presented and pursued, constitutional in nature and maintain due deference to property rights and the needs of industrial capitalism. Such concessions are reflected in freedom of association or organisation (as provided for under the 1937 Constitution), rights to collective bargaining and to take industrial action. However, the first Free State Government did display some disdain for entitlements granted by their

British counterparts, as it proceeded to alienate most working-class voters and reject the application of Whitley procedures to Ireland, i.e. the provision of third-party arbitration machinery for the Civil Service (Lee, 1980; Thomason, 1984). In fact, it was not until 1950 that advances of any significance were made in this regard. In line with this eventual adherence to an 'auxiliary' or accommodative strategy, the State largely supported the voluntarist principle in labour relations by mainly confining legal interference to the provision of mediation services. This strategy, whilst successfully isolating trade union militancy and dampening popular support for the route to revolutionary socialism, has forced the trade union movement to (generally) separate and seek its ideologically driven aspirations through a political wing (i.e. the Labour Party) or via tripartite or corporatist structures.

The Irish Labour Party was established at the Trades Union Congress in 1912, at the initiative of James Connolly and James Larkin. However, between a preoccupation with the burning 'national' question and a negligible industrial base (at least until the 1960s), the scope for the development of strong working-class communities and culture was restricted. Of further significance to the relatively modest influence of the Labour Party is the fact that it, together with the Irish Trades Union Congress, decided not to contest the 1918 General Election. This decision has been attributed to the party's lack of funds, interested candidates, political organisation and political direction. There was also a very definite reluctance among trade union and labour leaders to oppose Sinn Fein candidates—who actually secured 73 of the 105 parliamentary seats in the eventual election. However, it is now argued that '. . . this policy of abstention removed Labour from centre stage in Irish politics for many years, as it sidestepped the great issue of the time, which was the struggle for independence' (Kavanagh, 1987).

In fact, so prominent has the national question been, according to Fitzpatrick (1977), that attempts to examine Labour's efforts to remain distinct from the mainstream of Republican politics become a review of 'the process whereby Labour and the Republican movement were sucked together'. For example, in 1945 the ITUC split, primarily as a result of tensions between Irish- and British-based trade unions operating in the country. Just as the 'national question' and related tensions have played, and continue to play a central role in Irish political matters, so also was it inevitable that it would affect the operation and current shape of the industrial relations system. By 1959 however, the ITUC split was resolved, and the Irish Congress of Trade Unions (ICTU) was established to represent the vast majority of trade unions operating in this country.

Of course a working class consumed with the sacrosanctity of relativities and occupational status was unlikely to fill the ranks of a vibrant left-wing opposition along Western European lines. A striking consequence of this void is that there has been little substantial difference in policy stances between successive Governments on economic issues. Accordingly, given the ideological similarities across the main political parties and Governments, there has been relatively mild opposition to the directions, policies and actions of the Govermental process. The absorption of working-class demands into the existing industrial and political structures has also facilitated the maintenance of widespread support for those parties representing the values and beliefs of liberal capitalism. Indeed, for the larger part of this century the State has adopted such an 'auxiliary' role, as it avoided direct coercive interference in the industrial relations process, leaving the parties to resolve their own differences via free collective bargaining. Furthermore, following on the British example, the Government addressed itself to the social problems arising from the deficiencies of industrial capitalism, opting for greater intervention to protect and improve the quality of people's lives. Of course, the gradual creation of a welfare state also facilitated the maintenance of political consensus, stability and legitimacy. The emergence of a corporatist or interventionist strategy on the part of the Government was accompanied by an integration of political, economic and social decision making. That is, the State adopted a strategy of public policy making which actively involved the upper echelons of the main interest groups. This strategy was based on the expectation that the leadership of these groups would 'deliver' their respective constituents when the time for actual implementation of the policies came to pass.

From the 1960s onwards this policy of corporate control became evident, as trade union representatives were invited to participate in consultative bodies like the National Industrial and Economic Council and the Committee on Industrial Organisation. The onset of tripartite consultations was adjudged to be important given the need for economic adaptation, restructuring and the establishment of appropriate and realistic planning targets. The Government, therefore, had to fall back on those interests involved on the ground in order to acquire the necessary information and understanding as well as to secure their co-operation in the implementation of policy. The emergence of national-level tripartite bargaining, involving Government, employers and trade unions, marked a new phase in the relationship between the State and the trade union movement. Sparked by economic management motives, the desire to control incomes and inflationary pressures gave rise to such tripartite arrangements as have officially prevailed since 1977, though the Government has played a significant role in the formulation of such agreements (at least) dating back to 1970.

Prior to the suspension of these arrangements, over the 1981–87 period, they had expanded in scope to accommodate a plethora of economic and social affairs under the title of 'national understandings'. The temporary demise of the consensual approach at national level, during the 1980s, can be primarily attributed to a hardened negotiating stance on the part of both employers and the State. Related to this was a change in Government, with the more populist or pragmatic Fianna Fail party being replaced by a Fine

Gael–Labour Coalition. A subsequent change of Government facilitated the resurgence of the social partnership approach from 1987 onwards, with representative national-level agreements again embracing the range of economic and social issues. It is interesting in this regard to note that, despite the broad ideological commonality across the main political parties, all major initiatives on pay and economic planning have emerged when Fianna Fail has been in Government: centralised pay bargaining (1947), national wage agreements (1970), national understandings (1979), the Programme for National Recovery (1987) and its successors. Furthermore, it is striking that, whilst their British counterparts are being left out in the cold, the Irish trade union movement has played a central role in decisions (on not just pay increases), but on wider national economic and social strategy matters. However, in the opinion of von Prondzynski (1988), the price of such trade union participation in these programmes ought to be costed against:

> . . . every evidence that the Programme was designed as a back-up to the Government's programme of expenditure cut-backs and income restraint; the intention was primarily to tie the hands of the trade unions in particular and make difficult any serious militancy in opposition to these policies . . . this approach is working rather well.

The participative model then, which was initiated by Sean Lemass and really took off in the late 1950s, now appears to be accepted in principle, at least by the trade union and employer organisations. This is reflected by their involvement in a variety of industry- and national-level tripartite fora. However, the commitment to a participative approach is less evident at firm level. The focus of attention by both sides to the industrial relations process at this level tends to be the size of the wage settlement—an element well capable of exposing the fragility of interest-group solidarity.

The decision to enter the European Economic Community (EEC) with effect from 1973 was an important development in the political environment of industrial relations. An immediate impact was felt in both the industrial development and individual labour law arenas (McMahon, 1990). In regard to the former, the influx of multinational enterprises is commonly accredited with a greater level of professionalism in the area of personnel or human resource management. This influx also increased trade union membership levels, which were attained primarily through 'pre-production agreements'. Such agreements, on terms and conditions of employment, were concluded between the employer and the union prior to the commencement of operations. In contrast, however, the emergence of non-union establishments, with sophisticated human resource management policies and practices can also be traced back to this influx. In regard to the latter (labour law) influence, significant revisions were prompted in such areas as employment equality, mass redundancy and worker participation. This development has certainly facilitated the emergence of prominent players on the industrial relations pitch in the form of the EC and the European Parliament. Furthermore, few doubt that the Community will play a key role in shaping the political agenda for the future. The passage of the Single European Act has focused the minds of most pressure groups in society on the implications of greater economic and political union across the Member States. Amongst the range of influences on the industrial relations environment, considerable attention is being devoted to the 'social dimension', or Social Charter, which spans a range of social and employment rights—including health and safety, equitable remuneration, equality, information and consultation entitlements and freedom of movement.

In the 1990s then, the unfortunate state of many important national economic indicators signals a new era in the management of industrial relations. Pressures exerted by a persistent international recession and constraints on remedial initiatives imposed through membership of, and adherence to, the EC and Single European Market respectively, restrict the scope for 'quick-fix' solutions. It should also be acknowledged that recent political developments—including the demise of socialism in Eastern Europe and the resurgence of *laissez-faire* individualism (with its emphasis on monetarism, free enterprise, open markets, deregulation, and privatisation)—have forced the recall and revision of many trade union ideological aspirations. This may well reinforce the merits, for trade unions, of operating inside the neo-corporatist model and furthering their demands under the auspices of the prevalent liberal capitalist political and economic system.

1.3. THE ROLE OF THEORY IN INDUSTRIAL RELATIONS

The role of theory in industrial relations is intended to facilitate the analysis and appraisal of the subject's processes, structures and institutions in as objective a manner as is possible with any of the social sciences. This section of the text attempts, therefore, to outline and evaluate the main academic theories which have been developed in an effort to provide a logical and consistent means of understanding and interpreting industrial relations realities. Particularly over the past twenty years there have been a series of prescriptions for change, designed to improve the conduct of industrial relations in this country, e.g. changes in strike laws, worker-participation/-involvement schemes, trade union rationalisation. Such proposals can often be highly contentious, and the theoretical bases upon which they are based rarely enunciated. Accordingly, this section of chapter 1 introduces and assesses the main theoretical perspectives and related value judgements on the nature of the world of work.

1.3.1. PLURALIST ANALYSIS

The pluralist and related analyses of industrial relations systems in Western societies have been in pole position for over thirty years now. This framework, or model, is based upon the existence of a 'post-capitalist' society, where industrial and political conflict have become institutionally separated. Ownership is distinguished from management, and authority and power in society are more widely distributed than ever before. In effect, this analysis views society as comprised of a range of individuals and interest and social groups, each in pursuit of their own objectives. As in society, the employing entity is also comprised of an accommodation or alliance of different values and competing sectional interests. Effectively then, it is only through this accommodation that work organisations can attempt to operate with any degree of continuity and success. Just as the political system is institutionalised and regulated through a party-political and parliamentary process, so also is the industrial system institutionalised and regulated through representative organisations and appropriately structured processes. The existence of competing organisational values and interests give rise to 'a complex of tensions and competing claims which have to be "managed" in the interests of maintaining a viable collaborative structure' (Fox, 1973). Hence, the emergence of a succession of temporary compromises—or collective agreements—as the opposing aspirations for higher profits and productivity or efficiency are aligned with improved pay and working-condition demands. Collective agreements then are the result of collective bargaining between employers and workers (or their respective representatives) over terms and conditions of employment. As Dubin (1954) summarises: 'Collective bargaining is the great social invention that has institutionalised industrial conflict. In much the same way that the electoral process and majority rule have institutionalised political conflict in a democracy, collective bargaining has created a stable means for resolving industrial conflict.'

This perspective acknowledges the legitimacy of trade union organisation, interests and the right to contest the managerial prerogative. In any case, it is contended that 'greater stability and adaptability is given to industrial relations by collective bargaining than by shackling and outlawing trade unions' (Clegg, 1975). The structures, formats and processes of labour relations are perceived as the manifestation of the power relations and conflict between employers, managers and trade unions. Accordingly, conflict is viewed as a logical and inevitable feature of the world of work and, consequently, requires management by a variety of role players or representatives, procedures, processes and specialist institutions.

A central feature of this post-capitalist perspective is that the class conflict (between the 'haves' and the 'have-nots') of the Industrial Revolution has now abated. Marxist analysis of the powerful capitalists and weak wage earners—of the socially elite and the socially weak—is no longer an appropriate model. Contemporary society, it is argued, is more open and mobile with the franchise extended for the further democratisation of politics, greater accessibility of educational opportunity opening hitherto closed occupational routes, and the advent of the welfare state, which serves to alleviate the worst extremes of deprivation and inequality. Such societal developments have combined to effectively undermine, and point to the need for a replacement of, the Marxist prognosis. Furthermore, the spread and diffusion of property ownership, status and authority in the post-capitalist society has irretrievably removed the sharp divisions between those who were once industrially and politically powerful and their counterparts, who were weak and powerless in both these crucial spheres. Therefore, with the opening-up of routes to a vast array of prized positions in society—whether they be in the political, industrial or professional arenas—the superior and subordinate classes in the employment context need no longer be synonymous with the political or social classes, either generally or through successive generations.

Consequently, with the separation of industrial and political conflict, collective bargaining has become the focus of attention for the regulation of relations at the workplace.

With the emergence, structuring and regulation of representative organisations on both sides of industry, appropriate fora have now been established to address the tensions and conflicts arising at all levels between these sectional interest groups (e.g. the ICTU and IBEC). In the event of failure to resolve differences at plant level, an array of third-party institutions provide a generally acceptable route for the resolution of contrasting objectives and conflicts (e.g. the Labour Relations Commission, the Employment Appeals Tribunal). In conjunction with this system, it is argued that the development of employee involvement or participative practices serve to further emphasise the distribution or diffusion of power and authority in industry. According to Dahrendorf (1959) these developments are well reflected in: '(1) the organization of conflicting interest groups itself; (2) the establishment of 'parliamentary' negotiating bodies in which these groups meet; (3) the institutions of mediation and arbitration; (4) formal representations of labour within the individual enterprise; and (5) tendencies towards and institutionalization of workers' participation in industrial management.' Though pluralists acknowledge the inevitability of conflict, they do, nevertheless, point to the relative stability of a society which institutionalises, manages and contains any differences via collaboration, negotiated compromises and mediation.

1.3.2. UNITARY ANALYSIS

The basic premise of the unitary perspective on the industrial relations system is that all employment units are, or should be, cohesive and harmonious establishments, with a total commitment to the attainment of a common goal. Being unitary in structure and purpose, with shared goals, values and interests, and one source of (managerial) authority, the staff relations are set upon a plinth of mutuality and harmony. That is, there is no conflict between those contributing the capital (i.e. the owners) and the contributors of labour (i.e. the employees). Consequently, all staff members agree unreservedly with the aspirations of the organisation and the methods and means deployed to give effect to these targets. Through this team, or complementary partnership approach, it is assumed that both sides of the equation can satisfy their common goals of high profitability and pay levels, job security and efficiency. Nevertheless, it is implicitly acknowledged that—as with any team approach—competent and strong leadership, or management, is a prerequisite to the pursuit of organisational effectiveness. In practice this may give rise to elements of paternalism and/or authoritarianism on the part of management, in their approach to employee relations matters.

Paternalism may be reflected in a managerial concern for staff needs, together with a rejection of union recognition and collective bargaining practices. Alternatively, authoritarianism may materialise in a dominant managerial value system, characterised by a minimal concern for employee welfare and outright opposition to union recognition and collective bargaining initiatives. In either scenario, trade-unionism is opposed as a threat to the organisation's unity of purpose and the (legitimate and rational) managerial prerogative, as it competes for employee loyalty and commitment. The consequent rejection of collective bargaining is, therefore, based upon managements' perceived legitimate prerogative to proceed without the incumbency of negotiation to attain consent to their decision-making initiatives and responsibility. In such a setting it is assumed that management will insert an appropriate communications structure to alert staff to organisational priorities, and to management expectations of staff in respect of same. In response, staff give effect to these instructions as they display their loyalty to the entity for the realisation of their common goals (e.g. job security).

In essence the unitary theory rejects the concept of enduring conflict or organisational factionalism, as such collisions, competition or opposition distract from what are assumed to be non-competing, co-operative initiatives. The existence of conflict is not perceived to be a structural feature of organisational life but:

> . . . is either (a) merely frictional, e.g. due to incompatible personalities or 'things going wrong', or (b) caused by faulty 'communications', e.g. 'misunderstandings' about aims or methods, or (c) the result of stupidity in the form of failure to grasp the commonality of interest, or (d) the work of agitators inciting the supine majority who would otherwise be content. (Fox, 1966)

The unitary philosophy is, therefore, predominantly managerial. It legitimises management authority under the heading of commonality, it largely attributes the source of conflict to subordinates and it serves as a means of justifying their decisions to any interested parties. Any opposition to management is adjudged to be either ill informed or perverse. The undoubted increase in levels of opposition to trade union recognition, and the associated rise in the number of non-union establishments, has significantly strengthened the prevalence and validity of this particular analytical model on the national scene. Whilst traditionally one might have identified the family-owned business, religious and charitable organisations, or the police and army, as reflecting this approach, more recent times have witnessed an influx of foreign (particularly American and Japanese) companies giving effect to the concept via outright opposition to trade unions and through 'sophisticated' people-management policies and practices.

1.3.3. MARXIST ANALYSIS

Though Marxist analyses of industrial relations are more a by-product of a theory of capitalist society and social change than of the labour relations system itself, they do have considerable implications and provide a useful framework for the interpretation of the relationship between capital and labour. That is, Marxism is more concerned with the structure and nature of society than with the actual workplaces which that society accommodates. Of course, when the original Marxist analysis of the nature and structure of society was conceived the phenomena of trade-unionism and collective bargaining were barely established. Consequently, the application of the original Marxist analysis to contemporary labour relations institutions and phenomena is primarily the product of neo-Marxist theoreticians.

These sources attribute the industrial relations system with a limited role, via the resolution of pay and condition issues and the delineation of the boundaries of managerial prerogative. The system does not have any central role in the Marxist prognosis—which envisages a fundamental change in the distribution of power and wealth in society. However, under Marxism, conflict in the industrial relations arena has at least a symptomatic value, in its reflection of the opposing economic interests engendered by capitalism.

This body of theory is then essentially an analysis of the evolution of society—of which the capitalist (or bourgeois state) is only one phase. That is, Marxism depicts a series of developments, or phases of social change, from the initial state of primitive communism through an era of feudalism to capitalism. The machinations of capitalism, it is predicted, will give rise to a class war (between the 'Bourgeoisie' and the 'Proletariat'), culminating in a dictatorship of the proletariat, before progressing to socialism, and eventually a Utopian classless society.

In essence, the Marxist perspective is based upon the premise that class (i.e. capital and labour) conflict is at the root of societal change. This conflict is not a simple consequence of contrasting demands and tensions at the workplace, but is the product of an inequitable distribution of power and wealth in wider society. Inequity is also reflected in society's social and political institutions, which serve to maintain the position of the dominant establishment group, i.e. the owners of the means of production. Therefore, social and political conflict—and social change—is the result of these central economic inequities and divisions within society, between the owner or capitalist and labouring classes. Accordingly, conflict reflects the difference between these social classes with their diametrically opposed economic and political interests. Class and political conflict are therefore inextricably linked with industrial conflict—which the Marxist perspective adjudges to be a permanent feature of capitalism. This persistent and unavoidable conflict is the result of these competing interests, seeking to consolidate and advance their relative positions in the economic power structure, as they contest the distribution of the entity or society's power, wealth and 'surplus value'.

In effect then, the industrial relations system, or the workplace, is the microcosm or marginal forum for the conduct of a class war. This will ultimately spill over into a more fundamental political revolution initiated by the working class. Trade unions are viewed, in this context, as a collective response to the exploitation of the capitalist system. They may perform a central role in the wider political process for the attainment of significant alterations to the economic and social system, on behalf of the proletariat.

The operation of (national, industrial and enterprise-based) bodies of joint regulation, with their agreed procedures and processes, is adjudged, however, by Marxists to accommodate, consolidate, legitimise and effectively enhance the managerial prerogative and power position. They allegedly project an image, or veneer, of power sharing. In effect then, the whole collective bargaining process is perceived to, at least temporarily, accept, facilitate and ultimately support the inherent contradictions of capitalism. Furthermore, the State's legislative framework is perceived by Marxists to be a related piece of armoury, designed to support managements' interests (Hyman, 1975).

In summary then, when evaluating prescriptions arising from other perspectives, the Marxists would argue that economic and political issues cannot be separated. Marxists place great emphasis on the antagonistic interests of capital and labour, and in sharp contrast with alternative analytical frameworks, focus on the importance of assessing the power held by opposing interests and the way it will alter over time.

1.3.4. SOCIAL ACTION ANALYSIS

The social action perspective on industrial relations 'stresses that the individual retains at least some freedom of action and ability to influence events', in the manner they adjudge to be most appropriate or preferable (Jackson, 1982). This theory emphasises the role players' or actors' definitions, perceptions and influences on reality. It is these definitions and perceptions which determine their relationships, behaviour and actions. Therefore, with this frame of reference, social and industrial relations actions are best understood in terms of their subjectively intended meanings. Concentration on observed behaviour at the workplace restricts the value of any interpretation, as it overlooks the deeper intent of the actors. The actors' decisions are determined then not just by the specific work situations they find themselves in, but by a plethora of wider and underlying influences—such as the attitudes, values, experiences and expectations developed over a lifetime, both inside and outside of the workplace. The central relevance of this particular perspective is that it attributes to the individual actors some prerogative or discretion to shape the actual workplace and society in which they exist along (their) desired lines. In this context, however, they are restricted by their own perception of reality. Thus, the social action analysis accords some control or priority to the individual over the structure or system in which they find themselves. It offers a frame of reference which concentrates on the range of industrial relations system outputs as being as much the end result of the actions of its constituent parts, as of the structure of the system itself. The social action theory is, in fact, rooted in a well-developed sociological school of thought which argues that just as 'society makes man . . . man makes society' (Silverman, 1970).

1.3.5. SYSTEMS ANALYSIS

The systems theory of industrial relations originated in the late 1950s in the United States when John Dunlop (1958, 1993) proposed: 'An industrial relations system at any one time in its development is regarded as comprised of certain actors, certain contexts, an ideology which binds the industrial relations system together, and a body of rules created to govern the actors at the work place and work community.'

Dunlop's construction of an integrated model is based upon a view of the industrial relations system as one which, though overlapping and interacting with the economic and political decision-making systems, is nevertheless a societal subsystem in its own right. This subsystem's output or product is comprised of a set of rules pertaining to the employment relationship, which spans their design, application and interpretation. Accordingly, the industrial relations system is primarily concerned with the output of rules covering all pay and condition matters, together with the installation of procedures for their administration and application. The systems theory of industrial relations is, therefore, based upon the standard input–process–output model, which Dunlop argues can be applied regardless of the economic or political system in place.

Under the 'input' heading Dunlop identifies three sets of influences: *actors*, *environmental contexts* and *ideology*. These combine in the bargaining, conciliation and legislative processes to yield a body, network or web of rules. The *actors* include the different worker categories (whether organised or unorganised), the various layers of management—together with their respective representatives—and the range of third-party agencies. The *environmental context* impinging on the state of the industrial relations system is comprised of technological, market/budgetary and societal power location and distribution variables. The technological impact is reflected in such factors as the workforce's size, skill and sexual breakdown, its concentration or distribution, the location and duration of the employment. The market or budgetary constraints, whether applied locally, nationally or internationally, impinge upon all enterprise types, not just upon the entity's management, but also ultimately on all of the system's role players. The 'power' input relates to the structural context of, or degree of autonomy afforded the industrial relations system by the wider society. This will, of course, be significantly influenced by the distribution of power in that society. The third, *ideological*, input recognises that, whilst each group of actors in the system may have their own set of ideas, these are sufficiently congruent for a level of mutual tolerance, common belief or unifying ideological compatibility to prevail.

1.3.6. CONCLUSION AND CRITIQUE OF MODELS

As each theory originates from a different base, or set of assumptions, it would be inappropriate to insist upon a single 'best' theory of industrial relations, or to force the student down a 'pick-and-choose' road in the construction of an analytical framework to fit with their own particular perspective or insight. Whilst insisting upon this discretionary prerogative, it would be remiss not to acknowledge the primacy of the pluralist analysis in Irish industrial relations practices and debates. This is reflected in the high levels of union density together with the central role of, and preoccupation with, collective bargaining—and its institutions—at establishment, industrial and national levels.

As evidenced by their contrasting premises and prognoses all of the models of industrial relations outlined above have been subjected to critical evaluation. The pluralist analysis for example, despite its prevalence and robustness, has been criticised for its ready acceptance of the social and political *status quo,* and a fundamental conservatism which assumes an illusory balance of power between the various interest groups (Fox,1973; Goldthorpe, 1974). Unlike both the unitary and Marxist theories, the pluralist analysis avoids making moral value judgements—a factor which actually both enhances its standing and detracts from it. Similarly, the unitary perspective is cautioned for its unrealistic Utopian outlook, limited applicability (e.g. to non-union entities) and a paternalistic management orientation, which assumes a generally accepted value system. The Marxist analysis is adjudged, in this 'post-capitalist' era, to be anachronistic. Beyond the recent demise of communism and socialism in Eastern Europe, this verdict is mainly based upon the fact that the nature of class conflict has substantially changed since the last century. Contemporary society, with its mixed economy and welfare state, is now more open and socially mobile. In addition to the subjectivity of Marxism, it is also argued that the distribution of power, property and social status in society is perceived to be more widely diffused today than it was in the nineteenth century and, consequently, this undermines the theory's simplistic classifications.

In regard to social action theory, critics point to its neglect of those structural features which influence the action of its actors. This oversight, it is argued, really reflects the theory's own inability to explain the very nature of the wider system inside which these actions occur. Systems theory has also been subjected to considerable criticism, refinement and modification. For example, it is contended that the model's narrow focus omits the reality of and mechanisms for the distribution of wealth and power in society. In effect, its convenient unifying ideology, cum *status quo* inclination—which takes society as given—merely accords the industrial relations system some functional role. This entails the maintenance of stability, and overlooks a range of issues including change in industrial relations, the source of conflict and the system's interrelationship with the 'outside' political, economic and social scene. It is also contended that its structural emphasis leads to an output or focus on rules at the expense of the actual decision- or rule-making processes. Additionally, it fails to explain the important behavioural variables (i.e. why actors act as they do). It is argued that the system's model should accommodate the significant role of the owners of business, who warrant inclusion in both an actor's capacity and contextual capacity. Wood (1978/79) also recommends that a modifying distinction be made to the model 'between the system which "produces" rules (i.e. the industrial relations system) and the system which is governed by such rules (i.e. the production system)'. Therefore, the revised approach recommends a focus upon both the narrower rule-making processes and the wider contextual influences, e.g. political, legal and social contexts.

In conclusion then, far from being a descriptive subject based upon common sense, a single analytical framework or a set of incontrovertible facts and statistics, political and theoretical controversy is inherent to the topic of industrial relations. There is a vast array of ways of interpreting what is going on, and a multitude of opinions about what ought to be happening in the area. However, the fact that there is no universally accepted global theory is evident and ought to be accepted by the student as an attractive dimension of a topic which easily lends itself to contrasting perspectives, opinions and debate. In recognition of this fact, however, this text attempts, as far as is possible, to present a factual and unbiased account of the various institutions, processes and issues. It is for the student to make up his/her own mind on these matters, as the book endeavours to take a neutral line, presenting available evidence and different sides of the various arguments.

CHAPTER TWO

The Role of the Law

2.1. INDIVIDUAL EMPLOYMENT LAW

The principal purpose of labour law is to regulate, to support and to restrain the power of management and the power of organised labour (Kahn-Freund, 1977). One may trace this process of legislative intervention in the employment relationship as far back as the 1349 Ordanance of Labourers. This initiative was designed to impose wage ceilings for both artisans and labourers in the 'Black Death' era of severe labour shortages. However, it was not until the nineteenth century that a range of protective statutes were enacted covering such matters as health and safety and the form that wage payments should take. Over the past twenty years there have been significant developments, particularly in the area of individual employment law. Each of these legislative initiatives may be viewed as a countervailing force, giving redress to the unequal bargaining power of the individual *vis-à-vis* the employing organisation.

Of course, at the root of the employment relationship is the common law contract of employment, with its power to command and duty to obey. Accordingly, it may be argued that statute law is accorded a marginal role in its attempts to regulate and co-ordinate this relationship. For example, though management retain the power to 'hire and fire', this prerogative is somewhat restrained by dismissal, redundancy and equality legislation. In an attempt therefore to cover the more salient and relevant aspects of 'individual' labour law this section of chapter 2 reviews the role of the employment contract, dismissal law, equality legislation and, finally, summarises other statutes of particular relevance to industrial relations at work. Accordingly, little attention is paid to those areas of the law which have had little usage, or have not given rise to controversy of any magnitude in recent years.

2.1.1. THE CONTRACT OF EMPLOYMENT

The contract of employment is the legal basis of the employment relationship and is central to the interpretation and application of statutory rights. As with the basic law of contract it requires that there be an offer from the employer which is accepted by the employee, that there be consideration—or remuneration—from the employer for work done, and that there be an intention to create a legal relationship. The contract may be concluded on an oral or a written basis. Common law attempts to distinguish between a contract of service (i.e. with an employee) and a contract for service (i.e. with an independent contractor; see table 2.1). This is of some relevance given that it is only the 'employee' who can avail of the protection afforded under labour law. Case law indicates that three tests may be applied to differentiate between these contract types:

– Control: Can the employer tell the employee what to do and how to do it?
– Integration: Is the employee's work integrated into the business, or is it a case of the independent contractor working for the business?
– Multiple: What is the nature of the entire arrangement between the employer and the worker? This would be reflected in answers to the following types of questions:
– Are there wages, sick and holiday pay? Who pays them?
– Are income tax and social security deducted under the PAYE and PRSI systems respectively by the employer?
– Does the worker share in the profits/losses?
– Who provides the tools and equipment for the job?
– Are there specific provisions relating to termination?
– Is the employer entitled to exclusive service?
– Is it a genuine case of self-employment or is there an attempt to avoid protective legislation?

Table 2.1. Key differences between contracts of service and contracts for service

Contracts of service	Contracts for service
Employer–employee relationship	Employer–independent contractor relationship
Usually a continuous relationship	A once-off piece-of-work relationship
Duty of care owed to employees	Duty of care arising from occupier's liability
Generally liable for the vicarious acts of employees	Generally not liable for the vicarious acts of independent contractors
Protective legislation applies to contract	Protective legislation does not apply (excl. Safety, Health and Welfare at Work Act 1989)
Wage/Salary payment method	Fee payment method
Subject of contract is to carry on continuous work	Subject of contract is once-off job

Source: Gunnigle et al., 1992.

Despite the variety of tests or issues which may be addressed when dealing with this matter Fennell and Lynch (1993) conclude that though '. . . the substitution and/or supplementation of the control test by one more attuned to modern employment conditions is warranted under Irish law; . . . a certain measure of confusion is evident from the decisions of the Irish courts as to what formulation should be preferred'.

Accordingly, the application or otherwise of individual labour law enactments to specific employees remains somewhat uncertain. Lord Wedderburn (1986) has concluded that the variety of legal 'tests' have come asunder on the judiciary and it is 'not practicable to lay down precise tests' or a 'hard and fast list'. Indeed, he suggests, most courts now appear to apply the 'elephant test' for the employee, i.e. an animal which is too difficult to define but easy to recognise when you see it!

2.1.2. DISMISSAL AND THE LAW

The Unfair Dismissals Act 1977 was an important development in Irish labour law due to the restriction it places on the employer's right to fire. Whilst employer organisations chide its alleged impact on job creation initiatives, this allegation is strongly contested (Department of Labour, 1986), and some even argue that the Act has had major beneficial consequences for the conduct of industrial relations in the country. According to Murphy (1989):

> The Act has been a considerable success and has contributed to more effective management in notoriously problematic areas of management decision making . . . in many areas of personnel administration and disciplinary control . . . [it] has strengthened collective bargaining at workplace level by creating a closer harmony between employer and trade union views of what constitutes a fair dismissal.

THE ACT'S PROVISIONS

It is estimated that the Act applies to over three-quarters of a million employees in Ireland. Under its provisions (as amended by the 1991 Part-Time Employees legislation, see below) once an 'employee' has been continuously employed for one year, and is normally expected to work for at least eighteen hours a week, he/she has a right of action for an unfair dismissal. In the event of a perceived unfair dismissal a case may be brought before either a Rights Commissioner or the Employment Appeals Tribunal (EAT) within six months of the date of dismissal. Under a 1993 Unfair Dismissals (Amendment) Act, however, either the Tribunal or a Rights Commissioner may extend this time limit by six months in exceptional circumstances. The option of going directly to the Tribunal only applies in the event of either party objecting to a Rights Commissioner hearing. It is estimated that, in recent years, between both the Rights Commissioners and the Tribunal over 1,000 claims of dismissal arise annually (Mulligan, 1993).

Either party may appeal the Tribunal's decision to the Circuit Court within six weeks from the date on which the determination is communicated to the parties. Of course, if the employee has taken the matter to the Labour Court, or has instituted proceedings for damages at common law for wrongful dismissal, he/she would not also be entitled to redress under the Act. All employees are covered by the Act's provisions, with a number of exceptions, which include those:

– with less than one year's continuous service with the same employer (note exclusions provided for under the Worker Protection (Regular Part-Time Employees) Act 1991, in regard to part-time workers (see below); and the Unfair Dismissals Act 1993, in regard to successive temporary contracts and fixed-term or specified purpose contracts;

– over the normal retiring age;

– close relatives of the employer who are members of his/her household and work in a private dwelling house;

– employed by the Defence Forces and the Garda Siochana;

– employed by, or under, the State (excluding those provided for under section 17 of the Industrial Relations Act 1969);

– serving apprenticeships/trainees with FAS;

– officers of local authorities or health boards (excluding temporary officers), and of vocational educational committees and committees of agriculture; and

– persons normally working outside the State.

The Act provides that a dismissal will automatically be deemed to be unfair if it can be attributed to (a) trade union membership or activities (including industrial action), (b) religious or political opinion, (c) involvement in civil or criminal legal proceedings against the employer, (d) race or colour, (e) sexual orientation, (f) age, (g) being a member of the travelling community, or (h) pregnancy. It is notable that even those employees with less than twelve months continuous service who are dismissed on account of trade union membership or activity, or on account of pregnancy, or matters concerned therewith, may still avail of the Act's provisions. In regard to the pregnancy exemption, however, it has been held that a dismissal is not unfair if the employer can show that it would give rise to a breach of statute or statutory instrument, or that the employee is incapable, on account of her pregnancy or related matters, of adequately or safely doing her job. However, should the employer have an alternative suitable vacancy in this instance, it must be made available to the employee.

The burden of proof in dismissal cases normally resides with the employer. Yet, the employee must show that he/she is actually covered by the Act's provisions. Where a constructive dismissal allegation applies, or where the employee claims that the dismissal is attributable to trade union membership or activity, neither the presumption of unfairness nor the employer's burden of proof apply. Generally, however, employers bear the brunt of the Act's regulatory force in so far as the onus of responsibility is on them to show that they have acted reasonably. The Tribunal then attempts to evaluate the employer's reaction and sanction with a view to determining whether it lies within the range of responses which a 'reasonable' employer might make. A common determinant of the Tribunal's decisions on the status of a dismissal is whether the employer followed fair and proper procedures prior to the dismissal. This requirement of procedural fairness is rooted in the common law concept of natural justice and in the provisions of the 1937 Constitution. The four basic obligations in regard to disciplinary procedural arrangements identified from case law by Fennell and Lynch (1993) are:

(1) *Investigation:* An inadequate investigation of the situation on the part of the employer may give rise to a dismissal being deemed unfair. Accordingly, a reasonable and fair investigation of the matter should be undertaken by the employer prior to the decision to dismiss.

(2) *Hearing:* The employer must put the relevant case before the employee, thus allowing him/her to respond. A refusal to allow trade union representation at such meetings is likely to render the dismissal unfair.

(3) *Warning:* Prior to dismissal for misconduct or poor performance the employee should be given a warning, thus providing him/her with an opportunity to improve.

(4) *Proportionate penalties:* A dismissal will be adjudged to be unfair where the employer is seen to overreact. That is, if a lesser penalty would have been more appropriate in the circumstances.

The normal reaction of the EAT to a failure to follow fair procedures, especially those laid down in a collective agreement, is to adjudge the dismissal to be unfair. However, the extent of the contribution on the employee's part to the circumstances resulting in the dismissal will be taken into account when the Tribunal decides upon the appropriate remedy. Consequently, even if the Tribunal concludes, for whatever reason, that a dismissal was unfair, it might consider it appropriate to make a 100 per cent deduction from the compensation which the employee would otherwise be entitled to! It is also notable, however, that the Circuit Court has concluded, in instances, that an otherwise 'fair dismissal' does not automatically become unfair due to its procedural defects. Nevertheless, a direct result of this 'procedural fairness' ingredient is that there have been widespread changes in companies' procedures, practices and decision-making processes, with disciplinary and dismissal procedures now commonplace (O'Connor, 1982).

FAIR DISMISSAL

Those areas where a dismissal may be justified can largely (but not exclusively) be categorised under the following headings: (1) conduct, (2) capability and (3) redundancy.

(1) *Conduct:* This may take the form of a single act of gross misconduct or a series of such minor acts where the employee disregards relevant warnings. Dismissal arising out of alleged employee misconduct is the most common

type of case coming before the Tribunal. A fair dismissal under this heading normally occurs where the essential employer–employee relationship of trust is undermined. It generally applies to matters of sick leave abuse, substance or alcohol abuse, criminal convictions, dishonesty, disobedience, loyalty/fidelity and violence or intimidation (see Madden and Kerr, 1990). The Tribunal has not, however, established any objective standard of 'unacceptable conduct' which justifies dismissal. Instead it opts to evaluate the dismissal decision on the grounds of 'reasonableness', given the particular circumstances of each case. Consequently, one cannot construct a comprehensive and rigid checklist of types of conduct which will be adjudged by the Tribunal to be unacceptable and warrant dismissal. The 'reasonableness' parameters inside which it will evaluate each case relate to the nature and extent of the investigation undertaken prior to the dismissal and the conclusion reached on the basis of the information yielded. Accordingly, the employer is obliged to carry out a fair and full investigation, whilst adhering to the aforementioned principles of natural justice (see above). It is also relevant under this heading that 'off-duty' conduct—where it has implications for the employer—has been adjudged by both the Tribunal and the Courts to constitute grounds for fair dismissal.

(2) *Capability:* Dismissal pertaining to the capability, competence or qualifications of the employee for performing work of the kind for which he/she was employed to do may be justified. Of course, capability- or competence-driven dismissals often require the employer to advise the employee in advance of the relevant failure, thus enabling him/her to improve. Competence-related dismissals tend to arise where the employee is alleged to demonstrate a substandard work rate. Capability-related dismissals normally surface under the guise of attendance at work. Employees who are persistently late, or fail to attend work regularly, are commonly adjudged by the Tribunal to be incapable of performing the work which they were employed to do. Indeed, even in those cases of persistent or extensive absence due to illness, the furnishing of medical certification will not normally protect one from a dismissal where the employer has satisfied him or herself that a timely return to work is not expected.

(3) *Redundancy:* Dismissals on the grounds of redundancy usually constitute fair dismissals. Accordingly, dismissal attributed to the employer ceasing business, reducing workforce size or no longer requiring the employee's kind of work is not unfair. The onus of proving that a genuine redundancy situation exists, however, resides with the employer. Nevertheless, an employee may contest the dismissal on the basis of unfair selection. In such circumstances the employee must show that the same scenario applied to one or more other employees who were not made redundant, and that the redundancy procedure was unjustifiably breached, or that the selection was driven by any of the reasons set down at (a) to (h) above. Effectively then, the employer is precluded from using arbitrary criteria when selecting staff for redundancy, though he/she may successfully plead special reasons for

departing from an agreed or traditional procedure.

CONSTRUCTIVE DISMISSAL

The term 'constructive dismissal' relates to those cases where the employee terminates the contract on account of the employer's conduct. For example, the employee would be entitled to terminate the contract where the employer's conduct constitutes a significant breach, going to the root of the contract, or in the event of the employer indicating that he/she no longer intends to be bound by one or more of its essential terms. Even in those cases where the employee is not legally entitled to terminate the contract a constructive dismissal may be identified if the employer has acted unreasonably. The reasonableness of the employee in refusing to accept changes in the terms of conditions of employment will be considered by the Tribunal in the light of the circumstances and of good industrial relations. However, the onus of proof, that there was an act or omission on the employer's part, constituting a breach of contract, resides with the employee. Case law precedent, however, has led some authorities to conclude that this concept of constructive dismissal was somewhat meaningless, and that the relevant criteria to be applied remain something of a mystery (Von Prondzynski, 1989b).

UNFAIR DISMISSAL REMEDIES

The Act provides for three remedial alternatives in the event of a dismissal being deemed to have been unfair: reinstatement, re-engagement and compensation.

Reinstatement enables the employee to resume in the same position, on the same contractual terms, as those applying prior to the dismissal event. A practical implication of this award is that the dismissal is effectively deemed never to have occurred. Accordingly, the relevant back-pay must be awarded, the employee's seniority maintained and pension rights restored. Furthermore, if there have been any changes in the interim in the terms and conditions of employment that would have been applicable to that employee, they must also now be enforced (e.g. pay rise). Reinstatement is usually awarded where the employee is adjudged not to have contributed to the dismissal in any way.

Re-engagement entitles the employee to resume in the same or in a reasonably suitable different position, on contractual terms which are deemed reasonable in the light of prevailing circumstances. Such awards do not normally date back to the date of dismissal. As a result, though the unfairly dismissed employee's continuity of service is not affected, the period elapsing between the dismissal and the engagement effectively constitutes suspension without pay. When deciding between a reinstatement or a re-engagement award the Tribunal tends to take account of the extent, if any, to which the employee contributed to the unfair dismissal. However, over the years 1988 to

1991 it is estimated that out of 3,502 claimants only 202 (6 per cent) were re-employed, that is, 27 per cent of cases successfully pursued (Mulligan, 1993). Accordingly, nearly 55 per cent (1,920 cases) were withdrawn before or during the hearing, 24 per cent (851 cases) were dismissed and the balance, 21 per cent (737 cases), were allowed (Mulligan, 1993).

Compensation or payment is therefore the most common remedial option, but may only be awarded up to a maximum of 104 weeks remuneration (including bonus payments) in respect of the employment from which the employee was dismissed. The size of payment was determined, up to 1993, by taking into account the estimated future loss and the actual net loss of remuneration incurred by the employee as reduced by tax, social welfare and any alternate employment earnings. Arising from the 1993 legislation, however, compensation calculations must disregard income tax rebates made by reason of the dismissal and unemployment, sickness, and occupational injury payments to an employee under the Social Welfare Acts 1981–93. Deductions are also likely to be made from the compensation figure awarded where it is adjudged that the employee's conduct contributed to the dismissal, or that the employee failed to take adequate steps to secure alternate employment. The practical consequence of these calculations is that, for example, over the four-year period 1988–91 the average compensatory award was £3,149 (Mulligan, 1993). However, arising from the aforementioned compensation calculation changes, together with the other provision under the 1993 amendment, whereby a basic award of up to four weeks' remuneration is payable to claimants held to be unfairly dismissed where no financial loss has been incurred, it is to be expected that this average award level will increase.

The Tribunal retains the prerogative to select whichever remedy it deems appropriate in the particular circumstances. Though the views of the parties to the case ought to be elicited by the Tribunal, it may still choose to overlook same and issue an alternate remedy. According to Madden and Kerr (1990) the factors which appear to drive this decision are: '. . . the poor nature of the relationship between the parties, the fact that the employee has made serious allegations about the employer, the fact that the employee is not fit to return to work, (and) the fact that changes in the work situation means that no suitable job is available.'

Where the Tribunal issues a reinstatement or re-engagement award it would appear to assume that the relationship between the parties is not beyond repair. Fennell and Lynch's (1993) review indicates, however, that whilst the 'Pyrrhic victory' of compensation is the preferred remedy, re-employment is ordered where the employer acted extremely badly or the applicant is in great hardship.

2.1.3. EMPLOYMENT EQUALITY AND THE LAW

As with many of the legislative initiatives pertaining to employment matters taken in recent years the introduction of equality legislation was primarily prompted by Ireland's membership of the European Community and the necessity to comply with its directives. Under this heading legal provisions in regard to maternity rights, equal pay and other terms and conditions of employment are of particular relevance.

EQUAL PAY

The Anti-Discrimination (Pay) Act 1974 entitles males and females to equal pay for like work. For such purposes pay is interpreted as basic pay, together with all direct and indirect financial benefits and incentives. Many female workers have successfully brought claims under this Act to show that the work they do is the same as, or broadly similar to, that done by a male, and that any differences therein are of no practical significance in relation to their terms and conditions of employment. Relevant conditions to be met when taking a claim under this enactment include:

– the claimant must be working under a contract of service;
– the claimant must be making comparisons with another 'real' person, of the opposite sex, working for the same or an associated employer in the same place/locality;
– the claimant can show that either his/her work is identical to the comparator, or that their job differences are insignificant, or that his/her work is greater than (since 1989), or equal in value in terms of skill, physical or mental effort, responsibility and working conditions to that of the comparator.

In the event of a claim for equal pay being successful employers are liable to pay arrears for a maximum three-year period from the date of the claim's lodgement with the Labour Court. Undoubtedly the anticipation and enactment of this legislation has contributed to the improved relative position of female workers in the national wage structure. For example, over the 1970–80 period average hourly industrial female earnings rose by 11 per cent against the equivalent male rate (McMahon, 1987a). However, with the average hourly female rate standing at 71 per cent of the male rate in 1992, it is apparent that there remains considerable scope for improvement. According to Fennell and Lynch (1993) the Act is 'fraught with difficulties' like 'the failure to specifically guarantee a remedy for indirect pay discrimination' (see below), together with the 'requirement of a male comparator' when pursuing claims. In 1992 just twenty cases were referred to an Equality Officer under this Act.

EMPLOYMENT EQUALITY

The Employment Equality Act 1977 is designed to protect against discrimination on the basis of sex or marital status in relation to terms and conditions of employment and access to employment, training schemes, benefits, facilities, services and promotion. Of course in those (limited number of) situations where the employee's sex constitutes an occupational qualification, then its occupancy by one gender would be legitimate grounds for discrimination, e.g. model, sperm donor.

Unlawful discrimination on the grounds of sex or marital status may be direct or indirect. Direct discrimination on the grounds of sex or marital status occurs where a person is treated, due to their sex or marital status, less favourably than a person of the other sex or a particular marital status is, or would be, treated in similar circumstances. Indirect sex or marital status discrimination occurs where a requirement, which is really not essential to the job, is set down for both sexes or for married and single people, but a considerably smaller proportion of only one gender or marital status can comply with it.

REMEDY ROUTES

Where an individual adjudges there to be a breach of either the 1974 or 1977 enactments they may apply to the Employment Equality Agency (EEA) for assistance in making a reference to the Labour Court or to an Equality Officer. Indeed the Agency itself is empowered to refer a case to the Court where it suspects that discrimination is being generally practised, or where it is not reasonable to expect the person in question to take a case themselves. Where a claim is lodged with the Labour Court it may refer the matter to an Equality Officer (of the Labour Relations Commission). This Officer makes a recommendation on the matter, though it may be appealed to the Labour Court. In such an event the Court hears the case in tribunal session and issues a legally binding determination—which may only be appealed, to the High Court, on a point of law.

It is also notable that the EEA may undertake, and has undertaken, formal investigations at its own initiative. That is, the Agency is legally empowered to apply quasi-judicial powers for the purpose of investigating employment practices to determine whether they constitute discriminatory practice. In addition, the Agency has published a Code of Practice (EEA, 1983) for employers, employees, trade unions and employment agencies designed to eliminate discrimination at work. This contains guidelines on a range of relevant matters including recruitment, training, promotion, equal pay, etc. Though the Code does not have any legal status it is utilised by a wide cross-section of employers in the adoption of equal opportunity policies. Similarly, the Agency's publication of a Model Equal Opportunities Policy in 1991, again covering the range of recruitment, promotion and retention matters, has exerted a significant influence on a number of organisations which have followed suit (EEA, 1991).

Despite this enactment, however, the absence of equal access to higher occupational status groups persists (McMahon, 1987a). For example, the majority of female workers remain confined to the lower paid, peripheral or secondary sectors of the economy and labour market. One survey conducted nearly a decade after the 1977 enactment, concluded that there had been little or no change in women's job status and responsibilities, whilst the pattern of job segregation and the allocation of jobs between the sexes indicated little legislative impact on some central features of discrimination (EEA, 1986). Despite the restrictions placed on some employment practices (particularly in regard to recruitment and selection, see McMahon, 1987a, 1988) it must be acknowledged that the potential of these legislative initiatives to counter many of the problems inherent to a gender-based society remains limited. In 1992 a total of thirty-seven cases were referred to the Equality Officers under the 1977 Act.

SEXUAL HARASSMENT

One of the more significant developments arising under the provisions of the 1977 Act pertains to the matter of sexual harassment. Sexual harassment involves verbal, physical or visual conduct or acts which are sexual in nature or which have a sexual dimension and are unwelcome to the recipient. Successive Labour Court decisions have determined that sexual harassment, though not specifically alluded to, is actually prohibited under the Act, as unfair treatment constituting less favourable conditions of employment. Allegations of such harassment are, however, unlikely to be successful in the absence of corroborative evidence, as the onus of proof is on the applicant. Interestingly, even where such harassment arises outside of the workplace it is still likely to be adjudged to be in breach of the Act given that it may well have repercussions for the employee in his/her work environment. Over the 1989–91 period the number of such substantive casework enquiries received by the EEA had increased substantially—from 24 to 105 (Frawley, 1991, 1992), whilst in 1993 as many as 40 per cent of the Irish Institute of Personnel Management members indicated that they had dealt with such incidents (Tiernan, 1993).

MATERNITY LAW

The Maternity (Protection of Employees) Act 1981–91 entitles female employees to a period of maternity leave of at least fourteen weeks, where the employer is notified at least four weeks prior to the expected 'confinement', and a medical certificate establishing the fact of pregnancy is supplied. In addition to this leave entitlement the employee may take up to four weeks' additional maternity leave. However, unlike the aforementioned fourteen-week period, there is no entitlement to social welfare maternity benefit during this additional period. Furthermore, there is no obligation on the employer to replace the employee for any of the leave period.

There is no qualifying service in order to secure the right to maternity leave. Whilst the exact dates of the leave can be chosen by the employee, the period itself must span the four weeks prior to and after confinement. Whilst on maternity leave the employee's continuity of service is not broken. She is entitled to return to her job after the birth, provided she notifies the employer of her intentions in writing at least four working weeks in advance of the envisaged date of return and confirms this again two weeks prior to the return. It is worth noting that the Tribunal has held, in some unfair dismissal cases, that this is a mandatory requirement. However, 'the procedural requirements for the exercise of the right to take maternity leave and the right to return to work' have been adjudged to be 'unnecessarily complex' (Kerr, 1987). This is evident from the significant differences of opinion arising between divisions of the Tribunal on a number of fundamental issues relating to the Act (Kerr, 1987). In 1992 the EAT dealt with thirty-seven cases under this Act.

2.1.4. HEALTH, SAFETY AND WELFARE AT WORK

The relevance of the health and safety topic is sharply reflected by the fact that during 1991 a total of 2,779 accidents—of which seventy-three were fatal —were reported to the Health and Safety Authority. In the same year, a survey conducted by the Federation of Irish Employers (FIE) indicated that, on average, member companies had thirty accidents per year, resulting in the loss of 139 working days per company. The total cost of claims in 1989, for the survey group, was over £4.5 million (FIE, 1991). Total employers liability insurance in this country—another indicator of the magnitude of the problem—is estimated to run at over £100 million per annum (Carroll and Byrne, 1992). Health and safety is also attracting increasing attention from the EC, and by the end of 1992—the European Year of Safety, Hygiene and Health Protection at Work—over twenty directives concerned with the subject had been adopted as Community law. Given that 8,000 Community workers die annually as a result of work injuries, and that as many as 30 per cent of Community's workers consider their health and safety to be at risk whilst at work, this focus is hardly surprising (Briscoe, 1992; European Foundation for the Improvement of Living and Working Conditions, 1991).

Legislation pertaining to health and safety at work is quite complex as, in addition to common law, it spans some twenty enactments together with approximately 200 regulations. Barrington (1982) has classified these provisions as follows:
– legislation which deals exclusively with the health and safety of workers;
– statutes concerned with the regulation of work hours;
– statutes not designed as worker protection measures exclusively, but nevertheless providing varying degrees of protection; and
– statutes on the borderline between issues of general environmental pollution and those of occupational health and safety.

Safety at work is the responsibility of everyone at the workplace, both employer and employee. The primary responsibility, however, rests with the employer. Most claims for personal injury following a work accident contend that the employer failed in one or more of his/her common law duties. Under common law the Irish courts have decided that employers are obliged to exercise reasonable care toward employees in relation to health and safety

matters. Common law takes effect after the event, and its primary function is to compensate staff for injuries received at work. The implications of common law for employers are that they must:
– provide a safe system of work;
– ensure the provision of competent fellow workers;
– provide safety equipment and effective supervision; and
– provide a safe place of work.

The provision of a safe system of work obliges the employer to show that the protection or system provided is in accord with the general practice of that trade. Accordingly, an employer would not be responsible solely because an accident occurred in the course of the job. The failure to provide competent fellow workers (including subordinates and supervisors) may, but rarely does, constitute the basis of a claim. According to Gunnigle et al. (1992) this duty obliges an employer to:
– clarify the personal qualities and skills required to do the particular job;
– ensure the existence of a systematic recruitment and selection procedure; and
– provide the necessary training to do the job and special remedial training where required.

Furthermore, the employer may be found to be liable for the careless action of one employee which causes injury to another employee (i.e. vicarious liability). The common law obligation to provide proper safety equipment, for the purpose of avoiding staff exposure to risk and injury, includes a requirement that management take reasonable steps—up to and including disciplinary action—to ensure the use of that equipment. The provision of a safe place of work demands that the workplace be organised in the interests of health and safety. This obligation also extends to a customer's premises. Consequently, if staff are injured whilst working on a customer's premises they may successfully claim against their own employer.

The most recent statute law of significance in the area, the Safety, Health and Welfare at Work Act 1989, is applicable to all types of employment. The Act sets down major principles which all employers and employees must observe. According to Gunnigle et al. (1992), it is the most significant piece of legislation within the employment sphere in recent years as:
– it is the first attempt to codify the law on safety, health and welfare, in over twenty-five years, and covers all types of workers and employment;
– it established the National Authority for Occupational Safety and Health, for the purpose of providing integrated co-ordination and monitoring of safety, health and welfare matters at work;
– it introduces flexibility in the area of employee representation and consultation;
– it emphasises the preparation of proactive safety, health and welfare policies within the organisation;
– it changes the emphasis of the inspectorate system from one with a punitive focus to a facilitative one. It also strengthens the powers of the inspectorate

where companies refuse to conform with the legislation; and
– it emphasises the formulation of voluntary codes of practice and regulations, and it broadens the scope from one with a safety bias to a consideration of occupational health and welfare issues.

It is essentially a 'framework Act', with a guiding philosophy and direction, to be supplemented by way of regulations and codes of practice. The new National Authority, which develops these regulations and codes, is primarily responsible for enforcing, advising, promoting and undertaking research in the area. The Authority's inspectorate has wide-ranging enforcement powers, which extend to the right to serve a prohibition notice—requiring that work should stop when there is a risk of imminent and serious injury to workers —and to prosecute employers. During 1991, for example, a total of 11,000 workplace inspections were conducted.

The Authority has also issued guidelines on the formulation of a Safety Statement. Under the 1989 Act, a Safety Statement, which details the manner in which the health, safety and welfare of staff will be ensured at the workplace, is obligatory on all employers. However, a survey carried out by the Authority in 1991 revealed that only 16 per cent of workplaces had satisfactory safety statements. Overall then, the Act obliges employers 'in so far as is reasonably practicable to':
– design and maintain a place of work which is safe and without risk to health;
– provide safe means of access to and egress from a place of work;
– provide and maintain plant and equipment which is safe and without risk to health;
– provide necessary information, instruction, training and supervision for safe and healthy working;
– provide and maintain suitable protective clothing or equipment where hazards cannot otherwise be controlled;
– prepare adequate emergency plans;
– prevent risks to health and safety in relation to use of articles or substances;
– provide welfare facilities; and
– acquire the services of a competent person when necessary to ensure the safety and health of employees at work.
From the employees' perspective there is an obligation that they:
– take reasonable care to ensure the safety of themselves and others;
– co-operate with their employer in relation to compliance with statutory requirements;
– use protective equipment, clothing or other means for securing safety, health and welfare; and
– report potential risks to the employer in the event of them becoming aware of any.

The Act also entitles staff to be consulted for the purpose of making arrangements for co-operation in promoting and developing health, safety and welfare at work. Furthermore, they have the right to make representations to their employer on such matters, and their views must be taken into account 'in so far as is reasonably practicable'. If the workforce so decide, they may appoint a safety representative to act on their behalf. Amongst other entitlements, the safety representative may inspect the workplace at an agreed frequency and may accompany a Health and Safety Authority inspector on a tour of inspection.

2.1.5. OTHER EMPLOYMENT LEGISLATION

As noted above there exists a large body of employment legislation in Ireland serving to provide a basic floor of rights for employees. Together with this subsection, table 2.2 provides a brief summary of the more salient of these enactments. However, owing to their inherent complexity it would not be practical to set down a comprehensive checklist of the legislation's key provisions, case law precedents or potential for amendment. Such information may be accessed from a range of alternative sources (see Fennell and Lynch, 1993; Gunnigle et al., 1992; or Von Prondzynski, 1989b), with basic entitlement data also available from the Department of Enterprise and Employment.

Table 2.2. Summary of other employment legislation in Ireland

Act	Scope
Safety, Health and Welfare at Work Act 1989	Health, safety and welfare standards
Conditions of Employment Acts 1936 and 1944	Work hours, overtime, shiftwork, breaks
Holidays (Employees) Act 1973	Annual leave, public holidays
Protection of Young Persons (Employment) Act 1977	Employment conditions for youths
Minimum Notice and Terms of Employment Acts 1973 and 1984	Employee information and dismissal notice rights
Payment of Wages Acts, 1979–91	Non-cash payments and unlawful deductions
Worker Protection (Regular Part-Time Employees) Act 1991	Extends protective employment laws to part-time workers
Pensions Act 1990	Employee pension rights
Redundancy Payments Acts 1967–91	Lump-sum payment on redundancy
Protection of Employment Act 1977	Consultation prior to redundancy
Safeguarding of Employees' Rights on Transfer of Undertakings	Protecting employees' rights in cases of ownership changes
Protection of Employees (Employers' Insolvency) Act 1984	Employee entitlement protection in insolvency cases
Data Protection Act 1988	Automated/computer data access/confidentiality

Source: Adapted from Gunnigle et al., 1992.

HOLIDAY AND YOUNG WORKERS' LAW

Under the Holidays (Employees) Act 1973—as modified by the Worker Protection (Regular Part-Time Employees) Act 1991—(most) workers are entitled to be given leave, on full pay, at the rate of six hours for every 100 hours worked, i.e. approximately three weeks per year. In addition they are entitled to a specified number of annual public holidays—or to time off or pay in lieu. The Protection of Young Persons (Employment) Act 1977 prohibits the employment of children under fifteen years of age. However, a child over fourteen years may be permitted to do light non-industrial work during school holidays, provided it is not harmful to health, development or schooling. The Act further provides for the setting of limits to the working hours of young people, for rest intervals and the prohibition of night work.

MINIMUM NOTICE LAW

The minimum notice legislation entitles employees to a minimum period (or to accept pay in lieu) of notice prior to dismissal. Those employees covered by the Act, with thirteen weeks service, are entitled to statutory minimum notice. This applies on a sliding-scale basis to employees, whereby the longer the service the longer is the notice period entitlement (i.e. up to a statutory maximum of eight weeks). An employer is also entitled to at least one week's notice from an employee with thirteen or more weeks service. A study of the Act by Gunnigle et al. (1992) reveals that the EAT has determined that:
– notice given must be sufficiently certain and precise, leaving no room for ambiguity or uncertainty;
– the precise expiry date must be specified; and
– employees to whom the notice provisions apply are entitled to the same rights during the minimum notice period as they would enjoy but for the notice.

The minimum notice right does not, however, preclude either side from terminating the contract without notice on account of what the EAT would adjudge to be 'severe misconduct' by the other party (Von Prondzynski, 1989b). Under the same Act employees have the right to information, within one month of the request, to certain of the terms of their employment set down in writing. These may include:
– the date of commencement of employment;
– details of pay, including overtime, commission and bonus and the methods of calculating them;
– whether pay is to be weekly, monthly or otherwise;
– conditions about hours of work and overtime;
– holiday entitlements;
– sick pay arrangements and pension schemes if any; and
– periods of notice or, if the contract of employment is for a fixed time, the date when the contract expires.
During 1992 the EAT dealt with a sum total of 4,469 cases under this Act.

WAGE PAYMENT LAW

Under the Payment of Wages Act 1991 seven legal wage payment methods are provided for, including payment by cheque, bank draft, credit transfer or similar method, postal order and, of course, cash. Provision is also made for those situations in which financial institutions are affected by industrial action. Where the employee is paid on a non-cash basis and the cash is not readily available, subject to the employee's consent, the employer must pay wages by another non-cash method. Should the employee not agree, the employer must pay the wages in cash. The circumstances in which deductions can legally be made from wages and payments made by employers are also set down. Effectively, deductions must be provided for in the contract or other written form, the employee must be made aware in advance that a deduction will be made and the deduction must be reasonable in relation to the employee's wages.

PART-TIME WORKERS' PROTECTIVE LAW

Arising from the growth of the secondary labour market or 'peripheral' workforce the Worker Protection (Regular Part-Time Employees) Act came into operation with effect from April 1991. All part-time workers are covered by the Act if they work at least thirteen weeks (not necessarily consecutive) with the same employer and are normally expected to work at least eight hours a week for that employer. The Act provides for the application to regular part-time workers of the redundancy, minimum notice, worker participation (see chapter 9), unfair dismissals, maternity, holidays and employers' insolvency legislation. It is estimated that the Act's extension of the holiday legislation has provided a statutory entitlement to about 40,000 employees for the first time, while the number coming under the other legislation for the first time has been estimated at 20,000 (Department of Labour, 1992).

PENSION PROVISIONS

The Pensions Act of 1990, whilst not making occupational pension schemes compulsory, does attempt to regulate those schemes already in existence, and those which will come into operation after 1990. Effectively, the legislation (Gunnigle et al., 1992):
– establishes a Pensions Board to monitor and supervise the new requirements under the Act;
– provides for the compulsory preservation of pension entitlements for employees who change employments;
– introduces a minimum funding standard for certain funded schemes;
– provides for the disclosure of information to scheme members;
– clarifies the duties and responsibilities of scheme trustees; and
– implements the principle of equal treatment for men and women in occupational benefit schemes.

DATA PROTECTION LAW

The Data Protection Act 1988 entitles individuals to establish the existence of automated personal data, to have access to such data in relation to them and to have inaccurate data rectified or erased. The Act also obliges the Data Controller (i.e. the organisation which uses automated personal data) to adhere to a number of obligations including the accuracy, relevance and use of such data. Furthermore, a Data Protection Commissioner is provided with a legal basis for intervening where an individual complains that the principles have not been observed. The relevant principles provided for in the Act are:
– that the Data Controller fairly obtains and processes the data;
– that the automated data be factually accurate and, where necessary, up to date;
– that the data is kept for one or more specified and lawful purposes;
– that the data shall not be used or disclosed in any manner incompatible with the specified and lawful purposes;
– that the data retained be attainable, relevant and not excessive in relation to the specified and lawful purposes;
– that the personal data shall not be kept for longer than is necessary for the specified and lawful purposes; and
– that appropriate security measures should be taken by data controllers and processors against unauthorised access to or attention, disclosure or destruction of the data, and against its accidental destruction or loss.

REDUNDANCY AND OWNERSHIP CHANGES

In the current recessionary era the subject of statutory redundancy entitlements constitutes a fertile area for disputes. For example, during 1992 687 cases under the Redundancy Payments Acts 1967–91 were dealt with by the EAT. This legislation entitles workers with at least two years of continuous service, who have not reached retirement age, to a redundancy payment in the event of being made redundant. The legislative provisions pertaining to redundancy are too numerous and detailed to document here, however, suffice to note that the payment itself is calculated as follows:
– a sum equivalent to the employee's normal weekly working remuneration, plus
– half of the normal weekly remuneration for each year of continuous employment between the date on which the employee turned sixteen years old and the date at which they turned forty-one (or up to the termination of the contract of employment), plus
– full weekly remuneration for each year of continuous employment from the date of the employee's forty-first birthday until the dismissal, i.e. up to the termination of the contract.
A week's pay in such circumstances is subject to a statutory ceiling of £250 per week (£13,000 per annum), though it is adjusted from time to time.

Where collective redundancies arise the provisions of the Protection of Employment Act 1977 come into force. These require the employer to supply the employees' representatives with specific information regarding the proposed redundancies and to consult with those representatives at least thirty days before the first dismissal takes place, to see if they can be lessened or avoided. The employer is also obliged to advise the Minister for Labour at least thirty days in advance of the first dismissal. Despite the apparent stringency of these requirements, however, the legislation is adjudged to be of limited value. Von Prondzynski (1989b) and Gunnigle et al. (1992) suggest that the wide exceptions provided for in the Act mean that its enforcement is least possible where it is most necessary. In the event of the employer becoming insolvent the Protection of Employees (Employers' Insolvency) Act 1984 comes into play. Subject to certain limits and conditions, monies due to workers by way of pay arrears (including holiday and sick pay), entitlements under the minimum notice, equal pay, unfair dismissals and employment equality enactments, and monies due from court orders in respect of wages, sick pay, holiday pay or damages at common law for wrongful dismissal may be paid out of the Redundancy and Employers' Insolvency Fund. Outstanding employee contributions to an occupational pension scheme up to a year prior to the insolvency date, which the employer deducted but did not pay over, are also protected. In 1992 the EAT had to deal with 276 cases under this Act. Where the employer's identity alters due to a transfer of ownership the European Community's (Safeguarding of Employees' Rights on Transfer of Undertaking) Regulations 1980 apply to protect the employees' rights, and oblige the (old and new) employers to inform and consult the employees. Under the Unfair Dismissals Act 1993, however, where employees accept and retain a redundancy payment in this type of situation they are adjudged to have broken their continuity of employment for the purposes of the dismissal legislation. Mainly on account of interpretative difficulties rooted in those major differences between Irish and European legal terminology, these regulations are adjudged to be 'fairly unsatisfactory' (Von Prondzynski, 1989b).

2.2. COLLECTIVE LABOUR LAW

Collective labour law establishes the legal framework for industrial relations. Collective labour law is distinguished from individual labour law in that it is concerned with regulating the relationship between employers and collectivities of employees (normally trade unions). Individual labour law, as we have seen, is concerned with the conferring of positive employment rights on workers and as such concentrates on the relationship between the individual worker and the employer or management (Fennell and Lynch, 1993). Von Prondzynski (1989b) and Kerr (1989) note that collective labour law in Ireland is largely governed by legislation which can be classified into two categories. The first category covers statutes which were enacted prior to Irish Independence in 1922. Article 50 of the Irish Constitution of 1937 provides that, subject to its provisions, the laws in force prior to 1937 should continue unless repealed or found to be repugnant to the Constitution. The pre-1922 Westminster legislation largely regulated the legal status of trade unions and the taking of industrial action. The second category describes the statutes which were enacted by the Oireachtas since 1922, which were in the main designed to deal with the perceived problem of trade union multiplicity and others to provide for the establishment of industrial relations institutions such as the Labour Court.

The most significant development in Irish collective labour law in recent years has been the enactment of the Industrial Relations Act 1990. This Act represents the most comprehensive revision of industrial relations, trade dispute and trade union law in the history of the State, and its development and provisions will be discussed in later sections. The following sections aim to give a brief overview of the evolution of collective labour law in Ireland from its pre-Independence Westminster heritage to its present framework.

2.2.1. THE EVOLUTION OF IRISH COLLECTIVE LABOUR LAW

In the last century, the emergence of trade unions was hindered and restricted by an openly hostile State and legal system which, as Kerr (1989) suggests, often viewed trade-unionists as 'rebels and revolutionists'. Up until 1871, with the enactment of the Trade Union Act of that year, the British Common Law doctrine of criminal conspiracy was the commanding influence in the relationships between employer and employee. Trade unions were regarded by the courts as criminal conspiracies and were judged to be in restraint of trade. By 1870, however, a growing acceptance of the trade union movement, facilitated by its ability to harness its members' voting power, enabled the unions to gain a concession from the Conservative Government of the day. The Trade Union Act of 1871 which resulted gave trade unions the first seeds of legal respectability. The Trade Union Act legalised the existence of trade unions but carefully refrained from giving them the status of corporate entities, that is, entities capable of suing and being sued in their own name. The Act declared that the mere fact that a trade union's aims are in restraint of trade is not sufficient to render any union member liable for the offence of criminal conspiracy. The Act also provided that contracts entered into by a trade union were contracts which the law would enforce. However, the courts were debarred from directly enforcing agreements between unions and employers, or agreements between unions and their members, or recovering damages for breach of any agreement between one union and another. Another objective of the Act, as von Prondzynski (1989b) points out, was to encourage the trade unions to register with the Registrar of Friendly Societies. Wallace (1994) suggests that the practical effect of the provisions of the Act was to allow trade unions to exist within the law, but to prevent legal regulation of their affairs. The 1871 Act, as subsequently amended, governs the legal status of trade unions in Ireland today.

The attempt of the Trade Union Act of 1871 to legitimate trade unions within the law was largely unsuccessful as it became evident from judicial decisions that, even though the existence of trade unions was legal, many of their activities were illegal. This arose because of the underlying common law concept of criminal conspiracy. For example, if two or more union members combined to threaten to withdraw their labour, this was held by the courts to be a criminal conspiracy. Furthermore, picketing of any description was held to be illegal. The effect was to significantly frustrate the operation of trade unions in their efforts to improve the pay and conditions of workers through collective action. Following a successful campaign, which saw the trade union movement again support the Conservative party of Disraeli in return for a promise to amend the legislation, the remit of the criminal law was considerably restricted by the introduction of the Conspiracy and Protection of Property Act 1875. The Conspiracy and Protection of Property Act 1875 provided

(1) that no one was liable for any act committed 'in contemplation or furtherance of a trade dispute' unless the act would also be a crime if committed by one person;
(2) that a breach of contract by workers of gas or water supply was to remain a crime in certain circumstances;
(3) immunity to peaceful picketing in connection with a trade dispute (that is picketing that does not entail violence or intimidation);
(4) that a breach of contract by any person which endangered human life, risked serious bodily injury or exposed valuable property to destruction, continued to be a crime.

The Trade Union Amendment Act of 1876 strengthened the legal position of trade unions by ensuring that trustees could be held accountable for union funds. The net effect of these legislative changes was to remove the taint of illegality from trade unions. The Acts of 1871 and 1875 virtually excluded the law of conspiracy from the field of trade disputes. Kerr and Whyte (1985) argue that the reaction of employers and the courts, when denied the use of criminal liabilities, was to develop the notion of civil conspiracy under the law of tort, which provided remedies against conduct deliberately aimed at causing financial loss. The new threat posed to trade unions was that their ability to take effective industrial action was hampered by the prospect of employers seeking awards of damages and orders of injunctions. The crime of conspiracy had been succeeded as an anti-union weapon by the tort of conspiracy. This significant threat to the unions was bolstered by a number of important decisions. In the case of Quinn v Leathem (1901), initially heard in Belfast, it was established that if two or more persons combine together without legal justification to injure another, they are liable for damages for conspiracy. In this famous case it was held that an official of a trade union was liable for combining to injure an employer by threatening to withdraw labour from one of his customers unless the latter ceased to do business with him. While no unlawful act had been committed by any of the defendants individually, the combination to injure was an unlawful conspiracy, entitling the plaintiff to recover civil damages for the loss he had suffered. The Conspiracy and Protection of Property Act 1875 was judged to afford no protection since it gave immunity only from criminal conspiracy. However, the judgement was against the union official Leathem and not the union.

From the perspective of the trade unions an equally disturbing development was the decision of the House of Lords in the case of the Taff Vale Railway Company v Amalgamated Society of Railway Servants (1901). The trade unions had been reluctantly accepting civil actions against union officers and members as in the Quinn v Leathem case, but did not believe that the trade union as an entity could be sued to meet the liabilities for torts committed by its officers. Until 1901 it was assumed that because a registered union was an unincorporated association having no legal identity distinct from that of its individual members, this placed the union's funds beyond the reach of the judicial process. The decision which emanated from the lawlords in the Taff Vale case was that the union's funds were not immune from suits of damages. The case itself arose as a result of a strike by members of the Amalgamated Society of Railway Servants in August 1900. Richard Bell, the union's general secretary, had persuaded 'blackleg labour' not to work, thus inducing them to breach their contract with the Taff Vale company. The company sought an injunction and damages against the union. The case was heard on appeal in the House of Lords, where it was held that a registered trade union, as constituted under the Trade Union Act of 1871, was a legal entity possessing sufficient attributes of corporate personality to enable it to be sued in its registered name for the torts of its servants or agents. This decision was a tremendous blow to the unions as it seemed likely to reduce them to impotence, since if they declared a strike they ran the risk of their funds being attacked by the law. In the Taff Vale case the union had to pay £35,000 in total as a result of the case found against it (£23,000 damages was awarded to the company).

During the subsequent five years it has been estimated that unions lost £200,000 in similar actions. The effect of the decision in the Taff Vale case was to destroy the legal rights of trade unions as established by the Acts of 1871 and 1875, and to make strikes illegal. The trade union movement in response to these and other cases again looked to the political arena for redress (Wallace, 1988b). They campaigned vigourously for parliamentary reform to overturn this judge-made law. In the 1906 elections the election of a Liberal Government led to the passing of the Trade Disputes Act 1906. The Trade Disputes Act 1906 provided protection to trade unions and their members by granting them immunity from the tort of civil conspiracy, legalising peaceful picketing and providing immunity against actions which would otherwise have been illegal at common law. Section 4 of the Act also provided that trade unions could not be held liable for any act under the law of tort. The Act in effect conferred a 'blanket immunity' on trade unions by prohibiting any actions in tort against them in their registered name. This meant that the decision in the Taff Vale case had been reversed, and union funds were immune from awards of damages. The immunities conferred in the Act are restricted to persons 'acting in contemplation or furtherance of a trade dispute', dubbed the 'golden formula' by Wedderburn (1965). Von Prondzynski (1989b) suggests that the Trade Disputes Act 1906 adopted a very simple technique, that is, it identified the main judicial decisions which had disabled trade unions and gave unions an immunity from legal action under these judicial precedents.

It is important to note that the Act did not give a positive right to strike. Kerr and Whyte (1985) report that the trade unions opposed the enactment of a comprehensive labour law code with positive rights and obligations, and opted for the more pragmatic immunities approach. The immunities approach adopted in the Trade Disputes Act gave a distinctly voluntarist orientation to British and Irish industrial relations, characterised by the essentially abstentionist role of the State in the system.

The final piece of Westminster collective labour legislation enacted before Ireland achieved Independence is the Trade Union Act 1913. The Act amended the definition and registration provisions for trade unions. Its most important provision was to allow the funds of a trade union to be applied for political purposes. The Act arose because of the decision of the House of Lords in the case of Osborne v the Amalgamated Society of Railway Servants (1911), which held that unions were not entitled to raise or expend funds for political purposes. The Act reversed this position, provided that political purposes were included in the unions' objects, and separate political funds set up from which members could opt out.

Table 2.3 summarises the legislative developments in Irish collective labour law since 1922. After Independence the Oireachtas was relatively slow to augment the collective labour framework that it had inherited. The eighteen years between 1922 and 1940 saw a period of legislative inaction with only one statute enacted—the Trade Union Act of 1935. This Act essentially enables trade unions to hold an unlimited amount of land. The trade union movement was largely happy with the protectionist legislation that existed and, as McGinley (1990) suggests, their main concern was to preserve their Victorian legacy embodied in the Acts of the UK Parliament to which we have referred.

The Trade Union Act of 1941 was enacted to the backdrop of great concern over the perceived structural defects in the trade union movement. The proliferation of trade unions was seen to be a significant catalyst in the creation of industrial unrest. Von Prondzynski (1989b) argues that there was also a widespread belief at the time that the large number of trade unions, fragmented and uncoordinated, and the substantial number of British-based unions operating here were hostile to the best interests of the State. The Trade Union Act of 1941 obligated trade unions who wished to engage in collective bargaining to have a negotiating licence and in so doing introduced for the first time the concept of an 'authorised trade union'. The Act confined the immunities contained in the Trade Disputes Act of 1906 to such 'authorised trade unions'. A number of conditions were specified for a trade union to qualify for a licence, which essentially entailed depositing a sum of money with the High Court.

Table 2.3. Collective labour legislation enacted by the Oireachtas

Statute	Provisions
Trade Union Act 1935	Trade unions allowed to own unlimited amount of land
Trade Union Act 1941	Negotiation licences, sole negotiation rights
Trade Union Act 1942	Exemptions from negotiation licences, appeals in sole negotiation rights situations
Industrial Relations Act 1946	Establishment of the Labour Court
Trade Union Acts 1947–52	Six Acts extending power to reduce deposits of Irish unions by 75%
Industrial Relations Act 1969	Enlargement of the Labour Court Office of Rights Commissioners
Trade Union Act 1971	New negotiation licence rules: £5,000 deposit, 500 members, 18-month wait
Trade Union Act 1975	Encouraged the amalgamation of trade unions
Industrial Relations Act 1976	Allowed agricultural workers' access to the Labour Court
Trade Disputes (Amendment) Act 1982	Extended immunities of the 1906 Act to all except the police and the army
Industrial Relations Act 1990	Labour Relations Commission, pre-strike secret ballots, immunities/injunctions curbed, trade union rationalisation

Source: McGinley, 1990.

The second essential feature of the Act provided for the establishment of a Trade Union Tribunal which could give sole negotiating rights to one or more unions. This second feature posed a significant threat to the British-based unions who could not get sole negotiating rights on their own. Both features of the Act were designed to exclude certain trade unions from operating by regulating the function of negotiation, licencing some unions for the purpose and excluding others (Von Prondzynski, 1989b). The aim of the Act was to discourage the formation of new unions and to cut down the number of existing ones.

The Trade Union Act of 1941 was the focus of much criticism when debated in the Dail, particularly from Fine Gael TDs who questioned the constitutionality of the Act. Prior to enactment, it was the subject of an intense campaign by the trade union movement, which culminated in a large protest march in Dublin. A Trade Union Bill was drafted in 1942, designed to address some of the concerns expressed about the Trade Union Act of 1941 and mindful of the fact that certain exemptions to the general provisions must exist. The Bill was passed without debate, with the Trade Union Bill of 1942 providing certain exemptions from holding negotiating licences and providing appeals machinery in sole negotiation rights situations.

The Trade Union Act of 1941 was to become the subject of a constitutional test case in 1946, when the ITGWU applied for sole negotiating rights in the road passenger and tramway services of CIE, where the British-based National Union of Railwaymen (NUR) also operated. The NUR challenged the constitutionality of Part III of the Act, which dealt with the issue of sole negotiation rights, and in July 1946 the Supreme Court on appeal ruled that it was repugnant to the Constitution. Part III was struck down, all that remained of the 1941 Act were the provisions for negotiating licences.

The Trade Union Act of 1971 amended many of the provisions for negotiating licences under the 1941 Act, as the Government continued to pursue its policy of discouraging the formation of new unions. The 1971 Act provided that a union must notify the Minister for Labour and the ICTU of its intention to apply for a negotiation licence eighteen months beforehand. The Act also required the union to have 500 members in the State at the date of application for a licence and eighteen months beforehand. The appropriate deposit held with the High Court, which varied depending on the size of the union, was now to be at a minimum of £5,000. The Trade Union Act of 1975 extended the policy of promoting trade union rationalisation by encouraging amalgamations between unions essentially providing financial assistance to trade unions who successfully merge.

The Industrial Relations Acts of 1946 and 1969 established certain third-party institutions, namely the Labour Court and the Rights Commissioners, whose function it is to principally assist employers and trade unions in the conduct of industrial relations, particularly in the case of trade disputes. The development and the provisions of these Acts will be described in chapter 3.

2.2.2. THE REFORM OF COLLECTIVE LABOUR LAW—THE DEBATE

The Industrial Relations Act 1990 passed into law on 18 July 1990 and is now the definitive piece of legislation governing relations between employers and employees and their representatives in this country. The Act is the most comprehensive revision of the law governing trade unions, trade disputes and industrial relations generally in over eighty years since the Trade Disputes Act 1906.

The Act is the culmination, however, of over fifty years of debate on the general role of the law in industrial relations, and more specifically on the need for reform of existing trade disputes legislation. Wallace (1991a) argues that the lack of legislative activity from Government up to 1990 masks a recurrent and persistent interest in legal reform of industrial relations. Since the late 1940s successive Governments identified the need to reform and update the existing legislation, but until 1990 none had achieved anything substantial. McCall (1988) notes that Lemass made considerable progress in the late 1950s, but his efforts were to no avail. Reform of Irish industrial relations and trade disputes law has been high on the agenda of the Department of Labour since its establishment in 1966 (Department of Labour, 1991b; Kerr, 1991a). Kerr (1991a) suggests that the persistence of the reform debate can be understood by the fact that the general state of industrial relations was perceived throughout the 1950s, 1960s and 1970s to be in serious disorder—unofficial strikes were widespread, there were frequent disruptions to essential services, and there were a significant number of inter-union disputes, all of which were afforded immunities under the Trade Disputes Act. One of the very first initiatives of the newly established Department of Labour was to draft a Trade Union Bill in 1966, which proposed to remove immunities from liability under the Trade Disputes Act from trade union members who engaged in unofficial action, and require the holding of a secret ballot before a strike. The Bill was subject to severe criticism from the trade union movement and did not receive a second reading. The Government chose not to pursue the Bill because of the lack of consensus, the Minister for Labour conceding that legislation in this regard can only be effective if it had the co-operation of the trade unions (Dail Debates, 1969).

In May 1978 the Government, faced with employer calls for action over the increasing incidence of industrial action, appointed a Commission of Inquiry on Industrial Relations. The Commission was charged with examining industrial relations generally, and specifically to report on the relevance of statute law to industrial relations. Since the early 1970s employers had been advocating radical reform of the law applicable to trade disputes. Kevin Duffy (1993) suggests that the demand for reform was also coming from the Industrial Development Authority, who argued to the Government that the perceived poor industrial relations record in Ireland was a deterrent to the attraction of foreign investment.

The Commission's trade union participants withdrew in protest at the delay in bringing forward legislation to extend the coverage of the Trade Disputes Act to the public service. The Commission, which reported in 1981, maintained that there were serious defects in the Irish trade union structure. Essentially their view was that trade union multiplicity was a major problem with too many small unions giving poor service to members. Inadequate levels of service then led to disaffection among members and frequently to unofficial action (Report of the Commission of Inquiry on Industrial Relations, 1981). The Commission concluded that voluntary means alone were incapable of governing Irish industrial relations. The Report of the Commission made a number of controversial recommendations in relation to collective labour legislation including (1) the immunities trade unions enjoyed under the 1906 Act be limited, (2) the withdrawal of immunities from disputes of rights, that is, disputes concerning dismissal, equality, union recognition and inter-union disputes, (3) the introduction of a mandatory disputes procedure, (4) the establishment of a Labour Relations Board and a Labour Relations Court, which would determine whether industrial action complied with the trades disputes provisions. While none of these recommendations were implemented, Wallace (1988b) argues that the report provided a central focus for the debate on reform which continued throughout the 1980s.

The Report of the Commission was subject to much academic criticism. For example, McCarthy and von Prondzynski (1982) condemned the Commission's lack of original work, and argued that it selectively used secondary data to support its conclusions. Kelly and Roche (1983) maintained that in advocating greater legalism the Commission ignored countries that had a great deal of legal regulation and a high strike record. Wallace and O'Shea (1987) argued that the Commission had incorrectly identified the cause of unofficial strikes. On a more general note, the serious problem with Irish industrial relations as identified by the Commission related to trade union structure, yet the prescriptions addressed the issue of trade disputes.

The 1980s saw a decade of discussions between the Department of Labour, the ICTU and the FIE. These discussions were led by various publications which emanated from the Department. There were four sets of proposals throughout the 1980s, the final set of proposals by the Minister for Labour of the day, Bertie Ahern, in 1988 formed the basis of the provisions found in the Industrial Relations Act 1990. The 1983 discussion document rejected most of the Commission's recommendations, particularly the removal of immunities, and concurred with the academic criticisms of the Commission's Report (Department of Labour, 1983). In the view of the Department any increase in the incidence of strikes indicated inadequacies in the industrial relations dispute settling machinery rather than defects in the law (Kerr, 1991a). A discussion document published in 1985 by the Department of Labour and expanded upon in 1986, proposed the establishment of a Labour Relations Commission charged with the statutory responsibility to promote good industrial relations. More fundamentally, the proposals advocated a radical move away from the immunities-based system to a 'positive rights' approach

(Department of Labour, 1985). This approach opted for a positive right to strike instead of the immunity from liability in the event of a strike. A complete defence was to be afforded when the right was used. These proposals were met with criticism from the trade union movement because of the feared limitations which would have been placed on the right to strike. For example, it was envisaged that the right would not apply in workmen versus workmen disputes, in the event of secondary picketing, in the case of industrial action involving one worker, a strike by a minority of workers where there had been a recent ballot against such an action, and occupation or damage to property, personal injury or trespass. It was also feared that more restrictive conditions might later be imposed on the exercise of the right to strike. The then president of the ITGWU, John Carroll (1986), argued that those who claim 'that an alternative to the present immunities approach would strengthen the trade union position' must be taken with a grain of salt.

The publication of the Industrial Relations Bill 1989 was preceded by yet another discussion document in 1988 which, as mentioned, bore a remarkable similarity to the eventual Act (Department of Labour, 1988). The immediate origins for the 1988 discussion document are to be found in the Programme for National Recovery, which committed the Minister for Labour to holding discussions with the social partners about changes in industrial relations which, in the words of the Programme, 'would provide a better framework for collective bargaining and dispute settlement and help to create conditions for employment generating investment' (Department of Labour, 1991b). The 1988 proposals reverted to an immunities-based approach, but the exceptions to the complete defence outlined in the 1985 proposals survived. Bonner (1987) explains that the primary reason for reverting to the immunities system was the unenthusiastic response of the ICTU to the positive rights approach. Wallace (1991a) argues that the consistency seen in the proposals for reform is probably indicative of a number of interrelated factors: firstly, the influence of the Commission of Inquiry in setting the agenda for reform, secondly, a certain continuity of thinking on the topic of reform within the Department of Labour, and thirdly, the influence of British legislation on Irish thinking. The proposals were put to both sides of industry as the Minister sought to achieve a balance which would reflect the rights and responsibilities of both employers and trade unions. Various modifications were made to the proposals during the detailed negotiations which took place, and a number of changes were also made in the text of the Bill during its passage through the Oireachtas. The Bill was generally well supported from across all political parties when debated in the Dail. The Workers' Party (see Rabbitte and Gilmore, 1990), however, were unhappy with the Bill and were of the view that it would lead to more intervention in industrial relations matters by the Courts.

2.2.3. THE INDUSTRIAL RELATIONS ACT 1990

A number of more immediate factors may help to understand the rationale for the introduction of the Act. While undoubtedly the problems of perceived disorder (for example unofficial strikes, inter-union disputes, strikes in essential services, etc.), which had persistently haunted the Irish industrial relations system, were very infrequent in the late 1980s, the Department of Labour felt it was no time to be complacent. In the light of the national consensus secured under the Programme for National Recovery the Department of Labour felt it was an appropriate time to press ahead with changes to the existing labour law designed to maintain the relatively good record of industrial peace.

The law in relation to trades disputes had become extraordinarily complex (Department of Labour, 1991b; Kerr, 1991b). A considerable volume of case law had arisen from the judicial construction of the Trade Disputes Act 1906. Indeed, so much case law surrounded the 1906 Act that the usefulness of the legislation in providing a guide as to what was or was not permissible in a trade dispute was considerably diminished.

A threat of a constitutional challenge to the Trade Disputes Act 1906 had also long existed. It was feared that the constitutionality of the blanket immunity in the Act may be tested in relation to article 34, which guaranteed access to the courts. The Department of Labour anticipated that the Industrial Relations Act 1990 would address this situation.

The policy of encouraging trade union rationalisation initiated under the Trade Union Act of 1941 and extended under the Trade Union Acts of 1971 and 1975 was believed to have played a significant role in promoting trade union mergers and amalgamations. It was hoped that the new legislation would further promote this process.

The purpose of the 1990 Industrial Relations Act as outlined by the then Minister for Labour, Bertie Ahern (1991a), 'is to put in place an improved framework for the conduct of industrial relations . . . [with the] . . . overall aim of maintaining a stable industrial relations climate' (Ahern, 1991a). The longer title of the Act sets out that the aim of the Act is 'to make further and better the provision for promoting harmonious relations between workers and employers'. Bertie Ahern (1991b) also maintained that the 'Act was aimed at tightening and clarifying the situation in relation to trade disputes'.

THE PROVISIONS OF THE ACT
The provisions of the Act can be broadly divided between trade union law and industrial relations legislation.

I Trade Union Law Provisions

A. TRADE DISPUTES
The approach adopted in the area of trade disputes law was to repeal the Trade Disputes Acts of 1906 and 1982 and to reintroduce the main provisions of these Acts with amendments. The main features of the provisions relating to trade disputes are outlined overleaf.

(1) *Individual disputes:* The Act withdraws immunities from one person disputes where agreed procedures have not been followed.

(2) *Secondary action:* This is now restricted unless the union can show that the secondary employer directly sought to frustrate the aims of the dispute.

(3) *Picketing:* Workers may now only picket their own employer at the employer's place of work.

(4) *Immunities:* The Act places limitations on the blanket immunity which existed under section 4 of the Trade Disputes Act 1906 in respect of tortious acts. The immunity now only exists for acts 'committed in contemplation or furtherance of a trade dispute'.

(5) *Worker versus worker disputes:* These no longer fall within the definition of a trade dispute.

(6) *Injunctions:* In trade dispute situations where a secret ballot has been held and one week's notice given, the granting of injunctions, particularly *ex-parte* injunctions is restricted.

B. SECRET BALLOTS
As of 18 July 1992 union rules must contain provisions for the holding of secret ballots before any form of industrial action can be taken. No injunction will be granted to an employer in the event of a secret ballot being held.

C. TRADE UNION RATIONALISATION
The Act makes a number of amendments to existing trade union law designed to encourage mergers and to discourage formation of new or breakaway unions. The Act essentially increases the minimum membership level required for a negotiating licence to 1,000 and alters the sum of money required to be held on deposit with the High Court. The amount required varies according to the size of the union, but the minimum deposit now stands at £20,000. The Act also amends the Trade Union Act of 1975 by offering grants towards the expenses incurred in a two-year period prior to a merger attempt even if the attempt fails.

II Industrial Relations Legislation
The Act provides for the establishment of the Labour Relations Commission and divides functions between it and the Labour Court. The Act also makes changes in the procedure for the referral of disputes to the Labour Court and amended procedures in relation to the operation of Joint Labour Committees, employment regulation orders and registered employment agreements. The industrial relations provisions of the 1990 Act will be described in the discussion of the role of third parties in chapter 3.

The Experience to Date

It may still be too soon to make an accurate assessment of the impact the legislation has had on the conduct of industrial relations, in light of the relatively short time the Act has been in existence. Moreover, two fundamental sections of the Act which deal with balloting and injunctions have only been in place since July 1992. We have experienced a period of relative industrial peace since then, with few strikes to test the Act's provisions. However, there have been some significant developments in relation to the trade disputes provisions. Despite the limited number of cases aired in the Courts arising from the Act, a number of them have given rise to particular concern amongst trade-unionists. Especially worrying has been the interpretation of the provisions on individual disputes and picketing by the judiciary. The 1990 Act withdraws immunities for one person disputes where agreed procedures have been broken. In the case of Westman Holdings v McCormack and Others (1991) the question arose as to whether a dispute involving seven employees constituted seven individual disputes. As there were no agreed procedures in the company, the question was left undecided. In Iarnrod Eireann v Darby and O'Connor (1991) an injunction was granted in a dispute in which the Court held that an individual worker, who was supported by his fellow workers, had not complied with agreed procedures. What seems particularly disturbing about this decision from the trade union perspective is that disputes with a strong collective element to them, for example the dismissal of a shop steward, have immunity withdrawn from them until procedures are exhausted (Wallace, 1991c).

In the case of Westman Holdings v McCormack and Others the question of picketing also arose. The Westman Holdings case is undoubtedly the most significant case to be heard involving the Act to date. The case involved the sale of a licensed premises, where the workers who were dismissed by the original owner, sought work with the new owner of the premises. Section 11 of the Act provides that workers may only picket *their* employer. Westman Holdings was able to obtain an interlocutory injunction restraining the employees from picketing the premises after establishing a fair case that he was not *their* employer. This decision was confirmed on appeal to the Supreme Court. The case was ultimately settled out of court during the trial and as such no definitive decision had been taken on whether the picketing was lawful under the circumstances. Kerr (1991b) describes the alarming possibility which the decision seems to offer employers, that is, by dismissing employees during a trade dispute, the employees would no longer be covered by the 1990 Act. Thus, in dismissing the employees and terminating their contract of employment the employer could claim that the employees were no longer his employees. Although the Department of Labour have asserted that if employers began to use the Act in this manner, the Act would have to be amended.

A number of other provisions of the Act may cause trade unions some difficulties. For example, secondary action, though allowed under the Act, is more restricted. Meenan (1991) describes the requirement that the secondary employer had directly sought to frustrate the strike as a 'very high onus' of proof. Meenan (1991) has also drawn attention to the complicated rules in respect of secret ballots, the need for ballots for secondary action, the complex provisions for the aggregation of votes in a multi-union ballot as among the multiplicity of factors which could be used to challenge the legality of the ballots. Indeed, there have already been calls for the amendment of the secret ballot provisions, particularly those relating to the provisions for aggregation of votes in a multi-union ballot, in response to the controversy surrounding the ballots in the recent Irish Steel dispute. On the other hand, the loss of injunctive relief was universally welcomed within the trade union movement. The injunctive remedy was the most frequent legal recourse used by employers. Von Prondzynski (1981) estimated that the number of injunctions were likely to be in excess of 40–50 per annum, although as Wallace (1991) points out, there is no general agreement that this figure is accurate. Duffy (1993) suggests that in the years prior to the enactment of the 1990 Act, the situation had got to the point where an injunction would be granted in almost every case in which it was applied for.

The response of the trade unions to the operation of the Act so far has been on balance largely favourable. There was some initial disquiet as evidenced by two motions put down at the 1991 ICTU Annual Delegate Conference condemning the Act. One of those motions submitted by the Irish Distributive and Administrative Trade Union committed the ICTU to 'lobby extensively to have the Act amended so that an equitable balance between the interests of employees and trade unions is achieved' (*IRN*, 1991). This may be seen as a knee-jerk reaction to the uncertainties which some of the initial cases may have created in trade union circles. Kevin Duffy, the (1993) Assistant General Secretary of the ICTU, however, claims to be unaware of any situation in which a union has found it impossible to deal with a dispute because of the provisions of this legislation, nor is he aware of any industrial action taken by a union which was less successful than it might otherwise have been because of the provisions of the legislation. On the whole, to date it would appear that the Act has had little impact on the long-established way of conducting industrial relations in this country. Wallace (1991c) argues that a continuation of the strict judicial interpretation of the Act would mean that the employers may have the opportunity to use the law in a wide range of circumstances. However, to date there has been little evidence of employers having increased their recourse to the law in industrial relations matters. As Wallace (1991) suggests a more fundamental uncertainty is to what extent employers will use the law even if the opportunities arise considering the traditional voluntarist nature of our system.

CHAPTER THREE

The Role of the State

3.1. INTRODUCTION

It should be evident from the discussion in the first chapter that the primary responsibility for the conduct of industrial relations rests with management, employees and their representatives. Indeed, the bulk of everyday industrial relations is conducted by these parties. Trade unions and employer associations will be discussed respectively in the succeeding chapters. In this chapter, our concern centres on the role of the State, the third major actor on the industrial relations stage, or the 'third force' as Poole (1986) describes it. The involvement of the State in industrial relations may not be as obvious as that of trade unions and employers, but in some respects its impact may be more potent. The State sets the framework within which industrial relations exist and it is the State alone which has the law-making powers which may substantially change the rules affecting the employment relationship (Crouch, 1982a).

Salamon (1992) defines the State as the 'politically based and controlled institutions of government and regulation within an organised society'. When we speak of the State in Ireland we refer to members of the Dail, the Government, Civil Service, judiciary, Garda Siochana and the defence forces. However, as Salamon points out, the Government of the day (the party or parties in power) is the most important element within the State as it 'determines the directions, policies and actions of the State machinery'.

The primary responsibility of the State is the management of the national economy in a manner conducive to economic growth and the furtherance of national prosperity. It tries to accomplish this by pursuing four objectives which may not always be compatible, namely, to maintain a high level of employment, to ensure price stability, to achieve a favourable balance of payments and to protect the exchange rate (Crouch, 1982a). The State also has social objectives which emanate from the ideological perspective and general view of the nature of society of the party in Government. The industrial relations strategies adopted by the State are then designed with general reference to the attainment of these twin economic and social aims, and the methods the State chooses to pursue these objectives are largely determined by the ideological perspective of the Government of the day. The State's role in industrial relations is more pronounced in certain countries than in others, depending to a large extent on the context, circumstances and traditions within each country. The role of the State in a particular country may also be more pronounced from one administration to another because of the political beliefs and differences of the various parties in power.

An individual's perceptions, assumptions and expectations of how the State should be involved in industrial relations and the degree to which the State's intervention in industrial relations is considered legitimate or otherwise, largely depends on the individual's frame of reference. For example, viewed from the Marxist and radical perspectives, the State is seen historically as serving class interests, i.e. those of the capital class, irrespective of the party in power. Marx exemplifies this in suggesting that 'the executive of the modern State is but a committee for managing the common affairs of the whole bourgeoisie'. Thus Marx argues that the State's role in the industrial relations sphere is seen as protecting and supporting capital and its workplace representatives, i.e. management. The function of the State is to preserve the capitalist system and to preserve the dominance of capital over labour. Similarly, Hyman (1975) argues that public policy is 'nothing more than the ideal expression of the dominant material relationships' in industry.

The contrasting pluralist perspective views the State as a neutral party, or indeed in many respects as a referee between the divergent interests of employers and employees. Central to this viewpoint is the notion of 'voluntarism', that is minimal legal interference by the State in the conduct of industrial relations matters, leaving employers and trade unions free to develop workrules and procedures to suit particular organisational and industrial contexts. From this standpoint, if the State is to intervene in industrial relations matters, it should be to impose certain minimum standards and to protect individual rights in the employment relationship and to protect the 'national interest' if the Government of the day regards it as threatened.

Although advocating a non-interventionist, generally passive role for the State and promotion of a *laissez-faire* economic philosophy, the unitarist perspective sees an increased role for the State's law-making powers in regulating certain areas of industrial relations. Fox (1973) argues that unitarists believe that 'increased legal intervention in industrial relations matters can and should take the form of regulating . . . behaviour directly and embracing this regulation by direct punitive legal sanctions'.

The aim of this chapter is to consider the approaches or strategies that the State may pursue in industrial relations, and to review the four main methods by which the State may intervene in industrial relations namely (1) as an industrial relations policy maker, (2) as a provider of dispute resolution machinery, (3) as a legislator and (4) as an employer.

3.2. STATE APPROACHES TO INDUSTRIAL RELATIONS

A useful analysis of the policy alternatives or approaches which may be pursued by the State in industrial relations has been suggested by Crouch (1982a). Crouch identifies four alternative approaches which may be adopted by the State in industrial relations, namely (1) market individualism, (2) liberal collectivism, (3) corporatism and (4) bargained corporatism. Crouch sees these alternative approaches as expressions of the interrelationship between the dominant ideology in the industrial relations system (be it liberal or corporatist) and the relative power and autonomy of trade unions (be they strong and autonomous or weak and regulated). These varying options obviously entail very different social, political and economic implications. These ideal State approaches to industrial relations are summarised in table 3.1 and are discussed in the subsequent sections.

Table 3.1. State approaches to industrial relations

	Political ideology	Trade unions	Employer–employee relationships
Market individualism	*laissez-faire*	weak and regulated	exploitative or paternalistic
Liberal collectivism	liberal	strong and autonomous	voluntarist, free collective bargaining
Corporatism	corporatist	weak and regulated	subordinated and controlled, trade unions agents of control
Bargained corporatism	interventionist	strong and autonomous	voluntarist and tripartite

Source: Adapted from Rollinson, 1993.

3.2.1. MARKET INDIVIDUALISM

The dominant economic philosophy in market individualism is *laissez-faire*. This philosophy sees the market forces of supply and demand as the ultimate arbitrator of the competitive interests of capital and labour. Thus, labour is seen as a commodity to be bought or sold at a price to be determined by the market mechanism. Trade union interventions in the form of collective bargaining are seen as distorting the operation of the market and are treated with open hostility by employers favouring such a strategy. The *laissez-faire* option means mitigating trade union strength other than by means of compromise and agreements, typically by increased legislation aimed at placing legal limitations on trade union freedoms. Hence, trade unions under market individualism tend to be weak and regulated. Thus, as Crouch (1982a) points out, market individualism subordinates employees to the control and authority of the owner and the relationship between them is at best paternalistic but at worst exploitative. In keeping with the *laissez-faire* doctrine direct involvement by the State in industrial relations matters is avoided. Roche (1989) refers to this State approach as the 'market control' strategy which sees the government's role as supporting the reconstruction of competitive labour markets and controlling inflation and hence wage settlements by managing the money supply.

3.2.2. LIBERAL COLLECTIVISM

Liberal collectivism describes a framework which sees the coexistence of a liberal political ideology and the development of strong autonomous trade unions. Such an accommodation sees the acceptance of autonomous trade unions (by management) which represent, bargain and reconcile conflicting interests with management through the collective bargaining process. However, as Salamon (1992) points out, the dominant interests of management are protected through the establishment of a boundary between issues to be decided by collective bargaining and issues to be determined by managerial prerogative. The concepts of 'voluntarism' and 'pluralism' are central to this State approach. In this approach the parties to industrial relations insist on settling their own affairs without State interference. Roche (1989) classifies this State approach as 'auxiliary State control'. The role of the State is primarily facilitative, confined to providing dispute resolution institutions to aid the reconciliation of conflicts of interests which arise, and legislating to provide employees with a 'floor or rights' or minimum standards which of course can be improved upon through the collective bargaining process.

3.2.3. CORPORATISM

The theory of corporatism has its origins in a concept or idea about society which was common in the late nineteenth century. The classical idea of corporatism was a model of social organisation which sought to provide a blueprint for society where the State would function in co-operation with organised social-interest groups. Corporatism was intended to chart a middleground between liberal capitalism and State totalitarianism. The classical corporatists argued that liberal capitalist societies were characterised by rugged individualism and endemic social conflict, whereas totalitarianism was intrinsically repressive.

Roche (1989) defines corporatism 'as a strategy or model of public policy-making in which the State seeks to co-opt the leadership of social-interest groups into policy formulation in return for assurances that the latter will seek to deliver their respective constituencies when it comes to the implementation or execution of policies developed in central talks or agreements'.

Lehmbruch et al. (1982) argue that the following statements would characteristically define a fully corporatised system:

(1) Interest organisations are strongly co-opted into governmental decision making.

(2) Large interest organisations (in particular unions) are strongly linked to political parties and take part in policy formation.

(3) Most interest organisations are hierarchically structured and membership tends to be compulsory.

(4) Occupational categories are represented by non-competitive organisations enjoying a monopoly.

(5) Industrial relations are characterised by strong concertation of unions and employer associations with the government involved.

Corporatism then, as Poole (1986) suggests, denotes heavy involvement of the State usually taking the form of general legal regulation of industrial relations and the incorporation of trade unions into the State apparatus. Crouch (1982a) argues that such incorporation weakens trade union power and finds employees subordinated with trade unions operating as agents of State control.

Two variants or types of corporatism have been identified, namely (1) State or pure corporatism, and (2) bargained corporatism.

State or pure corporatism is facilitated by a concentration of powers in Government, monopoly forms of capital, the absence of associations of labour and political systems with a single party. This form of corporatism either involves massive State coercion or sufficient societal unity to make coercion unnecessary. In particular a unity of view must exist among employers, the State and the trade union leadership. As Poole (1986) contends 'corporatism is nurtured by a commitment to harmony and identity of interests at a cultural or ideological level reflected in a range of ethical and political philosophies that include catholicism, conservatism and social democracy'.

The corporate State is one which is often associated with totalitarian regimes of Fascist Italy and Germany in the 1930s and 1940s, and the former eastern-bloc Communist countries.

3.2.4. BARGAINED CORPORATISM

Bargained corporatism, often referred to as societal or liberal corporatism, describes a State approach to industrial relations which evolves in the presence of a dominant interventionist political ideology and strong autonomous trade unions. It represents the outcome of centrally organised interest groups and of open political systems. Such an approach involves increased Government consultation, negotiation or political exchange with both employer associations and organised labour through established tripartite corporatist forums at national level. This approach involves the Government, in effect, becoming a third party to the collective bargaining process interposed between the trade union movement and employer associations.

It is the voluntary nature of bargained corporatism and the consequent lack of compulsion and independence of trade unions which differentiates it from pure corporatism. In totalitarian Communist or Fascist regimes non-cooperative trade unions are often disbanded and membership of co-operative ones made compulsory. Co-operative trade unions often granted a deliberate representational monopoly. Centrally derived policies on industrial relations matters are enforced on affiliated organisations and in turn on the general body of members. Bargained corporatism, however, entails trade union acceptance of and commitment to strategies which may restrain the pursuit of their members' sectional interests. This restraint may take the form of voluntary wage controls to aid the government's efforts to manage inflation, relaxation of restrictive practices in the interests of improving productivity, a commitment to avoid industrial conflict, etc. In a bargained corporatist regime, the trade unions endeavour to deliver its constituents consent to such restraint in return for Government concessions. These concessions will usually give the trade union movement political influence in the policy formulation process of social and economic issues which normally cannot be attained through free collective bargaining, for example increased investment and job creation. Employers are similarly enticed into participation in the process in return for such political influence and Government commitments to control inflation, taxes, etc.

Roche (1989) has also identified two variants of corporate State involvement, i.e. a legislative variant and a social contract variant. His legislative variant is more akin to State corporatism where the State defines and controls the operations of the corporate bodies by statute, including the corporate bodies' ascendency over their members. The social contract variant essentially equates to what has been described as bargained corporatism.

O'Shea (1983) contends that corporatist systems differ from liberal collectivist or pluralist ones by virtue of their more orderly and planful structure and their more intimate and more dependent relationship with the State. O'Shea argues that a central hypothesis of the theory of corporatism is that corporatist systems are more governable and better able to absorb fundamental industrial change.

3.3. THE CHANGING NATURE OF IRISH STATE STRATEGIES

The dominant State approach to industrial relations in Ireland at the beginning of this century was market individualism. More widespread collectivisation and a greater degree of trade union organisation prompted the State to alter its stance to one of liberal collectivism or what Roche terms 'auxiliary State control'. In discussing Irish State strategies since the Second World War, Roche (1989) argues that there has been a drift from auxiliary State control to attempts at corporate control, which can be best understood in terms of two phases. Roche suggests that the first phase, during the 1960s, saw the trade unions becoming involved in a number of largely consultative bodies such as the Employer Labour Conference and the National Industrial and Economic Council. Throughout this period, however, liberal collectivism and 'collective bargaining remained inviolate', with any attempt by the State to intervene in pay determination being perceived as hostile by the trade unions, who used the threat of withdrawing from these consultative bodies as a means of repelling such corporatist advances. Roche suggests that it was during this phase that the strategic and institutional basis for further State intervention into industrial relations was established. Roche argues that the second phase in the movement towards attempts at corporate control of the bargained or social contract variety entailed the repeated negotiation of National Wage Agreements and two tripartite National Understandings in the 1970s and early 1980s. This period was characterised by active State involvement in the process of collective bargaining together with trade union participation in the process of government. Liberal collectivism or the auxiliary State resurfaced during the period 1982–87 with a return to decentralised bargaining. The Programme for National Recovery, followed by the Programme for Economic and Social Progress and the current Programme for Competitiveness and Work have seen a recommitment by the State and the social partners to pursuing a strategy of bargained corporatism. In comparative terms, Ireland would appear to be weakly corporatised when compared to the highly corporatised systems of Austria, Sweden or Norway. The issue of politics and the development of State policy in Irish industrial relations has been addressed in depth in chapter 1, and the role of the State in collective bargaining in Ireland is discussed in greater detail in chapter 6.

3.4. THE STATE AS A PROVIDER OF DISPUTE RESOLUTION FACILITIES

A second major role for the State in industrial relations is that of provider of dispute resolution facilities. The voluntarist nature of the Irish system of industrial relations ensures that the parties are free to settle their disputes through the process of collective bargaining by negotiation and compromise. In the event of their failing to resolve any differences they may prefer to avoid resort to industrial action and refer the matter to an independent third party for either conciliation, adjudication or arbitration. The State has provided for the settlement of trade disputes in this manner by the establishment of a number of specific institutions. Indeed, from the time of Independence in 1922, the State has provided third-party assistance in industrial relations. As Forde (1992) notes, the establishment of State-sponsored specialised bodies to resolve trade disputes is a feature of most advanced industrial societies.

A policy of non-intervention by the State will not always extend to the point where it can completely opt out of industrial relations matters. The 'public interest' (which in some sense the Government has to represent) and electorate opinion may often charge the State with the role of industrial peacemaker with the settlement of damaging and socially disruptive disputes seen as a direct responsibility of the State (Farnham and Pimlott, 1990).

Figure 3.1. State institutions for dispute resolution

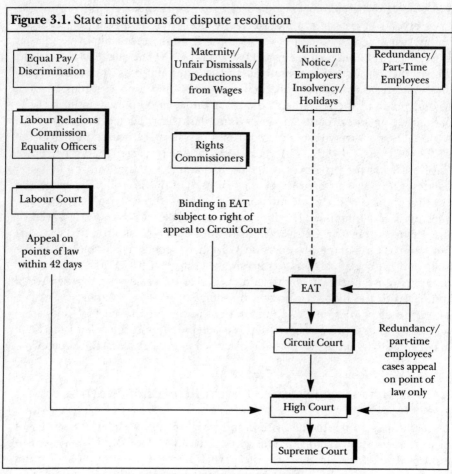

Source: Adapted from Wallace, 1987.

In the area of dispute resolution then, the State has established the following institutions: the Labour Court, the Employment Appeals Tribunal, the Labour Relations Commission, Rights Commissioners and Employment Equality Officers. Figure 3.1 charts the framework under which these institutions operate in the industrial relations field.

3.4.1. THE LABOUR COURT

The Labour Court is the principal institution in Ireland which facilitates the resolution of trade disputes. Article 37 of the Irish Constitution authorises the establishment of tribunals outside the court system with limited functions and powers of a judicial nature in non-criminal matters (Forde, 1992). The Labour Court was established by the Industrial Relations Act of 1946, with the aim as outlined in the Act's longer title 'to make further and better provisions for promoting harmonious relations between workers and their employers and for this purpose to establish machinery . . . for the prevention of trade disputes (Industrial Relations Act 1946). Provisions of that Act relating to the Court's constitution and operations were amended by the Industrial Relations Act of 1969 and by the Industrial Relations Act 1976. The effect of these Acts was to significantly expand the role of the Court in the industrial relations system. The role of the Labour Court changed significantly with the introduction of the Industrial Relations Act of 1990 which assigned many of its previously held functions to the Labour Relations Commission, which was established under the 1990 Act.

The principal role of the Labour Court in the Irish industrial relations scene is to investigate and make recommendations on cases referred to it by parties in dispute. These are normally issues where the parties have failed to reach agreement or compromise at local level. The Court has a number of other functions including:
– the registration of certain agreements;
– the establishment and servicing of Joint Labour Committees, and the ratification of conditions of employment by these committees;
– the provision of services in relation to the operation of Joint Industrial Councils;
– hearing appeals against a Rights Commissioner's recommendations and appeals against an Equality Officer's decision.

The Labour Court's referral procedure requires that in the first stage the parties in dispute are obliged to avail of the services of the conciliation service of the Labour Relations Commission. Should an issue remain unresolved after conciliation, it may be then referred to the Labour Court for investigation. The Industrial Relations Act 1990 provides that the Court may normally investigate a dispute only in one of the following situations:
– if it receives a report from the Labour Relations Commission that no further efforts on its part will help resolve the dispute, or
– if it is notified by the Chairperson of the Commission that the Commission

has waived its function of conciliation in the dispute.

The Court may also investigate a dispute:

– if it is hearing an appeal in relation to a recommendation of a Rights Commissioner or an Equality Officer, or

– if it decides after consultation with the Commission that exceptional circumstances of the case warrant a Labour Court investigation, or

– if it is referred to under Section 20 of the Industrial Relations Act 1969.

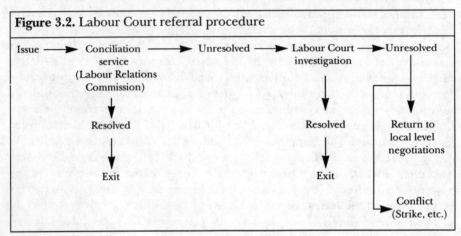

Figure 3.2. Labour Court referral procedure

Source: Gunnigle and Flood, 1990.

In addition, the Court may investigate a dispute at the request of the Minister for Enterprise and Employment.

The Court at present consists of a chairman, three deputy chairmen and nine ordinary members, all of whom are appointed by the Minister for Enterprise and Employment. The ordinary members are nominated for appointment by organisations representative of trade unions and employer associations. The ordinary members are required to always be available to the Court and are not permitted to hold any other employment which would prevent them from fulfilling their responsibilities to the Court.

For the speedy dispatch of business the Court may sit by division. At present there are three divisions of the Court. The operation of a fourth division was suspended in 1992. A division is comprised of a chairman or deputy chairman, and two ordinary members, one of the latter being a workers' representative and the other an employer's representative. A Labour Court hearing is normally presided over by such a division.

The title 'Labour Court' has often been noted as something of a misnomer; indeed, von Prondzynski (1989b) suggests that the title is misleading. The Labour Court itself has asserted that 'the procedure and general atmosphere prevailing at a hearing by the Court, for the purpose of the investigation of a trade dispute, bears little resemblance to the formalities of a court of law'.

Hearings are generally held in private, unless one of the parties concerned requests a public hearing.

> Formalities are reduced to a minimum. Written submissions are normally made by both parties, before the Court investigation commences. These written submissions are read at the Court hearing by the main spokesperson for each side, but the fact that certain aspects of the dispute may not be covered in the written submission does not prevent a party from covering these additional aspects by the way of a supplementary oral submission. Any points on which clarification or elaboration is required will be dealt with by way of questions by members of the Court. The more fully facts and arguments are given in the written and oral submissions, the less the need there will be for members of the Court to put questions. Written submissions are required to be in the hands of the Court a few days before the hearing. (Labour Court, Explanatory Hand-out)

Witnesses may be summoned before the Court and be examined under oath, and may be required to produce to the Court any document in their possession or control. However, these provisions are rarely used. When the Court feels it has adequately investigated a dispute, it will conclude the hearing and set about issuing a recommendation. Section 19 of the Industrial Relations Act 1969 outlines that 'the Court having investigated a trade dispute may make a recommendation setting forth its opinions on the merits of the dispute and the terms on which it should be settled'. Prior to the enactment of this piece of legislation the Court under section 68 of the 1946 Act was obliged to have regard to the public interest, the promotion of industrial peace, the fairness of the terms to the parties concerned and the prospects of the terms being acceptable to them. This section was repealed in 1969, as from very early in the operation of the Court it became clear to the Court that it was almost impossible to reconcile all of these criteria (Kerr and Whyte, 1985). This was highlighted by R.J.P. Mortished, the first Chairman of the Court, in commentating 'a settlement acceptable to the parties might be against the public interest and one which was not acceptable to the parties would not promote industrial peace' (Labour Court, Third Annual Report).

A Labour Court recommendation normally takes the form of a summary of the case submitted by each party to the dispute followed by the Labour Court deliberations with regard to the basis for settlement. The Court occasionally makes an oral recommendation at the end of the hearing or from time to time it may issue its recommendations by letter. The recommendations of the Court are generally not legally binding on the parties to the dispute. They are merely recommendations, not judgements which may be accepted or rejected by the parties. McCarthy (1984) described a Labour Court recommendation as 'essentially a third view' for the parties in dispute to consider, and that the

Court was established 'as a body whose purpose was to promote accommodation . . . to act as an honest broker, neither to apply law nor to create it'. However, in the event of the Court hearing an appeal of the decision of a Rights Commissioner or an Equality Officer, or where workers or their trade unions refer a dispute to the Court for investigation under section 20 (i) of the Industrial Relations Act 1969 (i.e. where the trade union refers the dispute on its own and agrees to be bound by the Court's recommendation) the recommendations of the Court are legally binding. This, in the eyes of the Court 'is in complete accord with the principle of free collective bargaining which underlies the establishment of the Labour Court. The Court's duty is to give a considered opinion as to the terms on which a particular dispute should be settled but the responsibility for the settlement rests at all times with the parties themselves' (Labour Court, Explanatory Hand-out).

Bearing in mind the voluntary nature of its recommendations, the Court has had a very satisfactory record with on average over three-quarters of its recommendations accepted by both parties. Even when Labour Court recommendations are rejected, their terms may often form the basis for a solution on return to local-level negotiations. Table 3.2 lists the numbers of recommendations issued by the Court each year since 1971.

Table 3.2. Labour Court recommendations

Year	No. of recommendations issued	Year	No. of recommendations issued
1971	162	1983	1,045
1972	n/a	1984	941
1973	326	1985	963
1974	365	1986	839
1975	403	1987	837
1976	474	1988	708
1977	462	1989	646
1978	546	1990	529
1979	575	1991	603
1980	866	1992	n/a
1981	766	1993	n/a
1982	975		

Source: Labour Court, Annual Reports.

The number of industrial disputes referred to the Labour Court rose dramatically throughout the 1970s, increasing from 162 cases in 1971 to 866 cases in 1980, and reaching a peak level of activity in 1983 when it issued 1,045 recommendations. This greatly contrasts with the situation in the 1960s when the Court heard on average 100 cases per year. The Court itself attributed this enormous increase in caseload to a general over-dependence on the Court and in many cases the failure of the parties to conduct full and meaningful negotiations at local level, the Court no longer being perceived as the 'court of last resort' (Labour Court, Thirty-first Annual Report). John Horgan, a former Chairman of the Court concluded that the increased reliance may have been due to 'negotiators losing the art of compromise' (Horgan, 1989). In commentating on this trend Wallace (1991c) suggests that

> . . . it seems largely unacknowledged the extent to which the greater proceduralisation of workplace industrial relations following the influence of the Donovan Commission 1965 to 1968 has contributed to this trend. Dispute procedures in Ireland now almost invariably contain a clause which restrains industrial action prior to referral to the Labour Court. This means that employers and unions can end up referring disputes to go to the Court, not because of any desire on the part of both parties to go to the Court, but because they must do so in order to comply with procedures.

Another telling factor in the dramatic rise of usage may have been the terms of the National Wage Agreements and National Understandings in the 1970s and early 1980s. Bonner (1989) suggests that these agreements contributed to increased reference to the Court. On the other hand, the significant decline in the activity of the Court since 1986 was felt by the then Department of Labour 'to be reflective of the improved industrial relations of recent years' (Department of Labour, Annual Report 1991). Although, it would be foolhardy to ignore the high levels of unemployment and the economic downturn experienced during the period and its effect on the relative strength of the trade unions as significant factors.

The Court was seen to depart from its broad role of promoting collective bargaining and resolving industrial conflict when it was given the role as determinant of disputes under the Anti-Discrimination (Pay) Act 1974 and the Employment Equality Act of 1977. Fennell and Lynch (1993) note that surprise was expressed in many quarters with the granting of such jurisdiction to the Court rather than to the Employment Appeals Tribunal. Despite initial reservations by von Prondzynski (1989b) and the Employment Equality Agency among others as to the quality of its early decisions, the general consensus is that the Court has discharged its functions well and has developed an expertise with regard to equality claims. A determination of the Court in relation to claims of discrimination may be appealed on points of law only within six weeks to the High Court.

Table 3.3 highlights the number of Labour Court determinations relating to the equality legislation since 1978. This table highlights a noticeable downward trend in relation to the number of Court determinations regarding equal pay, being as low as two in 1990. This may be due to a number of factors, but as Wallace (1991b) argues, most probable to the greater familiarity industrial relations practitioners have with the Act. The number of Labour Court determinations in relation to the Employment Equality Act 1977 has traditionally been very low. Since its enactment there have never been more than ten such determinations a year.

Table 3.3. Labour Court determinations, 1978—92				
	Employment Equality Act 1977		Anti-Discrimination (Pay) Act 1974	
Year	No.	In favour of claimants	No.	In favour of claimants
1978	2	2	18	8
1979	1	1	23	12
1980	8	3	39	26
1981	6	4	15	9
1982	9	5	10	2
1983	7	2	10	2
1984	4	2	9	3
1985	5	2	11	5
1986	2	1	8	3
1987	2	1	6	5
1988	1	1	7	2
1989	3	2	4	4
1990	4	1	2	2
1991	6	1	8	2
1992	10	4	4	4

Source: Employment Equality Agency, various annual reports.

3.4.2. THE EMPLOYMENT APPEALS TRIBUNAL

The Employment Appeals Tribunal (EAT) was initially established under section 39 of the Redundancy Payments Act 1967 as the Redundancy Appeals Tribunal. Its initial role was to adjudicate in disputes about redundancy and to administer the system of redundancy compensation introduced by the 1967 Act. The Minimum Notice and Terms of Employment Act 1973 extended the jurisdiction of the Tribunal to hearing applications brought under that Act by dismissed employees for compensation for loss sustained by them by reason of their employer's failure to give them the statutory period of notice. The Tribunal's jurisdiction was further extended by the Unfair Dismissals Act 1977 with regard to hearing claims for redress for unfair dismissals. It was retitled the Employment Appeals Tribunal under section 18 of the Unfair Dismissals Act 1977. The EAT currently also adjudicates upon and interprets a number of other Acts, namely the Maternity (Protection of Employees) Act 1981, Protection of Employees (Employers' Insolvency) Acts 1984 to 1991, the Payment of Wages Act 1991 and the Worker Protection (Regular Part-Time Employees) Act 1991. The EAT also hears appeals of the decisions of Rights Commissioners.

Table 3.4. Summary of appeals referred in 1993 and the outcome of the appeals disposed of in 1993

Act	Number of appeals referred*	Allowed	Dismissed	Withdrawn during hearing	Withdrawn prior to hearing	Total number of appeals disposed of
Redundancy Payments	967	444	202	162	142	950
Minimum Notice and Terms of Employment	3,425	2,609	368	174	329	3,480
Unfair Dismissal (Direct Claims)	1,145	223	199	239	275	936
Maternity (Protection of Employees)	23	0	8	9	9	26
Protection of Employees (Employers' Insolvency)	100	266	6	1	4	277
Worker Protection (Regular Part-Time Employees)	50	3	21	8	9	41
Payment of Wages	0	0	n/a	n/a	n/a	0
Total	5,710	3,545	804	593	768	5,710

* Some appeals disposed of in 1992 were not referred in 1991. Some appeals referred in 1992 are not yet disposed of. Unfair Dismissals appeals against the Recommendation of Rights Commissioners are excluded.

Source: Department of Enterprise and Employment, 1994

Table 3.4 sets out the workload in terms of referrals and the outcome of claims and appeals heard by the EAT in 1993. As can be seen, 5,710 claims and appeals were referred to the Tribunal during that year, 967 under the Redundancy Payments Act, 1,145 under the Unfair Dismissals Act, 3,425 under the Minimum Notice and Terms of Employment Acts, 23 under the Maternity (Protection of Employees) Act, 100 under the Protection of Employees (Employers' Insolvency) Acts, 50 under the Worker Protection (Regular Part-Time Employees) Act 1991 and none under the Payment of Wages Act. In addition, there were 82 appeals to the Tribunal against Rights Commissioners' recommendations (Department of Enterprise and Employment, 1994).

The composition of the Tribunal consists of a chairman and twelve vice-chairmen. The chairman is required under statute to have at least seven years experience as a practising barrister or solicitor. This statutory requirement does not apply to the serving vice-chairmen, but in practice they tend to have similar legal experience. These members are appointed by the Minister for Enterprise and Employment. The Tribunal also consists of a panel of thirty-eight ordinary members, drawn equally from nominees of employer associations and the Irish Congress of Trade Unions. The EAT, in similar fashion to the Labour Court, operates in divisions consisting of a chairperson or vice-chairperson and one member from the trade union and employer sides, in accordance with section 39 (ii) of the Redundancy Payments Act of 1967. A clerk attends each EAT hearing, whose function it is to offer mainly administrative support to the Tribunal.

Applications to the EAT are made on special forms (RP51A) available from the Tribunal or the Department of Enterprise and Employment. Employees must give their name and address, the name and address of the employer, the name of the Acts under which they are claiming, the grounds of the application and the redress sought (von Prondzynski, 1989b). Employees must also give the name and address of their representative (if any). With regard to representation, an applicant to the EAT may present their case in person, may be represented by counsel or a solicitor or by a representative of a trade union or employer association (Fennell and Lynch, 1993). Of the 683 claims and appeals heard under the Unfair Dismissals Act in 1992, 598 employees (87.6 per cent) were represented (96 by trade unions and 502 by solicitor or counsel) and 566 employers (82.9 per cent) were represented (76 by employer organisations and 490 by solicitor and/or counsel) (EAT, Twenty-fifth Annual Report). Employees must observe the time limits specified under the Act that they apply—otherwise they may lose their right to bring a claim.

The procedures adopted by the EAT are similar to court proceedings but there is a greater amount of informality. Fennell and Lynch (1993) describe the approach of the EAT when hearing an applicant as 'legalistic, individualistic, rights-based, heavily reliant on common law notions of fair procedure and assessment of reasonableness'. Rules of procedure for the EAT are outlined in the Redundancy (Redundancy Appeals Tribunal) Regulations 1968, the Unfair Dismissals Act 1977, and the Maternity Protection (Claims and Appeals) Regulations 1981. These regulations, however, are accompanied by and subject to the principles of 'constitutional' or 'natural justice' (Forde, 1992). Under the various regulations it is possible for a party to make an opening statement, call witnesses, cross-examine any witnesses called by any other party, give evidence and address the Tribunal at the close of the evidence. Evidence is normally given under oath. Hearings of the EAT are usually held in public, but may be held *in camera* at the request of either party.

The decision of the EAT (called a determination) can be given at the close of the hearing, but more usually it is issued some time later in written form.

The EAT maintains a register of its decisions, which may be inspected free of charge by any employer or employee. Should an employer fail to carry out the terms of an EAT determination, proceedings may be taken by the Minister for Enterprise and Employment to the Circuit Court in order to ensure compliance. EAT determinations are not subject to the principle of precedence as in a court of law. Table 3.5 highlights the number of cases referred to the EAT since 1978.

Table 3.5. Number of EAT referrals, 1978–93	
Year	**Number of cases referred**
1978	1,506
1979	1,410
1980	2,478
1981	2,658
1982	4,029
1983	5,357
1984	5,654
1985	9,741
1986	8,019
1987	8,537
1988	6,099
1989	4,474
1990	5,938
1991	4,921
1992	6,508
1993	5,710

Source: EAT, annual reports.

For applicants under the Unfair Dismissals and Maternity Protection legislation the Tribunal issues determinations which may be appealed to the Circuit Court within six weeks. At the Circuit Court the case is heard *de novo*, i.e. that there is a full rehearing of the case. Appeals in relation to the other Acts such as redundancy, protection of employees, minimum notice and part-time workers, falling under the jurisdiction of the Tribunal, can only be made to the High Court on a point of law.

An examination of the effectiveness of the Tribunal cannot ignore its value as a forum which endeavours to provide a speedy and inexpensive method for individuals who wish to seek remedies for alleged infringements of their statutory rights. Hence the approach of the EAT 'is one concerned with the vindication of a worker's rights rather than the conciliation of conflicts of interests' (Fennell and Lynch, 1993). A perceived difficulty (particularly in trade union circles) with the operation of the Tribunal as a forum of dispute resolution, is that it often translates labour disputes which may have a high collective validity, e.g. the dismissal of a shop steward, into claims based on individualistic rights.

3.4.3. THE LABOUR RELATIONS COMMISSION

As discussed in the previous chapter, the enactment of the Industrial Relations Act 1990 heralded the first significant institutional reform in the dispute resolution machinery in Ireland since the Industrial Relations Act of 1969. The Act provided for the establishment of a new body, namely the Labour Relations Commission, which took over many of the functions previously performed by the Labour Court. It is a tripartite body with trade union, employer and independent representation, and has been given the overall responsibility for promoting good industrial relations in this country. To this end the Commission provides a range of services which are designed to help prevent and resolve disputes. Apart from taking over the management, co-ordination and policy direction of the existing conciliation, Rights Commissioners and equality services (roles previously discharged by the Court), the Industrial Relations Act 1990 also charged the Commission with some newly established functions:

– to provide an industrial relations advisory service;
– to prepare codes of practice relevant to industrial relations matters;
– to offer guidance on codes of practice and help to resolve disputes concerning their implementation;
– to conduct or commission research into matters relevant to industrial relations;
– to review and monitor industrial relations developments;
– to assist Joint Labour Committees and Joint Industrial Councils in the exercise of their functions.

The then Minister for Labour, when speaking of the rationale for the establishment of the Commission, referred to the need to have a body with the primary responsibility for promoting better industrial relations. Thus, the Commission was expected to highlight examples of good practice and encourage others to adopt similar practices (Dail Debates, 1989). Kevin Bonner, Secretary at the Department of Labour, and a key architect of the 1990 Act, argued that 'a body such as the Labour Court with responsibility for investigating and issuing recommendations is constrained from adopting a more forceful role in the promotion of good industrial relations' (Bonner, 1989). Bonner also cites the support of some prominent academics for the establishment of a new independent body with this mission. McCarthy (1982), in criticising the previous institutional arrangements, urged the creation 'of a system by which better practices would be promoted'. Hillery (1979) in a similar vein suggested the establishment of a new institution which he believed 'could play an important role in improving the quality of industrial relations acting as an agent of change'.

Another reason for the reform of the institutional structures (and continuing to be a major objective of the Commission) was 'to encourage and facilitate a more active approach to dispute prevention and resolution', thus placing a new emphasis on the settling of disputes at local level. Another related objective of the Commission was 'to restore the original purpose and status of Labour Court investigations and recommendations' (Dail Debates, 1989). The stated rationale for the separation of the role of the Commission and that of the Labour Court was to restore the role of the Labour Court as a 'court of last resort'. Kieran Mulvey, Chief Executive of the Commission, argues that the setting up of the Commission had the clear intent of changing 'the almost automatic reference (of disputes) to the Court' (Mulvey, 1991a). In debating the 1990 Act in the Dail, the then Minister for Labour noted the central role which the Court had developed in the 1970s in the resolution of disputes which arose from the terms and the interpretation of national wage agreements. The Minister contended that the industrial relations actors had developed the habit of referring disputes to the Court and had found it difficult to revert back to settling their own problems. Relatively trivial matters were being heard by the Court, which had assumed the mantle of 'court of first resort'. It was intended that the Court would revert to its original function, i.e. 'the final authoritative tribunal in industrial relations matters whose recommendations would once again be documents with great moral authority with the main responsibility for dispute resolution being shifted back to the parties themselves' (Kerr, 1991a).

Kevin Duffy (1993) argued that 'in the past the conciliation service was often used as a formality in order to advance to the Labour Court, and the real negotiation took place after the Court had issued its recommendation'.

The establishment of the Labour Relations Commission was not greeted enthusiastically by all. Fianna Fail TD and UCD Professor of Industrial Relations, Brian Hillery, expressed the concern that the Commission may, far from becoming a significant agent in the promotion of good industrial relations, become 'just another layer of bureaucracy' (Hourihan, 1990). Wallace (1991c) speculated that, should the Labour Relations Commission become successful in promoting high levels of settlement at local level (at conciliation or in the workplace), the cases coming to the Court would be those that management were unwilling or unable to give concessions, in other words, hopeless cases. This, he feels, might lead the Court to fall into disrepute with the trade unions in the likely event of the unions losing a high proportion of these cases. The Labour Court itself was highly critical of the establishment of the Commission when the Department of Labour first published proposals for the body in 1988.

In a published response to the Minister's proposals, the Court expressed difficulty in understanding:

> . . . how the effectiveness of the conciliation service or the quality of its work could be better achieved under the proposed Labour Relations Commission than is possible under the Court. The same staff would be involved, their terms of reference would be the same and the outcome

of their work would be unchanged—either the case would be resolved or referred to the Court. (Labour Court, Forty-second Annual Report)

The Court concluded that it could not 'envisage the setting up of a Labour Relations Commission as establishing an improved dispute settling service to the constituents of the social partners on either qualitative or administrative grounds'. In fact, the Court asserted that the proposed Commission 'would profoundly diminish the effectiveness of the Court by divorcing from it the right to determine the cases it will hear and separating from it the conciliation service which has always been regarded as an integral part of the Court' (Labour Court, Forty-second Annual Report).

THE CONCILIATION SERVICE

The Labour Relations Commission's most public and arguably most important function and, as Mulvey (1991b) suggests, the major on-going area of the demand for services of the Commission, is the conciliation service. As mentioned previously, the conciliation service was formerly provided by the Labour Court.

The origins of conciliation in the UK and Ireland trace back to 1860, when A.J. Mundella persuaded both parties to a dispute to set up a permanent conciliation and arbitration board (Farnham and Pimlott, 1990). Official conciliation has been in operation since 1896 with the enactment of the Conciliation Act of that year. Kelly (1989b) reports that during the 1920s and 1930s the Department of Industry and Commerce contained a small staff of conciliators whose purpose was to aid employers and trade unions in dispute. The Conciliation Act was repealed in 1946 by the Industrial Relations Act, of which section 16 empowered the Labour Court to appoint individuals to act as Conciliation Officers. The Industrial Relations Act of 1969 retitled these officers Industrial Relations Officers and provided that they 'shall assist in the prevention and settlement of trade disputes and in the establishment and maintenance of means for conducting voluntary negotiations between employers and workers either generally or in particular industries or particular areas or between particular employers and their workers'.

Conciliation has been described as the involvement of an independent third party in the negotiation of the settlement to a dispute (Kerr and Whyte, 1985). The conciliator has no power to compel the parties to reach agreement. Conciliation as opposed to adjudication does not entail the offering of proposals by the conciliator as to how the dispute should be settled.

This voluntary nature and the informality of the conciliation service has led to its considerable appeal with both employers and workers. It is best viewed as an extension of the direct negotiations at local level. The efficiency of the service depends almost entirely on the measure of co-operation which is forthcoming from the parties themselves.

The normal procedure at a conciliation conference is for an Industrial

Relations Officer (IRO) to preside over a meeting of the conflicting parties as a means of learning each side's point of view. Having listened to both parties, the IRO may hold separate meetings (often referred to as side conferences) with both parties to get a better idea of the basis for the dispute and what is required to resolve the issue. The IRO acts as a facilitator and will try to guide the parties along certain lines in the search for an acceptable solution.

As can be seen from table 3.6 success rates in resolving issues at conciliation have fluctuated over the years. The conciliation service had an average success rate of approximately 50 per cent for much of the 1980s but this has more recently increased to over 60 per cent and achieved a high of 74 per cent in 1990. More recent figures from the Labour Relations Commission suggest that the success rates at conciliation are continuing to improve.

Table 3.6. Conciliation service referrals, 1971—92

Year	No. of disputes in which conciliation conferences were held	No. of disputes settled at conciliation (% in parentheses)	
1971	628	429	(68)
1972	713	443	(62)
1973	855	487	(56)
1974	951	646	(68)
1975	1,108	576	(52)
1976	1,071	581	(54)
1977	1,175	638	(54)
1978	1,288	651	(51)
1979	1,301	633	(49)
1980	1,375	693	(50)
1981	1,582	766	(48)
1982	1,855	927	(50)
1983	2,090	1,114	(53)
1984	1,750	1,037	(59)
1985	2,021	1,355	(67)
1986	1,892	1,268	(67)
1987	1,787	1,151	(64)
1988	1,571	1,064	(68)
1989	1,450	1,019	(70)
1990	1,552	1,143	(74)
1991	1,880	1,598	(85)
1992	1,935	1,451	(75)

Source: Labour Court and Labour Relations Commission Annual Reports.

The relocation of the conciliation service under the auspices of the Labour Relations Commission was designed to give a new impetus to the role of conciliation and to encourage the parties to take more responsibility for the resolution of disputes (Department of Labour, 1991b). One possible reason for the increasing success rates is that, because of this increased emphasis on the settling of disputes at conciliation, Industrial Relations Officers are now less willing to allow unions or management to use the conciliation service as a stepping stone to full Labour Court investigations. There had been frequent criticisms over the years of both employers and trade unions abusing the system through their unwillingness to settle at conciliation. The gatekeeper role assigned to the Commission by the Industrial Relations Act 1990 is expected to ensure that only issues of substance proceed to the Labour Court where they are not settled at conciliation.

The on-the-ground evidence of this change in the process of conciliation may be seen in the increased number of conciliation conferences held. Prior to the establishment of the Commission, Duffy (1993) contends that parties to a dispute

> . . . may have expected to attend one or maybe two conciliation conferences on a dispute, after which the dispute, if not resolved would be referred to the Labour Court. We are now finding that conferences are being adjourned and re-convened until the Commission is satisfied that every effort has been made to resolve the dispute.

The ratio of meetings to cases has risen from 1.19 in 1987 to 1.5 in 1991 (Mulvey, 1991a). The increased workload of the Commission has seen the levels of activity of the service rise to its 1985 record levels.

THE ADVISORY SERVICE

The Industrial Relations Act 1990 made provision for an 'industrial relations advisory service'. The legislation states that 'the Commission may, if it thinks fit, on request or on its own initiative provide for employers, employers associations, workers and trade unions such advice it thinks appropriate on any matter concerned with industrial relations'. This is arguably the most innovative feature arising from the formation of the Commission, and is an innovation which has been advocated by academic commentators in the past, (Wallace, 1991c). Wallace suggests that the rationale for the advisory service is as follows: 'A small number of companies are responsible for a disportionate number of the difficulties which arise in the area of industrial relations. By focusing on these organisations and conducting industrial relations audits and providing expert advice, it should be possible to lower the incidence of industrial action at a national level.'

Disputes are often merely a symptom of a greater underlying problem in the workplace and such problems often remain after a dispute has been settled. The main focus of the conciliation service is to deal with the immediate dispute. The brief of the advisory service on the other hand is to help identify the underlying problems giving rise to recurring industrial relations unrest where impartial advice from a third party acceptable to management and unions could help to resolve such issues (Department of

Labour, 1991a). In the past the Labour Court was not always able to examine underlying problems at workplace level, which can give rise to frequent disputes.

The conception of an advisory service operating in such a manner is undoubtedly to be commended. However, Wallace (1991c) draws attention to a number of possibly significant problems and limitations in operationalising the idea. He notes that persistent problems which arise in organisational settings are more likely to be associated with structural factors, e.g. relating to the nature of the work, the size of the organisation, economic or financial pressures, the stage that a product may be located in its lifecycle, etc. Many such structural factors are likely to be outside the scope of the advisory service's influence. Wallace also questions the criteria which the advisory service will use in approaching its investigations. He argues that the envisaged mode of operation of the service presupposes that 'good' industrial relations can be objectively defined and can be brought about by a 'set of techniques'. Most industrial relations theorists would challenge these notions. Wallace also points to the fact that in-depth studies have been undertaken in the past with, at best, mixed results. For example, the inquiry into the Banks dispute in 1971 and the 1972 investigations into the ESB did not prevent further disputes arising in these industries in the 1970s.

CODES OF PRACTICE
One of the principal new functions of the Labour Relations Commission is to prepare codes of practice on an unspecified range of matters in industrial relations. It can do so at the request of the Minister for Enterprise and Employment or of its own volition. Codes such as these have long been a feature of industrial relations in Britain and Northern Ireland. Under the terms of the Industrial Relations Act 1990 the Commission is charged with drafting codes of practice in consultation with employer and trade union organisations and other interested parties. When approved by the Commission the draft is then submitted to the Minister for Enterprise and Employment who can make a statutory instrument declaring the code to be a code of practice for the purposes of the 1990 Act. While codes of practice are set in a statutory framework they are not directly enforceable in that a breach of the code will not attract any civil or criminal sanction. The codes of practice are intended to give guidance to employers and trade unions on particular issues and are intended to have strong moral authority but no more. Thus the drafting of the codes of practice under the terms of the Act is unlikely to address the problem raised by the Commission of Inquiry on Industrial Relations in their report in 1981, namely 'that voluntary codes possess the serious disadvantage of being least likely to be adopted in the very circumstances where they are most needed'. Codes of practice can, however, be admissible in evidence and can be taken into account by the courts or the dispute settlement agencies in determining any issue to which they may be

relevant. Duffy (1993) claims that there is some confusion as to what is intended by allowing codes to be 'admissible in evidence'. Much will depend on the manner in which the Labour Court and other bodies apply the right to take codes into account when determining cases that come before them.

To date one code of practice has been prepared dealing with disputes procedures and procedures for resolving disputes in essential services. That code of practice sets out the type of procedures which should be followed in processing disputes on all collective and individual issues. The code in the essential services proposes the use of arbitration systems so as to avoid the likelihood of the service being disrupted by an industrial dispute.

The Minister has also suggested the following areas to the Commission to be possibly covered by codes:
– protection and facilities for worker representatives in the company;
– provision of information to and consultation with employees on the activities of the undertaking and on decisions likely to affect employees.

The Industrial Relations Act 1990 also assigned the Labour Relations Commission with the responsibility for assisting Joint Industrial Councils (JICs) and Joint Labour Committees (JLCs) in the discharge of their functions. The Commission's role is essentially to provide Industrial Relations Officers to act as chairpersons to a number of JICs and JLCs.

Joint Industrial Councils are permanent voluntary negotiating bodies whose task it is to facilitate collective bargaining at industry level in certain industrial sectors (Gunnigle and Flood, 1990). They are composed of representatives of employers and trade unions within the industry. Joint Industrial Councils may be registered with the Labour Court. Kerr and Whyte (1985) contend that registration only offers marginal advantage to the JIC, as accommodation in the premises of the Labour Court and secretarial services are made available to both registered and unregistered JICs alike. At present there are three registered JICs in existence for the footwear and construction industries, and one for the Dublin wholesale fruit and vegetable trade. Of these, the Construction Industry Joint Industrial Council has been suspended since July 1982, due to an unresolved difference between employer and union representatives. The Joint Board of Conciliation and Arbitration for the Footwear Industry has been suspended since October 1983. The JIC for the Dublin Wholesale Fruit and Vegetable Trade has not formally met since the early 1970s.

In addition to these registered councils there are eleven unregistered JICs. They exist in respect of the following industries: bacon curing, bakery and confectionery trade, banks, electrical contracting, flour milling, grocery provision and allied trades, hosiery and knitted garments manufacture, printing and allied trades in Dublin, State industrial employees, woollen and worsted manufacture and Telecom. Approximately 83,000 workers are represented by these councils (Labour Relations Commission, 1993).

Joint Labour Committees are statutory bodies comprised of employer and trade union representatives and independent members, and regulate wages and conditions of employment in areas where collective bargaining is poorly established (Gunnigle and Flood, 1990b). There are currently fifteen Joint Labour Committees (JLCs) in existence covering approximately 88,000 workers (Labour Relations Commission, 1993). Joint Labour Committees exist in respect of the following industries: aerated waters, agriculture, brush and broom, catering (excluding Dublin), contract cleaning (Dublin), hairdressing (Cork), hairdressing (Dublin), handkerchief and household goods, hotels (excluding Dublin and Cork), law clerks, provender milling, shirtmaking, tailoring, women's clothing and millinery. A JLC for the catering industry in the County Borough of Dublin and the Borough of Dun Laoghaire was the most recent addition to this list in November 1992. JLCs are charged with determining the legally binding minimum wages and conditions of employment for those workers represented by it. The JLC submits proposals to the Labour Court for fixing minimum wage rates or for regulating conditions. If the Court accepts the proposals then it makes an Employment Regulation Order (ERO) giving statutory effect to the proposals. Employment Regulation Orders are enforced by inspectors appointed by the Minister for Enterprise and Employment.

3.4.4. RIGHTS COMMISSIONERS

The office of the Rights Commissioner was created by section 13 of the Industrial Relations Act 1969. The Rights Commissioners' service was originally attached to the Labour Court, and their function was to intervene in and to investigate industrial disputes with the view to promoting settlement. Rights Commissioners were primarily established to reduce the workload of the Labour Court and to provide a 'prompt adjudication service for what may be regarded as the less major industrial relations issues' (Kelly, 1989b). The clear intention at the time was that the Rights Commissioners would be a more informal avenue for dealing with industrial disputes than a full Labour Court investigation. The rationale for the establishment of an office which appeared to duplicate the functions performed by Conciliation/Industrial Relations Officers is still unclear. Forde (1992) argues that they played a valuable role in resolving disputes which were caused by incidents with one or a small group of employees. Since the enactment of the Industrial Relations Act of 1990 the Rights Commissioners' service has operated as part of the Labour Relations Commission but is totally independent in the performance of its functions. Rights Commissioners are appointed by the Minister for Enterprise and Employment from a panel submitted by the Commission, and under the terms of the Industrial Relations Act 1969 may investigate a trade dispute provided that:
– it is not a dispute connected with the rates of pay, hours or times of work, or annual holidays of a body of workers;

– it is not a dispute concerning persons who do not have access to the Labour Court;

– a party to the dispute does not object in writing to such an investigation;

– the Labour Court has not made a recommendation about the dispute.

There are five Rights Commissioners currently in office. They are available to parties in dispute provided both agree to such a hearing and to accept the Commissioner's decision. In practice, Rights Commissioners mostly investigate disputes concerning individual employees. They follow their own procedures and adopt their own practices, having no statutory guidelines to direct their activity and operate individually (Von Prondzynski, 1989b). Investigations are held in private with Rights Commissioners being obliged to issue a written recommendation outlining their opinions on the merits of the dispute. The Industrial Relations Act 1990 provides that an objection to an investigation by a Rights Commissioner must be notified in writing to the Commissioner within three weeks.

The role of the Rights Commissioners has significantly expanded since 1969 with the enactment of further employment legislation giving them additional functions. They now have a statutory role in investigating cases under the Unfair Dismissals Act 1977, the Maternity (Protection of Employees) Act 1981 and, since 1992, the Payment of Wages Act 1991.

A recommendation by a Rights Commissioner is not legally binding but in practice they tend to be observed by employers and trade unions. However, disputes heard under the Industrial Relations Act 1969 may be appealed to the Labour Court, which results in an order which is binding on the parties to the dispute. An appeal against a Rights Commissioner's recommendation must be notified in writing to the Labour Court within six weeks from the date of the recommendation. Cases in relation to the other Acts in which they have a role can be appealed to the Employment Appeals Tribunal. Similarly, an appeal against the recommendations of the Rights Commissioner under these Acts must be made within six weeks.

As can be seen from table 3.7, the number of disputes disposed of by the Rights Commissioners far exceeds the number of recommendations issued in any given year. This is accounted for by the fact that many cases investigated do not result in a recommendation. Kelly (1989b) argues that this is a testimony to the success of the Rights Commissioners in resolving disputes upon intervention.

There was a dramatic growth in the number of cases disposed of by the Rights Commissioners in the early 1980s reaching a peak level of activity in 1981 of some 2,057 cases. In 1990 Rights Commissioners dealt with 1,202 disputes and issued 434 recommendations. The number of recommendations which are appealed to the Labour Court has averaged approximately 16 per cent in recent years.

The Rights Commissioners service has been received favourably by all sides of industry, by practitioners and industrial relations experts alike. Kelly

(1989b) reports that academic analyses of the service tend to be complimentary with little adverse comment. Noted advantages of the service are its perceived impartiality, flexibility and accessibility, providing a quick and efficient mechanism for dealing with problems which have proved intractable at local level.

Table 3.7. Rights Commissioner activity, 1979–91

Year	Disputes dealt with under Industrial Relations Act 1969	Recommendations issued by Rights Commissioners	Appeals to Labour Court (% in parentheses)
1979	1,699	506	36 (7.1)
1980	2,025	661	86 (13)
1981	2,057	639	73 (11.4)
1982	1,931	531	63 (11.9)
1983	1,637	583	100 (17.2)
1984	1,445	687	118 (17.2)
1985	1,431	679	109 (16.1)
1986	1,708	603	107 (17.7)
1987	1,732	630	98 (15.6)
1988	1,477	550	76 (13.8)
1989	1,149	455	91 (20)
1990	1,202	434	64 (14.7)
1991	1,521	n/a	n/a

Source: Department of Labour and Labour Court Annual Reports.

3.4.5. EQUALITY OFFICERS

Section 6 of the Anti-Discrimination (Pay) Act 1974 created the Office of the Equal Pay Officer attached to the Labour Court. The title was subsequently changed to Equality Officer under the Employment Equality Act of 1977. Equality Officers deal with issues relating to discrimination on the grounds of sex or marital status arising under the Anti-Discrimination (Pay) Act 1974 and the Employment Equality Act 1977. The Anti-Discrimination Act entitles women to equal pay for 'like work', while the Employment Equality Act prohibits discrimination against women on the grounds of sex or marital status in non-pay areas like recruitment, training, promotion and working conditions. Equality Officers operate within the scope of the Labour Relations Commission but are independent in the performance of their functions. When a dispute is referred to an Equality Officer, they will carry out an investigation and issue a recommendation, based on the merits of the case. In the course of an investigation the Equality Officer examines written submissions made by the parties, meets the parties and visits premises to inspect work in progress. Equality Officers are empowered to enter premises, examine records or documents, seek information and inspect work in progress in the premises. To impede an Equality Officer in his/her investigation is an offence subject to a substantial fine. If either party is dissatisfied with this recommendation, they may appeal to the Labour Court within forty-two days. The Court's determination in such circumstances is final and legally binding on the parties. There is also a right to appeal the determination of the Labour Court to the High Court on a point of law.

Table 3.8 highlights the number of Equality Officer recommendations issued from 1978 to 1992. During the year 1990 the Equality Officer service issued thirty-five recommendations in cases under the Employment Equality Act 1977. This represented a large increase on the 1989 figure and departs from the slight increase since 1986. A noticeable downward trend can be seen in the number of recommendations issued by the Equality Officer in relation to the Anti-Discrimination (Pay) Act 1974.

Table 3.8. Number of Equality Officer recommendations, 1978–92

	Employment Equality Act 1977		Anti-Discrimination (Pay) Act 1974	
Year	No.	In favour of claimant	No.	In favour of claimant
1978	5	2	52	n/a
1979	14	8	52	38
1980	14	9	65	48
1981	20	9	55	42
1982	12	2	27	18
1983	22	11	28	12
1984	28	10	27	7
1985	18	7	17	2
1986	8	3	19	8
1987	11	8	14	7
1988	11	5	16	9
1989	12	8	12	5
1990	35	11	13	5
1991	22	16	8	4
1992	22	12	14	4

Source: Employment Equality Agency, Annual Reports.

The Employment Equality Act 1977 also provided for the establishment of another institution of the middleground, the Employment Equality Agency. This agency is responsible for the promotion of equality of opportunity, the elimination of discrimination between men and women, married and single, in relation to employment and to keep the two pieces of equality legislation under review. The Employment Equality Agency is also empowered to offer guidance to claimants who bring a case to the Labour Court. The Agency also has the sole right to initiate proceedings in cases of discriminatory advertisements and where there is a general policy of discriminatory practices.

3.5. THE STATE AS LEGISLATOR

One of the key functions of the State is to pass laws regulating the conduct of the people and organisations it controls (Brewster, 1989). Labour law in Irish industrial relations falls into two broad categories, namely collective labour legislation and individual employment legislation. Both have been discussed in detail in the previous chapter, therefore this section aims to revisit the topics by means of a summary of the salient points to describe each category.

COLLECTIVE LABOUR LEGISLATION
Collective labour legislation deals with the relationship between employers and collectivities of employees (normally through trade unions) and until recently was almost entirely based on earlier British legislation. Article 50 of the Irish Constitution of 1937 provides that, subject to its provisions, the laws in force prior to 1937 should continue unless repealed or found to be repugnant to the Constitution. Consequently, Irish Trade Union and Trade Disputes Law, until the introduction of the Industrial Relations Act of 1990, had remained largely similar to that which applied in 1922 in Britain and Ireland.

The most significant development in the area of collective labour legislation in recent years has been the enactment of the Industrial Relations Act 1990. This piece of legislation has been described as an important benchmark in trade union law. As well as the subject of institutional reform, the Act deals with trade disputes, immunities, picketing, secret ballots, injunctions and trade union rationalisation.

INDIVIDUAL EMPLOYMENT LEGISLATION
Some of the personal fundamental rights of the citizen are outlined in article 40 of the Constitution and include the right of citizens to freely express their opinions and conviction, and to form associations and unions. The citizens' right to form associations and unions is qualified by the State's right to enact laws in the public interest governing its exercise. The citizens' right includes that of not being forced into joining or leaving, or being dismissed because of trade union membership. The Unfair Dismissals Act 1977 additionally provides that the dismissal of an employee because of trade union membership or activity shall be deemed unfair. The constitutional guarantee does not preclude employers and employees (or their trade unions) from making agreements specifying which union, or one of a number of unions, workers in the particular employment will join. However, the constitutionality of such closed-shop arrangements remains open to question.

The contract of employment through its common law provisions constitutes the legal basis of the employer–employee relationship. More recently legislation has had a significant impact on this relationship with the passing of a number of Acts affecting individual employee rights at work. Since the 1970s several important Acts have been passed and a large number of regulations and statutory instruments introduced under existing employment legislation. Much of this change has been in the area of dismissals and sex discrimination. These pieces of legislation were dealt with in detail in the preceding chapter.

There is a considerable body of employment protection legislation in Ireland providing a basic floor of rights to individual employees. This legislation is marked by several inconsistencies particularly the differing periods of service required to qualify and the different adjudicating mechanisms.

3.6. THE STATE AS AN EMPLOYER—INDUSTRIAL RELATIONS IN THE PUBLIC SECTOR

Apart from its legislative and facilitatory functions, the State plays a significant role as the country's major employer. It accounts for about one-third of all employees in a range of areas principally composed of the Civil Service proper, education, local authorities and health boards, security forces, and State-sponsored bodies. Most of these employees are organised into trade unions or staff associations (Department of Public Services, 1987).

In some public sector areas, distinctive industrial relations features have developed but, as Cox and Hughes (1989) note, it would be inappropriate to view public sector industrial relations as inherently different from those pertaining in the private sector. Indeed the Report of the Commission of Inquiry on Industrial Relations (1981) suggests that personnel problems in both the public and the private sectors are similar although differences tend to occur in the procedural responses made.

In relation to the negotiation of pay and conditions of employment, a notable distinction may be drawn between those public sector areas subject to agreed Conciliation and Arbitration (C&A) schemes and those which come within the scope of the Labour Court. Conciliation and Arbitration schemes date from the 1950s, and currently different schemes operate for categories such as the (non-industrial) Civil Service, teachers, gardai, local authorities and health boards and the Vocational Educational Committees. A unique feature of the Civil Service scheme is the network of staff panels that evaluate any claims from recognised unions or staff associations before these are forwarded to conciliation. Conciliation consists of joint councils of management and employee representatives which consider claims before them and issue an agreed report. The composition and specific role of conciliation councils differ between schemes, and only specific issues may be referred to conciliation. These issues include pay, allowances, working hours, overtime, grading, and policies on recruitment, promotion, discipline, pensions and sick pay. Most claims exclude issues relating to individual employees. The vast majority of issues are resolved at conciliation, but those which are not may proceed to arbitration provided they are arbitrable under the terms of the appropriate Conciliation and Arbitration scheme. An Arbitration Board normally consists of an agreed chairman (often legally qualified) and two representatives from both the management and staff side. Detailed written submissions are made by both sides and these are supplemented by oral submissions and witnesses as appropriate. The finding of the Board is sent to the Minister for Finance and the other appropriate Minister, who have one month to approve the report or submit it to the Government. The Government has the option of accepting the report or moving a Dail motion to reject or amend it—a course of action which is normally seen as exceptional. The Local Authority and Health Board scheme differs from the above format in that the management or staff side have the option of rejecting the decision of Arbitration.

Table 3.9. Access to adjudication bodies in the public sector

	Arbitration Boards		Labour Court	
	Category	No. (approx.)	Category	No. (approx.)
Civil Service: non-industrial industrial	Grades up to assistant secretary –	30,800 –	– All categories	– 8,000
Gardai	All ranks excl. commissioners	11,400		
Teachers (1st and 2nd level, and RTCs)	All categories	43,000	–	–
Other educational groups	VEC clerical, etc., staff	1,000	Other categories	8,000
Health Boards (a)	Officer grades (incl. general nurses)	23,500	Manual and craft grades, psychiatric nurses	16,000
Voluntary hospitals (b)	–	–	All categories	16,000
Local authorities	Officer grades	10,000	Non-officer grades	25,500
Non-commercial State bodies	–	–	All categories	9,000
Commercial State bodies: ESB An Post Telecom Eireann	– – Temporary voluntary C&A scheme for most grades, civil service arbitrator	– 8,500 18,000	All categories in theory, seldom used (b) Legal entitlement to go to Court waived temporarily	12,000
Others	–	–	All categories	49,200
Total		146,200		143,700

Source: Cox and Hughes, 1989.

In addition to the specific grades in the public sector discussed above, employees in most State-sponsored bodies have access to the Labour Court. Exceptions are An Post and Telecom Eireann, that have a separate Conciliation and Arbitration scheme. A notable characteristic of public sector industrial relations is the role of the Department of Finance (previously this role was executed by the Department of the Public Services). It acts as the Government's adviser on matters relating to public sector pay and employment-related matters. It will critically review pay claims, lay down appropriate policy guidelines and oversee their implementation through direct and indirect negotiations. The Department represents the State as employer at the Employer Labour Conference and is involved in many of the Conciliation and Arbitration hearings.

Another important actor on the management side in the public sector is the Local Government and Staff Negotiations Board (LGSNB), whose role is to assist local authorities and health boards in industrial relations. Representatives of the board act on behalf of management on the appropriate Conciliation and Arbitration scheme and in major negotiations with non-officer grades.

CHAPTER FOUR

Trade Unions

4.1. INTRODUCTION

This chapter considers the nature and role of trade unions in Irish industrial relations. The types of unions, their objectives and their governing structures are discussed and examined. The chapter subsequently examines the issues of trade union density, recognition and influence using recent research evidence. The chapter then considers current issues and challenges facing the Irish trade union movement with particular emphasis on the impact of so-called human resource management (HRM) practices. This latter issue is further considered in chapter 8. Firstly, we begin by briefly exploring the historical development of trade unions in Ireland.

4.2. THE HISTORICAL DEVELOPMENT OF TRADE UNIONS

The historical development of trade unions is inextricably linked to the development of industrial relations. The current nature of the trade union movement in Ireland has its origins in the dramatic changes brought about by the Industrial Revolution beginning in Britain in the eighteenth century and later spreading to Europe and North America. Developments in technology, particularly the use of steam power, improved machinery and sources of raw materials allowed for the production of goods in larger quantities for wider consumer markets. These developments heralded a gradual change from a largely peasant society based on agriculture and craft production to an industry-based society with new social divisions, where the bulk of the people worked in the 'factory system' and relied on wages for their existence. Thus, people now worked together in much larger numbers and on much more tightly defined tasks. This scenario led to the emergence of modern management as a result of the need to plan, control, direct and organise the use of equipment, capital, materials and people in the factory system.

By and large the early factory owners adopted quite authoritarian approaches to workers. Working conditions were very poor and the term 'sweated labour' has come to characterise the conditions under which the early wage labourers worked.[1] Workers themselves could not do much about this situation as they had little or no economic or political power. The legal system favoured the owners of capital and it was not until the growth of organised labour through the trade union movement that employee concerns could command the attention and action of factory owners and management.

The trade union movement had become well established in Ireland by the early 1900s in many industries in Dublin, Belfast and Cork (McNamara et al., 1988), and especially after the passing of the 1906 Trade Disputes Act. The growth in influence and power of the 'new unionism' was most obviously manifested in the leadership skills of Jim Larkin and the Irish Transport and General Workers' Union. The festering conflict between employer and worker interests came to a head in the lock-out of 1913. An important effect of this turbulent period was that it served to accelerate the organisation of employees into trade unions and employers into employer associations and thus placed an ever-increasing emphasis on industrial relations. After the difficulties and confrontation of 1913, labour relations moved towards a more constructive approach based on negotiations and mutual agreement. The union movement had arrived and employers had to take steps to accommodate it. This was done through multi-employer bargaining via employer associations, and through the employment of labour relations officers to deal with personnel and industrial relations matters at organisation level.

In Britain, the aftermath of the First World War was marked by an initial period of economic expansion which helped strengthen the new 'model' unions. This soon gave way, however, to a prolonged period of trade depression and industrial conflict. Employers found themselves in the driving seat with little pressure to pay any great concern to employee needs. The dominance of an autocratic management style combined with poor pay and working conditions led to poor industrial relations. Strikes were common with the unrest culminating in the General Strike of 1926 in Britain. In this period workers and their trade unions became increasingly suspicious of management motives in introducing welfare initiatives in the workplace. The unions became particularly 'anti-welfare' as they saw it as a managerial strategy to prevent worker organisation. Now, with the demise of welfare, trade unions —particularly the new general unions—stepped up their organisation drives and, helped by the numerous grievances of industrial workers, saw their membership increase gradually throughout the 1930s. As unemployment began to fall, the position of the unions was reinforced and collective bargaining became more widespread. Employer reaction to these changes moved slowly from one of initial opposition to tolerance and later acceptance of the new order. In many organisations this shift was manifested in the establishment of a personnel function but with the emphasis on labour relations management rather than welfare. While the labour relations aspect of management has its roots much further back in the early attempts to organise workers in the new factories of the eighteenth and nineteenth centuries, it was not until the inter-war years that management–union relations became an established element of the managerial role. The position of the trade union movement as a powerful actor in the industrial relations framework was firmly established in Britain by the end of the Second World War. In an environment of full employment and competition for labour, unions found themselves in a strong bargaining position and their involvement in collective negotiations was actively supported by Government.

In Ireland too trade union membership increased steadily from the early 1930s. During the war years wages were controlled under emergency powers orders. These ended in September 1946 and marked the start of a new era for Irish industrial relations with the establishment of the Labour Court under the terms of the Industrial Relations Act of that year. By the 1960s levels of unionisation among manual workers had increased significantly. The shop-steward movement began to emerge as a significant factor in establishing plant-level bargaining as a central component of workplace industrial relations (Marsh 1973). This situation was accentuated by the growth in white-collar trade-unionisation since the 1960s (Bain, 1970; Kelly, 1975). Increasingly workers in administrative, supervisory and other 'staff' categories joined trade unions and demanded bargaining rights with their employers. The 1960s were also characterised by a marked increase in levels of industrial conflict. The increased industrial unrest experienced over the two decades since 1960 may be partially explainable by the huge increase in the pace of industrialisation. Ireland moved in a relatively short period from being a primarily rural, agriculture-based economy to one which has experienced a rapid increase in levels of urbanisation, industrial and commercial employment, living standards and education. Inevitably, such dramatic change will create difficulties for a rapidly evolving economy and similar difficulties have been encountered in many other countries.

The onset of the 'national wage agreement era' in 1970 marked a transformation from the rather unclear system of wage rounds which had existed since the end of the Second World War. A key effect of national wage agreements was to move major pay bargaining issues away from the level of the organisation. Initially this was seen as freeing management from complex negotiations with trade unions and giving them more certainty in corporate planning. At a time of relative economic prosperity and substantial growth in union membership, the key role for the trade union in the workplace—pay bargaining—was removed. However, union officials still needed to justify their role to the membership. With the expectancy that pay increases would be derived via National Agreements, attention was increasingly focused on matters that could be negotiated at local level; employment conditions, pay anomalies and productivity. Far from eliminating plant bargaining, national agreements merely changed its focus. Various types of productivity deals were negotiated throughout the period. In fact, productivity became an important means for work groups to gain pay increases above the stated maxima in national wage agreements. These contributed to a high level of wage drift in the national agreement era whereby actual levels of wage increases exceeded the maximum levels in individual agreements (McCarthy, 1977; O'Brien, 1981, 1989b). Indeed the emphasis on industrial relations continued to expand throughout the era and one of the great advantages claimed for national agreements, namely reduced levels of industrial conflict, failed to materialise. Concurrently, the incidence of strike activity continued to increase in the 1970s.

Another important development which has had a significant influence on trade unions is the impact of foreign multinational companies (MNCs). The beginnings of MNC investment in Ireland came from a reversal of previous Government policy of protectionism, and a movement towards an open-market economy in the late 1950s. The increase in MNC investment took off in the 1960s and mushroomed for much of the 1970s. O'Malley estimated that the foreign industry sector grew at an average rate of 21.4 per cent per year in the 1960–74 period compared with a rate of 5.6 per cent for all industry (O'Malley, 1983). For many of the newer MNCs operating here—especially those of US origin—the Irish industrial relations framework represented a new experience. High levels of unionisation, reliance on voluntary collective agreements and non-binding arbitration, multi-unionism and differing employment legislation represented new challenges for such organisations. Of particular concern was the question of unionisation. For many US companies in particular, the prospect of dealing with trade unions was a new departure. Many such organisations had a clear preference for non-union status (Murray, 1984). Even companies who had dealt with unions before were often unhappy about the prospect of dealing with a number of unions representing different categories of workers. Thus, where unions were recognised, this was generally achieved through recognition of a single union or a limited number of unions as prescribed in a written procedural agreement which incorporated post-entry closed shop (Enderwick, 1986).

The onset of the harsh economic climate of the 1980s dramatically changed the industrial relations environment. This changed economic climate, characterised by widespread redundancies and high unemployment, significantly altered the bargaining environment with adverse consequences for trade unions. Increasingly employers sought to address issues such as payment structures and levels of wage increases, the extent of demarcation and restrictive work practices and, ultimately, the erosion of managerial prerogative by trade unions. Restrictive trade union legislation in Britain and hard-line management approaches in many firms indicated a more offensive approach to dealings with trade unions. The outcomes of the strikes by miners in Britain and air traffic controllers in the US reflected this changed climate in the early 1980s. Trade union membership began to fall in many Western countries. Many of the newer and apparently successful companies had evolved a management style and a corporate culture which rejected collective dealings with trade unions. The term 'employee relations' gradually gained acceptance in the management vocabulary signifying the subtle but significant change from collective management–union interactions to individual management–employee interactions. Unions themselves had to adapt to their changing environment. Merger activity increased dramatically throughout the 1980s as unions attempted to both rationalise their activities and improve service to members (Roche and Larragy, 1986). The most significant merger was that between the Federated Workers' Union of Ireland (FWUI) and the Irish Transport and General Workers' Union (ITGWU) to form the Services Industrial Professional and Technical Union (SIPTU). There is also evidence that employer opposition to union recognition also increased in the 1980s (McGovern, 1988, 1989a, b; Gunnigle, 1992c, 1994), which presented additional challenges to unions in attracting members.

4.3. THE NATURE AND ROLE OF TRADE UNIONS

4.3.1. ALTERNATIVES TO TRADE UNION ORGANISATION

Trade unions have historically been the most prominent means of representing worker interests to employers, Government and other parties. However, there are alternative approaches which workers may adopt. For example, workers may deal with employers on an individual basis (individual bargaining). This may be attractive to workers who are in a strong bargaining position such as those with skills or knowledge which is highly valued by employers. It may also be attractive in organisations where management place a high priority on individual employee needs and provide attractive pay and conditions of employment. In general, however, it is felt that individual workers are at a severe disadvantage in bargaining terms *vis-à-vis* employers, and thus individual bargaining is not the best approach for most workers.

Another alternative for workers is to form work-based or staff associations or groups to represent their interests to employers. Staff associations have traditionally been comprised of white-collar employees such as professional and managerial staff, who are not trade union members. The officers of a staff association usually represent their members through consultation with the company's senior management on collective as well as individual issues, and have several characteristics of trade unions. They have been viewed by some managers and employees as an alternative to traditional trade-unionism. Joining a staff association is often seen as an improvement on individual bargaining since by joining together workers can present a united front to employers and redress some of the bargaining imbalance inherent in individual bargaining. Another perceived advantage of staff associations is that they provide a collective voice for employees without the introduction of a third party (trade union) into management–employee relations. Some employees may prefer to join staff associations for particular reasons. For example, the traditional perception of trade unions as catering for 'blue-collar' workers may create a 'snob value' which encourages employees to join/remain in staff associations. From an employer perspective staff associations are often perceived as less difficult to deal with and less likely to engage in confrontational/adversarial bargaining approaches. However, work-based associations have been criticised because of their lack of independence from the organisation. Another disadvantage is the absence of an external organisation structure and resources with which to provide bargaining expertise or legal advice. Very often traditional trade-unionists take a cynical view of them, seeing them as a poor apology for real trade union organisation. These factors may often combine to limit the bargaining power of staff associations in their interactions with management.

The major contrasts between trade unions and staff associations are summarised in table 4.1. It is important to note that these generalisations may not characterise all trade unions or staff associations.

Table 4.1. Trade unions and staff associations: contrasts

	Trade unions	Staff associations
Objectives	1. Replace individual bargaining with collective bargaining	Similar, but less ideological commitment
	2. Improve pay and employment conditions	Similar
	3. Political	Non-political
Controlling authority	Union headquarters; normally strong role for ICTU	No external authority
Rules/ procedures	Detailed constitution; sometimes with strong political dimension	None or brief constitution; oriented to firm
External resources	Access to external expertise and resources; influence on national issues (e.g. incomes policies)	None except by contracting in
Methods	Collective bargaining: adversarial orientation	Consultative orientation
Use of sanctions	Prepared to use strike weapon	Most unlikely to use strike weapon
Services to members	May have range of services	Limited services

4.3.2. THE ROLE AND OBJECTIVES OF TRADE UNIONS

Trade unions have traditionally been seen as the most effective means of countering employer power and achieving satisfactory pay and working conditions for employees. Their role is well established in the Irish context with most legislation dealing with the legal position of trade unions dating back to pre-independence days. Partly as a consequence of the perceived inadequacies of both individual bargaining and staff associations many workers have come to view trade unions as the best mechanism for representing their interests to employers through collective bargaining and to Government and employer organisations on a broader political level.

Essentially unions are organisations that aim to unite workers with common interests, while seeking to define those interests, express them, safeguard and advance them through their interactions (particularly via collective bargaining) with individual employers, employer associations, Government, Government agencies and other parties. The basic strength of a union, therefore, lies in its ability to organise and unite workers. By joining trade unions employees provide themselves with the collective means to redress the imbalance in bargaining power which otherwise exists between individual workers and their employer. The Webbs, who wrote the first comprehensive history of trade unions and early collective bargaining, came up with what was long accepted as the most comprehensive definition of a trade union (Webb and Webb, 1920): 'A continuous association of wage earners with the objective of improving or maintaining conditions of employment.'

While this description aptly describes the workplace collective bargaining role of trade unions, it fails to explicitly address the broader societal role of trade unions in advancing worker interests in the political arena (see Salamon, 1992). For our purposes trade unions may be viewed as permanent associations of organised employees whose primary objectives are to:
(a) replace individual bargaining by collective bargaining, thereby redressing the balance of bargaining power in favour of employees and reducing management prerogative in employment-related matters;
(b) facilitate the development of a political system where workers have a greater degree of influence on political decisions resulting in an economic and social framework which reflects the interests of wage earners and the working class;
(c) achieve satisfactory levels of pay and conditions of employment and provide members with a range of services.

4.3.3. LEGAL POSITION
The legal position of trade unions, particularly in relation to their operation and formation, has been an issue of some debate in the context of Irish industrial relations. The main legislation dealing with the formation and operation of trade unions in Ireland are the Trade Union Acts of 1941 and 1971, and the Industrial Relations Act 1990. However, the legal definition of trade unions provided for in the legislation is very broad ranging and extends to employer organisations (see Kerr, 1989; Kerr and Whyte, 1985). This legislation stipulates that, apart from certain 'exempted' bodies, only 'authorised' trade unions holding negotiating licenses are permitted to

engage in collective bargaining on pay and working conditions. This legislation also specifies the conditions which a union must fulfil before it will be issued with such a licence. The granting of negotiating licences is subject to a number of restrictions. Trade unions may only gain a negotiating licence where they register with the Registrar of Friendly Societies and meet the notification (eighteen months), membership (at least 500 members) and financial deposit (minimum IR£5,000) criteria set out in the legislation. Trade unions with headquarters outside the Republic of Ireland need not register as outlined. However, they must be legally recognised trade unions in their country of origin and meet some prescribed guidelines in relation to their controlling authority. Otherwise such unions must meet the notification, membership and deposit requirements set out above. The legislation also provides for the operation of a number of 'exempted bodies'. These 'exempted' bodies are not required to hold a negotiating licence to engage in collective bargaining and include workplace ('staff' or 'house') associations/unions, some Civil Service associations and teachers' associations (Kerr and Whyte, 1985).

The major piece of legislation governing trade union operation is the Industrial Relations Act 1990. This Act deals with trade disputes, immunities, picketing, secret ballots, injunctions and trade union rationalisation. The Act provides for the protection of persons who organise or engage in trade disputes from civil liability. The Act further provides for the protection of trade union funds against actions for damages and the legalisation of peaceful picketing in trade dispute situations. The Act requires trade unions to conduct secret ballots of all members of the union who could be reasonably expected to take part in industrial action, prior to engaging in such action. The Act only provides for secondary picketing (i.e. picketing an employer other than the primary employer involved in the dispute) where it is reasonable for workers to believe that the second employer was acting to frustrate the industrial action by directly assisting the primary employer.

4.4. TYPES OF TRADE UNION

Irish trade unions have traditionally been organised on an occupational basis. This meant that employees tended to join a particular union because they worked in a particular job or trade. In Ireland trade unions were traditionally categorised as catering for either craft, general or white-collar workers (see Kelly and Bourke, 1979). It is important to note that it is extremely difficult to categorise unions as 'pure' craft, general or white-collar as most unions will deviate from a tight definition of their union category on some dimension. For example, general unions may have white-collar and craft workers in membership and not all 'craft' unions operate a recognised apprenticeship system. Thus, the categorisation discussed below should be read as indicative of union types in existence in Ireland rather than as a tight definition. Clearly other types of trade union classifications exist, such as enterprise unions in Japan whereby both white- and blue-collar workers are represented by a union whose sole membership comes from the enterprise in which it operates, or independent business unions in the US. Indeed, in the UK context, Turner (1962) suggests that a more appropriate categorisation of union types is based on whether union membership is 'open' to employees regardless of occupation, or 'closed' to all employees except those working in a defined trade requiring a prescribed apprenticeship or training period. However, the craft, general, white-collar categorisation provides a convenient benchmark upon which to analyse Irish trade unions as discussed below.

4.4.1. CRAFT UNIONS

Craft unions were the earliest form of union organisation and have their origins in the early unions which emerged in Britain at the start of the nineteenth century. These new 'model' unions, as they were termed, confined their membership to skilled categories such as printers and carpenters who had served a recognised apprenticeship in their particular trade. The Amalgamated Society of Engineers was the first British 'model' union to organise workers in Ireland. It established five Irish branches in 1851, and by 1858 it had ten branches here with a membership of 1,300 (Boyd, 1972). These early craft unions represented a relatively small proportion of the labour force. In Ireland it is estimated that by 1890 there were only about 17,500 trade union members in total, all of whom were skilled workers (Boyd, 1972). However, the significance of the 'model' unions was that by becoming accepted as important actors in the industrial relations system they created a 'vital bridgehead' in ensuring the acceptance of trade unions as part of the political and organisational framework.

Craft unions cater for workers who possess a particular skill in a trade where entry is restricted through apprenticeship or otherwise. Prominent examples of occupational categories who are organised in craft unions are electricians and fitters. It is suggested that such unions, by controlling entry to the craft, have traditionally held considerable negotiating power. For this reason craft unions tend to be vigilant in ensuring that only qualified people holding union cards carry out certain types of skilled work. This often led to criticisms of restrictive and inefficient work practices and sometimes to demarcation disputes. Increased mechanisation and consequent de-skilling has had a detrimental impact on the membership and power of craft unions as reflected in the reduction of their share of union members from a high of 17 per cent in 1940 to approximately 11 per cent in the late 1980s (Roche and Larragy, 1989a,b). Indeed, a number of traditional crafts have effectively been rendered obsolete and their associated trade unions have often ceased operations or merged with larger craft or general unions. Nonetheless, craft unions remain an important grouping within the Irish trade union movement. Figures from the Irish Congress of Trade Unions suggest that the three main engineering craft unions (Amalgamated Engineering and Electrical Union—AEEU, Technical, Electrical and Engineering Union —TEEU and the National Union of Sheet Metal Workers of Ireland —NUSMWI) have 6 per cent of ICTU members, while the major building unions (Union of Construction and Allied Trades and Technicans—UCATT, Building and Allied Trades' Unions—BATU and the Operative Plasterers' and Allied Trades' Society of Ireland—OPATSI) account for just under 4 per cent of total ICTU membership (ICTU, 1993).

4.4.2. GENERAL UNIONS

The origins of general trade unions are rooted in the increased number of unskilled or general workers employed in the large factories and other large organisations which characterised late nineteenth- and early twentieth-century Britain. These 'new' unions tended to be more militant than their 'model' union predecessors. They initially organised categories such as general labourers and dock workers, and were noted for both their aggressiveness and political consciousness in attempting to improve pay and working conditions for their members. General unions catering for unskilled workers such as labourers and dockers existed in Ireland from the 1860s. However, general unions began to play a more active role in Irish industrial and political life in the early 1900s (Boyd, 1972):

> The years 1907 and 1913 are outstanding in Irish trade union history for they are the years in which the unskilled labourers, at first in Belfast and then in Dublin, asserted their right to belong to trade unions. In each city this right was bitterly contested by employers . . . on the workers' side was Jim Larkin. He led the struggles for free trade-unionism and will be remembered as long as there is a Labour movement in Ireland.

Jim Larkin was involved with the National Union of Dock Labourers (NUDL) in Liverpool and moved to Belfast as a union organiser in 1907, and later extended his organising activities to Dublin and other Irish cities. After a dispute with the NUDL Larkin left the union and established the Irish Transport and General Workers' Union (ITGWU) in 1909. The ITGWU and other general unions catered for categories of workers such as dockers, caterers and railway workers. They became engaged in a series of strikes in 1911 and 1912, culminating in the Dublin lock-out of 1913. While this initially dealt a severe blow to the general unions they slowly recovered and reorganised. Union membership grew from 130,000 in 1914 to 300,000 in 1922 and the ITGWU accounted for 130,000 of these members (Boyd, 1972; McNamara et al., 1988). After leaving the ITGWU Larkin founded the Workers' Union of Ireland in 1914.

Although general unions are sometimes perceived as comprising all workers regardless of occupational or industrial classification, they have traditionally catered mostly for semi-skilled and unskilled workers. In recent years, however, some general unions have attracted white-collar and some craft categories into their membership. They are common in all types of organisations and industrial sectors with the best known example being the Services Industrial Professional and Technical Union (SIPTU). This is by far the largest trade union in Ireland with a membership of 199,000 (Department of Labour, 1993). SIPTU was created in 1990 as a result of the merger of the, then, two largest trade unions in the country, the Irish Transport and General Workers' Union (ITGWU) and the Federated Workers' Union of Ireland (FWUI). General unions tend to be the largest unions and account for approximately half of all trade union members. Recent figures from the Irish Congress of Trade Unions (ICTU) suggest that the three general unions —SIPTU, ITGWU, MPGWU (Marine Port and General Workers' Union) —represent some 45 per cent of all ICTU members.

4.4.3. WHITE-COLLAR UNIONS

White-collar unions normally cater for professional, supervisory, technical, clerical and managerial grades. White-collar unions experienced a significant growth in membership, particularly in the late 1960s and into the 1970s. The share of union members in white-collar unions increased from 24 per cent in 1940 to over 35 per cent in the 1980s, and in the period 1966 to 1976 white-collar unions increased their membership by 71 per cent as compared to an overall growth in union membership of 30 per cent over that period (Roche and Larragy, 1989a,b). The dramatic growth in the services sector (particularly the public sector) was a significant factor facilitating the growth of white-collar unionisation. Kelly (1975) also identified negative circumstances at work, particularly poor job design and general quality of working life as important factors facilitating white-collar unionisation. While traditionally white-collar workers were generally reluctant to join trade unions, changing attitudes combined with the significant advances in pay and conditions secured by blue-collar unions encouraged hitherto 'conservative' white-collar workers to unionise. The period also witnessed a growing awareness among some unions of the white-collar sector. The British-based Association of Scientific Technical and Managerial Staffs (ASTMS) attracted a large number of Irish insurance workers and other professional staff into its membership. The Irish Transport and General Workers' Union became the first general union to explicitly develop a white-collar section under the now TD Pat Rabbitte. White-collar categories thus represented a relatively 'greenfield' opportunity for union membership drives in the 1960s and 1970s.

In evaluating union membership statistics it is difficult to differentiate between white-collar and blue-collar workers. However, the major areas of concentration of white-collar workers are the public sector and the financial services sector. Recent figures from the Irish Congress of Trade Unions (ICTU) suggest that the five largest public sector unions (Irish Municipal,

Public and Civil Trade Union—IMPACT, Communications Workers' Union —CWU, Irish Nurses' Organisation—INO, Civil and Public Services Union —CPSU, and the Public Services Executive Union—PSEU) account for almost 17 per cent of ICTU members, while the three key teacher unions (Irish National Teachers' Organisation—INTO, Association of Secondary Teachers of Ireland—ASTI, and the Teachers' Union of Ireland—TUI) account for over 8 per cent of ICTU members. Turning to the financial services sector we find that the two major unions here (Irish Bank Officials' Association—IBOA, and the Manufacturing Services and Finance Union—MSF) account for another 8 per cent of ICTU membership. Other important unions catering for white-collar employees include the Irish Distributive and Administrative Trade Union (IDATU) and the Irish National Union of Vintners, Grocers and Allied Trades Assistants (INUVGATA).

4.5. TRADE UNION STRUCTURE AND GOVERNMENT

While it is always difficult to generalise about the structures of different organisations, it is possible to identify a number of common characteristics in the organisation structure of the majority of Irish trade unions. A basic characteristic of the governing structure of most Irish trade unions is that ultimate decision-making authority is vested in the membership and executed through resolutions passed at the Annual Delegates Conference (ADC). It is then the job of the union executive to carry out policy thus decided. The union officials' primary task is to carry out the operational aspects of the unions' role, servicing the membership through assistance and advice. The branch is the basic organisational unit in the union structure and it may be organised on either a geographic (catering for several companies) or establishment basis. A typical union structure is outlined in figure 4.1. The structure and personnel of trade unions in Ireland can be described at three levels, namely the workplace, branch and national level.

A. WORKPLACE LEVEL

At workplace level the *shop steward* is the key union representative. Their role is to represent employee interests on workplace issues, liaise with union officials, and keep members *au fait* with union affairs. In practice shop stewards may become involved in much workplace bargaining involving local grievances or disputes. On more major issues, their role is to support the trade union official and give feedback to the membership. The shop steward has been described as 'an employee who is accepted by management and union as the lay representative of the union and its members with responsibility to act on their behalf in industrial relations matters at the organisational level' (Salamon, 1992).

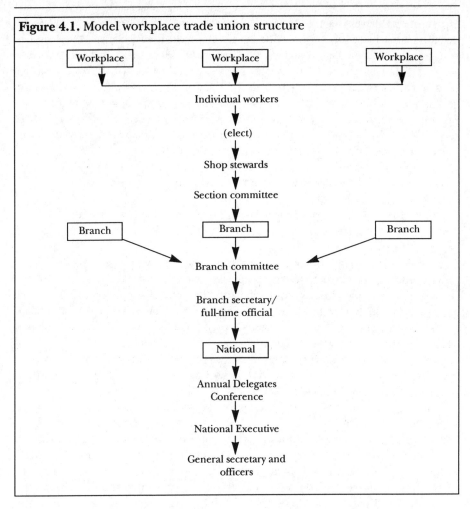

Figure 4.1. Model workplace trade union structure

An employee's first personal contact with a trade union will normally occur in the workplace. This usually happens when a shop steward invites new employees to become union members. The shop steward is the main trade union representative in the workplace. Shop stewards are elected by fellow trade union members at elections, which normally take place once a year. A number of shop stewards may be elected to represent different sections within an organisation.

Shop stewards are also employees of the organisation and, as such, must perform their normal job. It should be noted that the Code of Practice (under the Industrial Relations Act 1990), issued in 1993 in respect of Employee Representatives, states that such representatives should be afforded *reasonable* time off to perform their representative duties. Equally, trade union representatives are charged with representing their members in a fair and

equitable manner. It has become custom and practice in a number of organisations for shop stewards to be given time off to perform their union role and have access to requisite facilities (e.g. secretarial and telephone). However, these are often minimal and it is extremely rare for shop stewards to be given substantial leave to perform their union duties as is the case in some established UK firms. This may be because the small scale of most Irish organisations does not facilitate such resources being afforded to shop stewards. In the context of the operation of trade unions, the shop steward performs a number of important tasks. These include:
– recruiting new members into the union;
– collecting union subscriptions from members in the absence of 'check-off' arrangements;
– negotiating with management representatives on behalf of members;
– acting as a channel of communication between members and the union central office;
– defending and advancing the interest of members at all times.

The number of shop stewards has grown considerably over the last twenty years and particularly in the period from the mid-1960s to the 1980s. This growth is probably due to a number of factors, particularly (1) the increased acceptance of shop stewards by management; (2) the increase in plant-level collective bargaining; (3) the increase in employment legislation and consequent attention to 'policing' employee rights in the workplace; and (4) the heavy demands of union officials and associated reluctance of some unions to appoint more full-time officials.

It is suggested that the vast majority of shop stewards may spend about an hour during the working day on their union activities, paid by their employers, and perhaps as much again unpaid. Research suggests that a considerable number of shop stewards take on the job because they feel they would be good at it, think it is important, or feel it would help them 'get on' (Flood, 1989; Marsh, 1973; Salamon, 1992). A considerable number, however, are persuaded into it. Despite their initial reluctance, they later become highly motivated, finding the role satisfying. Sometimes managers may perceive shop stewards as the source of grievances. However, they are often better seen as the person whose role it is to articulate grievances felt by members. Because of their role they may be more attuned to problems, and likewise they may 'squash' grievances which they feel are not worth progressing. Shop stewards have a difficult situation in that they have to maintain the support of their members while at the same time maintaining a position with management from which they can negotiate effectively. Furthermore, they often perform their job with limited training or direction from their union.

The *section committee* is a group of trade union members elected by fellow trade union members who work in a specific section of the organisation. The section committee's main activity is to help shop stewards to perform their tasks effectively. Shop stewards within an organisation frequently form themselves into a committee, so that they can meet regularly, discuss common problems and decide on policy. Such a committee is called a Shop Stewards' Committee. All of the shop stewards are members of the same trade union, and if the shop stewards are members of different trade unions the committee is called a Joint Shop Stewards' Committee. Joint Shop Stewards' Committees can regulate conflict between unions, support and, if necessary, sanction individual stewards. They also constitute a more powerful and unified body for negotiating with management.

B. BRANCH LEVEL
The branch is a group of trade union members. Sometimes all the members of a branch work in one large business enterprise, but as is more often the case in Ireland, a branch is made up of people from different companies who work in a particular area. Figure 4.1 indicates how individual trade union members and their elected representatives are grouped together into a trade union branch. The branch is the basic unit of trade union organisation. It is usually divided up into several broad sections according to the grade or type of worker. The union branch carries out two important functions:
(1) it manages the internal affairs of the union;
(2) it strives for improvements of the terms and conditions of branch members.

Branch policy is decided by the branch at ordinary general meetings and at the branch Annual General Meeting (AGM). The affairs of the branch are managed by a branch committee, which is normally part-time. This committee is elected at the AGM, which also elects delegates to attend the Annual Delegates Conference of the union. The branch committee and all branch members are served by a branch secretary. In larger unions the branch secretary will have assistance and they are normally permanent employees of the union. If this is the case, then they are known as full-time branch officials whose primary functions are (a) the administration of branch affairs, and (b) negotiating terms and conditions for all branch members with management representatives.

C. NATIONAL LEVEL
The election of union officers takes place at the Annual Delegates Conference. Motions concerning the union and its policies are also discussed and voted upon. The motions are usually branch resolutions, and a motion that is approved at the Annual Delegates Conference becomes a resolution of the conference and so the policy of the union. Figure 4.1 illustrates that the Annual Delegates Conference is comprised of branch delegates who elect the union's National Executive Council and the union's General Council.

The National Executive Council is responsible for carrying out the decisions of the Annual Delegates Conference. In particular, it appoints the union's full-time branch officials and appoints staff employed by the union.

The general officers of a union are usually full-time employees of the union and they do not have another job. In some unions they are appointed to their position by the National Executive Council and in others they are elected at the Annual Delegates Conference or by a ballot of union members. The general officers usually consist of a general president, a general secretary, a general vice-president and a general treasurer.

4.5.1. IRISH CONGRESS OF TRADE UNIONS (ICTU)

The Irish Congress of Trade Unions (ICTU) is the central co-ordinating body for the Irish trade union movement with 97 per cent of trade-unionists in membership of unions affiliated to Congress (ICTU, 1993; *Irish Industrial Relations Review*, 1993). While Congress acts as representative of the collective interests of the Irish trade union movement, individual unions retain a large degree of autonomy and the ICTU relies on the co-operation of affiliated unions in promoting its overall goals. The Annual Delegates Conference decides on key policies and the executive is responsible for policy execution as well as general administration. Ultimate decision-making power within Congress is vested in the Annual Delegates Conference. Here delegates from affiliated unions consider various resolutions presented by union delegates, and those adopted become ICTU policy. The executive is responsible for policy execution as well as general administration.

The ICTU plays an extremely important role at national level, representing and articulating union views to Government and other institutions. The role of the ICTU is particularly significant in centralised pay negotiations. Along with the other social partners (Government and employer representatives), it is party to national negotiations on pay and other aspects of social and economic policy. It is the vehicle through which trade unions decide on participation in centralised pay bargaining, approve any agreement thus concluded, and ensure affiliated unions' adherence to the terms of such agreements. The ICTU also represents trade unions on several national bodies and provides union nominees for conciliation and arbitration services.

Various committees operate under the auspices of the ICTU. These include the Disputes Committee, which deals with inter-union disputes about membership, the Demarcation Tribunal, which deals with inter-union disputes in relation to work boundaries and the Industrial Relations Committee, which has the particularly important responsibility of granting an all-out picket in disputes. Such a picket obliges all union members employed in an organisation with which the dispute is, not to pass the picket, provided that the picket is peaceful, at the place of work of the employer and 'in contemplation or furtherance of a trade dispute'. Furthermore, a secret ballot of all union members must be held, and the aggregate majority must be in favour of such industrial action. Individual unions can only sanction a 'one-union picket', whereby only members of the union in dispute are obliged not to pass.

Trade unions not affiliated to the ICTU include the National Bus and Rail Workers' Union (NBRWU), the Psychiatric Nurses' Association (PSA) and the Dairy Executives' Association (DEA).

4.5.2. TRADES COUNCILS

These are voluntary groupings of unions on a regional or local basis. They are made up of officials and members of local unions who meet regularly to consider matters of regional and, sometimes, national significance. They can be extremely influential in determining union policy and are often perceived to relate more closely to membership needs than Congress. Trades councils may become particularly active in relation to certain political issues and were very much to the fore in the PAYE protests of the early 1980s. Forty-two trades councils were affiliated to Congress in 1988 (twenty-nine in the Republic).

Table 4.2. Trade union membership, 1945–90

Year	Membership	Employment density*	Workforce density**
1945	172,300	27.7	25.4
1960	312,600	49.6	45.4
1975	448,800	59.3	52.3
1980	527,200	61.8	55.2
1981	524,400	61.5	53.5
1982	519,900	60.3	51.4
1983	513,300	61.1	49.7
1984	500,200	60.7	48.2
1985	483,300	59.9	46.6
1986	471,000	58.0	45
1987	457,300	56.2	43.1
1988***	470,644	57.1	44.2
1989	458,690	55.6	43.4
1990	462,451	54.6	43.2

* Employment density = trade union membership/civilian employees at work x 100.
** Workforce density = trade union membership/civilian employee workforce x 100.
*** Figures for 1988–90 are estimates and are derived from the annual affiliated membership of the Irish Congress of Trade Unions and the Department of Enterprise and Employment.

Source: DUES Project UCD, Roche, 1992a.

4.6. TRADE UNION MEMBERSHIP

The total number of trade unions in Ireland amounts to some sixty-five unions catering for a total membership of around 460,000, or 43 per cent of the workforce in 1990 (see table 4.2). The period since 1980 has witnessed the most serious decline in trade union density since the 1930s. Trade union membership in the Republic of Ireland fell by over 51,000 members, or almost 10 per cent, in the 1980–85 period (Roche, 1989). However, this decline is principally attributed to macroeconomic factors, most notably economic depression, increased levels of unemployment and changes in employment structure characterised by decline in traditionally highly unionised sectors (the manufacturing industry and the public sector) and growth in sectors which have traditionally posed difficulties for union penetration, such as private services (see Roche, 1992a; Roche and Larragy, 1989a,b). A study by McGovern (1989a,b) points to increasing opposition to union recognition in the 1980s, suggesting that management approaches to unionisation have either hardened in line with the 'anti-union' style or become 'more subtle' in attempting to avoid unionisation.

In terms of current trends in union membership, it is interesting that provisional figures from the Department of Enterprise and Employment (formerly the Department of Labour) based on returns from unions affiliated to the Irish Congress of Trade Unions suggest that figures for trade union membership rose from over 470,000 in 1988 to some 477,000 in 1992, and the Department suggests that this trend has been sustained in 1993 (Department of Enterprise and Employment, 1993; ICTU, 1993). This increase in membership appears to reflect the fact that more people are now at work than ever before, though, ironically, unemployment is at a record high. Reasons for growth and decline in trade union membership are discussed later in this chapter. It is important to add a note of caution in relation to union membership figures based on returns from unions affiliated to the Irish Congress of Trade Unions. These figures are subject to confirmation and have not been subjected to detailed scrutiny of the DUES data series covering union membership trends for the period up to 1987 and led by Professor Bill Roche at University College Dublin (see Roche, 1992a; Roche and Larragy, 1989a,b). However, it is also worth pointing out that figures for Irish trade union membership do not include the estimated 25,000 members of the Garda and Army representative associations. Clearly, the inclusion of these figures would increase the levels of trade union density in Ireland.

Looking more closely at the breakdown of trade union membership by size of union it is evident that there is a notable imbalance in distribution of trade union members (see table 4.3). At one extreme we find a relatively small number of quite large unions representing almost three-quarters of the total union membership. At the other extreme there are approximately forty small unions catering for 11 per cent of total membership. Increasingly, these smaller unions are losing members while growth in trade union membership belongs to those larger unions. This may be a vindication of Government policy in the Industrial Relations Act 1990 to encourage the reduction of small unions. A related factor has been the increase in union merger activity. Union mergers clearly facilitate some rationalisation in the trade union movement but can also be a source of discontent due to the potential loss of identity and influence of individual trade unions. The ten largest trade unions in terms of membership are outlined in table 4.4.

112

Table 4.3. Trade union membership by size of union,* 1991

No. of members	No. of unions	% of total membership
Less than 1,000	17	1.3
1,001 – 2,000	10	3.0
2,001 – 5,000	11	6.7
5,001 – 10,000	6	9.7
10,001 – 15,000	3	8.0
Over 15,000	8	71.3

* This table only refers to trade unions holding negotiating licences under the Trade Union Acts and excludes a number of other representative bodies who do not hold such a licence but who operate as trade unions.

Source: Department of Enterprise and Employment, 1993.

Table 4.4. Large trade unions in Ireland

Name of union	Membership
1 Services Industrial Professional and Technical Union (SIPTU)	198,905
2 Irish Municipal, Public and Civil Trade Union (IMPACT)	27,493
3 Technical Engineering and Electrical Union (TEEU)	22,042
4 Manufacturing Services and Finance Union (MSF)	20,219
5 Irish National Teachers' Organisation (INTO)	19,884
6 Amalgamated Transport and General Workers' Union (ATGWU)	18,620
7 Communications Workers' Union (CWU)	16,601
8 Irish Distributive and Administrative Trade Union (IDATU)	16,562
9 Association of Secondary Teachers of Ireland (ASTI)	13,133
10 Irish Nurses' Organisation (INO)	12,902

Source: Department of Enterprise and Employment, 1993 (trade unions holding negotiating licences, 31 December 1992).

4.7. TRADE UNION DENSITY

As discussed above a useful index of union penetration in a country is trade union density. Measures of trade union density are twofold: (a) the percentage of the workforce who are trade union members; (b) the percentage of employees who are trade union members. As we can see from table 4.2, trade union workforce density in Ireland (measured by the proportion of the workforce who are trade union members) fell from a high of 55 per cent in 1980 but currently would appear to be stabilising at approximately 43 to 44 per cent. [Employment density in Ireland is estimated at *c.* 55 per cent.] Levels of union density and possible reasons for changes in union density in Ireland are discussed in some depth below. The level of trade union density in Ireland compares favourably with union density in the UK, which is currently some 40 per cent, and is considerably higher than in the US, where employment density as a proportion of the non-agricultural workforce stands at approximately 16 per cent, and is confined to a small number of industrial sectors such as the automotive and transport areas (see table 4.5).

Table 4.5. International employment union density (in %)

Australia	42	Italy	40
Austria	46	Japan	27
Belgium	53	Luxembourg	50
Canada	35	Netherlands	25
Denmark	73	New Zealand	42
Finland	71	Norway	57
France	12	Sweden	85
Germany	34	United States	16
Great Britain	40		

Source: OECD Outlook, 1991.

4.7.1. TRADE UNION MEMBERSHIP AT ORGANISATION LEVEL

In examining levels of trade union density at organisation level (the number of employees in a given organisation who are trade union members) the Price Waterhouse Cranfield (PWC) Project provides the most useful source of data (Brewster and Hegewich, 1994; Gunnigle et al., 1994). This study found that levels of union density in Irish organisations were quite high, and were consistent with the aggregate national statistics (Gunnigle et al., 1994; Price Waterhouse Cranfield Project, 1992). The PWC Project figures for Ireland are outlined in table 4.6, and were based on a survey of the top 1,500 trading and non-trading organisations in Ireland. As we can see, the levels of trade union density in the surveyed companies are high with almost two-thirds of respondent firms reporting that more than 50 per cent of their staff were trade union members. The PWC Project found that average union density across the companies was approximately 55.9 per cent. This compares closely with a union density of approximately 55 per cent of the employed national labour force (i.e. the number of union members as a percentage of the employed labour force; see Roche, 1992a; Roche and Larragy, 1989a,b).

Table 4.6. Trade union density (N = 269)

Proportion of employees in trade unions	% of respondent firms
0	18.4
1 – 25%	6.4
26 – 50%	10.9
51 – 75%	18.0
76 –100%	42.3
Don't know/missing	4.1

Source: Price Waterhouse Cranfield Project, 1992; Gunnigle et al., 1994.

A large proportion (60.3 per cent of the sampled companies) had union membership levels in excess of 50 per cent of their workforce. The exclusion of the non-unionised establishments increases union density to 69 per cent.

Given an aggregate union density among the employed labour force of 56 per cent it is not surprising to find a high level of union density in the top 1,500 trading and non-trading establishments where concentration of employees is greatest. This is particularly evident in the case of public sector establishments, which account for 42 per cent of the most highly unionised establishments but only 24 per cent of the sample in the PWC Project (see table 4.7).

Table 4.7. Level of union membership by sector

Level of union membership	% of firms by sector (actual numbers in parentheses)		
	Private	Public	Total
0%	22	1	16.9 (40)
1 – 25%	8	2	6.3 (15)
26 – 50%	14	2	11.4 (41)
51 – 75%	19	12	17.3 (41)
76 –100%	35	78	45.6 (108)
Don't know	2	5	2.5 (6)
Total	100 (179)	100 (58)	100 (237)

Source: Price Waterhouse Cranfield Project (Ireland), 1992; Gunnigle et al., 1994.

Table 4.8. Union membership by size

	% of firms (actual numbers in parentheses)						
Size	0%	1–25%	26–50%	51–75%	76–100%	Don't know	Total
1–50	38.6	20.5	4.5	9.1	25	2.3	100 (44)
51–100	27.5	10	27.5	17.5	17.5	0	100 (40)
101–200	12	2	12	24	48	2	100 (50)
201–500	15.3	4.2	8.3	18.1	50	4.2	100 (72)
501–1,000	10	0	6.7	20	60	3.3	100 (30)
1,001 +	7	0	7	19	67	0	100 (27)
Totals	19 (50)	6.5 (17)	11 (29)	17.9 (47)	43.3 (114)	2.3 (6)	100 (263)

Source: Price Waterhouse Cranfield Project (Ireland), 1992; Gunnigle et al., 1994.

4.7.2. FACTORS AFFECTING UNION DENSITY

A number of structural variables have been advanced to account for variations in union membership across industries and single establishments (Bain and Price, 1983; Hirsch and Berger, 1984). Variations in union levels are associated with shifts in the gender, occupational and industrial composition of potential union membership (particularly shifts in employment in the public/private and manufacturing/services sectors) and changes in industrial structure such as employment concentration, single- or multi-establishment status, product markets and capital intensity.

Size, sector, industry and the *proportion of white-collar, part-time* and *female workers* have all figured prominently as significant explanatory variables in the empirical literature on union density (Bain and Elias, 1985; Bain and Elsheikh, 1979; Bain and Price, 1983; Booth, 1986; Deery and De Cieri, 1991). Drawing from this literature Turner (1993) suggests that in the Irish context we can hypothesise that unionisation will vary negatively with the proportion of white-collar and part-time workers in an establishment, but positively as size increases, positively if it concerns a public-sector establishment and positively in specific industries such as manufacturing, transport and utilities. Less prominent but also relevant explanatory variables in the literature are establishment status, product market and capital intensity.

It has been suggested that *single independent establishments* are more likely to have a negative impact on unionisation than establishments which are owned or controlled by a large firm or multinational (Bain and Elsheikh, 1980). It is argued that a single establishment is more likely to relate to its employees in a paternalistic manner, in which the terms and conditions of employment are determined in a personal and informal way rather than by formal rules applied impersonally to all, which facilitates collective organisation.

It has also been suggested that unionisation is affected by the *nature of the market* in which the product of the establishment is sold (Bain and Elsheikh, 1979), with levels of unionisation being inversely related to the competitiveness of the market. The competitiveness of the product market and the ease or difficulty of unionisation within establishments is essentially related to whether the product market is local as distinct from national, or international.

Finally, the *country of origin* may have a significant impact on unionisation at establishment level. In particular, American-owned companies in the electronics industry are reputed to pursue an active strategy of union avoidance (McGovern, 1989a,b) or the marginalisation of trade unions through the use of such processes as direct employee communication and the prompt handling of grievances (Gunnigle, 1994). Indeed, Gunnigle (1994), in a survey of firms established since 1987, found that non-unionism among larger organisations was predominantly confined to US-owned firms. We might expect that foreign ownership or at least companies originating from the US may exert a drag on the level of unionisation.

In their analysis of union density levels in Ireland Turner et al. (1994) found that the level of unionisation was positively related to the size of company (number of employees) with large employers more likely to have higher levels of union density. As the authors point out, this finding is consistently supported by most of the empirical research on the determinants of unionisation. The authors found that union density levels were higher in the public sector. Their study suggests that the proportion of white-collar workers in an establishment has a significant and negative effect on union density. Four industrial sectors were positively related to union density with traditional manufacturing having the strongest effect, as perhaps could be expected. Transport and communications is a traditionally highly unionised sector, while banking in the Republic of Ireland is also highly unionised with the employees in the four largest banks covered by a single trade union.

4.8. TRADE UNION RECOGNITION

Despite the relatively high level of unionisation there are no specific statutory provisions to govern the process of collective bargaining and particularly trade union recognition in the Republic of Ireland. The constitutional guarantee of freedom of association embodied in article 40.6.1. of the Constitution confers the right on workers to form or join associations or unions. This provision has also been interpreted to include an implied right not to join trade unions where individuals do not wish to do so. The implications of this provision were demonstrated in a Supreme Court case of 1961 involving industrial action by a section of a company's workforce to enforce a 'closed shop' (i.e. compulsory union membership for all employees). In this case it was held that while the Constitution conferred on employees the right to join trade unions it also included an implied right not to join and on this basis found against the union and its actions (Educational Company of Ireland v Fitzpatrick and Others (1961)). This finding renders suspect many post-entry closed-shop agreements, although pre-entry closed-shop agreements (where union membership is a condition of the job offer) would seem to be in line with the provisions of the Constitution (see Abbott and Whelan v Southern Health Board (1981), unreported).

However, while the Constitution supports the freedom of workers to organise into associations or unions there is no apparent obligation on employers to recognise such unions or bargain with them (Report of the Commission of Inquiry on Industrial Relations, 1981). Neither is there any specific provision for recognition in the Trade Union Acts of 1941 and 1971. These Acts stipulate that, apart from certain bodies, only 'authorised' trade unions holding negotiating licenses are permitted to carry on negotiations in relation to pay and employment conditions. These Acts also specify the conditions which a union must fulfil before it will be issued with such a licence. The Labour Court may issue a recommendation in recognition disputes. However, this does not have legal effect. There are no statutory guidelines existing on the circumstances which should apply when an authorised trade union holding a negotiation licence seeks recognition from an individual employer.

In spite of the lack of any statutory mechanism for securing trade union recognition this issue does not appear to have been a great source of difficulty for the majority of managements or employees. Indeed, many employers appear to have been traditionally quite happy to recognise and conclude collective agreements with trade unions. This may be a result of our tradition of dealing with industrial relations through collective bargaining with unions (Roche, 1989). However, with the declining membership and power of Irish trade unions the issue of recognition has become increasingly contentious in recent years. There is substantial evidence of increased management opposition to unionisation in recent years particularly among some multinational organisations (especially US-owned firms in the high-technology sectors) and indigenous small firms (Gunnigle, 1994; Gunnigle and Brady, 1984; McGovern, 1989a,b).

4.8.1. TRADE UNION RECOGNITION AT ORGANISATION LEVEL

Despite some adverse commentaries on the level of trade union recognition and density in Irish organisations the evidence from the Price Waterhouse Cranfield (PWC) Project suggests the union membership in Ireland is quite robust. The PWC Project found that the great majority of Irish organisations surveyed recognised trade unions (see table 4.9). We have also seen above that union density levels were also quite high with almost two-thirds of respondent firms reporting that more than 50 per cent of their staff were trade union members. However, recent research evidence on trade union recognition in more recently established firms in the manufacturing and internationally traded services sectors presents a contrasting picture with a much lower level of trade union recognition (Gunnigle, 1992c). These issues are discussed below.

The PWC Project found that a total of fifty-seven (see table 4.9) companies, or 21 per cent of the sampled companies, did not recognise a trade union for collective bargaining purposes while seven of these companies acknowledged the presence of trade union members in their establishments. In the private sector there were a total of 183 companies surveyed in the PWC Project of whom fifty (or 28 per cent) did not recognise a trade union (Turner, 1993). An examination of the distribution of companies not recognising a trade union reveals the prominence of such firms in advanced manufacturing industries (see table 4.10). It would thus appear that firms in the advanced manufacturing sectors are less likely to recognise unions than those in traditional sectors.

Table 4.9. Trade union recognition

Trade union recognition	No. of firms (N = 269)	% of firms
Yes	207	77
No	57	21
Missing/Don't know	5	2

Source: Price Waterhouse Cranfield Project (Ireland), 1992; Gunnigle et al., 1994.

Table 4.10. Union status by industry (in %, actual numbers in parentheses)

Sector	Non-union	Unionised	Total (N=182)
Agriculture	37.5	62.5	(8)
Non-energy, minerals	16.7	83.3	(18)
Advanced manufacturing*	43	57	(35)
Other manufacturing	8.5	91.5	(59)
Building and civil engineering	33.3	66.7	(3)
Distribution trades	10	90	(20)
Transport and communications	25	75	(4)
Banking and finance	81.8	18.2	(11)
Personal and other services	50	50	(6)
Health and education	40	60	(5)
Fire, police, quangos	38	62	(13)

* Manufacturing is divided into two groups: metal manufacturing, which mainly covers the electronic and computing industry and which we label as 'advanced manufacturing' and 'other manufacturing', which refers to all other manufacturing areas and can be labelled as traditional manufacturing.

Source: Price Waterhouse Cranfield Project (Ireland), 1992; Gunnigle et al., 1994.

Turning to the impact of country of origin on trade union recognition, table 4.11 indicates that US firms are less likely to recognise trade unions. As already pointed out much of the literature on union recognition in Ireland has emphasised this fact. However, the differences identified in the PWC Project are quite small and would seem to suggest that US companies are only marginally more unlikely to recognise trade unions. However, this finding, which presents a relatively positive picture of union recognition in Ireland, contrasts with the findings of a recent study of new ('greenfield') firms established since 1987 (Gunnigle, 1994). Here the incidence of non-unionism was much higher with almost 53 per cent of firms not recognising trade unions (as opposed to 21 per cent in the PWC Project: see table 4.12). This study of industrial relations in greenfield sites found that the incidence of non-union status was mainly related to ownership and industrial sector. Indeed, non-unionism was predominantly confined to US-owned firms—only four of the twenty-seven US-owned firms recognised trade unions. Most Irish and European companies recognised trade unions. Senior management in European and Japanese-owned companies seemed less concerned than their US counterparts with the issue of union recognition. An interesting theme to emerge in interviews with the European and Japanese-owned companies was their preference for single-union recognition or 'one grieving voice' as stated by the general manager of a large Japanese company. It was interesting that only one of the twenty-three US-owned firms operating in the 'high-technology' sectors recognised a trade union. Of the four unionised US firms there seemed to be particular reasons in each instance which facilitated union recognition. In three cases the new greenfield companies were wholly owned

119

subsidiaries of US corporations which had established operations in Ireland over a decade ago and had recognised trade unions in those companies. This experience was instrumental in the decision to recognise trade unions in the greenfield sites. The other US firm which recognised unions operated in a craft-based sector employing skilled employees which were traditionally highly unionised, thus making union recognition probable. Interviews among non-union firms revealed that, for the great majority, the decision to pursue the non-union route was determined at corporate headquarters. In general it seemed that the impact of corporate headquarters in influencing establishment-level industrial relations was greater in non-union firms than in unionised firms. In the greenfield study most firms which recognised trade unions had closed-shop agreements with one or more trade unions. Also, union recognition was generally confined to manual grades.

The impact of ownership on union recognition is also considered in the following section in the context of a broader evaluation of factors impacting upon trade union recognition.

Table 4.11. Union recognition by origin of company (in %, actual numbers in parentheses)

	US	Ireland	EC	Rest	Total
Non-union	31.9	30.6	21.9	0	27.6
Unionised	68.1	69.4	78.1	100	72.4
Total	100	100	100	100	100
	(47)	(85)	(32)	(10)	(174)

Source: Price Waterhouse Cranfield Project (Ireland), 1992; Gunnigle et al., 1994.

Table 4.12. Union recognition in established and greenfield companies (in %, actual numbers in parentheses)

	Established		Greenfield	
Unionised	77.0	(207)	47.2	(25)
Non-union	21.2	(57)	52.8	(28)
Missing/Don't know	1.9	(5)	0.0	(0)
Total	100.0	(269)	100.0	(53)

Source: Price Waterhouse Cranfield Project (Ireland), 1992; Gunnigle et al., 1994;
Gunnigle, 1992c.

4.8.2. FACTORS AFFECTING UNION RECOGNITION[2]

Turner (1993) suggests that in general the factors which were found to be determinants of inter-establishment variations in the level of union membership are similar to those that account for the presence or absence of union recognition in an establishment (Bain and Elsheikh, 1980; Beaumont and Harris, 1989). However, Green (1990) distinguishes between the supply of an available union to each workplace and the demand for a union, that is, the decisions of individuals as to whether to join. The presence of a union at a workplace acts as a 'gateway' enabling employees to join. The determinants of whether there is a recognised union in an establishment, 'the determinants of coverage', are viewed as a distinct stage in a two-stage process, the second being the determinants of union membership. On the supply side, according to Green (1990) the *structural factors* associated with the *job itself* determine whether there is a *recognised union available*, and on the demand side, *individual characteristics* also determine whether an employee joins an available union. But, overall, his results 'reaffirmed' the importance of such structural factors as *industry, sector, occupation, firm size, gender typing* and *proportion of part-time workers* in determining union status (Turner, 1993; see also Beaumont and Harris, 1991).

In Milner and Richards' (1991) survey of firms in the London docklands, *size, ownership* (negatively if foreign) and *age of the establishment* (negative if started after 1983) significantly affected the probability of union recognition, while the proportion of women, white-collar workers and part-time workers, sector (service or manufacturing), single or multi-establishment unit, had no significant effect. Beaumont and Harris (1991), using data from the 1984 workplace survey of private sector firms, also found *size and age of establishment* (for non-manual workers) to be significant, but not ownership. The proportion of *part-time workers, women and manual workers* were also significant in affecting the probability of union recognition. But in a survey of private sector electronic plants in Scotland (Sproull and MacInnes, 1987) the proportion of females in a workforce did not influence the probability of unions being recognised, even after controlling for part-time workers. Significant variables were size and proportion of part-time workers; variables that had no significant effect were age of establishment, ownership (UK or foreign), and the proportion of females and employees on staff conditions. Obviously, some variables are more peripheral than others in affecting the probability of union recognition and are more related to the particular focus and level of the data/survey being analysed with contingencies such as region, ownership and proportion of part-time/white-collar and female workers, being chiefly a matter for empirical verification, while such factors as *size of establishment, sector* and *industry type* are more central both conceptually and empirically.

In analysing the PWC Project (Ireland) findings Turner et al. (1994) found that the significant factors affecting union recognition were size and workforce characteristics. Increases in organisation *size* were positively associated with union recognition and an increasing proportion of *white-collar workers* in an establishment was negatively associated with union recognition. Companies in what might be termed the advanced manufacturing sectors and the Banking and Finance sector had the largest negative impact on union recognition and thus appear more likely to be non-union compared to other sectors. However, given the small number surveyed in Banking and Finance the chances of an unrepresentative sample inhibits the reliability of the findings for this sector.

4.9. TRADE UNION INFLUENCE

While analyses of trade union density and recognition are relatively straightforward and objective, assessing trade union influence is an altogether more complex task. Firstly, and unlike membership and recognition, influence is largely perceptual. Secondly, influence can differ depending on the nature and type of influence we are talking about. For example, it would generally be accepted that the existence of centralised agreements on pay and related matters since 1987 has greatly facilitated high levels of union influence on national affairs, particularly in the area of economic policy. Turning to the issue of trade union influence in workplace industrial relations, again we find the major source of data is the PWC Project. The picture emerging in relation to trade union influence from this study does not appear as bleak for trade unions as some commentators have indicated (see table 4.13). While 23 per cent of Irish firms felt that trade union influence has decreased in recent years, 66 per cent felt there had been no change and 10 per cent felt that union influence had actually increased.

Table 4.13. Change in trade union influence: organisational level

Influence of trade unions	No. of firms (N = 265)	%
Yes, increased	19	7
Yes, decreased	51	19
No, the same	137	52
Missing/Don't know	58	22

Source: Price Waterhouse Cranfield Project (Ireland), 1992.

In examining the changes in trade union influence in the public and private sectors the PWC data identified a greater perceived decrease in the influence of trade unions in the private sector. Here 29 per cent of private sector firms reported a decrease in union influence with the corresponding figure for public organisations being 18 per cent. However, a more interesting and unanticipated finding is the perceived stability of trade union influence in both sectors. Despite a severe economic recession and the tenuous nature of employment tenure in many private-sector firms, 63 per cent of respondents in this sector indicated no change in trade union influence.

The recent study of employee relations practices in new greenfield companies discussed above (Gunnigle, 1994) examined the impact of trade unions upon workplace-level employee relations in companies (greater than 100 employees) established since 1987. In this study it is significant to note that respondents in 40 per cent of unionised firms felt that trade unions had either 'minor' or little impact. This was particularly the case among the small number of US-owned firms which recognised trade unions.

4.10. CURRENT ISSUES FACING IRISH TRADE UNIONS

4.10.1. DECLINING MEMBERSHIP

A particular issue in the context of changing patterns of industrial relations concerns trade union recognition and the future role of collective bargaining. The period since 1980 has witnessed a most serious decline in trade union density. As indicated earlier this decline has principally been attributed to macroeconomic factors, most notably economic depression and increased levels of unemployment and also changes in employment structure characterised by decline in traditionally highly unionised sectors (typical employment forms in manufacturing industry and the public sector) and growth in sectors which have traditionally posed difficulties for union penetration—such as private services (Roche, 1992a; Roche and Larragy, 1989a,b). Opposition to union recognition also appears to have increased in the 1980s (Gunnigle, 1992c; McGovern, 1989a,b). Some of these issues have been considered in our earlier discussion on trade union density and recognition in Ireland. However, a significant issue worthy of consideration in the context of developments in trade union membership is the influence of human resource management (HRM). This factor is considered below in the context of trade union membership and recognition, and is also the subject of broader analysis in relation to developments in Irish industrial relations in chapters 8 and 9.

4.10.2. TRADE UNION RATIONALISATION

A common criticism of the Irish trade union structure is that there are too many unions relative to total membership. It has been suggested that this causes problems for management, who have to deal with a number of unions, and also leads to inter-union rivalry and conflict as they compete with each other for membership. At an aggregate level Ireland does have a large number of unions dealing with a small membership (some sixty-five unions catering for approximately 460,000 members in 1990). However, a closer examination of aggregate union membership statistics indicates that the vast majority of trade-unionists are members of a few large trade unions with the remainder in very small unions catering for a very small proportion of total union membership (see tables 4.3 and 4.4 above). Rationalisation of the trade union structure has been high on the agenda of successive Governments. The recent merger of the ITGWU and the FWUI, which represented the two largest trade unions in the country forming SIPTU, headed a wave of negotiations by trade unions on the topic of possible mergers and amalgamations. It is suggested that SIPTU, the largest union in the State, caters for almost 40 per cent of total trade union membership. Indeed, the number of trade unions in the Republic has declined dramatically in recent years because of the pace of mergers and rationalisations. The total number of trade unions in Ireland has fallen from over ninety unions in the 1960s to some sixty-five unions in 1991 (see table 4.14). This trend seems set to continue as evidenced by the more recent merger between the National Union of Journalists and the Irish Print Union. However, we may also concurrently experience some dissatisfaction with merger activity due to a loss of identity and influence of some unions as a result of union mergers, particularly those involving the merger of small unions with much larger ones.

Table 4.14. Numbers of trade unions in Ireland, 1980–90

Year	Number of unions	Year	Number of unions
1980	86	1986	77
1981	86	1987	76
1982	83	1988	74
1983	80	1989	68
1984	78	1990	65
1985	77		

Source: Department of Enterprise and Employment, 1992.

4.10.3. BRITISH AND IRISH UNIONS

A unique characteristic of the Irish trade union structure in EU terms is that there are many unions from another EC Member Country (Britain) which operate in the Republic of Ireland. Recent figures from the Irish Congress of Trade Unions (ICTU) suggest that there are some thirteen British-based unions operating in the Republic of Ireland. Congress estimates that these thirteen unions account for some 63,000 members or some 14 per cent of total membership of trade unions affiliated to the ICTU. These include major unions such as the Amalgamated Transport and General Workers' Union (ATGWU) and the Manufacturing Services and Finance Union (MSF). Because trade unions rely primarily on current income from membership subscriptions, these unions are often in a strong financial position to service their Irish membership. On the other hand major policy decisions in such unions are taken in the UK and there has been debate on the priority accorded to the concerns of the Irish membership. Roche and Larragy (1989a,b) note the declining trend in the share of union members catered for by British unions but attribute this to changes in the structural composition of the workforce rather than any factors deriving from their national base.

4.10.4. TRADE UNION DEMOCRACY

Another common criticism of trade unions is that they fail to exercise adequate control over their membership or that militant minorities exercise undue influence over union affairs. These often refer to situations where it is alleged that a particular group of trade union members pursue a course of action which is at odds with the wishes of either the majority of the membership or the union officialdom. An implication of this line of thought is that unions can exert a type of autocratic control over the membership. This fails to appreciate the internal structure and operation of trade unions within our voluntarist tradition. The very existence of trade unions is centred on meeting the needs of the membership. If they fail to do this, then their very *raison d'être* diminishes.

Trade union discipline and control is based on a moral set of acceptable practices and the union hierarchy will be keen to ensure these are upheld through persuasion rather than compulsion in order to retain membership confidence (Kelly and Brannick, 1989). While it is true that unions do have power to decide on issues, it seems that control works in both directions (Flood, 1989, 1990a,b; Marchington, 1982). A union can exert a certain degree of control over its members in deciding on an appropriate line of action and it also has a disciplinary role in certain circumstances. However, the membership also has the right to decide on policy and they can exert control over the union to get it to serve the needs as perceived by that membership (e.g. by withholding subscriptions or threatening to join another union). In a multi-union environment trade unions must be very circumspect to meeting those needs lest they experience an exodus of membership.

4.10.5. TRADE UNIONS AND HUMAN RESOURCE MANAGEMENT (HRM) PRACTICES

The development of human resource management and its impact on industrial relations is considered in some depth in chapter 8 of this text. Human resource management is felt to have a significant impact upon the nature of workplace industrial relations and particularly on the role of trade unions. This final section considers the impact of human resource management (HRM) on trade union recognition. Broader issues relating to human resource management and industrial relations are considered in chapters 8 and 9.

Generally, human resource management (HRM) strategy is aimed at increasing the identification and commitment of the employee to the organisation and is sometimes held to be incompatible with the collectivist ethos of trade union recognition and collective bargaining (Beer et al., 1984; Guest, 1987, 1989a,b). Fiorito et al. (1987) argue that HRM practices are often part of attempts by employers to either substitute for, or avoid, unions. Indeed, the results of their research support the view that HRM policies affect unionisation. Turner (1993) suggests that a pertinent hypothesis is that the use of HRM practices inhibits union recognition in establishments. Using a comprehensive index of twelve measures of HRM practices Fiorito et al. (1987) conclude that such practices do inhibit unionisation but that the impact of specific policies varies considerably, with those in the area of communications and participation having the greatest adverse impact on union organising success. However, Milner and Richards (1991) found a significant positive association between companies that recognised unions and the greater use of employee involvement techniques such as quality circles, joint consultative committees, suggestion schemes and a regular newsletter. They suggest that recognising a union can facilitate the introduction of employee involvement by providing a ready-made organisational structure and, more importantly, an authority structure among employees which can be utilised to increase the chances of employee involvement techniques succeeding. Turner (1993) hereby suggests that an alternative, if weaker hypothesis is that unionisation is both compatible and supportive of the use of HRM practices.

In a review of American literature on HRM Beaumont (1991) found that the chief or at least most frequently cited components of HRM strategy are: a relatively well-developed internal labour market (in matters of promotion and employee development); flexible work organisations; contingent (performance-related) compensation practices; individual and group participation in task-related decisions and extensive internal communications arrangements. There is little empirical investigation of the impact of HRM practices on industrial relations and in particular trade union recognition and membership in Ireland. However, recent work by Turner (1993) provides some interesting findings. Using data from the PWC Project (Ireland) Turner (1993) examines five indicators, namely (1) the presence of an explicit HRM strategy; (2) employee development (training); (3) contingent compensation practices; (4) communications and (5) flexible work practices, to measure the extent of HRM practices in establishments. Structural variables found to be significant determinants of union density (discussed earlier) were also included in order to control for such factors as size, sector, proportion of white-collar workers and industry type which could possibly influence the use of HRM practices.

In the Irish context Turner (1993) suggests that an explicit *HRM strategy* is more likely to indicate some level of integration as well as indicating developed HRM policies and practices. In the PWC Project respondents were asked whether their organisation had a written or unwritten HRM strategy or none at all. Companies with a documented HRM strategy are defined as having a comprehensive strategy. While the existence of an explicit strategy may be a proxy for the components of HRM rather than a separate factor it can clarify the interesting question of whether companies who have explicit HRM strategies actually follow through in their employment practices. The existence of a written policy on HRM strategy was found not to have a significant effect on unionisation. In this respect Roche and Turner (1994) found that union non-recognition in the private sector was more associated with traditional managerial anti-union attitudes rather than the influences of current HRM thinking.

The *employee development* dimension was measured by the proportion of salaries and wages currently spent on training. Turner divided companies into those who spend more or less than 5 per cent of their company's annual salaries and wages budget on training. Training and development of employees is seen in HRM literature as an essential component of the flexible firm, improving functional flexibility and also binding the employee to the organisation particularly where the training is firm specific (Guest, 1987, 1989a,b). Although most trade unions encourage the training and development of their members the relationship between training and union recognition may be negative where the training and development undertaken becomes part of a union substitution strategy. Turner (1993) found that establishments which allocate over 5 per cent of annual salaries on training were more likely to have a lower level of unionisation.

Contingent *compensation practices* were measured by the presence of performance-related pay schemes and profit-sharing schemes for clerical and/or manual employees. Turner found that the existence of profit-sharing schemes and/or performance-related pay was negatively related to the level of unionisation. Trade unions are traditionally ambivalent to profit-sharing schemes and explicitly hostile to performance-linked pay systems. Given their collectivist orientation, trade unions aim to standardise wages across worker categories and prefer the use of such criteria as seniority and the 'going rate' for the job to determine pay levels. The strength of this attitude is perhaps reflected in the fact that pay was found to be the second largest influence on levels of unionisation. In analysing the PWC Project data Gunnigle et al. (1993) found that the nature of payment systems (in this case performance-related pay (PRP) schemes and profit sharing) was the only employment practice which differed significantly between union and non-union firms. There was no significant difference between union and non-union firms in the use of the remaining HRM practices. However, Roche and Turner (1993) in another study on the private sector found that only the existence of performance-related payment methods could be associated with union non-recognition in Ireland. This was qualified in that study in relation to the existence of a preference for engaging in local bargaining within that organisation. Gunnigle et al. (1994) found that the use of profit sharing and performance-related pay for all employees regardless of union status was broadly similar. However, when only clerical and manual employees were included there were substantial differences, with non-union companies making greater use of profit sharing and PRP for lower-level employees (table 4.15). A significant proportion (37.2 per cent) of companies in the private sector indicated an increase in the use of variable pay as a share of the total reward package offered to employees in both union and non-union companies. However, the conclusion that pay systems are the distinctive factor separating the employment practices of union and non-union firms must be evaluated in the context of the actual measures used. The HRM measures in the PWC Project did not encompass every aspect of the factor being measured (i.e. content validity is a problem). Unfortunately, this is a common problem with empirical studies of HRM practices and partly occurs from the lack of conceptual development in this area. At the same time there are cogent and convincing reasons for expecting performance-related pay (PRP) to prevail to a greater extent in non-union firms reflecting as we have already noted a tension between trade union notions of pay and PRP schemes. Indeed, pay practices are more strongly associated with union recognition than size or the proportion of white-collar workers.

Table 4.15. Union status and utilisation of merit pay and profit-sharing schemes (in %, actual numbers in parentheses)

Type	Non-union	Union	Total
Profit sharing	16 (8)	12 (16)	13 (24)
Merit pay	60 (30)	53 (69)	55 (99)
Clerical and manual*	56 (28)	36 (46)	41 (74)

*This measures the combination of performance-related pay schemes and profit-sharing schemes for clerical and manual employees.

Source: Price Waterhouse Cranfield Project (Ireland), 1992.

Flexible work patterns were measured by examining the level of increase in utilisation of both functional and numerical flexibility. Respondents in the PWC Project were asked to indicate whether jobs had been made wider/more flexible over the last three years for either clerical or manual employees or both. This measure of HRM practice, along with the measure of communications were found to have no significant relationship with union density in the establishments studied in the PWC Project. Surprisingly, union density does not vary between establishments where more than 20 per cent of the workforce was either part-time, temporary/casual or fixed-term employment contracts and other establishments. However, Gunnigle et al. (1994) stressed that the measurement of these practices cannot be considered to be empirically extensive or conceptually well developed. Functional flexibility broadly refers to the extent to which employees are flexible in the types of work they perform and the range of skills they can use. The measure of flexibility used in the PWC Project did not assess the extent of flexibility but rather whether the perception was that functional flexibility was increasing or decreasing. Obviously there may be a significant difference in the extent of functional flexibility which the measure used by the researchers in the PWC Project failed to establish.

Numerical flexibility was assessed using the proportion of employees on part-time, temporary or casual and fixed-term contracts of employment. Companies are divided into two categories, those with more than 20 per cent of any one or more of these type of employees in the workforce and those with less. There was no significant relationship between union density and numerical flexibility, with 60 per cent of the establishments which use some form of numerical flexibility having a density level above 76 per cent. Numerical flexibility was slightly more prevalent in public sector establishments with 22 per cent compared to 16 per cent of establishments in the private sector. It was least prevalent in establishments of US origin (8 per cent) and relatively equally prevalent across the rest (Irish 21 per cent; EC 22 per cent; others 25 per cent). Employees on such contracts in the public sector are more likely to be union members given the high level of unionisation in this sector, thus reducing union opposition to numerical flexibility.

Turner (1993) also found that union and non-union firms exhibited similar patterns in the use of numerical flexibility. However, when the trend in specific flexible employment practices is examined, a number of differences emerge between union and non-union firms (see tables 4.16 and 4.17).

Table 4.16. Union status and numerical flexibility (in %, actual numbers in parentheses)

	Numerical flexibility		
	No	**Yes**	**Total**
Non-union	86.0	14.0	100 (50)
Unionised	82.2	17.8	100 (129)
Total	83.2	16.8	100
	(149)	(30)	(179)

Number of missing observations: 4

Source: Price Waterhouse Cranfield Project (Ireland), 1992.

Primary flexibility can be differentiated from secondary flexibility and defined as non-standard employment contracts where flexibility is built into the job contract. Non-standard employment contracts include part-time work and temporary/casual work. Secondary flexibility refers to such practices as overtime and shift work, which can be utilised within the standard employment contract. Union opposition to part-time and casual work encourages the extraction of flexibility from the existing permanent workforce in the form of overtime/shift work and the use of subcontracting and fixed-term contracts. According to this logic flexibility in unionised firms is more likely to be of a secondary nature with additional flexibility being sought through subcontracting and fixed-term contracts. The pattern in table 4.17 indicates that the use of overtime has increased more in unionised (25 per cent) than in non-unionised (12 per cent) environments. However, the decrease is also greater in unionised organisations (33 per cent), suggesting perhaps that, while unionised organisations continue to rely heavily on overtime, they may also be turning to other methods in an attempt to enhance flexibility and to improve cost structures. Part-time work also appears to be more common in unionised companies. While 26 per cent of unionised companies suggest that they do not use part-time work, about 50 per cent of non-union organisations suggest it is not used. Also, part-time work appears to have increased significantly more in unionised companies (38 per cent) than in non-union companies (22 per cent). Other important issues emerging from table 4.17 are that temporary or casual work has increased most in non-union companies, and fixed-term contracts appear more popular in unionised companies. The trends identified in table 4.17 may possibly reflect the ability of trade unions to unionise regular part-time workers, and/or the fact that part-time workers do not pose a threat to a permanent unionised workforce. However, this is less likely to be the case with casual workers, who are often in a less secure position than regular part-time workers, and can provide a pool of labour which is capable of replacing existing permanent workers.

Table 4.17. Union status and flexible employment practices (in %, actual numbers in parentheses)

	Non-union				Union			
Work practices	Increased	Decreased	Same	Not used	Increased	Decreased	Same	Not used
Overtime	12 (6)	20 (10)	55 (28)	14 (7)	25 (49)	33 (65)	38 (74)	3 (7)
Part-time work	22 (4)	4 (2)	26 (13)	49 (25)	38 (71)	81 (14)	28 (51)	26 (48)
Casual work	45 (24)	9 (5)	28 (15)	15 (8)	36 (67)	16 (30)	39 (74)	9 (16)
Sub-contracting	26 (14)	4 (2)	34 (18)	36 (19)	34 (63)	5 (9)	29 (54)	30 (56)
Fixed contracts	26 (13)	–	25 (13)	47 (24)	37 (68)	4 (7)	31 (57)	28 (51)

Source: Price Waterhouse Cranfield Project (Ireland), 1992; University of Limerick, 1992.

The extent of *employee communication* with manual and non-manual employees was measured by whether clerical and/or manual employees or both were formally briefed about the strategy and financial performance of their company. As table 4.18 shows, there is no significant difference between union and non-union firms with regard to managerial, professional/technical and clerical employees. However, in companies where a union is recognised manual workers are more likely to be briefed on strategic and financial matters. This may reflect the ability of unions to represent the interests of those furthest from the source of such information. In any case it indicates a significant difference which warrants further research. It must be noted, though, that non-union companies have traditionally relied extensively on direct verbal and written communication with their employees. Thus, we must be cautious in the interpretation of the large increases in these methods in unionised establishments noticeable in table 4.19.

Table 4.18. Union status and provision of financial information/business strategy information to employees (in %)

| | Type of information | | | |
| | Financial Information | | Business strategy | |
	Union	Non-union	Union	Non-union
Grade of employee:				
Management	93	90	91	96
Professional/Technical	60	62	65	76
Clerical	43	42	48	46
Manual	38	28	35	34

Source: Price Waterhouse Cranfield Project (Ireland), 1992; Gunnigle et al., 1994.

Table 4.19. Union status and trends in communication

| | | Non-union | | | | Unionised | | |
Mode	Increased	Decreased	Same	Total*	Increased	Decreased	Same	Total*
Staff bodies (incl. trade unions)	16	2	18	36	13	18	50	81
Direct verbal	46	2	46	94	62	2	28	92
Direct written	30	2	44	76	45	4	35	84

* The percentages in the table are constructed as a proportion of all union and non-union firms.

Source: Price Waterhouse Cranfield Project (Ireland), 1992; Gunnigle et al., 1994.

While the rate of change is greatest in unionised firms, the prevalence of direct communication processes is likely to be less extensive than in non-union firms. However, the trend testifies to increasing change in unionised companies towards communication patterns traditionally associated with non-union firms and includes for many firms a more direct relationship with their employees, which includes briefing on strategic and financial matters. Whether this suggests a more co-operative climate between management and employees and that unionisation is both compatible and supportive of the use of HRM practices (Turner, 1993) is a mute question and will depend on, among others, factors such as the nature and extent of the information provided to employees. Post-hoc and limited information on strategic and financial affairs is of little use and more often can actually lead to a climate of distrust and calculative behaviour on the part of employees. Unfortunately, the data does not distinguish between managerial, clerical and manual employees but it is probable that such increases apply mainly to managerial and professional staff.

A combination of the employment practices discussed above provides a general measure of the incidence of HRM approaches. As such the evidence discussed in relation to the Irish context suggests that HRM practices do not significantly influence union density. Equally, there are few significant differences between union and non-union firms in the use of HRM practices although there are some interesting, if minor, differences.

4.11. CONCLUSION

This chapter has broadly examined the historical development and current nature of trade-unionism in Ireland. This chapter has served to highlight that, in fact, union strength in Ireland is quite robust considering the broader economic climate and international trends in unionisation levels. Equally, it also seems that HRM practices have not sounded the deathknell of Irish trade-unionism. This latter issue of human resource management and its impact on industrial relations is considered further in chapters 8 and 9. However, in the next chapter we turn to the issue of employer organisation and particularly the role of employer associations in industrial relations.

NOTES
1. It is noteworthy that the origins of our current Joint Labour Committee system (outlined in chapter 3) lie in concerns about the use of 'sweated labour' at the turn of the century and resulting in the establishment of Trades Boards to enforce the minimum pay rates in certain occupations. See for example McMahon (1987b, 1989).
2. This discussion is largely based on the work of Tom Turner (1993). The authors would like to acknowledge Mr Turner's co-operation and permission to use his work in this analysis of factors affecting trade union membership and density in the Republic of Ireland.

CHAPTER FIVE

Employer Associations

5.1. INTRODUCTION

As with worker organisations, employers are equally likely to combine for purposes associated with employment and labour matters (Smith, 1970). This chapter considers the role of employer associations in Irish industrial relations. In particular we examine the operation and structure of employer associations, the legal definition of employer associations in Ireland, employer association membership and the range of services provided by such associations. We begin, however, by considering the objectives of employers in industrial relations. This helps crystallise the reasons why employers join associations for industrial relations and other purposes, and the objectives and structure of such organisations.

5.2. EMPLOYER OBJECTIVES IN INDUSTRIAL RELATIONS

The primary concern for organisations operating in a competitive environment is to maximise organisational effectiveness and generate satisfactory returns for the owners/stakeholders. Such returns are often expressed in terms of cost effectiveness and, for the commercial organisation, profitability. Management's primary role is to organise the factors of production, including labour, to achieve these objectives. Consequently, it must make decisions in a variety of areas to facilitate the achievement of corporate goals. Industrial relations is one such area where management must decide on optimal structures and practices.

It is difficult to assess the degree to which employers have specific industrial relations objectives or adopt related workplace strategies. Organisations vary so greatly in terms of structure and philosophy that it would be impractical to suggest a comprehensive set of industrial relations objectives. Indeed, it is clear that a particular organisation's industrial relations priorities and approach are heavily influenced by a combination of internal and external variables such as product market conditions and business goals, which differ considerably between organisations. This theme is further developed in chapter 9, which considers management approaches or styles in industrial relations. Nevertheless, it is worthwhile considering some general beliefs common among employers. Thomason (1984) identifies a number of employer beliefs or objectives in industrial relations as follows:

(1) *Preservation and consolidation of the private enterprise system:* This has larger political overtones and relates to the concerns of employers to preserve an environment conducive to achieving business objectives at enterprise level. They will be particularly concerned that principles such as private ownership, the profit motive and the preservation of authority and control are maintained.

(2) *Achievement of satisfactory returns for the owners:* This relates directly to the organisation's primary business goals. For commercial organisations to survive in the long term satisfactory profit levels must be achieved. Thereby, managerial approaches and strategies will always be influenced by this primary concern. Non-profit-making organisations will be equally concerned with cost effectiveness and the quality of their product or service.

(3) *Effective utilisation of manpower resources:* Manpower is a key management resource and its effective utilisation is central to the management process.

(4) *Maintenance of control and authority in decision making:* Employers will strive to ensure effective control and authority in executing its management role particularly in strategic decision making.

(5) *Good management–employee relations:* Employers will also strive to maintain good working relations with employees but this must be achieved within the operational constraints of the organisation. The scope to agree attractive remuneration levels and conditions of employment, etc., will vary according to the organisation's market position and profitability as well as its personnel philosophy. Good industrial relations will be a priority since they are an important ingredient in ensuring the organisation achieves its primary business goals as well as being laudable in itself.

To help achieve such objectives employers have found it beneficial to combine into permanent organisations. At the outset it is necessary to distinguish *employer associations,* which are concerned with industrial relations issues, from *trade associations,* whose objectives are largely confined to trade or commercial issues. Oechslin (1985) defines employer associations as 'formal groups of employers set up to defend, represent or advise affiliated employers and to strengthen their position in society at large with respect to labour matters as distinct from commercial matters'.

This chapter considers the role of such employer associations and particularly focuses on their involvement in Irish industrial relations.

5.3. The Historical Development of Employer Organisations

Employer organisations of a sort undoubtedly existed before the growth of trade-unionism and some possibly had connections with the guilds of the Middle Ages. As Adam Smith observed as far back as 1776 employers are likely to combine into associations for purposes related to employment and labour matters generally (Smith, 1970).

The major impetus for the growth of employer associations as defined above was the perceived need to react to and deal with the 'new unionism'. This helps distinguish between employer organisations whose precise *raison d'être* was to deal with labour matters (employer associations) from those where trade and commercial reasons were the main reason for their existence and development, and which are most commonly referred to as trade associations.

A related and traditional reason why employers have formed representative associations is to prevent harmful economic competition with each other, particularly in relation to pay, and to counter the power of trade unions. Other reasons include the increasingly complex nature of collective bargaining and employment legislation and the desire for a forum for the exchange of views among employers.

In their early attempts to grapple with organised labour and employment matters, employers, after initially dealing with such issues on an individual enterprise basis, soon found it opportune to combine either on an *ad hoc* or temporary basis or to form permanent associations. The reasons behind the formation of such associations were largely functional. Most of the early business enterprises were owner managed by the traditional entrepreneur/master. It has been argued that entrepreneurs have a weaker spirit of association than other social groupings and therefore any attempts at combination would need to have a solid rationale (Oechslin, 1985). Consequently, many of the early employer associations were forums for exchanging views and opinions, and this role later developed into one of joint strategy formulation. Such organisations mostly operated on a regional/industry-wide basis. Central umbrella associations were a later development. Thus, the early employer organisations were largely Masters' associations for particular industrial sectors and/or regions, who had combined for a variety of reasons not necessarily related to labour matters. While some of these exist today, the more important contemporary employer associations are those of corporate employers with specific employment-related objectives.

5.4. Employer Associations in Ireland

As discussed above employer organisations in Ireland are classified into two categories—employer associations and trade associations—both of whom must register with the Registrar of Friendly Societies. Employer associations are involved in industrial relations and must hold a negotiating licence under the terms of the Trade Union Acts. This distinguishes them from trade associations, which are not required to hold such a licence. Employer associations are in effect trade unions of employers and fall within the same legal definition as a trade union. While this may not initially seem significant, it can have important implications for the role and membership of employer associations. In particular, it suggests an approach to industrial relations which emphasises the role of collectives or combinations as opposed to individuals.

In 1993 the Department of Enterprise and Employment records indicated that there were thirteen employer associations as defined above (shown in table 5.1).

Table 5.1. Employer associations in Ireland, 1993

Name of association	No. of members
Construction Industry Federation	2,188
Cork Master Butchers' Association	42
Dublin Master Victuallers' Association	184
Irish Business and Employers' Confederation	3,279
Irish Commercial Horticultural Association	59
Irish Hotels Federation	514
Irish Master Printers' Association	39
Irish Pharmaceutical Union	1,222
Irish Printing Federation	52
Licensed Vintners' Association	624
Limerick Employers' Association	6
Petroleum Employers' Association	5
Society of the Irish Motor Industry	1,212

Source: Department of Enterprise and Employment, 1993.

While the number of employer associations is considerably less than their trade-union counterparts, there is considerable diversity in membership composition. One can find within this listing examples of traditional Masters' associations, industry-based associations, and a general association which is national in scope.

5.4.1. THE IRISH BUSINESS AND EMPLOYERS' CONFEDERATION (IBEC)

By far the largest employer association in Ireland is the newly formed Irish Business and Employers' Confederation (IBEC), which was formed on 1 January 1993 through the merger of the Federation of Irish Employers (FIE —formerly the Federated Union of Employers) and the Confederation of Irish Industry (CII). The Irish Business and Employers' Confederation (IBEC) represents business and employers in all matters relating to industrial relations, labour and social affairs. Over 3,700 firms are in membership. These firms employ some 300,000 people or approximately 60 per cent of the country's labour force excluding agriculture, the public service and the self-employed. As the country's major representative of business and employers, IBEC seeks to shape national policies and influence decision making in a way that protects and promotes member employers' interests. This is clearly shown in the Confederation's Mission Statement in box 5.1.

Box 5.1. Mission statement—Irish Business and Employers' Confederation

The Mission Statement of the Irish Business and Employers' Confederation is . . .

> to influence vigorously the formation of policy at national, European and international levels towards the development of an enterprise culture, the creation of economic and social conditions favourable to the profitable growth and effectiveness of Irish business and employers, and the development of productive employment, whilst having due regard to the interests of the wider community

and

> to provide quick response assistance, information, advice and representation for members in protecting their interests and maximising performance.

Unlike the old FIE, IBEC's role is not confined solely to industrial relations. In addition, IBEC represents industry in matters of trade, economics, finance, taxation, planning and development. IBEC develops and reviews policy on this wide range of topics through consultation with members, research and expert advice and opinion. A major role of IBEC is the representation of employer interests on these issues to Government and the public at large. It also maintains employer representation on various national and international bodies.

In all, the Confederation represents business and employers on over eighty separate organisations, institutions and committees. Representatives are chosen from the National Executive Committee elected by members, managers with particular experience and expertise, and senior executives from the Confederation. IBEC also acts as Ireland's business and employer representative within UNICE, the European employer representative body, the International Organisation of Employers (IOE) and the International Labour Organisation (ILO). In this role IBEC evaluates European and international developments and their effect on its affiliated membership.

IBEC's industrial relations, advisory and consultation services are organised on a regional basis. The Industrial Division and the Distribution and Services Division both operate from its Dublin headquarters, while the five regional offices operate independently with back-up facilities provided from Dublin. Designated executives are often assigned to deal with individual company needs. Particularly important among these services is IBEC's role in representing member firms at mediation, conciliation and arbitration hearings but IBEC also provides a range of specialist services in areas such as management training, health and safety, and legal advice and representation.

5.4.2. CONSTRUCTION INDUSTRY FEDERATION (CIF)

The Construction Industry Federation (CIF) is the second largest employer association in Ireland. Unlike IBEC, which represents employers from a range of industrial sectors, the CIF is essentially an industry-based association dealing with both trade/commercial matters and industrial relations affecting the construction industry. Its affiliated membership totals just over 2,000 firms, representing over 46 per cent of all those in the construction industry. These firms are estimated to employ around 50,000 workers or 75 per cent of all workers in privately owned construction firms.

In the area of industrial relations, the main role of the CIF involves monitoring and handling industrial relations on all large sites, dealing with any matters referred to it by member organisations, negotiation of national registered agreements, representing members at conciliation and arbitration, and providing information and advice to affiliates (Pollock and O'Dwyer, 1985).

5.4.3. OTHER EMPLOYER ASSOCIATIONS IN IRELAND

Most of the other employer associations are primarily concerned with trade and commercial issues although some are quite involved in industrial relations. The labour relations role of the *Irish Hotels Federation* is largely confined to representing employer interests on the Hotel Joint Labour Committee and providing general industrial relations advice to members. It does not involve itself in local bargaining. Similarly, the *Society of the Irish Motor Industry* is mostly concerned with trade and commercial issues but does provide a personnel/industrial relations advisory and assistance service. The *Licensed Vintners' Association* provides a range of services to Dublin publicans, one of which involves industrial relations. It conducts negotiations on pay and working conditions with the Irish National Union of Vintners, Grocers and Allied Trades Assistants and also provides affiliated members with a personnel advisory service covering areas like personnel policy, discipline/dismissal and redundancies.

The involvement of the remaining employer associations in industrial relations is limited. However, an interesting association is the *Limerick Employers' Federation*, which is a rare example of a regional association involved in industrial relations. It is largely representative of retail and distribution organisations in the greater Limerick area, and in addition to its trade/commercial role, it provides advice and assistance, and acts as a forum for the exchange of views on industrial relations and personnel matters generally.

5.4.4. THE IRISH EMPLOYERS' CONFEDERATION

The Irish Employers' Confederation (IEC) was set up in 1969 just prior to the advent of centralised pay bargaining and at a period of considerable industrial unrest. One of its purposes was the desire to present a united employer front on industrial relations issues and to rationalise multi-unionism on the employer side. This latter issue was particularly noteworthy at the time as employers had frequently criticised Irish trade unions for their multiplicity. At the time of its foundation there were twenty-one employer associations holding negotiation licences under the Trade Union Acts. While this was considerably less than the ninety-odd trade unions operating in the State at that time, it was still a cause for concern that there was no central employer body. The initial membership comprised of seven major employer associations including the Federated Union of Employers (subsequently the FIE, and now IBEC), the Federation of Builders, Contractors and Allied Employers (now the CIF), and the Limerick Employers' Association, but the major driving force seemed to be the FUE.

During the period of centralised bargaining (1970–81) the IEC played an important role in representing employer interests at the Employer–Labour Conference. While the Employer–Labour Conference was initially established as a bipartite forum for discussion of pay, prices and general industrial relations matters it became most widely known as the mechanism for the negotiation of successive national wage agreements. The employer side of the conference was represented by the IEC together with representatives of State-owned enterprises and Government (in its role of employer). Since the early 1980s the role of the IEC has become increasingly ambiguous. In 1990 its membership consisted of eleven affiliates, only four of which were employer associations with the remainder mostly semi-state organisations. Its current role seemed totally overshadowed by the FUE, and the subsequent merger in 1993 of the FIE (formerly the FUE) and the Confederation of Irish Industry (CII) to form the Irish Business and Employers' Confederation (IBEC) has made the latter body the *de facto* voice of Irish employers on industrial relations issues. Thus, while the IEC played a significant role in centralised pay bargaining in the 1970s and early 1980s it never really reached the status of a federation for all employer associations and today seems even further from that role, the most significant employer association in Ireland being the Irish Business and Employers' Confederation.

5.4.5. OTHER EMPLOYER GROUPINGS

While this chapter is primarily concerned with formal employer associations operating in the area of industrial relations, it is also important to note, as discussed earlier, that employers may also establish and combine in less formal groupings. Such associations or groups are generally used by employers as a forum for the exchange of views and information on industrial relations issues and also as a mechanism for co-ordinating employer approaches to specific industial relations issues. Such groupings have the advantage of informality and cohesiveness while conferring none of the obligations or costs attached to formal assocation membership. Such associations may be formed on a regional (e.g. the Limerick/Shannon Personnel Managers group) or industrial basis (e.g. the electronics sector) and may meet on either a semi-permanent basis or only when a significant issue arises. The Institute of Personnel and Development (IPD), which is the major professional association for management practitioners in industrial relations, may also act as a forum for representing employer interests in industrial relations.

5.5. OBJECTIVES OF EMPLOYER ASSOCIATIONS

Some common employer objectives in industrial relations were outlined above and include:
– support for the private enterprise system;
– achievement of satisfactory returns for the owners of the organisation;
– effective utilisation of manpower;
– maintenance of management prerogative in decision making;
– ensuring good employer/employee relations.

Most employers would subscribe, with varying degrees of commitment, to these general objectives and many have found that through combination they can portray a common front and more effectively achieve employer goals at both the micro and macro levels.

However, beyond these common objectives Windmuller (1984) argues that it is inappropriate to refer to the views and approaches of employer associations as constituting a specific ideology, and suggests that employer associations unlike trade unions, do not subscribe to some ideal economic and social system and are not part of a quasi-political movement. While it may be valid to say that employer associations do not affiliate to a particular political party (as trade unions often do) employer associations do have broad economic, social and political objectives which they pursue and their role —particularly of national associations—is not just confined to micro-level issues but also to larger societal-level matters such as political control, economic and social policy. Similarly, at organisation level they will seek to provide members with a range of services to help them deal more effectively with industrial relations issues. A summary classification of broad employer association objectives is outlined in box 5.2.

In a political era where lobby groups are becoming increasingly important, employer associations have assumed a significant role in representing employer interests on national issues. They provide a mechanism through which governments can solicit employer views on areas such as labour legislation and are important vehicles for influencing public opinion on more general political issues. This political role of employer associations is most clearly associated with their desire to influence broad economic decision making. Employer organisations will generally support what could be termed conservative economic policies which serve to protect the interests of capital and ensure freedom from an excess of State intervention in business. In the area of social policy the approach of employer organisations will be largely pragmatic. On the one hand, they will generally attempt to prevent, or at least lessen, the effects of protective labour or social legislation such as legal moves towards extending industrial democracy or information disclosure; on the other hand, they will accept some degree of social and legislative reform provided their perceived effects on the interests of capital are not adverse.

Box 5.2. Objectives of employer associations

1. *Political:* to effectively represent employer views to Government, the general public and other appropriate bodies so as to preserve and develop a political, economic and social climate within which business objectives can be achieved.

2. *Economic:* to create an economic environment which supports the free-enterprise system and ensures that managerial prerogative in decision making is protected.

3. *Social:* to ensure any social or legal changes best represent the interests of affiliated employers.

4. *Employee relations:* to ensure a legislative and procedural environment which supports free collective bargaining and to co-ordinate employer views and approaches on employee relations matters, and provide assistance to affiliated employers.

Turning to the specific role of employer organisations in industrial relations, this may be categorised into four broad areas:

(1) *Exchange of views:* We have already suggested that many of the early employer organisations were traditional masters' associations, who initially came together to discuss labour relations and related issues. Such associations provided a useful forum for opinion exchange and discussion. As the impact of trade unions increased and the State became more active in economic and social affairs, the role of such associations became even more important. Employers now came together not only to exchange information but to agree common policies and strategies. This led to a greater formality in the organisational structure of employer associations. This role is still important today. However, it is practically difficult to get a wide input into any general discussions on policy issues of national significance. Such opportunities can possibly be afforded at regional level. However, for larger associations, policies and positions are generally decided by a limited representative body of employer opinion.

(2) *Representation of employer views to Government and its agencies:* As the political philosophy of *laissez-faire* receded and Government became more active in economic and social affairs, employers saw a need for their views on such issues to be effectively represented to Government. This need became even

more pressing with the extension of the welfare state in the post-war era and the growth in social and—particularly—employment legislation. As Munns (1967) remarked in his research paper on employer associations to the Royal Commission on Trade Unions and Employers' Associations (1968), under the chairmanship of Lord Donovan (hence referred to as the Donovan Commission):

> All of the national organisations regard the representation of members' views to Government as an important and growing part of the function. The general importance arises from the fact that much legislation has a direct bearing on industrial affairs and associations take very seriously their responsibility to seek amendments to existing or proposed legislation which would have a harmful effect on their members, or to improve the practical execution of the Government's intentions.

Employer associations, particularly at central level, will therefore seek to influence the direction and nature of labour legislation and Government policy generally so that the position of affiliated employers is adequately protected. Such efforts have been most obvious on issues such as industrial democracy and financial disclosure, and have contributed to either the dropping or dilution of such legislation.

This representative role in Ireland is largely filled by the major employer associations involved in Irish industrial relations discussed earlier in this chapter. Again the Irish Business and Employers' Confederation (IBEC) plays a particularly prominent role representing business and employer views on bodies such as the National Economic and Social Council, which was established by the Government as a forum for the discussion of the principles relating to the efficient development of the national economy; the Central Review Committee, which monitors issues arising from nationally agreed arrangements (such as the Programme for Competitiveness and Work —PCW); FAS (Foras Aiseanna Saothair), the Training and Employment Authority; the Employer–Labour Conference, which was established to allow the various interest groups to deal directly with industrial relations issues; the National Authority for Occupational Safety and Health, which controls the operation and enforcement of occupational health and safety legislation in Ireland; and the Employment Equality Agency, which is the statutory authority with the responsibility for the promotion of equality between men and women in employment.

This political representation role of employer organisations is now well established in many countries. Consequently, when Government wishes to get the views of employers, it will approach the appropriate employer organisation. As Oechslin (1985) suggests, such a practice is a recognition of both the technical expertise and the representative character of the employer association. Thus it is important that employer organisations present a representative front so that Governments can readily identify their source of advice and also identify representatives of employer interests for appropriate bipartite or tripartite bodies such as arbitration councils, Government commissions, international organisations, etc. In Ireland IBEC plays the leading role in nominating employer representatives to such bodies as the Labour Court and the Labour Relations Commission, the Employment Appeals Tribunal, and the Irish Productivity Centre.

(3) *Representation of employer interests to the public:* Allied to the political representational role of employer associations is their role in representing employer views to the public at large on relevant issues. This will be done through the general media or the association's own publications. It is increasingly important that employer opinion on issues be adequately represented and this public relations-type function is particularly relevant for central employer organisations. Relations with the media are an important element of this role, as is a competent research and publications section.

(4) *Provision of specialised services to members:* Employer associations will provide a range of specialised industrial relations services for their affiliated membership. Sisson (1983) suggests that the main industrial relations services provided by employer associations are (1) negotiation of pay and conditions of employment; (2) operation of disputes procedures; (3) advisory and consultancy services, and (4) representation.

The issue of employer association membership is discussed below, while the nature and utilisation of the industrial relations services of employer association services is considered later in this chapter.

5.6. MEMBERSHIP OF EMPLOYER ORGANISATIONS

While the distinction between trade associations and employer associations is useful, it does not fully cater for situations where some organisations play a dual role in dealing with both trade and labour issues. Also, some countries may have a central organisation which represents employer interests in both commercial and labour areas, for example the Irish Business and Employers' Confederation in Ireland and the Confederation of British Industry in Britain. This section considers issues relating to membership and structure of employer associations. In particular it focuses on factors influencing membership and structure such as industry/regional issues, ownership and size of firm, and then considers the government of employer associations.

Employer associations are comprised of a regionally, industrially and structurally diverse membership. Such regional and industrial diversity was manifested in the establishment of traditional Masters' associations, which were particularly common in the building and butchering trades and whose objectives were largely confined to local trade- and employment-related matters. While some such associations still exist today many have amalgamated with larger national associations. While not a prerequisite for the representation of employer views at national level, the formation of a central representative confederation is an important mechanism for more effectively co-ordinating and articulating employer views. Of course the role of such a confederation is dependent on numerous factors—not least the locus of collective bargaining. In countries dominated by industry-wide bargaining, such as Germany, the role of the industry-wide employer associations may be dominant. However, a co-ordinated employer voice may also be necessary and this is generally provided by a central confederation. In Ireland this role is provided by the IBEC and is particularly prominent during periods of centralised pay agreements.

Turning to the specifics of membership of employer associations, Thomason (1984) differentiates between entrepreneurs who essentially own (at least partly) and run their businesses, and abstract corporate entities that are run by professional managements. He argues that the change in composition of employer association membership from entrepreneur owner-managers to corporate business forms run by professional management partly explains the changing role of employer associations. The corporate business form has replaced the older entrepreneurial-type firm as the prevalent type of organisation in membership of employer associations. Thomason suggests that this mix partly explains the different philosophies and roles of different employer associations.

There are also some tentative indications that ownership may influence employer association membership (Brown, 1981). A study of newly established companies in Ireland found that US-owned firms were less likely to join employer associations (Gunnigle, 1992c). This may be related to the corporate approach to trade unions and collective bargaining. Where this involves a preference for non-union status, such organisations may be reluctant to join an employer association (Oechslin, 1985; Purcell and Sisson, 1983). This issue is discussed in greater depth later in this chapter.

The issue of public sector organisations becoming members of an employer association is a relatively recent phenomenon. While initially it might seem incompatible for public sector organisations to join an employer association (traditionally a bastion of free enterprise) many have adopted a pragmatic approach by utilising employer association services in certain areas (Oechslin, 1985). In Ireland the Department of Finance and the Local Government Staff Negotiations Board fulfils the key advisory and assistance role for management in many parts of the public sector. However, some public sector organisations and particularly the semi-state sector have increasingly taken up membership of employer associations as a result of an increase in the levels of unionisation in the public sector and the consequent need for expertise and advice on industrial relations issues.

As is the case in relation to unionisation it has been argued that organisation size is a key determinant of membership and utilisation of employer associations. For example, it has been suggested that small firms have more to gain by joining employer associations (International Labour

Organisation, 1975). The major reasons are related to cost and resources. When a small organisation reaches the stage where it becomes involved in formalised collective bargaining, it may be particularly attractive to join an employer association as it is generally not in a position to employ personnel specialists, and the owner-managers of such firms may not have either the necessary time or expertise to effectively handle such matters. Since the cost of joining an employer association is generally related to the size and/or profitability of the individual firm, it may be relatively inexpensive for small firms to join. However, despite the apparent validity of this line of argument there is no conclusive evidence to support the view that small firms are more likely to join employer associations (Government Social Survey (UK), 1968). In fact the research evidence on workplace industrial relations suggests that employer associations are not more frequently used by smaller organisations (Brown, 1981; Daniel and Millward, 1983; Gunnigle, 1992c). Brown (1981) suggests that ' . . . one theory that can be dismissed is that employers' associations are primarily used by the smaller establishment who lack specialist resources'.

Thus, the employer association literature seems to suggest that larger firms are more likely to join and utilise the services of employer associations and that employer association membership is positively correlated with size of the organisation, ownership, trade union recognition and the presence of a specialist personnel/industrial relations management.

5.7. ADVANTAGES AND DISADVANTAGES OF EMPLOYER ASSOCIATION MEMBERSHIP

We have already considered some of the factors influencing an organisation's decision to affiliate to an employer association for industrial relations purposes. Clearly a key factor influencing employer association membership and utilisation is the desired managerial approach and philosophy towards workforce management. Contextual factors like industry, size, market position and history/ownership will also influence decisions on employer association membership. It is clearly a decision for the senior management of a particular enterprise to critically evaluate its own position and decide if membership of an employer association is appropriate to its own particular circumstances. However, at a general level it is useful to outline the main advantages and disadvantages of employer association membership for individual organisations. These are summarised in table 5.2.

The next section reviews the services provided by employer associations and these correlate closely with the advantages of employer association membership. Below some of the reasons why organisations may choose *not* to join an employer association are considered.

One of the *disadvantages* of employer association membership is a *potential reduction of autonomy* in decision making for the individual organisation.

Employer associations will be keen that members maintain a standard line in negotiations on pay and conditions of employment through the development of agreed policy guidelines (e.g. organisations may be expected to keep pay increases below 3 per cent in a given period). These guidelines will reflect the needs of a diverse membership (in terms of organisation size, profitability, etc.). The individual organisation must decide if such norms are appropriate to its particular needs. For example, an organisation may wish to negotiate a pay increase which breaches the common strategy of the employer association.

Table 5.2. Advantages and disadvantages of employer association membership

Advantages	Disadvantages
• Collective approaches and uniform policy	• Cost of membership
• Advice on trade union matters	• Loss of autonomy
• Technical advice and information	• Loss of flexibility
• Skilled negotiators	• Comparisons with other firms
• Expert advisory and consultancy services	• Greater acceptance of role for trade unions
• Standardised pay and employment conditions	• Greater formalisation in industrial relations
• On par with regional/industry norms	
• Assistance in industrial relations difficulties	
• Influence on Government, national affairs	

Comparability is also an important factor. By virtue of association membership an organisation's pay and conditions will be closely reviewed in relation to other member firms. Trade unions will use the terms of collective agreements struck with some member firms as 'leverage' to secure similar terms with other organisations.

These issues reflect the difficulties employer associations face in developing common policies for a diverse membership. They also highlight the difficulties employer associations face in enforcing policy guidelines and raise the issue of control over affiliates. Breaches of agreed policy guidelines by individual member organisations can detrimentally affect the credibility of such guidelines and may incur the wrath of sections of the affiliated membership. This has occasionally resulted in firms withdrawing from membership or being disaffiliated by the association. Such breaches of discipline are almost inescapable in associations where membership is voluntary and general policies are laid down for a diverse membership. Like trade unions, employer associations will strive to ensure maximum organisation of its potential members and in practice exercise a more informal authority over members relying on persuasion and peer pressure to secure adherence to common policies. Employer associations are generally reluctant to punish non-conforming members and particularly so when expulsion is considered. Should a large number of enterprises or even a few significant employers not join an employer association its representativeness is clearly called into question.

Sisson (1983) notes some important British organisations which have either withdrawn from membership or never joined employer associations (e.g. Esso, Daily Mirror, British Leyland and Ford). Here too, there is some evidence of notable enterprises not in association membership. These are often major employers and exert considerable influence on local pay trends and general industrial relations matters. An important factor in such decisions seems to be related to the degree of influence such organisations believe they might have on association policy and the restrictions that membership would place on their flexibility of manoeuvre.

It is also important to evaluate how association membership fits in with the *corporate personnel philosophy*. This issue is also discussed below in assessing employer association membership and utilisation in new ('greenfield') companies. Employer associations are in effect trade unions of employers and generally prefer to deal with their employee counterparts through collective bargaining. However, some firms have a clear preference for the non-union route. In recent years Ireland has seen considerable growth in the 'high-technology' sector. This has largely been the result of foreign firms (particularly US-based) establishing manufacturing plants here. Non-union US companies such as Digital, Motorola and Microsoft are now an integral part of the manufacturing scene. Some of these firms have brought with them a particular corporate approach to industrial relations which places the emphasis on dealing with employees on an individual basis rather than through trade unions. For such firms membership of an employer association (i.e. a union of employers) would be totally incompatible with a management approach based on direct contact with the individual.

The Irish Business and Employers' Confederation seems acutely aware of the need to attract into membership employers who have an explicit preference for greater individualism in management–employee relations. A recent development in relation to this issue has been the creation of 'individual client relationships' which allow such affiliates to maintain flexibility in decision making while availing of personnel/industrial relations services and engaging in less formal policy co-ordination. Employee Relations Services Limited (ERS) has been established by IBEC as a subsidiary company. Although this organisation is quite new, it appears that companies that might otherwise not be members of IBEC subscribe to the ERS to avail of specialist services in areas such as management strategies and payment systems (e.g. PRP), etc. ERS also provides an industrial relations auditing service designed to provide senior managers with an evaluation of industrial relations in their enterprise. ERS clients pay a similar fee to IBEC and have free access to IBEC's other services. Many non-union companies may be more comfortable with membership of ERS as it maintains their 'non-union' stance.

A more pragmatic reason for non-membership is related to *cost* (see table 5.3). An important issue here may be that firms pay the full cost of membership regardless of services used. By contrast, an organisation which uses consultants simply pays for services rendered. Most association subscriptions are related to size of firm (number of employees) and costs can be substantial for larger organisations (Ridgely, 1988). For example, companies' annual subscriptions to IBEC are typically as follows: £1,406 for a company with 75 employees; £5,553 (300 employees), £13,665 (750 employees), and £22,700 (1,500 employees). Related to this may be the feeling among firms with a developed personnel function that they do not need association services and that, as Reynaud (1978) suggests, employer associations become '. . . an organisation of services for the small undertakings paid for by the big ones'. We have seen above that the research evidence does not support this view and it seems that large firms use employer associations as much, and often more than small ones (Brown, 1981; Daniel and Millward, 1983).

Table 5.3. Per capita subscription rates IBEC, 1994

1st year minimum payment	IR£600.00
Minimum subscription per annum	IR£475.00
and/or	
First 200 employees	IR£ 19.96
Next 800 employees	IR£ 19.02
Next 1,000 employees	IR£ 9.58
Remaining employees	IR£ 4.73

5.8. THE GOVERNING STRUCTURE OF EMPLOYER ASSOCIATIONS

In general, employer associations are organised so that ultimate decision-making power resides with the affiliated membership. However, there is a high degree of complexity in the structural arrangements of employer associations with various models of internal government structure in evidence. Therefore, we can merely generalise on common themes in the internal governing structures of employer associations. Windmuller (1984) suggests that the governing structures of the major employer associations will be composed of three to four levels:
– assembly or general meetings;
– general or executive council;
– executive board or management committee;
– presiding officer (president/general secretary/chairman).
Windmuller suggests that this structure attempts to cater for membership participation while allowing day-to-day management to be carried out by full-time staff. Windmuller suggests that general assemblies or meetings, because

of their large and unwieldy nature, will rarely meet more than once a year and are largely a vehicle through which the membership influence and communicate with the central administration of the association. They help decide upon general policy issues and elect the various committees. Windmuller, in commenting on their role, suggests that: 'Hardly anywhere do general meetings exercise real power beyond the election of executive bodies.'

In contrast, the executive council is much smaller. It will normally comprise of elected representatives and some office-holders, and will often be representative of various industrial, regional or sectional interests, and will meet with more frequency (possibly four to five times per year). Its main role is to monitor and give general direction. The executive council appoints the various committees and monitors their work and the general running of the association. Again Windmuller comments that: 'Councils carry some weight but still lack the continuity and compactness to be the decisive element in policy formulation.'

Possibly the most important layer in the governing structure of employer associations is the management or executive committee/board. This is normally much smaller and meets regularly (possibly on a monthly basis). Its membership consists of representatives elected on a regional basis, from the various branch/industrial divisions, from the major enterprises, and some office-holders of the association. Such bodies may also elect the various standing committees (finance, industrial relations, law, etc.) depending on whether there is a general council or not. These committees often have the power to co-opt members, which is often used to bring in prestigious and influential people from the business community who can make a valuable contribution to committee work. The executive board or general council will exert considerable influence on association policies and approaches, and together with the association president and the senior staff will be primarily responsible for policy formulation and execution.

For many associations the position of chairman or general secretary remains a part-time position held by a senior manager from an affiliated enterprise. However, with the increasing demands of association work this often creates a dilemma for the incumbent as this job requires considerable time away from his company. Depending on the demands of the position the relationship between the president and full-time senior manager of the association (director-general/managing director) will be a crucial one. Generally, the director-general will be expected to administer all the association's affairs according to the policy guidelines laid down by the general assembly, the general council and/or the executive committee. The post-holder will be expected to work closely with the association's president and take his advice on general policy matters. A primary role for the director-general will be to manage the professional staff of the association. Professional association staff have increased dramatically and now cover areas like Labour

Law, Health and Safety, Negotiations, Research, and Administration (Commission on Industrial Relations (UK), 1972).

In general, therefore, while employer association structure reflects an impression of active participatory democracy this may be somewhat misleading. For pragmatic purposes control and direction of association affairs is vested in the hands of a small number of the affiliated members, who, together with the president and full-time staff, oversee the general running of the association. That is not to say that employer association affairs take little account of the wishes of the membership. On the contrary, since affiliation to employer associations is voluntary and because associations continually strive to be the authentic representative voice of their constituency, such associations must be very circumspect to the needs and wishes of their membership.

Like trade unions, the primary source of revenue for employer associations is membership subscriptions, which is used to cover the main costs of running the association—mainly payroll. Contributions by member firms are usually related to some measure of profitability and/or company size. The most common measures are the wage bill, number of employees, sales/output, or value added. Other sources of revenue are training programmes, publications, payments for specialist services. However, given the lack of hard information on employer association finances it is difficult to estimate the value of such sources or the breakdown of association expenditure.

In deciding to join an employer association an individual enterprise is in effect agreeing to delegate some of its decision-making role in industrial relations to the association. Since it is the role of an employer association to represent the collective interests of its affiliated membership it must by definition seek to exercise authority and—ultimately—discipline on those members whose actions are detrimental to the desires of the general membership. While in some countries (especially in Scandinavia) central employer associations have extensive power and influence to control the activities of member firms, the more widespread situation is that the control and influence exercised by employer associations over their membership is becoming ever more tenuous.

Probably the most difficult issue related to the running of employer associations is the question of authority and control over member firms. Most employer associations will be comprised of a varying and diverse membership, and will attempt to service and assist firms of varying size, profitability, management structure and philosophy. Consequently, there will be various factors which serve to inhibit the association's goal of common policies and approaches. For instance, companies may seek to gain competitive advantage through the labour market, which will affect common pay strategies. Also, unions will use their bargaining power to secure above the norm deals with stronger companies which they can then use subsequently as precedents in later negotiations. Some such companies may indeed be willing to strike such agreements with unions rather than incur industrial unrest. However, such agreements may be in breach of the policy guidelines of the employer association. As discussed earlier, this can result in some firms withdrawing from membership or being disaffiliated by the association. It would seem that more and more associations are attempting to circumvent this problem by offering a non-conforming membership status entitling firms to use the services of the association but not obliging them to strictly adhere to policy guidelines on issues like pay negotiations and conditions of employment.

5.8.1. THE GOVERNING STRUCTURE OF THE IRISH BUSINESS AND EMPLOYERS'
CONFEDERATION

Within the organisation structure of the Irish Business and Employers' Confederation, the role of the general membership of affiliated organisations is to elect a National General Council comprising 250 representatives, who then determine general policy and appoint the National Executive Council. The Council itself is comprised of office-holders and nominees from the various regions and branches, totalling fifty in all. It is primarily responsible for overseeing policy formulation and implementation, appointing the key specialist committees and the permanent secretariat in conjunction with the director-general and federation secretary. The director-general and the full-time staff are responsible for carrying out the primary activities and services of the association (see figure 5.1).

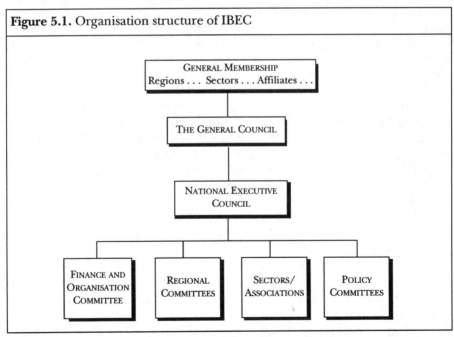

Figure 5.1. Organisation structure of IBEC

Source: Daly, 1994.

5.9. EMPLOYER ASSOCIATION MEMBERSHIP AND MANAGEMENT APPROACHES IN INDUSTRIAL RELATIONS

Membership of employer associations is also seen as a useful indicator of preferred management approaches to industrial relations. Membership of employer associations has traditionally been associated with the pluralist industrial relations model. A recent study of industrial relations in new, 'greenfield' companies in the manufacturing and traded services sectors found that the majority of firms surveyed were employer association members, in all but one instance the Irish Business and Employers' Confederation (Gunnigle, 1992c). The decision to join an employer association was largely associated with country of ownership and trade union membership (see tables 5.4. and 5.5). While just over half the US-owned and Irish-owned firms were employer association members, over 86 per cent of 'other' foreign-owned companies were members of employer associations. As expected, companies which recognised trade unions were significantly more likely to be employer association members. Of the greenfield companies surveyed, 88 per cent of unionised firms were employer association members while only 39 per cent of non-union firms were members. Some 36 per cent of the companies who were members of employer associations used association executives directly in workplace industrial relations interactions. The general pattern was for organisations to use the employer association primarily as a source of information and advice across a range of personnel issues including industrial relations. Research evidence suggests that employer associations, in relation to utilisation of association services, are most relevant in the private sector and that membership is positively related to trade union recognition, increased company size and the presence of a specialist personnel function (Brown, 1981; Daniel and Millward, 1983; Gunnigle, 1992c). Indeed, trade union recognition appears to be a key factor. Formalised collective bargaining arrangements, procedural agreements and developed shop-steward system (all characteristics of the traditional pluralist industrial relations model) appear to be positively related to employer association membership and extensive utilisation of association services is probable. Even in the smaller organisation the prospect of employer association membership may become increasingly attractive when such firms reach a stage of development where trade union recognition has been granted and there is a move towards formalising the company's approach to industrial relations management (Gunnigle, 1989; Gunnigle and Brady, 1984).

It is argued in chapter 9 that this evidence in relation to employer associations may be indicative of change in the role of collectivism in industrial relations management. Employer associations have traditionally been integral to the pluralist industrial relations model. However, growth of the non-union sector, particularly in greenfield sites, and a related expansion of individualistic Human Resource Management-type policies means that, for such companies, membership of an employer association (in essence a union of employers) is often perceived as incompatible with a management approach based on individual dealings with employees. The Federation of Irish Employers (now IBEC) initially responded to this development by establishing an advisory and consultancy service (namely the ERS discussed above) designed to cater for non-union firms while not conferring the usual status of association member. The evidence from this study seems to indicate that this strategy has met with some success but has not, as yet, convinced the majority of new non-union companies to become employer association members.

Table 5.4. Employer association membership and utilisation by country of ownership in greenfield companies (actual numbers of firms, N = 53))

| | Employer association membership | | Utilisation of employer association services | | |
	Yes	No	Direct involvement in establishment level employee relations	Employee relations advice	General Per/HR advice
Ireland	6	5	2	5	5
US	14	13	2	14	14
Japan	4	2	1	4	4
Europe	8	0	7	8	8
Other	1	0	0	1	1
Total	33	20	12	32	32

Source: Gunnigle, 1992c.

Table 5.5. Employer association membership and utilisation by trade union recognition in greenfield companies (actual numbers of firms, N = 53)

| | Employer association membership | | Utilisation of employer association services | | |
	Yes	No	Direct involvement in establishment level employee relations	Employee relations advice	General Per/HR advice
Non-union	11 (39%)	17 (61%)	0	11 (100%)	11 (100%)
Union	22 (88%)	3 (12%)	14 (56%)	21 (84%)	21 (84%)

Source: Gunnigle, 1992c.

5.10. EMPLOYER ASSOCIATION SERVICES

It was suggested earlier that employer associations provide a range of industrial relations services for their affiliated membership particularly in the area of negotiations, research, advice and representation of employer interests. These services are discussed below.

RESEARCH AND ADVISORY SERVICES

In reviewing the UK context Sisson (1983) suggests that the major expansion in the work of employer organisations in the UK has been in the provision of various advisory and consultancy services (Commission on Industrial Relations (UK), 1972; Gladstone, 1984; Sisson, 1983). These advisory and consultancy services fall into three broad categories: (a) legal; (b) pay; (c) specialist consultancy. This trend seems to point to the increasing importance of the provision of advisory services by employer associations.

The growth of both collective industrial relations legislation and protective employment legislation since the early 1970s has led to a significant increase in employer demand for specialist legal advice on these matters. Employer associations are expected to provide specialist legal advice and assistance to members in areas such as dismissal, redundancy, employment conditions, employment equality and industrial disputes. It is now usual for larger employer associations to have a specialist legal section which provides such advice and assistance, and which also publishes information guidelines on legislation for the general membership. In Ireland IBEC publishes a range of materials on a wide variety of topics to keep its members abreast of developments in the employment area. The Confederation also provides services to various sectors and monitors national policies through a committee structure.

Possibly a more traditional employer association service is the provision of information and advice to member firms on basic wage rates and levels of wage increases. Most employer organisations carry out various types of surveys and analyses of basic wage rates and fringe benefits for differing occupations, regions and size of organisation. Consequently, they are able to provide member firms with up-to-date information on local, regional and national pay trends, and advise such firms on reward issues. The Research and Information Service of IBEC gathers information and data on all aspects of work and employment (e.g. annualised hours, absence figures, etc.). It interprets the information it collects (e.g. *The IBEC/ERSI Monthly Industrial Survey*) in an employer context at a national level (e.g. prospective changes in social welfare).

In addition to legal and pay advice, many employer associations will also provide members with specialist advice and assistance on particular issues. This role is a general one and varies between associations. However, areas of specialist assistance include job evaluation, productivity schemes, work study, bonus schemes and recruitment. In an Irish pilot study Butler (1985) found that advisory and consultancy services are seen by members as the most useful function of employer associations, and that those dealing with legislation, pay and redundancy were most widely utilised. These findings are summarised in table 5.6.

Table 5.6. Utilisation of the advisory and consultancy services (in %)

Services	Percentage of companies utilising services
Recruitment	7.7
Education and training	32.5
Labour legislation	100.0
Work study, bonus schemes	15.4
Job evaluation	0.0
Redundancy policy	77.0
Local pay levels	100.0
National pay levels	84.5
Incomes policy	38.5
Others	7.7

Source: Butler, 1985.

REPRESENTATION

Apart from providing member firms with information and advice, employer associations will directly assist members by acting on their behalf in collective bargaining negotiations. This role can be important at several levels. Employer associations can represent members in plant-level negotiations on, for example, the introduction of new technology. They can also play a more extensive role in representing their affiliates in either industry or national-level bargaining. This function of representation will also apply to mediation and arbitration, where employer associations can represent affiliates in tribunal hearings, conciliation meetings and arbitration hearings. Given the growth in employment legislation and the greater complexity of collective negotiations this role is an increasingly important one.

The representational role of employer associations involves both a political dimension and third-party representation. Representing employer views to Government, State institutions, trade unions, the general public and other interested parties is a key role of employer associations. In general one often finds a clear distinction between employer representation on trade/commercial issues and employer representation on industrial relations matters. Indeed, this was the case in Ireland until 1993. Up to this time the Confederation of Irish Industry (CII) operated as the national organisation representing employer interests in matters of trade, economics, finance, taxation, planning and development. However, the CII did not involve itself in industrial relations. This latter role was primarily executed by the then Federation of Irish Employers (previously the FUE). The merger of the CII and FIE in 1993 consolidates these dual roles into one employer body, the Irish Business and Employers' Confederation, which is consulted by and makes representations to Government on labour and general business/commercial matters. While it represents employer interests on various national committees and institutions it also provides employer representation on various mediation and arbitration bodies such as the Labour Court and the Employment Appeals Tribunal. Apart from IBEC, industry-based associations also carry out representative functions related to their own sector.

An equally important representational function of employer associations occurs at conciliation and arbitration fora. Representation of affiliated employers at the Labour Relations Commission, Labour Court, Employment Appeals Tribunal and other third-party hearings is a valued and important service of employer associations, as is evident from the extent of such activities as demonstrated in the annual reports of employer associations such as IBEC and CIF, and those of the Labour Court and Labour Relations Commission (see table 5.7). Affiliated firms will generally use the services of their employer association if involved in third-party proceedings, although such utilisation may only involve obtaining advice and direction. At Labour Court hearings in particular it is common for the employer case to be presented by an employer association official. This may also occur at Employment Appeals Tribunal hearings although there is a tendency for employers to increasingly opt for legal representation.

Table 5.7. FIE/IBEC involvement in mediation, arbitration and negotiations

	No. of cases per year							
	1984	1985	1986	1987	1988	1989*	1992	1993
Labour Court investigation	458	420	538	488	386	394	217	219
Labour Court conciliation	1,176	963	1,470	1,146	874	1,014	684	765
Employment Appeals Tribunal	241	302	396	190	n/a	216	258	235
Rights Commissioner	439	312	586	429	n/a	346	266	278
Equality Officer	16	16	28	35	n/a	72	18	11
Consultation with members	7,203	8,155	6,400	6,919	6,726	5,864	4,804	4,737
Trade union negotiations	3,590	2,664	2,928	2,842	2,702	2,540	1,286	1,220

* 1990, 1991 figures not available in annual reports.

Source: IBEC Annual Reports, 1984–89; 1992–93.

The industrial relations arm of IBEC is involved in providing industrial relations advice and assistance to members. The provision of such advice/assistance may involve direct IBEC participation in negotiations with trade unions and would also cover research and specialist advisory services as well as assistance with the preparation of employment agreements, consultation on particular personnel issues and the provision of premises and facilities for consultation and negotiation. The industrial relations aspects of IBEC essentially encapsulate the previous roles of the Federation of Irish Employers (FIE). The Confederation's staff provide advice in response to membership enquiries and also engage in direct consultation with members in all aspects of employment such as pay, contracts, conditions of employment, recruitment, discipline and dismissal. This includes direct negotiation and bargaining on behalf of members and usually takes the form of representation before hearings of the Labour Court, the Labour Relations Commission, Rights Commissioners and the Employment Appeals Tribunal.

EDUCATION AND TRAINING

It is now common for the larger employer associations to conduct training programmes for their membership. Particular emphasis is often placed on training personnel/industrial relations specialists. Associations will try to keep the membership up to date on current developments in labour law and collective bargaining. Associations not extensively involved in training and education, will normally provide advice or assistance. Associations may also run joint ventures with national or regional management training centres which eases the demand on resources while meeting the needs of the membership.

COLLECTIVE BARGAINING

By far the most obvious role of employer associations is in the actual conduct of collective bargaining. The role of employer associations in representing members in collective bargaining is important at two levels: multi-employer bargaining and establishment-level bargaining. The issue of bargaining levels is central in determining the role of employer associations in collective bargaining. Traditionally the central role of employer associations has been in the conduct of multi-employer bargaining, especially at industry or national level. In the UK context the Donovan Commission (1968) remarked that: 'The practice of industry-wide bargaining is closely bound up with the existence of employers' associations.' It went on to conclude that the major reason companies continued to remain members of employer associations was their support for multi-employer bargaining: '. . . membership of employers' associations is a consequence of unquestioning commitment to maintain the formal system of industrial relations. The system provides for industry-wide bargaining; employers' associations are essential for this; therefore companies belong to employers' associations.'

While this argument has some foundation, it is also true to state that where the focus of bargaining has shifted upwards to national level or downwards to enterprise level, the role and importance of employer associations in collective bargaining has remained prominent. Multi-employer bargaining on an industry-wide basis has traditionally meant a key role for the appropriate employer association in conducting negotiations over pay and related issues on behalf of its constituents. This form of bargaining was particularly common in Britain but now seems to be on the wane with greater emphasis on enterprise or plant-level bargaining (Brown, 1981). It still remains a common format for collective bargaining in other countries such as Germany and is practised in some industrial sectors in Ireland. The Construction Industry Federation, for example, continues to dominate collective negotiations in the general building sector.

The apex of multi-employer bargaining will involve collective negotiations at national level involving central employer association(s), trade unions and, possibly, Government. Such a situation gives a very prominent role to employer associations. During periods of centralised pay agreements in Ireland (1970–82, 1987–date), employer associations, particularly the Irish Business and Employers' Confederation (IBEC), play a pivotal role in representing employer opinion to the other social partners. In effect this means that individual affiliated members delegate bargaining responsibilities to their employer associations thus making the employer association and not the individual employer the main actor on the employer side in industrial relations negotiations on pay and associated issues.

In the post-war period collective bargaining in Ireland has been characterised initially by the wage-round system and later by a series of national agreements. Between 1946 and 1970 there were twelve wage rounds, five of which were negotiated centrally between employer representatives and trade unions, giving a prominent role to employer associations. The remainder were characterised by periods of intensive collective bargaining at either industry or enterprise level with wage increases permeating through to most organised employees.

In the 1970–82 period employer associations, largely through the Irish Employers' Confederation and the Federated Union of Employers (now IBEC), played a major role in the negotiation of a series of centralised pay agreements. When this system ended in 1982 there was a return to so-called 'free' collective bargaining on an enterprise basis. This changed the role of employer associations from being the key employer actor in pay negotiations to a more supportive role in providing advice and assistance to individual enterprises and co-ordinating approaches to pay negotiations. The current pattern of centralised national agreements on pay and related issues was initiated by the Programme for National Recovery as negotiated by the 'social partners' in 1986–87 and helped restore the then FUE (now IBEC) and, to a lesser extent the CIF, to their pivotal position in national pay bargaining. The Programme for Economic and Social Progress (PESP, 1990–93) provided for local bargaining, which also facilitated a significant role for employer association involvement in the conduct of establishment-level industrial relations on pay and related matters.

Thus it is apparent that, while enterprise-level collective bargaining was sometimes thought to leave little for employer associations, this is demonstrably not the case in the Irish context. Where the focus of pay bargaining has shifted to enterprise level, as in the 1982–87 period in Ireland, there was little evidence of a dramatic reduction in the role of employer associations. Indeed, it appears that employer associations have a very important role to play in single-employer bargaining. This role incorporates the co-ordination of policy on pay- and employment-related issues, formulating general guidelines for affiliated employers; supplying research data and information for use in negotiations, and providing expert personnel to either conduct the negotiations or advise and assist local management. This supportive and co-ordinating role at establishment level is an important one from an employer viewpoint. By giving advice on pay trends and related issues employer associations provide the basic information with which the individual organisation enters the bargaining process. By co-ordinating employer approaches, it establishes a framework for the conduct of such negotiations, and by providing negotiating personnel it may either conduct the negotiations or advise/assist management in such negotiations.

5.10.1. DISPUTES PROCEDURES AND ADJUSTMENT

Closely associated with the prevalence of multi-employer bargaining is employer association involvement in the operation of disputes procedures. This role seems particularly important in some sectors of industry in the UK, but is a less prominent function of employer associations in the Irish context. However, employer associations do tend to actively promote the use of workplace grievance and disputes procedures which cater for dispute referral to third-party conciliation and arbitration. Unlike Britain, however, the operation of external disputes procedures by employer associations never played a significant role in the Irish industrial relations framework. Here disputes procedures are normally negotiated at enterprise level. The role of employer associations is primarily to assist and advise members on the formulation and operation of such procedures.

The provision of strike insurance or other types of mutual defence schemes for employers involved in an industrial dispute has been a traditional function of employer associations. Again practice varies widely from informal commitments of support, through mutual aid agreements, to standard insurance schemes.

5.11. SUMMARY

This chapter has considered the role of employer associations in industrial relations. Particular emphasis has been placed on the nature and role of Irish employer associations such as the Irish Business and Employers' Confederation and the Construction Industry Federation. The chapter has also reviewed the main advantages and disadvantages of employer association membership for individual organisations and considered the main industrial relations services provided by such associations.

Employer associations clearly play a very significant role in both national- and enterprise-level industrial relations. Of course individual employers are also responsible for the development and implementation of industrial relations policies and practices within their own individual organisations and workplaces. Recent literature has highlighted a marked increase in emphasis on developing linkages between business strategy and industrial relations, and, particularly, the growth of so-called human resource management (HRM) approaches. Contemporary developments in management approaches to industrial relations are considered in depth in chapter 8 and, particularly, chapter 9 of this book. However, the next chapter deals with what has traditionally been seen as the most significant aspect of industrial relations, namely collective bargaining.

Chapter Six

Collective Bargaining

6.1. What Is Collective Bargaining?

For the purpose of this book, collective bargaining refers to the process through which agreement on pay, working conditions, procedures and other negotiable issues are reached between organised (unionised) employees and management representatives (Gunnigle and Flood, 1990). Collective bargaining represents a mechanism through which divergent interests in organisations, namely the interests of employees and employers, are reconciled through an orderly process involving negotiation and compromise.

The principal feature of collective bargaining is that employees do not negotiate with their employers on their own behalf but do so collectively through representatives, and that various aspects of a worker's contract of employment are determined not individually but collectively. Clearly then a number of prerequisites must be fulfilled for collective bargaining to function successfully, namely

(1) employees must have the freedom to associate, enabling workers to join together in trade unions which are not in any way under the control or influence of employers; and

(2) employers must be prepared to recognise trade unions and accept the constraints placed upon their ability to deal with employees on an individual basis.

The process is called 'bargaining' because both employers and employees can apply pressure on the other. Clegg (1976) contends that this element of pressure is vital to collective bargaining and argues that mere representation of views or appeal for consideration is not bargaining. The requirement that collective bargaining is conducted with the view to reaching agreement does not exclude from the definition negotiations that may break down and result in a strike or lock-out, provided, of course, there was a genuine attempt to reach agreement.

The industrial relations systems of most industrialised countries are founded upon collective bargaining arrangements which act as the primary mode of union–management interaction and industrial relations government. However, many variations are apparent in the collective bargaining systems of any organisations, industries or countries chosen for examination. The conduct of collective bargaining may vary considerably between organisations but will remain essentially voluntary in nature, that is, it relies on the moral commitment of the participants.

Collective bargaining is by no means the only method of determining conditions of employment or regulating industrial relations. Even in countries where it is most dominant it nearly always exists side by side with other mechanisms, including individual bargaining between employer and employee, regulation by the Government (legislation), the unilateral imposition of terms of employment by management or, similarly, the imposition of terms unilaterally by trade unions. While these other methods do exist as realistic and sometimes successful alternatives to collective bargaining, there is a strong view that collective bargaining is in fact the most satisfactory way for employers and employees to determine conditions of employment. For example, the Donovan Commission clearly expressed its preference in stating that 'collective bargaining is the best method of conducting industrial relations' (Royal Commission on Trade Unions and Employers' Associations, 1968).

Individual bargaining refers to the situation which arises when an individual negotiates with an employer in the classically contractual sense over the conditions of his or her employment. It is not unusual for individual employees to be able to negotiate their own contract of employment. For example, employees at management or executive levels often negotiate their own terms or conditions as individuals. For the majority of employees, however, rates of pay, hours of work, etc. are predetermined by company union agreements and cannot be haggled over to suit individuals.

In this chapter we are initially concerned with some of the different perspectives surrounding the nature of collective bargaining and with the issue of structure in collective bargaining, but the chapter will centre on the development of the institution of collective bargaining and pay determination in Ireland.

6.2. THE NATURE OF COLLECTIVE BARGAINING

The credit for coining the expression 'collective bargaining' belongs to Beatrice Webb, who first used it in her study on the co-operative movement of Great Britain (Webb and Webb, 1897). Of course, it has long since become firmly established in the vocabulary of industrial relations and trade-unionism. The practice itself had, however, existed well before the term came into existence, with the earlier forms of collective bargaining erroneously being known as 'arbitration' or 'conciliation' (erroneous as no independent third party took part in the proceedings; Jensen, 1956). The precise nature of collective bargaining, however, has been the subject of much debate in academic circles over the years. Put simply, this debate has centred on whether collective bargaining may be best described as an economic or as a political activity. Farnham and Pimlott (1990) argue that in practice this theoretical distinction between collective bargaining as an economic or political activity has little conceptual or empirical validity. However, the following sections aim to briefly highlight some of the arguments central to this debate.

It is the Webbs who may also take credit for the first attempt at developing a comprehensive theory and definition of collective bargaining in their seminal work *Industrial Democracy*, first published in 1897. The Webbs saw collective bargaining as one of the means utilised by trade unions in pursuing their objective of 'maintaining and improving the conditions of their members' working lives'. Collective bargaining is one category of three observed activities of trade unions which the Webbs identified in their research in nineteenth-century Britain. The other activities were identified as mutual insurance and political activity. As Flanders (1968a) later commented: 'For the Webbs collective bargaining was exactly what the words implied: a collective equivalent and alternative to individual bargaining.' The Webbs saw collective bargaining as basically a process by which the individual contract is replaced by the collective agreement. The Webbs argued that collective bargaining can fundamentally best be seen as an economic activity because collective bargaining in their view is essentially a means of contracting for the sale of labour. Its purpose is to determine under what terms labour will continue to be supplied to a company by its existing employees and by those newly hired.

The Webbs' description of collective bargaining has been challenged, most notably by Alan Flanders (1968a). Flanders argued that in dealing with collective bargaining the Webbs inaccurately defined the practice as 'a collective equivalent and alternative to individual bargaining'. Quite simply, Flanders' belief is that when discussing individual and collective bargaining, the Webbs were not 'comparing like with like'. Flanders (1968a) argued that in essence collective bargaining is a rule-making activity (with no proper counterpart in individual bargaining) whose function is to regulate, but not replace, individual bargaining. In other words, the end product of the individual bargain is a contract, while the outcome of collective bargaining is a set of rules. Flanders' description of collective bargaining as being essentially a rule-making process concurs with the views of other authors. For example, the International Labour Organisation (ILO) sees the overriding purpose of collective bargaining to be 'the negotiation of an agreed set of rules to govern the terms of the employment relationship, as well as the relationship between the bargaining parties themselves' (ILO, 1973). Flanders concedes that collective bargaining often replaces individual bargaining but suggests that they are not, however, complete alternatives (that is mutually exclusive) as the Webbs inferred, and he suggests that collective bargaining and individual bargaining can coexist.

Flanders' second point of departure from the Webbs' view of collective bargaining surrounds their belief that collective bargaining is primarily an economic process. Flanders differed by suggesting that collective bargaining is in essence a political activity. He agrees with Harbison (1966) who proposed that an essential characteristic of collective bargaining is that it is 'a power relationship between organisations', and as such sees collective bargaining as best described 'as a diplomatic use of power'. The strike is seen to represent a strategic use of the power relationship between the organisation and union members, and as such is seen as a bargaining ploy. In Flanders' eyes, there is no equivalent in the individual bargaining situation.

Flanders' view of collective bargaining as primarily a power relationship between organisations has found support in the work of many authors from varying perspectives throughout the literature. For example, Stevens (1963) defines collective bargaining as a 'social control technique for reflecting and transmitting the basic power relationships which underlie the conflict of interests in an industrial relations system'. Perlman (1936), proposes that collective bargaining is not just a means of raising pay and improving conditions of employment but 'above all a technique whereby an inferior social class or group carries on a never slackening pressure for a bigger share in the social sovereignty', highlighting the power struggle which he feels is in essence collective bargaining. Indeed, Perlman does not see collective bargaining as being confined to the industrial arena but manifesting itself 'equally in politics, legislation, court litigation, Government administration, religion, and education'. On a similar note, Hyman (1975) argues that collective bargaining is merely a means of social control and an institutionalised expression of the class struggle between those owning capital and those selling labour in industry. An obvious but important point highlighted by these definitions and others is that much of the debate on the nature of collective bargaining will be coloured by the theoretical perspective or frame of reference on industrial relations adopted by the author.

More recently, Alan Fox (1975) has come to the defence of the Webbs and tried to rehabilitate their perspective by attempting to answer many of the criticisms levelled by Flanders. Put briefly, Fox takes issue with Flanders' claim that collective bargaining can be differentiated from individual bargaining in that it is a rule-making activity. Fox argues that the individual bargain defines the rules which will be observed by both parties if the contract is entered into, and these are reviewed in the course of the continuing relationship and as such 'the individual contract is just as much a rule-making instrument as its collective counterpart'.

Anthony (1980) argues that the notion of collective bargaining as fundamentally a rule-making process (as Flanders views it) may be problematic in that it suggests that there is an equal distribution of power between employer and union as a precondition for the existence of collective bargaining. Anthony admits that relationships encompassing a rough balance of power between the parties to collective bargaining are often found in industrial situations; however, 'collective bargaining also exists in different circumstances, where power is unevenly distributed, where control is more unilateral, where responsibility is barely jointly exercised'.

Fox feels Flanders' contention that collective bargaining is distinguished from individual bargaining by being a 'diplomatic use of power' is equally unacceptable. Fox asserts that the individual bargain can also embody a diplomatic use of power as evidenced by an employer or an employee who may temporarily have a bargaining advantage choosing to bring or not to bring their superiority of bargaining power to bear in the individual bargain for reasons of expediency. Fox (1975) argues that since both collective and individual bargaining involve a rule-making process and diplomatic use of power they are in fact similar, and 'that the former is indeed a collective version of the latter'. Fox disagrees with the major conclusion of Flanders' line of reasoning, that is, that the main function of collective bargaining and trade-unionism is political rather than economic. Fox argues that the major bargaining preoccupation of trade unions relates to securing increased financial reward and improved conditions. Indeed, it is in this economic activity that trade unions find their major justification in their members' eyes.

6.2.1. THREE THEORIES OF COLLECTIVE BARGAINING

Chamberlain and Kuhn (1965) adopt a more holistic approach in attempting to develop a generic definition of collective bargaining. In reviewing the various theories of collective bargaining, they concluded that collective bargaining is (1) a means of contracting for the sale of labour, (2) a form of industrial government, and (3) a method of management. This conception of collective bargaining Chamberlain and Kuhn defined as the marketing theory, the governmental theory and the managerial theory of collective bargaining.

The marketing theory is essentially similar to the classical view of the Webbs, which sees the individual contract as being replaced by the collective agreement. The purpose of collective bargaining is to determine the terms and conditions under which labour will be supplied to an organisation by its employees. Central to the marketing theory is the belief that collective bargaining is necessary to redress the inequity of bargaining power between employer and employee.

The governmental theory views collective bargaining as a form of industrial government. The governmental theory views collective bargaining in a manner similar to that described by Leiserson (1922), who argued that the principal function of collective bargaining 'is to set up organs of government, define and limit them, provide agencies for making, executing and interpreting laws for industry and means for enforcement'.

The managerial theory stresses the functional relationship between union and company, suggesting that they combine 'in reaching decisions on matters in which both have vital interests'. The theory emphasises 'mutuality', namely that those who are integral to the conduct of an enterprise should have a voice in the decisions which affect them. So, collective bargaining is viewed as a method of management, serving the interests of both parties. Collective bargaining serves employer interests of controlling the labour market and facilitating greater managerial control. From the trade union perspective, collective bargaining serves the interests of union members by regulating or checking the making of managerial decisions.

Chamberlain and Kuhn did not suggest that these three theories were mutually exclusive or incompatible alternatives, but rather that they may be seen as reflecting different stages in the development of collective bargaining. As Flanders (1968a) suggests:

> Early negotiations were mainly a matter of fixing terms for sale of labour. . . . Later came the need for procedures for settling disputes on these and other issues between the parties. . . . Only when eventually agreements were made on subjects that entered into internal decision making processes of a business enterprise was there a basis for the managerial theory of collective bargaining.

Chamberlain and Kuhn (1965) also emphasise that collective bargaining is essentially a collaborative relationship describing it as requiring 'that some agreement be reached . . . some agreement must ultimately be forthcoming if collective bargaining continues. Thus neither party is independent under collective bargaining. Neither can perform its function without the other'.

The notion of consensus or agreement is central to many of the definitions of collective bargaining found in modern textbooks. For example, Hawkins (1979) describes collective bargaining as 'the resolution of conflict through compromise' (compromise inferring that the process is based on agreement). The ILO has referred to collective bargaining as 'negotiations about working conditions and terms of employment between an employer, a group of employers, or one or more employer organisations on the one hand, or one or more employee organisations on the other with a view to reaching agreement' (ILO, 1960). The definition offered at the beginning of this chapter echoes this view in describing collective bargaining as 'the process through which agreement on pay, working conditions, procedures and other negotiable issues are reached between organised employees and management representatives'. Green (1991) discusses collective bargaining as fundamentally consisting 'of an employer, or a group of employers negotiating the terms and conditions of employees with the representatives of one or several worker organisations and reaching agreement on these issues'.

6.3. The Structure of Collective Bargaining

Bargaining structure refers to the stable or permanent features that help to distinguish the collective bargaining process in any particular system (Parker et al., 1971). It refers to the framework in which negotiations between employers and organised workers takes place. Parker et al. submit that variations in the bargaining structure of industrial relations systems can be accounted for by the differences which arise in respect of four aspects, namely bargaining levels, bargaining units, bargaining forms and bargaining scope. Bargaining structure in any particular system is dynamic, and variations in one or more of these dimensions will alter the structure of collective bargaining from time to time. Figure 6.1. below outlines the different levels where collective bargaining may take place.

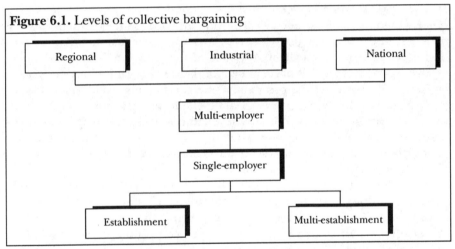

Figure 6.1. Levels of collective bargaining

Source: Gunnigle et al., 1992.

6.3.1. Bargaining Levels

By definition collective bargaining requires collective action on the part of employees. However, it does not necessarily require collective action on the part of employers. Individual employers as well as employer associations may form a bargaining group with trade unions. Trade unions may bargain with one employer, a group of employers or with representatives of an employer association. Hence, collective bargaining may take place at multi-employer or single-employer level. Multi-employer bargaining can take place at national or regional levels, or at the level of the particular industry. Single-employer bargaining can also take place at a number of levels depending on the structure of the organisation. The individual employer can be involved in both bargaining at establishment level (largely referred to as workplace bargaining) and at a multi-establishment level (if the organisation is a multi-site operation). In addition, collective bargaining at the level of the single-employer might involve negotiations either with an individual union or in a multi-union environment with representatives from a group of unions. Frequently an employer may be involved in collective bargaining at both single-employer and multi-employer levels. For example, in certain industries agreements may be negotiated at several levels to determine different elements in the employment package (Farnham and Pimlott, 1990); for instance, pay increases may be negotiated through multi-employer bargaining at national level between employer associations and trade union federations, with hours of work being handled through single-employer negotiations at establishment level.

Some efforts have been made to explain why an employer may have a preference for either single- or multi-employer bargaining. There are certain benefits of multi-employer bargaining which may help to explain its attractiveness to some organisations. For example, multi-employer bargaining relieves employers of the need to deal with annual wage negotiations, leaving members of the management team free to devote their time to other areas of importance. The standardising of rates of pay and conditions amongst a group of employers avoids pay competition between organisations, regulating an important aspect of the competitive market. Gunnigle and Flood (1990) argue that at a more strategic level multi-employer bargaining concentrates union attention at trans-company level, thereby separating the locus of management decision making from the locus of collective bargaining, effectively denying unions' access to key management decision makers at the organisational level.

Gunnigle and Flood also suggest that for organisations in comfortable trading positions multi-employer bargaining is a relatively painless way of dealing with industrial relations. These advantages, associated with multi-employer bargaining, may, however, involve certain trade-offs. While standardising rates of pay can be seen as beneficial in some ways, it may cause organisations to miss out on some important opportunities. For example, the capacity for single-employer bargaining to allow management negotiators to more closely relate wage rates to establishment-level issues like increased productivity, cost reductions, regional norms and so on. In addition, if organisational members are directly involved in the negotiation process it can be argued that it increases the likelihood there will be a greater commitment to observe the terms of any agreements reached.

Pierson (1961, cited in Sisson, 1987) tries to throw light on the choice of level by reference to industrial structure. He observed that in the US 'multi-employer bargaining appears to thrive in those industries in which employers tend to be small relative to their union counterparts, product competition either on a national or local basis is intense, capital requirements relative to labour requirements are low, and profit margins are narrow'. Multi-employer bargaining may offer significant economies of scale to the smaller employer in sharing the costs of trained experts (employer associations) to deal with trade unions and to give advice on industrial relations issues.

Pierson also identified the circumstances which, in his view, lead to single-employer bargaining: 'Production units tend to be large, capital constitutes an important part of total costs and is relatively immobile, and product competition is less intense.'

Similar studies in the UK by Deaton and Beaumont (1980) suggest that multi-employer bargaining is associated with a high regional concentration of organisations operating within a similar labour market, having a high union density with many unions operating within the same industry, single-employer bargaining being associated with larger establishments, multi-site organisations, foreign ownership, organisations operating within non-competitive product markets and the existence of specialist industrial relations managers at a senior level.

A multi-establishment organisation must also address itself to the issue of whether to negotiate at multi-establishment (corporate level) or at the level of the establishment (individual enterprise). Kinnie (1986) suggests that competitive pressures have led to two possible employer responses. On the one hand, corporate management may seek to exert central control over costs and work practices through greater centralisation in industrial relations management. At the same time many employers wish to decentralise control to create individual cost centres and delegate responsibility for increased efficiency. Kinnie (1986) argues that while the trend in managerial control is for greater centralisation, this does not necessarily involve a move away from establishment bargaining, suggesting that organisations are trying to strike a balance between pressures for centralisation and decentralisation recognising the need to co-ordinate strategic decision making at corporate level while allowing greater operational discretion at local level.

6.3.2. BARGAINING UNITS, FORMS AND SCOPE

A bargaining unit refers to the group of workers to be covered by a particular bargained agreement. A bargaining unit may cover a narrow group, e.g. all supervisory staff in one company, or it may cover a larger group, say, all manual employees in an industry or all unionised workers in a country. A bargaining unit may also involve a single union, a group of unions or, for that matter, an association of unions that acts as bargaining agent at the negotiating table on behalf of employees. Bargaining units will vary according to the bargaining level at which the negotiation takes place. For example, a single union may negotiate at establishment level, whereas an association or federation of unions is more likely to negotiate at national level.

Bargaining form describes the degree of formality of an agreement. This may vary from an informal approach which relies on unwritten agreements on the one hand, to a very formal approach which utilises comprehensive written agreements on the other. It appears that the higher the bargaining level within a country, industry or organisation, the higher the degree of formality.

Bargaining scope relates to the range of issues to be covered, such as basic pay, shift premiums, overtime rates, holidays, hours of work, disciplinary procedures, etc., and may be comprehensive or restrictive in its range. A comprehensive scope implies that scope of bargaining covers the entire range of employment issues affecting employees, while a restrictive scope suggests a focus on particular or problematic issues.

The end product of the collective bargaining process is the collective agreement. Collective agreements are frequently regarded as covering two different kinds of arrangements, those that deal with *substantive* issues and those that are *procedural* in nature. The scope of substantive agreements will obviously vary widely from company to company, but substantive terms usually concern pay, work quantity and quality specifications, hours of work, overtime premiums, shift allowances, holiday entitlements, sick benefits and allowances. However, this list is by no means exhaustive. Anthony (1980) describes procedural arrangements as determining the ways in which terms and conditions of employment are arrived at, and the ways in which differences over the application of agreed terms and conditions are settled. Such procedural arrangements may cover discipline, grievances, disputes, rule changes, the way in which wage claims are to be processed and other constitutional matters.

6.4. COLLECTIVE BARGAINING—AN APPRAISAL

The International Labour Organisation (ILO) has argued that collective bargaining offers a number of advantages which, the ILO believes, explains its prevalence and broad acceptance in many countries (ILO, 1973).

The first of these advantages lies in its flexibility. It is suggested that collective bargaining is far more flexible than other methods of industrial relations government, for example statutory control. This is clearly evident from the diversity of agreements which can emerge from collective bargaining negotiations. Collective bargaining may be adopted to cope with the varying requirements of many different organisations and industrial sectors.

It has also been argued (particularly by pluralists who are the main advocates of collective bargaining) that collective bargaining redresses the undoubted disparity in bargaining power which exists between the individual employee and the organisation which is his or her employer. Collective bargaining is portrayed as an instrument which contributes to an approximate balance of power between organisations and their employees. The existence of collective bargaining arrangements can protect the individual worker against possible exploitation which may arise through individual dealings with an organisation because of the employer's superior bargaining position.

Collective bargaining allows workers to participate in the setting of the terms under which they are to work by ensuring their involvement in organisational decision making. The collective bargaining process also involves eliciting the consent of those who live under the terms of any agreement. This consent ensures stability between the parties, thus reducing the potential for problems to arise which may cause conflict in the workplace. A related advantage of collective bargaining lies in its potential usefulness for solving problems arising from conflicts of interests over the distribution of scarce resources. Collective bargaining arrangements can be seen as a means of airing grievances and differences of opinion on contentious issues through orderly negotiation aimed at securing eventual agreement. It can be argued that the absence of such mechanisms for processing and resolving potential disputes would be detrimental to any notions of good industrial relations.

Whatever its potential advantages, the institution of collective bargaining has been criticised by individuals from varying theoretical perspectives and shades of opinion. Beaumont (1990b) has highlighted some of these negative commentaries. For example, those viewing industrial relations from the unitarist frame of reference have long contended that collective bargaining arrangements are totally unnecessary, as they emerge from an employer's failure to satisfy his/her employees' job needs. Unitarists believe that collective bargaining will inevitably result in undesirable conflict and also introduces a competing focus of loyalty for employees within the workplace, that is, a union.

Those supporting the radical school of industrial relations have attacked collective bargaining for its inherent conservatism in that it promotes consensus and discourages social change. They see collective bargaining (with its emphasis on negotiation and compromise more often than not in relation to substantive issues) operating to reinforce the prevailing 'status quo' and not challenging the structures of ownership and control in society. Beaumont suggests that radical scholars, for example Hyman (1975) and Fox (1974a), believe that collective bargaining has the effect of (1) producing only marginal improvements in the terms and conditions of employees, (2) lowering union members' expectations with regard to what is realistically negotiable, (3) making industrial conflict more manageable through the process of procedural regulation, and (4) constraining the development of a cohesive working-class consciousness orientated towards larger political and economic change.

The economic efficiency of collective bargaining has also been called to question. A view often advanced is that collective bargaining is inflationary in that rising wage settlements contribute to an increased overall level of prices which is damaging to society in general. Flanders (1967) argues that collective bargaining at particular periods took inadequate account of the public interest in having a relatively low rate of inflation, and suggests that collective bargaining arrangements should be designed to minimise wage inflationary pressures. Phelps-Brown (1971) argues that wages under collective bargaining may be 20–25 per cent higher than they otherwise would be, but this advantage to the worker is not financed by the employer but is achieved at the expense of the consumer, that is, other workers, through increased prices.

Beaumont (1990b) reports that collective bargaining has been criticised for being 'too strike prone' in particular systems at particular periods of time. It has been argued that collective bargaining produces an unacceptable level of conflict and industrial disputes. This view is often advanced by those who believe that an optimal level of strike activity should exist in the public interest, that is, a level that is socially tolerable and acceptable.

Collective bargaining has also received criticism because of its voluntary nature (particularly in Ireland and Britain) which renders collective agreements legally unenforceable. This, at least in some people's eyes, coupled with the extent of the legal immunities granted to trade unions, is seen to contribute to an overly adversarial system of collective bargaining.

6.5. COLLECTIVE BARGAINING IN IRELAND

Collective bargaining has been described as the central institution regulating behaviour between unions, employees and employers in Ireland (Turner, 1988). The Irish system of collective bargaining is characterised as being essentially a voluntaristic system. There is no legal obligation on trade unions and employers to engage in collective bargaining on pay or any other issue at any level. The system relies on the moral commitments of the participants, with collective agreements being regarded as 'binding in honour only'. The Commission of Inquiry on Industrial Relations (1981) noted that the Irish system reflects the view that collective bargaining and not the law should be the primary source of regulation in the employment relationship, and should be based on the assumption by all parties that recourse to the law will be avoided.

Employers are not legally obliged to recognise trade unions at the workplace. However, the high degree of unionisation has meant that employers have accepted collective bargaining with unions if they are representative of the workplace (Income Data Services, 1992).

Collective bargaining arrangements in Ireland are strongly grounded in the pluralist tradition, that is, they are based on the assumption that a conflict of interests exists in the workplace between management and employees, with a primary reliance on adversarial collective bargaining to resolve temporarily the conflicting interests.

Another characteristic of the Irish model is the tendency towards centralised bargaining. Calmfors and Drilfill (1988) define centralised bargaining as 'the extent of inter-union and inter-employer co-operation in bargaining with the other side'. Centralised bargaining essentially describes institutionalised negotiation between representatives of trade union confederations (in Ireland the ICTU) and employer associations (in Ireland primarily IBEC) about wages and other issues. Since achieving Independence in 1922, there has been a changing emphasis on different levels of bargaining, essentially oscillating between national and enterprise level, which will be discussed in later sections. In more recent times, centralised bargaining in Ireland has been typified by attempts to adopt a corporatist approach to collective bargaining. Corporatist arrangements are distinguished from centralised bargaining in that corporatism integrates (1) Government intervention in collective bargaining so that negotiations become tripartite, (2) a debate over broader issues such as macroeconomic concerns, and (3) the existence of consensus in the national interest. As evidence of this corporatist experimentation, pay determination in Ireland since 1970 has predominantly been negotiated with reference to some centrally bargained wage agreement between employer associations and the trade union movement (except the period of decentralised bargaining between 1982 and 1987), with varying degrees of Government involvement up to and including direct negotiations as evidenced by the Programme for National Recovery, the Programme for Economic and Social Progress and the most recent Programme for Competitiveness and Work.

Even in the presence of centralised bargaining, collective bargaining in Ireland is largely conducted at company level. The function of the national agreements (for example the current Programme for Competitiveness and Work) is to set out agreed national-level guidelines for wage increases and other related issues. The national agreement may also allow scope for supplementary productivity bargaining at establishment level. However, these guidelines are always subject to the outcome of negotiations at company level, though, admittedly, the experience since 1987 has been that local-level settlements have largely complied with the norms set out in the centralised agreements.

Industry-wide bargaining, though widespread in the 1960s, is no longer a major factor, as many of the industry-wide bargaining groups have since disbanded.

6.6. THE DEVELOPMENT OF COLLECTIVE BARGAINING AND PAY DETERMINATION IN IRELAND

The development of the institution of collective bargaining in Ireland can be traced with reference to a number of distinct temporal spans, namely the late nineteenth century to 1941, 1941 to 1946, the wage rounds from 1946 to 1969, the sequence of national wage agreements from 1970 to 1981, the period of decentralised bargaining between 1982 and 1987, and the current period of national bargaining which was initiated by the Programme for National Recovery in 1987 and continues under the Programme for Competitiveness and Work.

6.6.1. THE BEGINNINGS

The emergence of the institution of collective bargaining in Ireland is inextricably linked to the economic and social developments which took place at the end of the last century. It is also undoubtedly closely associated with the growth of trade unions and (to a lesser extent) with the subsequent and often consequential growth of employer associations. The historical development of trade unions has been discussed in an earlier chapter.

The process of collective bargaining grew slowly from the first signs of its emergence in the 1890s. The early evidence of such bargaining was practiced by members of the craft unions, who, at the turn of the century, were the only organisations capable of surviving the adamant resistance of employers and the open hostilities of the State. The forerunner to what we now understand as collective bargaining often involved organised skilled workers trying to regulate their wages by unilateral action. They would devise union standard wage rates ('price lists') and present them to employers as a demand, and would oblige their members not to work for less. They would also undertake to strike if their demands were not met. This bore little resemblance to what we now understand as collective bargaining, but represented a kind of ultimatum (ILO, 1960). Faced with such an ultimatum, employers had either to accept the union rates or risk a strike.

Some employers chose to negotiate with the emergent trade unions, especially in times of prosperity, and conclude collective agreements with them as a means of avoiding industrial action. However, they would not necessarily agree to bargain in all circumstances, particularly in times of poor performance or depression, when in fact wages were often reduced without consultation. The existence of structures for collective bargaining were therefore often dependent on the vagaries of the business cycle or the goodwill of the employer (ILO, 1960).

The passing of the Trade Disputes Act in 1906 reiterated the legality of trade unions, provided immunity from actions in tort to trade unions and legalised peaceful picketing. This key piece of legislation saw the trade union movement gain an increased foothold in many industries in Dublin, Belfast and Cork, particularly with the foundation of (what was to become) the Irish Transport and General Workers' Union in 1909.

The process of recognition of the developing 'new unions' was gradual, the initial reaction of employers being to resist this new wave of trade-unionism as they had resisted the craft unions before them. The resistance was both ideological and philosophical, unions were seen to be interfering with the employers' freedom to run their businesses as they pleased, contrary to the principles of economic liberalism.

The first decade of this century also saw the emergence of the first employer associations, the Cork Employers' Organisation in 1909 and the Employers' Executive Committee in Dublin, whose explicit purpose it was to put up a common front in the resistance to trade-unionism. The issue of union recognition, of course, eventually resulted in confrontation in 1913 with the Dublin lock-out.

After the problems and trauma of this six-month strike, relations between employers and trade unions moved on to a more constructive approach based on negotiations and mutual agreement. The employers' systematic resistance to trade-unionism and to the notion of joint dealings led to the frequent use of the strike. The heavy losses experienced by both sides heralded the gradual abandonment of resistance as an employer strategy in favour of collective bargaining. Employers had come to the realisation that the union movement had arrived, and employers had to take steps to accommodate it.

The acceptance of the trade unions' role was reinforced in Britain by the Whitley Reports (1917–18) which favoured strong management–union relations and helped to establish permanent joint consultation procedures for various industrial sectors. At this time there was a notable 'about-turn' in public policy which 'swung around to at least a benevolent tolerance of collective bargaining, and increasingly to its active promotion' (ILO, 1973).

By 1920, two important prerequisites for the effective functioning of collective bargaining were fulfilled in Ireland, namely freedom of association (which was later strengthened by the Constitution of 1938) and trade union recognition (which to this day continues to be voluntary).

The period between the two World Wars saw collective bargaining still in its infancy in this country. Wages and conditions were still generally fixed by individual bargaining. Trade union density being relatively low, the majority of collective bargaining that did occur was carried out at the level of the individual firm, with less taking place through multi-employer bargaining via employer associations. O'Brien (1989b) describes this phase of collective bargaining as being 'uncoordinated and rather haphazard'.

6.6.2. THE WAGE ROUNDS

The onset of the Second World War brought a temporary cessation of collective bargaining in Ireland, wage determination being governed by the Wages Standstill Order (No. 83) of 1941, which was issued under the Emergency Powers Act of 1939. Prices rose steadily during the war period, which led to an erosion of purchasing power. The suspension of this order upon the ending of the war led to bargaining groups throughout the country lodging claims for substantial wage increases. The Government, in anticipation of the potential problems that might arise, set up the Labour Court to adjudicate on disputes that developed in relation to wage claims. The subsequent negotiation of these wage increases resulted in a general upward movement of wages, which came to be known as the first wage round. McCarthy et al. (1975) define the notion of a wage round as 'a general upward movement in wages and salaries which (a) is usually completed in an active bargaining period of between 3 to 12 months, (b) recurs at regular intervals, (c) typically covers all bargaining groups and (d) results in wage increases of the same general order of magnitude'.

Collective bargaining during the period 1946–69 was to be dominated by a series of wage rounds that were negotiated at fairly regular intervals, approximately every two years. The duration of the round was largely dependent on economic conditions and the bargaining power of respective groups, but a time frame was not generally specified. There were twelve principal bouts of collective bargaining over the period, the majority of which were decentralised in format. Eight of these wage rounds were negotiated at either plant or industry level, that is, they represented periods of free collective bargaining where the parties negotiated their own agreements without interference. The remaining four were bipartite agreements negotiated between the Federated Union of Employers and the Irish Congress of Trade Unions at national level. Hardiman (1988) suggests that these centralised agreements, were 'quite rudimentary and unsophisticated' and bore little resemblance to the national agreements which were to emerge in the 1970s. The first three of these centralised agreements were negotiated in the late 1940s and 1950s, (1948, 1952 and 1957) and were evaluated as being little more than '*ad hoc* responses to particular economic circumstances' (O'Brien, 1981).

As already mentioned, the wage rounds were open-ended and thus no specific termination date was set for the round. Open-ended agreements persisted until the mid-1960s when fixed-term agreements became standard, and generally consisted of flat-rate cash increases. Termination dates of individual agreements varied widely between different bargaining groups. As a result, the negotiating procedures became quite complicated with wage rounds often overlapping each other. The termination dates differing by up to twenty-one months or more by 1970.

Table 6.1. The bargaining level for wage rounds 1946–70

Year in which implementation commenced	Wage-round number	
	Local-level or decentralised bargaining	National-level or centralised bargaining
1946	1	
1948		2
1951	3	
1952		4
1955	5	
1957		6
1959	7	
1961	8	
1964		9
1966	10	
1968	11	
1970	12	

Source: Adapted from O'Brien, 1981.

Wage rounds were by no means synchronised, being largely unplanned, but, as Hillery (1989) contends, they became institutionalised into the Irish model of collective bargaining. The terms of wage rounds were usually accepted relatively quickly by industry, particularly if the Labour Court issued a recommendation up-holding the level of the wage round increase. Table 6.1. describes the bargaining level at which the wage rounds between 1946 and 1970 took place.

The following are the characteristics reported by McCarthy et al. (1975) in their study of the wage-round experience in Ireland during the period 1959–70.

(1) Wage rounds involved virtually every bargaining group. However, the increases took longer to filter through to some groups.

(2) The process did not result in identical settlements in each case, but it did result in the establishment of a minimum rate of increase (usually defined in money as opposed to percentage terms). The effect was to compress the overall wage structure. Thus, in 1959 the highest paid bargaining group received approximately four times as much as did the lowest, but by 1970 this ratio was cut in half (OECD, 1979).

(3) In addition to the primary round a supplementary process was identified. Some groups were able to gain additional increases which were aimed at restoring differentials, that is, the difference between different rates of pay for different types of labour, the supplementary process being a response to specific labour market pressures and exceptional status claims.

(4) Another feature of the system was that the level of settlements rose during the period whilst their duration fell.

(5) Less 'important' or powerful groups in the round waited for the results of others before lodging their claims.

(6) The study by McCarthy et al. also identifies that some 'key wage bargains', that is, the settlements of the more powerful bargaining groups (wage leaders) were the motive force of the wage rounds. When such claims were met this led to a chain reaction by competitive unions seeking to restore relativities. For example, thus the maintenance craft workers' agreement of October 1966 set the pattern for the eleventh round. The wage leaders in each round, because of their relatively powerful bargaining position, established a high norm for the round, which contributed to a high general level of wage increases through comparability claims.

6.6.3. THE EVOLUTION OF THE WAGE ROUNDS

The earlier wage rounds of the 1940s and 1950s were described by one commentator as 'sprawling untidy affairs, typical teenagers, one might say. Collective bargaining was little better than horse trading. Some union officials fought their way through rounds with the same mind set reminiscent of the late nineteenth century' (O'Brien, 1989a).

In the early 1960s the Irish economy advanced at an average 4 per cent growth rate per annum. In the five-year period between 1958–63 industrial exports rose by 46 per cent. This new-found prosperity, however, led to an 'intensification of distributive bargaining' (Hardiman, 1988) and an increase in wage competition between bargaining groups, self-interest and sectional interest, as O'Brien (1989a) suggests, being pushed to the fore at the expense of the national interest. The period of the 1960s brought with it changed attitudes and increased expectation for Irish people, which inevitably manifested itself in increased pressure for higher wages, the threat to the national interest being that the upward thrust to wage claims created inflationary pressures on the economy, which threatened economic growth.

These economic fears prompted the Government of the day to review options aimed at modifying the system of wage rounds. The Government published a White Paper entitled 'Closing the Gap', which proposed wage controls and implied that they might be enforced by the Employer Labour Conference (ELC) (a bipartite employer–employee consultative forum established in 1962). The trade union representatives of the ELC withdrew from the body in protest.

In December 1963 Sean Lemass proposed in the Dail that future wage rounds should 'be based on an intelligent understanding and interpretation of the national interest (through national wage agreements) rather than through the procedures of horse trading and strikes as in the decentralised wage rounds' (Dail Debates, 1963).

Lemass's efforts secured the fourth centralised wage agreement of the wage-round era, the 1964 National Wage Recommendation (NWR). The NWR was innovative in that it introduced for the first time the idea of a particular wage-round increase for a fixed term (two and a half years). Because of imprecise drafting and the issue of admissibility of non-wage claims (specifically the issue of the forty-hour week) the recommendation floundered and, to quote the Minister for Labour of the day, ended 'in a shambles' (O'Brien, 1989a).

The first Maintenance Craftsmen's Agreement in 1966 was also for a fixed term and set a precedent which has bound bargainers at every level since, namely agreements of fixed-term duration. The introduction of fixed terms into the wage rounds between 1966–70 did nothing, however, to combat competitive wage bargaining, which was particularly prevalent in the craft sector, protection of relativities and differentials, being deeply embodied in Irish collective bargaining, no more so than in craft unions. The end of the decade culminated in the maintenance craftsmen's dispute. The dispute between the Federated Union of Employers and the maintenance craft unions centred on efforts to establish a national-level multi-employer agreement covering craft workers, and largely concerned an unsuccessful attempt by the Federated Union of Employers to break the relationship between contract craft and maintenance craft workers. The strike which resulted was historic, it lasted for six weeks and, as Breen et al. (1990) argue, damaged the reputation of the trade union movement both internally and externally. It was unprecedented in its bitterness, and relations between craft and general unions were strained to virtual breaking—a split in the Irish Congress of Trade Unions at the time became a real possibility.

The chief lesson emerging from the operation of collective bargaining in the 1960s was that decentralised wage rounds as they operated were by their nature unstable and prone to inflation. The Irish system of wage determination had reached something of a crisis in its evolution—high levels of wage settlement and industrial action in pursuance of wage increases in the 1960s adding to the perception of disorder in collective bargaining, problems which were apparent to both sides of industry.

6.6.4. THE EMERGENCE OF NATIONAL WAGE AGREEMENTS

From the mid-1960s the National Industrial and Economic Council (a body established in 1963 consisting of employer and employee representatives, senior civil servants and academics whose brief was to give the council's views on the principles that ought to be applied for the development of the national economy) produced a series of reports which argued that one of the main tasks of the Government was to control domestic inflation. In its report No. 27, published in April 1970 (Report on Incomes and Prices Policy), they proposed the establishment of a bipartite body to interpret national policy guidelines for wage increases.

The Government responded quickly to this proposal and reconstituted the Employer Labour Conference (ELC). At its inaugural meeting the ELC appointed a working committee to draft proposals which might initiate national-level negotiations. Although the terms of reference for the reactivated ELC were approved by the ICTU, the debate on the move at the following Annual Delegates Conference of ICTU withheld approval from the concept of an incomes policy. An impasse on the question of a national wage agreement had been reached, despite threats of drastic action from the Government.

Again the response of the Government was almost immediate. On 16 October it published a Prices and Incomes Bill which proposed statutory control of all incomes, limiting increases to 6 per cent or £1.80 per week until the end of 1971. In announcing the bill the then Minister for Finance made reference to the 'truly staggering' claims already submitted at industry level, e.g. 30 per cent for maintenance craftsmen, 40 per cent for builders, 66 per cent and 93 per cent from competing electricians unions (Dail Debates, 1970). The prospect of statutory control of Irish collective bargaining would have been a dramatic divergence from all that had come before it.

The threat was effective and the First National Wage Agreement was painfully hammered out, which gave 10 per cent for twelve months and 4 per cent for a further six months. The Government made a number of concessions to the ICTU and agreed to withdraw the bill (Breen et al., 1990). This process of moral suasion and threats to legislate was to form an integral part of Government industrial relations strategy throughout the 1970s.

6.6.5. THE NATIONAL WAGE AGREEMENTS

The National Wage Agreement (NWA) of 1970 was a watershed in the evolution of Irish collective bargaining. It marked the departure from the traditional method of decentralised collective bargaining and saw the 'beginning of a prolonged suspension of free collective bargaining' (Roche, 1989).

The National Wage Agreements set the agreed rate of wage increase for the entire national workforce in all industries and sectors. The initial agreements (1970–76) were bipartite employer–union agreements, with the Government represented only in its capacity as public-sector employer. As the decade progressed the Government came to become more directly involved in the negotiation of agreements. In all, between 1970 and 1978 seven National Wage Agreements were negotiated followed by two National Understandings in 1979 and 1980. The National Understandings differed from the National Wage Agreements in that they included two elements, a union–employer pay agreement and an agreement between the unions and Government on non-pay issues.

The principal clause of each agreement was the clause governing the basic norm for pay increases, the amount payable and the phasing of the implementation of the agreement. The substantive terms altered from one agreement to the next, the basic pay increase, of course, subject to the greatest variation. Virtually every NWA norm was biased in favour of the lower paid. However, no lasting improvements were made in their position in the course of the agreements.

Each NWA set out the conditions by which a bargaining group could pursue above the norm cost increasing claims, that is, claims which represented increases above and beyond the levels specified in the NWAs. These essentially related to anomaly (equity-based), productivity-based claims and improvements in the conditions of employment. O'Brien (1989b) suggests that these anomaly and productivity clauses 'were tried and tested to the point of exhaustion'. Such claims contributed to a high level of wage drift in the period where actual levels of wage increases exceeded the maximum levels in individual agreements. Claims under these clauses were particularly prevalent in the public sector. Indeed, the Minister for Finance in his budget statement in 1981 remarked that the cost to the Government of anomaly awards had outran the costs of the agreement norms (Dail Debates, 1981).

The second and subsequent agreements allowed employers to claim inability to pay what became known as the 'below the norm' clause. Employers thought that they might have a wide variety of grounds for such pleas; however, the criteria for the use of the clause were very restrictive and little use was made of it.

All the centralised agreements of the 1970s were negotiated through the offices of the Employer Labour Conference. The ELC was also charged with monitoring the implementation of the agreements. The Steering Committee of the ELC initially heard any problematic cases that arose. The ELC then referred the case to either its Interpretation Committee, whose function it was to clarify the meaning of the terms of the agreements, or to its Adjudication Committee (since 1974), whose task it was to rule on issues deemed to be in breach of the agreements.

Disputes that arose as a result of the agreements were required to be referred to the Labour Court. Each agreement with the exception of the 1978 agreement prohibited the taking of industrial action in pursuance of above the norm claims.

6.6.6. THE EVOLUTION OF THE NATIONAL WAGE AGREEMENTS

The 1970 National Wage Agreement set the pattern for subsequent national bargaining in Ireland. The ratification of the 1970 National Wage Agreement was considered no less than miraculous given the background of some of the claims from the more militant bargaining groups and the complexities and tensions that had to be overcome. The agreement ran for eighteen months and provided for two payments or phases of twelve- and six-month duration, the first being for £2 a week for all adult male workers and the second on a percentage basis.

Table 6.2 summarises the terms and conditions of the National Wage Agreements.

Table 6.2. The terms and conditions of the National Wage Agreements

Year	Round No.	Phase	Details
1970	13	1	£2 a week for men, £1.70 for women
		2	4% plus cost of living escalator of £33 a year
1972	14	1	9% on first £30 a week, £2.50 minimum for men, £2.25 for women; 7.5% on next £10 a week and 4% on the remainder
		2	4% plus cost of living escalator supplement of 16p for each 1% increase in the CPI
1974	15	1	9% on first £30 a week; 7% on next £10 a week; 6% on next £10 a week – minimum £2.40 a week
		2	4% plus 60p a week; cost of living escalator 10%
1975	16	1	8% – minimum of £2 a week plus a quarter of 2nd phase of 14th round
		2	5% – minimum increase of £1 a week
		3	No increase except one-quarter of 2nd phase of 14th round
		4	2.8%
1976	17	1	3% of basic pay plus £2 a week, subject to a maximum of £5 a week or £3 a week if greater
1977	18	1	2.5% plus £1 a week, minimum increase of £2 a week, maximum increase £5 a week
		2	2.5% plus £1 a week, minimum increase of £2, maximum increase of £4.23 a week
1978	19	1	8% minimum increase £3.50 a week
		2	2%

Source: Adapted from OECD, 1979, and McGinley, 1989b.

Even though there was no formal commitment to enter into discussions for a further agreement, both employer and trade-union representatives negotiated a second agreement in 1972, which was ratified on similar lines to that of the agreement of 1970. It provided for improved increases for women and the lower paid, who had not fared particularly well during the period of decentralised bargaining (Hillery, 1989). The agreement was also for an eighteen-month duration.

At the conclusion of the Second National Wage Agreement average rates of pay had risen by 19 per cent compared to 17 per cent under the first NWA. This increase, coupled with lower rates of productivity and price increases, saw the Second NWA as being more inflationary.

The Second NWA, as already mentioned, saw the introduction of an inability to pay clause, for employers who could not meet the terms of the agreement because of their particular economic circumstances. This clause was to be replicated in all subsequent agreements.

Both sides of industry again voluntarily agreed to enter into negotiations for a third agreement in 1974. This agreement proved to be more difficult to negotiate than its predecessors given the background of the aforementioned inflationary pressures. A draft agreement by the ELC was rejected at a special delegates conference of the ICTU, largely because of dissatisfaction with the level of the pay increase on offer. It was only with the intervention of the employers, who increased their offer by 3 per cent, and the securing of agreement from the Government to alter income tax relief, reform taxation and increase social welfare spending in the coming budget that the deal was finally ratified.

This Third National Wage Agreement was for the shorter duration of twelve months. It included the principle of indexation (that is linking the level of pay increase directly to movements in official prices), which was to prove very costly. The period of the agreement saw inflation rise to unforeseen levels mainly as a result of 'imported inflation' caused in the main by the oil crisis following the Arab-Israeli War in 1973. The rate of inflation rose from 11.4 per cent in 1973 to 17 per cent in 1974. The pay agreement accorded pay average increases in the region of 30 per cent (OECD, 1979).

The Third National Agreement in 1974 also saw the initiation of a successful attempt to narrow the spread of termination dates which had varied greatly because of the legacy of the wage-round system. The range of termination dates fell from twenty-one months to about three months. This was achieved by a system of so-called 'substitution payments'.

The negotiation of the Fourth NWA in 1975 saw the Government of the day make an explicit input into the terms of that agreement. The Government's influence on previous NWA negotiations was limited to efforts to indirectly influence the level of settlements through the budgets. An agreement, which was essentially an indexation agreement, was ratified in April of 1975. However, it soon became apparent that the terms of the agreement would cause considerable difficulties for employers and would also pose significant cost to the Government in the light of the public sector pay bill.

In response to the situation and in addressing the mounting pressure from the FUE for discussions on integrating pay, taxation and social policy, and union concerns over income tax, the Government suggested having tripartite discussions on these issues.

In June of that year the Government introduced a supplementary budget that removed Value Added Tax from certain items and introduced price subsidies as a package aimed at breaking the inflationary spiral. The Government, using the supplementary budget as bargaining leverage, threatened to revoke these price reliefs if the Fourth National Wage Agreement was not renegotiated. It was, and the eventual agreement was a turning-point in that a 'standstill agreement' was negotiated. The previous agreements had afforded larger increases than (1) their predecessors and (2) the rates of inflation of the day.

The renegotiation established the new sequence of having the budget precede the NWA negotiations and, as Hardiman (1988) suggests, 'created a degree of expectation that NWAs and budgets might be closely linked again in the future'.

Talks on a Fifth NWA in 1976 opened in March again under the auspices of the ELC, amidst widely disparate views. The Government had made an appeal for a voluntary pay pause, which, understandably, was supported by the employers who suggested a nine-month pay pause followed by a flat-rate increase of £2.40 a week. The unions wanted an agreement to run back-to-back, that is, they did not want a pay pause. In any event, a draft agreement was achieved which was to be for thirteen and a half month duration with an annualised increase of 14 per cent, and which restricted special increases in the public sector. A special delegates conference rejected the proposals, essentially because of the restrictions placed on special pay increases. In the light of this rejection the FUE proposed more favourable terms, namely 3 per cent plus £2 a week and the inclusion of a two-month pay pause, and was notably less restrictive on the issue of special pay increases. These proposals by the employers were contingent on the Government and the ICTU partaking in tripartite discussions to work out a framework for a total pay policy for 1977–78 within the context of a general economic and social programme for the development of the economy. The Minister for Labour responded positively to the proposals and an interim agreement was worked out, which would be for seven-months duration. As well as the above-mentioned substantive terms it also included a clause indicating that a further national agreement be agreed subject to tripartite discussions and essentially be budget linked.

The Sixth NWA of 1977 was the first in which a pay agreement was explicitly negotiated with reference to budgetary provisions. In January 1977 the Minister for Finance, in the course of his budget, announced a variety of tax concessions and measures to improve employment. All of these provisions were contingent on the NWA being ratified (Dail Debates, 1977). This was a clear example of bipartite talks on pay increases being conducted against a background of a tripartite arrangement involving the Government and involving issues other than pay. At the tripartite conferences the Government outlined its willingness to give £50 in tax concessions in return for moderate increases.

The terms of the agreement ratified were for 2.5 per cent of basic pay plus £1 a week increase in phase 1 and phase 2. The agreement was to last for fourteen months with a three-month pay pause between the expiration of the Fifth and the beginning of the Sixth NWA.

Although the text of the Sixth NWA makes no specific reference to the budget, it was generally accepted that the tax concessions were integral to its acceptance (Breen et al., 1990; O'Brien, 1989b).

The round of negotiations for a Seventh NWA in 1978 also had tax inducements and Government commitments central to its acceptance. Again these concessions were contingent on the negotiation of an acceptable pay agreement. This, however, looked very unlikely as negotiations had reached a deadlock by the time of the February budget in 1978. The new Fianna Fail Government confirmed its commitment to the process of centralised bargaining when, as an inducement to ensure the ratification of a new agreement, it withdrew its strict limit of 5 per cent which it had put on pay increases.

The ensuing talks were difficult, but an agreement was reached in March 1978 and involved a basic norm of 8 per cent. The agreement was accepted by the ICTU by a slender margin. Hardiman (1988) suggests that the unions were generally unhappy with the above the norm clauses, which were stricter than before at a time when most sectors were doing quite well. As a concession to the unions, the 1978 agreement introduced a new feature which provided for the negotiation of pay increases up to 2 per cent extra at local level. It also permitted for the first time industrial action in certain circumstances in pursuance of above the norm increases.

6.6.7. THE NATIONAL UNDERSTANDINGS

By 1978 there was growing disillusionment within the trade union movement with the system of NWAs. Trade unions in particular felt that they were enduring excessively strict limitations and not getting enough in return. As von Prondzynski (1992) points out, some unions had always seen centralised bargaining as a mechanism that inhibited trade unions from realising their full bargaining potential. At a special delegates conference in November 1978 the ICTU rejected the opening of talks on a national agreement for 1979. The prospect of a return to decentralised 'free for all' bargaining loomed. The Government responded with a budgetary package aimed at renewing the unions' interest and invited the trade unions to discuss a 'National Agreement for Development', which included increasing tax-free allowances, modifying tax bands and extra public spending on employment creation. The ICTU again convened a special delegates conference to discuss the Government's intentions and to construct some policy proposals which it would use as the basis for negotiation with the Government. Their principal concerns dealt with the nature of taxation which they perceived to be inequitable but also included proposals on employment and participation.

In March 1979 negotiations got underway that eventually resulted in a first National Understanding called the 'National Understanding for Economic and Social Development'. The ICTU's executive council, mindful of the fact that they had no mandate to openly engage in talks for a new national agreement, 'explained that they were simply engaged in talks on trade union policy proposals' (Roche, 1989). These talks involved a series of working parties. The trade union and employer talks centred on pay, and trade union representatives met with ministers on a variety of non-pay issues including taxation, employment, health and education.

A package of proposals resulted from these tripartite working parties, which were placed before a special delegates conference in May 1979, and were surprisingly rejected. The proposals failed to gain acceptance because the ITGWU felt that the arrangements for tripartite consultation were not far-reaching enough (ICTU, 1975).

The Government felt that securing a national agreement was essential to the economic development of the country, and threatened to introduce statutory pay guidelines for the interim period (in effect a 7 per cent pay limit). The FUE, fearing a return to the 'nightmares' of 'free for all' bargaining, increased their pay offer and, with other minor revisions, ensured the acceptance at an ICTU special delegates conference in July.

The National Understanding of 1979 represented something of a new departure in Irish collective bargaining. For the first time the Government became involved in national pay talks as a Government, where previously it had been involved in its capacity of public sector employer. The NU of 1979 also for the first time introduced a major non-pay element into national agreements. Table 6.3. summarises the terms and conditions of the National Understandings.

Table 6.3. The terms and conditions of the National Understandings

Year	Round No.	Phase	Details
1979	20	1	9% minimum increase of £5.50 a week
		2	2% plus amount related to CPI movement, minimum increase £3.30 a week
1980	21	1	8% plus £1 a week
		2	7%

Source: McGinley, 1989b.

The First National Understanding covered a period of fifteen months in two phases. Phase 1 provided for a basic increase in pay of 9 per cent subject to a minimum of £5.50 a week. Phase 2 provided for a 2 per cent increase in basic pay and included provision for changes in the Consumer Price Index during the period (which, as it transpired, meant an actual increase paid under phase 2 of 7 per cent plus £2.40 a week).

A second National Understanding was negotiated in 1980. This time around the ICTU received an overwhelming mandate to pursue another national agreement. However, the FUE, which had previously been an enthusiatic supporter of the central agreements, began to express dissatisfaction with their performance. A number of factors help to explain the FUE's new-found reluctance. They believed that an unsatisfactory balance had been achieved between the central norms of the agreements and local-level bargaining. They were also disturbed by the high level of industrial disputes, and became increasingly critical of the cost of the non-pay elements of the agreements (Fogarty et al., 1981).

Nevertheless, a series of bipartite and tripartite talks ensued, through different institutional channels than the first Understanding. The pay talks used the offices of the ELC and non-pay elements were taken up directly with the Taoiseach and members of the Cabinet. These talks were only completed successfully after the intervention of the Government with guarantees to the employers on the contents of the 1981 budget. The Second National Understanding was therefore completed with, as Roche (1989) suggests, the FUE 'openly resentful of undue political pressure', which they felt was brought to bear on them.

The Second National Understanding was ratified in October 1980, and, as its forerunner, had a pay and a non-pay element to it. It provided for increases in two phases: phase 1 granted an increase of 8 per cent of basic pay and £1 a week for 8 months; phase 2 granted an increase of 7 per cent for a period of six months after the end of phase 1.

The expiration of the Second National Understanding heralded the suspension of centralised bargaining in Ireland. Although formal talks opened towards negotiating a new understanding, an impasse was soon reached on the pay terms between the ICTU and the FUE, and the newly elected Fine Gael–Labour Coalition Government was unwilling to intervene to avert a breakdown. What followed was a return to decentralised bargaining.

6.6.8. THE PERFORMANCE OF CENTRALISED BARGAINING, 1970–81

The National Wage Agreements and National Understandings were generally accepted as being unsuccessful attempts at centralised bargaining. Admittedly, they attempted to address many of the shortcomings of the wage rounds in the 1960s. In particular, they were a much more structured system: levels of pay were set in specific terms, the duration of the agreements was fixed and machinery was provided to deal with disputes arising out of the terms of such agreements and to deal with any anomalies. As von Prondzynski (1992) suggests 'they had basically stabilised what had become a chaotic picture'. However, the system was felt to be unsuccessful in that the principal objectives of each of the social partners were not achieved. The agreements were seen by the Government as opportunities to pursue national economic objectives. However, on these criteria it would appear that little success was achieved. In spite of Government and employer assurances to the trade union movement, unemployment rose sharply. In 1969 unemployment stood at 4 per cent of the labour force, but by 1982 it had reached 10.7 per cent (Conniffe and Kennedy, 1984). Another objective of all parties to the process of centralised bargaining was the reduction in the levels of industrial unrest: although a claimed advantage of national agreements, this objective was not achieved. While the agreements contained procedures to promote industrial peace, the level of working days lost regarding matters covered by the NWAs climbed in the second half of the 1970s. After some success in the early stages of national agreements, Ireland's strike record continued to deteriorate throughout the 1970s with man-days lost up by 30 per cent on the previous decade. The annual average number of days lost per year rose from 353,769 in the period 1960–69 to 430,759 in 1970–79 (Fogarty et al., 1981). Another associated and worrying development was the increased tendency for unofficial action, which over the period accounted for over two-thirds of all strikes (Wallace and O'Shea, 1987), a phenomenon that also reflected increased workplace organisation and power of trade unions.

In spite of the reports that national agreements were anti-inflationary by nature, the Government was unable to deliver on its commitments, and inflation actually rose throughout the 1970s, reaching 20 per cent by 1981. The perception of the Government's ability to honour its commitments was severely damaged, as evidenced by John Horgan's reference (while still Chairman of the Labour Court) to the National Understandings as 'Notional Understandings' (McGinley, 1989a).

The ICTU pressed throughout the period for changes to the system of taxation; however, at the end of the period of national agreements there had been little change in the overall burden of taxation on wage and salary earners (which in fact rose from 30 per cent in 1979 to 45 per cent in 1981). Also, the proportion of personal taxation to personal income rose from approximately 7 per cent in the mid-1960s to 12 per cent in 1974 and over 15 per cent in 1976 (Conniffe and Kennedy, 1984). From the employer perspective, calls for wage moderation were unsuccessful. Wage rises were seen as being higher than appropriate for the period, and employers were particularly aggrieved at what they called the excessive use of the above the norm clause.

6.6.9. THE EXPERIENCE OF DECENTRALISED BARGAINING, 1982–87

When the long series of centralised national agreements finally ended in 1982 it was to be replaced with a short period of decentralised bargaining at enterprise level. The collapse of centralised bargaining, however, did not involve a return to the system of collective bargaining which predated it and indeed bore little resemblance to that which took place before 1970. Collective bargaining throughout the wage round era has been described as amounting to little more than 'splitting the difference between initial offers and claims' (O'Brien, 1989a), the function of trade union claims being to impress members and potential members. The claims were more often concerned with notions of equity or comparability than with the companies' financial performance and ability to pay.

Foley and Gunnigle (1994) argue that the return to decentralised bargaining, however, saw viability and economic performance become the key criteria shaping wage increases. Wage increases now had to be earned through better company or individual performance. Hence, settlements varied widely throughout industries, with no wage-round norm being established; indeed, many commentators questioned the existence of the wage-round concept in the private sector between 1982 and 1987 (McGinley, 1989a). The FUE sought to shift collective bargaining away from the notion of a specific norm in each wage round and away from the idea that wage rounds ought to follow each other automatically. Their position was that pay increases should be closely tied to what the individual firm could bear (Hardiman, 1988). The Government attempted at times to impose a norm through pay guidelines but these were largely ignored by private sector negotiators and, as von Prondzynski (1985) argues, were best seen as the Government's opening position in the public sector pay negotiations. Table 6.4 highlights the reported average increases achieved in the private sector over the period.

Table 6.4. Private sector pay increases, 1981–87*

Round	Average cumulative increase (%)	Average length (months)
22	16.4	14.9
23	10.9	13.5
24	9.3	12.75
25	6.8	12.0
26	6.0	12.0
27	6.5	15.4

* It is important to bear in mind that these figures may disguise large disparities within and between rounds.

Source: McGinley, 1989b.

O'Brien (1989b) suggests that the return to decentralised bargaining saw industry and trade agreements, which were prevalent in the 1950s and 1960s, becoming less fashionable in many areas. During the 1960s there were sixty industrial bargaining groups which covered the country. Many of these groups fell into disuse during the period of centralised bargaining, and were disbanded and failed to be reactivated during the 1980s. No new industry/trade groups were formed with a new Joint Labour Committee, contract cleaners being the only notable exception. The focus of bargaining activity was quite clearly fixed at the level of the individual firm.

A notable feature of the period was the reduction over the rounds in the number and the range of supplementary cost-increasing claims (above the norm claims). Irish wage costs per unit rose by only 7 per cent between 1980 and 1985, compared with an average 37 per cent increase in competing countries (Hardiman, 1988). There was also consistent support by both employers and trade unions for one-year agreements and a progressive movement towards single-phase agreements. This came about possibly in response to the uncertain economic conditions that prevailed and employers' needs to tie wage bargaining to the annual budgetary process.

The union negotiating agenda lengthened, with non-wage conditions of employment taking on a greater significance in negotiations than before. The content of union claims changed with a shift away from pure pay claims to claims in relation to hours of work, bonuses, leave and general working conditions (Income Data Services, 1992). Employers countered with equally pressing demands, particularly in relation to working practices and methods, to which there seemed amongst trade union ranks 'to be a growing willingness to accept the need for changes' (FUE Annual Report, 1986).

The return to decentralised bargaining coincided with a dramatic rise in the unemployment rate, ever-increasing redundancies (standing at over 30,000 per annum by 1984), falling trade union membership, coupled with recessionary conditions. All of these factors led to a much weakened trade union movement. Indeed, it has been argued that the deteriorating economic circumstances introduced a 'new realism' into employer–employee relationships, which was to transcend all facets of organisational activities including collective bargaining (Foley and Gunnigle, 1994). The capacity of unions to engage in industrial militancy was reduced, and the period saw a notable drop in the level of strikes.

Management during the period clearly regained the initiative, with productivity improving strongly, often as a result of rationalisation. Overall, private sector employers did much better than they had hoped when local-level negotiations resumed in 1982. In successive wage rounds pay norms followed falling inflation downwards. There was certainly no private sector employer push for a return to national agreements—indeed, as O'Brien (1989b) argues, in the light of the advantageous bargaining position of employers there were very considerable doubts about it.

6.6.10. THE PROGRAMME FOR NATIONAL RECOVERY (PNR)

The prime motivating factor for the reactivation of the process of national bargaining in 1987 was, undoubtedly, the growing crisis in public finances.

The three principal elements in current Government expenditure were foreign debt service, social welfare and the public sector payroll. At the end of 1986 the national debt of £24 billion was three times larger than it had been in 1980, and represented 148 per cent of annual GNP. Unprecedented levels of unemployment saw Government expenditure in social services increase from 28.9 per cent of GNP in 1980 to 35.6 per cent in 1985 (NESC, 1986). Many commentators warned that the country appeared to be heading for economic and financial disaster. Because of the perceived difficulties in tackling debt service and social welfare, the public sector payroll became the central focus of Government action. The experience of decentralised bargaining from 1982 saw more modest pay increases negotiated in the public sector. Also, in an attempt to contain the Government's pay-bill, a career-break scheme and an embargo on recruitment (designed to reduce numbers through natural wastage) were introduced.

The National Economic and Social Council (NESC), a consultative forum comprised of representatives of the main interest groups in the economy—the trade unions, employers and farmers—produced a report entitled *A Strategy for Development 1986–1990*. This report emphasised the need for cogent action to address the 'twin problems of mass unemployment and chronic fiscal imbalance', and was to become central to future Government thinking on the nature of national bargaining and incomes policy (NESC, 1986). The NESC report did not make any explicit recommendations on pay because the employer representatives on the council expressed the view that negotiations at the level of the firm was the most appropriate means of determining pay.

The beginning of 1987 brought the election of a Fianna Fail Government, whose economic strategy was to be broadly guided by the principles and priorities established in the NESC report. The Government, in its initial budget, announced a number of measures to improve the position of the public finances including restrictive measures in relation to public sector pay. In the course of a number of consultative meetings with the Government after the general election it became apparent that it was interested in attaining a three-year pay agreement.

In April of 1987 the ICTU proposed to the Government that there should be discussions about a national plan for growth and economic recovery, public finances and social services. Interest in returning to a national agreement was expressed by a number of prominent trade union leaders throughout 1986 (such as John Carroll of the ITGWU and Bill Atley of the FWUI). A number of factors may help to understand the ICTU's interest in the negotiation of a new national agreement. Issues such as employment, tax reform and social welfare were now central to the ICTU's agenda, as it would appear that the political and economic objectives of trade unions had long since converged. Congress were now particularly concerned for the plight of low-paid employees, who were suffering most in the recessionary conditions of decentralised bargaining in the 1980s because of their weak competitive bargaining position. The trade union movement was also mindful of the situation which had developed in Britain, where British unions had suffered under the premiership of Thatcher and repressive Tory legislation. Bill Atley, the General Secretary of the FWUI, warned at the ICTU Annual Delegates Conference that the trade union movement was in serious danger of being marginalised (ICTU Annual Report, 1987). The trade unions looked to the prospect of a new national agreement to 'beef up' their role and status in Irish society. They had feared that the trade union movement might go the way the unions had gone in Britain and be excluded from the national scene.

Dineen and Wallace (1991) argue that the decision of the trade unions to participate in the negotiation of the Programme for National Recovery (PNR) must be seen in the light of falling membership levels between 1980 and 1987. This decline focused the attention of unions on the threat that unemployment posed to membership levels. By collaborating with Government policy and entering into a national agreement the unions would be seen to be getting wage increases, albeit modest ones, which they hoped would help to retain members and to attract new ones.

The ICTU was also troubled by the state of the public finances and the Government's need to control the public sector payroll, which could only be achieved by either cutting numbers of employed or by freezing public sector pay rates, or, indeed, by both. The prospect of having a pay freeze in the public sector, which represented approximately half of the trade union membership, while the private sector locally negotiated even moderate increases, posed a serious threat to the unity of the trade union movement.

On the employer side, the FUE were initially less than favourable towards the idea of a further national agreement. They were especially concerned about the proposal for a reduction in working hours and the fact that a national agreement would be too rigid. They, however, 'had been gradually wooed into support of the Government's wider economic policies, in general . . . the cuts in public spending were the kind the private sector employers have been urging for years' (*Business and Finance*, 1987). It would be accurate to suggest that the employers were under an amount of political pressure to negotiate a new agreement. However, in the final analysis their support for such an agreement was secured by their recognition that the likely terms of any proposed agreement would be advantageous to their affiliated companies. Indeed, the view expressed was that little was to be achieved by abstaining from the process and participation, at least, had some potential.

The negotiations that followed were eventually concluded in October 1987 and resulted in the Programme for National Recovery. The programme was to cover the period up to the end of 1990 and entailed the following provisions:
– the creation of a fiscal, exchange and monetary climate conducive to economic growth. This included a commitment that the ratio of debt to GNP should be reduced to between 5 and 7 per cent;
– movement towards greater equity and fairness in the tax system;

– measures to generate employment opportunities. Notably, no extra expenditure was to be committed to this;
– reduction of social inequalities.

The PNR covered proposals for pay agreements in both the public and private sectors. The public sector agreement provided for a six-month pay pause and for increases in basic pay for the three-year programme of 3 per cent on the first £120 of basic weekly pay and 2 per cent on the balance. A minimum increase of £4 per week in basic pay for full-time adult employees was also agreed.

The private sector agreement provided for the same substantive terms. The £4 minimum, however, was to be subject to local negotiations. It also committed bargaining groups not to advance any further cost-increasing claims on employers for the duration of the agreement. The minimum cash increase was aimed at benefiting low-paid employees.

It was also agreed to facilitate an objective of the trade unions, that discussions would take place between the Government, FUE and CIF, and the ICTU on the development of a general framework for reducing working time by one hour for those working forty or more hours per week.

The PNR was markedly different from the earlier centralised agreements. O'Brien (1989a) argues that 'a whole host of old conventions were ditched and new conventions forged'. These included the following:
– a three-year agreement—previously unheard of;
– a pay increase at or even slightly below inflation—previously unheard of;
– no provision for below the norm or above the norm payments;
– a national commitment to pursue the reduction of working hours—previously unknown;
– no institutional monitoring of the agreement as the ELC had in the 1970s.

The pay terms were not fixed norms but guidelines which, in the private sector, had to be agreed through local-level bargaining. This met a major employer concern on the flexibility of the pay arrangements. The PNR also differed from its predecessors of the 1970s in that the terms concerning economic and social policy were expressed as specific targets and not as binding commitments.

The PNR was generally viewed as a considerable success in that the terms of the agreement were largely satisfied. Wage increases that were achieved at local level ran roughly parallel to those suggested by the PNR. During the three years covered by the programme manufacturing output and exports grew steadily creating a major balance of trade surplus. There was an advancement in economic growth of more than 4 per cent per annum on average, and inflation reached its lowest level in thirty years in 1988. The debt–GNP ratio was stabilised falling from 131 per cent in 1987 to 111 per cent in 1990, and net job gains were achieved reversing the trends of the early 1980s. Strike levels declined considerably, with a particularly significant fall-off in the level of unofficial strikes. Some questions have been raised by economists as to whether the success of the Irish economy experienced between 1987–90 was due to the PNR or to the generally buoyant international economy. As with most macroeconomic issues the nature of the causation is difficult to ascertain.

Amongst the trade unions there was continuous criticism that the resources being generated were not being sufficiently channelled into employment creation. For example, the 1988 ICTU Annual Delegates Conference saw three motions debated, all largely critically of the PNR. However, two years into the programme the ICTU voted to continue to support it and, with the end of the three-year PNR in sight, decided in favour of entering talks on a new agreement.

6.6.11. THE PROGRAMME FOR ECONOMIC AND SOCIAL PROGRESS (PESP)

In October 1990 the ICTU again took the initiative and proposed that the Government, the employers, the farming organisations and trade unions should agree on a ten-year development strategy for the country. The result of the subsequent negotiations was the Programme for Economic and Social Progress (PESP).

The PESP covered the period from the expiration of the PNR to the end of 1993. The key objectives of the PESP were:
– sustained economic growth and the generation of greater income;
– a substantial increase in employment;
– a major assault on long-term unemployment;
– the development of greater social rights within health, education, social welfare and housing services;
– the promotion of social responsibility in relation to discharge of tax liabilities;
– the development of worker participation, women's rights and consumer rights.

The agreement set out that increases were to be awarded annually for three years on the basis of:
– 4 per cent of basic pay in the first year of the agreement;
– 3 per cent of basic pay in the second year of the agreement;
– 3.75 per cent of basic pay in the third year of the agreement.

Where the application of this formula resulted in increases in basic pay for full-time employees of less than £5 per week in the first year, £4.25 per week in the second year or £5.75 in the third, then the percentage increase could be adjusted by local-level bargaining. These increases were to be negotiated through the normal industrial relations machinery with regard to the economic and commercial circumstances of the particular firm.

The PESP also provided for local bargaining in 'exceptional cases'. In such circumstances employers and trade unions could negotiate further changes in the rates of pay or conditions of employment which were up to but not exceeding 3 per cent of the basic pay of the group of employees concerned.

As was the case with the PNR, the PESP provided that no cost-increasing claims, in addition to the ones outlined above, could be made on employers in the course of the agreement. Unions were not precluded under the agreement from making claims for the introduction of pension or sick-pay schemes where none existed. The PESP committed employers, trade unions and employees to promoting industrial harmony. Where the parties could not reach agreement on any issue covered by the PESP, it was agreed that they could jointly refer the matter to the Labour Relations Commission/Labour Court or to other agreed dispute resolution machinery.

Since its negotiation, the PESP had been subject to critical commentary from some quarters. Barret (1991), for instance, argued shortly after its publication that the PESP represented a continuation of the Government's 'slide back to borrowing and wasteful public expenditure', and marked an abandonment of the expansionary fiscal rectitude which appeared to have bolstered the economy under the PNR.

The public sector unions experienced some problems in the operation of the PESP, most notably the Government hinting that it was considering reneging on the pay aspects of the programme as a result of lower than expected growth at the beginning of 1992. A concerted protest strike throughout the public sector resulted from the Government's attempt to demand a flat-rate increase of £5 instead of the 3 per cent under the programme (Von Prondzynski, 1992).

Perhaps the most significant critical aspect of the PESP, however, was its performance in relation to some of the objectives or targets outlined in the agreement. For example, the PESP had a substantial increase in employment as an objective. This did not occur; in fact, an ESRI analysis suggests that employment was reduced by 5,000 between 1990 and 1993 (Barret, 1993). A major assault on long-term unemployment was promised. However, in September 1992 there were 49,000 more long-term unemployed than in 1990 (Barret, 1993). Under the terms of the PESP the standard tax rate was to be reduced to 25 per cent by 1993, but in fact it was 27 per cent plus a 1 per cent 'temporary' income levy. The public sector pay-bill, which increased by over 27 per cent between 1990 and 1993, was also the source of much discontent. In hindsight it can be argued that the Government may have been a bit ambitious in their forecasts for the programme. Maurice Doyle, the Governor of the Central Bank, criticised the Government for not renegotiating the PESP when circumstances such as weak growth and rising unemployment required it. The attainment of the targets in the programme was undoubtedly hindered by such unforeseen developments as the currency crisis at the end of 1992, which would have been almost impossible to plan for.

The PESP was undoubtedly accompanied by more positive aspects. The fundamentals of the economy, that is, interest rates and inflation, were still relatively good. The national consensus developed under the PNR was continued. The relative industrial peace, a feature of the PNR, also continued under the PESP. However, as Sheehan points out, 'there is no firm evidence one way or the other that centralised bargaining helps to secure industrial peace' (Sheehan, 1991). The Government have also argued that a significant number of jobs were saved during the term of the PESP through Ireland's improved competitiveness in wage costs relative to its main trading partners.

While it may still be too soon to offer a complete assessment of the impact of the PESP, it would be fair to say that the performance of the Irish economy for the duration of the PESP compares unfavourably to the relative success of the economy for the duration of its immediate predecessor, the PNR. It would be reckless in the extreme, however, to suggest that the PESP was solely responsible for the economic problems of the country experienced since 1991. The performance of the PESP must be seen in the light of a depression in the international economy, which was experienced for the duration of the programme. Indeed, given that the PNR was in effect when international conditions were favourable, and that the results of the PESP were much less impressive when the international situation was less favourable, there would appear to be a strong argument that the success of such national agreements is contingent upon external factors.

6.6.12. THE PROGRAMME FOR COMPETITIVENESS AND WORK (PCW)

Prior to the expiration of the PESP in December 1993, the parties to the programme set out their positions regarding the negotiation of further national agreement. The unions advanced some preconditions for a renegotiation of a follow-on agreement, principally that the Government remove the 1 per cent 'temporary' levy and that certain limitations placed upon social welfare payments be rescinded, both measures introduced in the budget of 1993. Mr Edmund Browne, a joint president of SIPTU, argued that, by introducing these measures, the 'Government had diminished the status of the social partnership', and added that the Government was presiding over and precipitating the end of the social consensus process. Initially, the Government was unwilling to accept these preconditions and the prospect of a return to decentralised bargaining was on the cards. In the final analysis, however, it seemed unlikely that these preconditions would necessarily prevent the trade unions from taking a place at the negotiating table, and the preconditions may best be viewed as bargaining tactics on the ICTU's behalf. It appears evident that the ICTU would have found it more advantageous to be party to a new agreement than to stay out of any new arrangements. An analysis completed by SIPTU in 1992 showed that take-home pay for the average worker had increased in real terms in the years since 1987, after a decline in the years 1980–87 (Sheehan, 1992). Sheehan contends that many union leaders believed that their best interests would be served within the context of an overall national agreement similar to the PESP (Sheehan, 1993). There were some outspoken members of the trade-union movement, for example, Michael O'Reilly, the General Secretary of the Amalgamated

Transport and General Workers' Union, who condemned the PESP and its forerunner, the PNR, as 'having laid the basis of marginalisation of the whole trade union movement', and argued that the 'new right' had prompted sections of the ICTU 'to advocate collaboration with employers and Government in controlling workers in order to create stability'.

The Government for their part had made it very clear that they wanted another national agreement to replace the PESP. The Minister for Finance, Bertie Ahern, stressed that pay moderation would have to be part of any new deal and expressed interest in securing a no-strike guarantee until the year 2001. The Government had been reported as saying that it was willing to offer a number of concessions to the unions as part of any new agreement including the following:
– electing workers to company boards;
– increasing the nine annual public holidays;
– introducing a uniform working week of less than forty hours;
– greater equality for women workers;
– better health, welfare and housing services.

The private sector employers were relatively happy with the PESP. Some may have complained about the level of pay rises involved, though they were thankful of the certainty it offered. Pay bargaining at local level in the private sector produced increases which largely complied with the pay terms suggested by the PESP. The Income Data Services (1992) report that 90–95 per cent of companies surveyed adhered to the pay guidelines outlined by the PESP. The local-level bargaining clause went well from the employers' point of view, as it was conceded in less than 50 per cent of workplaces. However, many did regard the process of negotiating these local rises as 'difficult and troublesome' (*Business and Finance*, 1993). According to a survey carried out by the Institute of Personnel Management (IPM), 95 per cent of senior personnel managers were in favour of a further PESP-type agreement (Yeates, 1993). The IPM stressed the positive benefits that centralised agreements had on improving competitiveness in the private sector and saw considerable prospects for obtaining low-pay increases in the light of low levels of inflation. Some employers argued for the need for greater flexibility to be built into any new agreement, as it was clear from the experience of the currency crisis at the beginning of 1993 that the external environment of many organisations has the capacity to change so rapidly that a moderate increase under a national agreement may become unsustainable in a relatively short space of time.

An accommodation was reached between the Government and the ICTU in relation to the unions' preconditions, and the outcome of the negotiations which ensued was the Programme for Competitiveness and Work (PCW), which was negotiated within the context of the long-term development strategy for the country. Table 6.5 sets out the pay terms agreed for the private sector and the public service for the duration of the programme, which runs from 1994 to 1997.

Table 6.5. Pay terms of the Programme for Competitiveness and Work

Category	1994	1995	1996	1994–97
Private sector employees, basic increases*	2% for 12 months on basic pay from 1 January	2.5% for 12 months on basic pay from 1 January	2.5% for first 6 months; extra 1% in second 6 months	Increase of 8% in basic pay over three years
Building sector, basic increases	5-month pause, then 2% for 12 months	2% for 12 months from 1 June	2% for 4 months; 1% for next 3 months; 1% for final 3 months	5-month pause, then 8% increase over 33 months; deal lasts 39 months
Public-service employees, basic increases	Freeze to 1 June, then 2% for 12 months	2% for 12 months from 1 June	1.5% from 1 June; 1.5% from 1 October; 1% from 1 January 1997; deal expires June 1997	5-month pause, then 8% rise in basic pay over 3 years to June 1997
Public-service awards local/special awards	1% rise payable from 1 April as down payment prior to completed negotiation	0.75% rise payable from 1 June after negotiation	0.75% rise payable from 1 June after negotiation; final 0.5% payable from 1 June 1997	Maximum of 3% rise in pay for productivity increases under this carry-over from PESP

* Excluding building and construction sector.

Source: Tansey, 1994.

6.6.13. A Note on the Future

The future of collective bargaining and pay determination in Ireland may only have three possible alternatives: another bout of decentralised bargaining, a sequel of some kind to the present PCW arrangements or a statutory norm. In considering the possibility of the Government intervening with a statutory pay limit, it is difficult, if not impossible, to conceive of the present national consensus declining to the point where legislation became necessary. While decentralised bargaining might suit some trade unions and employers, it has almost always resulted in a slow but accelerating escalation of wage settlements (and industrial conflict) to unsustainable levels (O'Brien, 1989b). The 'free for all', also often bringing with it the exploitation of the low-paid, obliviousness to the plight of the unemployed and reduction of international competitiveness.

Another option outside the structure of a further national agreement may be the determination of pay with reference to some guidelines imposed by the ICTU or the Government. Such voluntarily agreed guidelines have been used in the past; e.g., in 1966 the ICTU agreed to limit claims to a £1 a week. The principal danger with this arrangement has been that unions often see the limit as a minimum as opposed to a ceiling, and press for supplementary claims.

CHAPTER SEVEN

Collective Bargaining Practice

7.1. INTRODUCTION

In the preceding chapter we have seen that at a general level collective bargaining incorporates the process through which managements, employees and their various representative bodies discuss and consider issues such as pay, working conditions, procedures and other negotiable matters. We have also seen that collective bargaining may take place at multi-employer or single-employer level. In Ireland the traditional focus of collective bargaining, on major issues has been on multi-employer bargaining, with supplementary workplace bargaining at establishment level. Since 1987 there have been three major national agreements on pay and other matters. However, this development does not mean that collective bargaining at the level of the workplace has become obsolete. Workplace bargaining remains very much a significant and integral component of industrial relations practice in organisations. Indeed, this has been faciliated under recent centralised agreements, which provide for the agreement of centralised pay guidelines while allowing management and employees in exceptional cases to negotiate further at establishment level.

Organisations may engage in local-level bargaining for a variety of reasons. From a managerial perspective, the pressure to be competitive, to control costs and to improve productivity and quality are common catalysts for local-level bargaining. This type of negotiation takes the form of unique arrangements between management and unions, to cater specifically for local needs. Personnel managers in Ireland overwhelmingly tend to consider that industrial relations activities form the most important part of their job (Gunnigle and Shivanath, 1988; Keating, 1989; Monks, 1992; Shivanath, 1987). In analysing the findings of her survey on the work of personnel practitioners in Ireland Shivanath (1987) commented as follows: 'Industrial relations . . . [was] identified by the respondents as the most crucial area of their work. Whether the question centred around importance of activity, value to the organisation or proof of contribution, in all instances the group of activities collectively called industrial relations [was] reported to be top of the list.'

The management of day-to-day industrial relations also means that senior and line management have to deal on an ongoing basis with a range of industrial relations issues. These may be contentious issues where a conflict of interest arises between employers and workers. In particular, the areas of grievance handling and discipline administration are very much a central part of workplace industrial relations and an important concern for those responsible for managing industrial relations at the level of the workplace. Alternatively, less contentious issues will also merit the attention of management, employees and their organsiations. These may be minor changes in working arrangement which require communication and discussion between the interested parties.

This chapter considers what are felt to be key aspects of collective bargaining practice at the level of the organisation, namely industrial relations negotiations, grievance handling, and discipline administration. The area of employee participation and involvement, incorporating management –employee communications is discussed in chapter 9.

7.2. INDUSTRIAL RELATIONS NEGOTIATIONS

The process of negotiation is both necessary for, and central to, collective bargaining. Many would, in fact, argue that the negotiation process is the single most fundamental aspect of collective bargaining. Industrial relations negotiations involve interactions between managers, employees and their representative bodies. The objective of negotiation is to reach agreement in relation to divisive issues under discussion.[1] While there are many somewhat diverse descriptions of industrial relations negotiations, Hawkins (1979) provides us with what is possibly the most widely quoted definition, describing negotiation as 'the process of resolving conflict through compromise'.

For the great majority of unionised organisations, management–trade union negotiations represent the primary vehicle for dealing with management–employee relations, and reaching agreement over a broad range of industrial relations issues such as pay and conditions of employment. Negotiations between unions and management over pay and conditions of employment are normally termed 'distributive bargaining' since they involve bargaining or haggling over issues where a favourable settlement for one party means an element of loss for the other (Walton and McKersie, 1965). This 'win–lose' approach represents the adversarial model of collective bargaining where each party pursues its own specific objectives and hopes to afford minimal concessions to the other party. It is most obvious in pay negotiations where concessions by management inevitably represent both a quantifiable

200

cost and a reduction in profits/dividends. On the other hand, negotiations can have a more joint problem-solving approach, sometimes referred to as 'integrative' or 'co-operative' bargaining, where both parties are concerned with finding a jointly acceptable solution resulting in mutual benefits for both sides. This is often referred to as a 'win–win' approach to industrial relations negotiations (Chamberlain and Kuhn, 1965; Walton and McKersie, 1965). Inevitably, workplace negotiations will involve a combination of both approaches with the 'mix' being influenced by the extent of trust and openness between the parties.

Figure 7.1. Adversarial and Co-operative model of negotiation

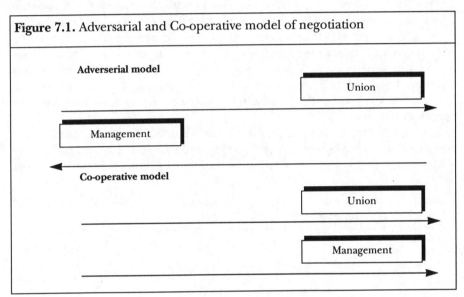

7.2.1. THE NEGOTIATING PROCESS

Normally, the formal initiation of industrial relations negotiations begins with one party presenting a claim to the other, and then meeting to discuss the issues raised. It is interesting to note that industrial relations negotiations tend to be a highly ritualistic process. Once one party presents a claim, subsequent negotiations will generally involve the various parties meeting and discussing the issues in a specific context, bargaining and haggling over the divisive issues and reporting back to their respective constituents. Such negotiations may conclude either by reaching a mutually acceptable agreement on the issues raised or, possibly, a failure to agree resulting in a breakdown of negotiations. Such an impasse may be resolved through further discussion, mediation/arbitration or use of sanctions, such as industrial action.

Whether or not the negotiating process reaches a successful conclusion depends on a number of factors. Most importantly, such issues like the willingness to compromise, the bargaining skills of both sides (including their persuasive abilities) and ultimately, the power balance between parties will all impact on the final outcome of the negotiation (Hawkins, 1979). It is important to note that negotiating is an ongoing process not limited to one particular issue or time. All parties will generally be concerned with the establishment of enduring and stable relations. The long-term relationship between both parties is often treated as more important than the particular issue upon which a single negotiating process is focused. Frequently, the maintenance of this relationship takes precedence over achieving a short-term 'victory'. Indeed, bargaining 'adversaries' such as trade union officials and personnel managers can, over time, build up a close working relationship which can be very facilitative in the resolution of many troublesome issues.

At a more informal level, industrial relations negotiations can be concerned with more individualistic issues such as grievances, disciplinary action and minor claims. These types of issues involve line management and employees and/or their representatives. The mechanism for handling claims, grievances or disputes may often be outlined in a formal procedure agreement (Wallace, 1989).

The negotiating process itself will generally follow a number of predictable phases. These may be categorised as (1) preparation for negotiations, (2) bargaining and (3) follow-up action as outlined in figure 7.2 and discussed below.

Figure 7.2. The negotiating process

Phase	Activities
1. Preparation	Agree objectives and mandate
	Research
	Choose negotiating team
	Assess bargaining power
2. Bargaining	Discover positions
	Expectation structuring
	Compromise and movement
3. Post–negotiation	Document agreement/disagreement
	Clarify
	Agree action plans
	Communicate
	Implement action plans
	Review

1. PREPARATION FOR NEGOTIATIONS

This phase, in which both parties prepare for the subsequent negotiations, is an essential prerequisite for success in industrial relations negotiations (Hawkins, 1979; Scott, 1981). Within the preparation phase there are several important criteria which should be satisfied. Nierenberg (1968) suggests that effective preparation involves gathering all relevant information and retaining this for use at the bargaining table as well as ensuring that any agreements/procedures are adhered to. Such preparation requires that negotiators be familiar with the details of the case and have a clear idea of their objectives and mandate before entering the bargaining arena.

Additional criteria for effective preparation include the following: adequate administrative arrangements, appropriate research, the participation of relevant team members and the development of key negotiating skills.

Adequate administrative arrangements: These should be in place before negotiations take place. This includes ensuring all parties are aware of the issues and timing of the negotiations. It also involves the provision of adequate physical facilities including the venue (spacious, free from interruptions, convenient), seating and adjournment arrangements (non-intimidating, caucus rooms) and back-up facilities (phone, fax, typing, etc). Most industrial relations negotiations take place within the organisation. However, there may be occasions when it is appropriate to move 'off-site' to provide a more neutral atmosphere, avoid on-the-job interruptions or leaks from the negotiations.

Appropriate research: Adequate back-up research helps ensure that the presentation of a case at negotiations is well substantiated. Clearly, the extent and nature of such research will vary depending on the issues involved. Of particular relevance are indices and trends of pay increases and working conditions, and comparable settlements/agreements in other organisations. Employer associations, trade union research units and some consultancy organisatons provide such information. This information may also be elicited through informal contacts with other firms, trade unions or other bodies. Adequate research support helps focus negotiations on facts rather than discussing opinions or value judgements (Fisher and Ury, 1986). Preparatory research might also incorporate an evaluation of the repercussions of likely settlement options and 'knock-on' effects of different potential outcomes of negotiations, including industrial action.

The participation of relevant team members: Where the issue for negotiation is relatively minor, the negotiating team will normally be comprised of line managers/supervisors and shop-stewards/individual employees. In such instances the role of senior management and trade union officials is generally restricted to the provision of advice and guidance as required. In larger unionised organisations the personnel manager will normally represent management with the trade union official leading the union side in major negotiations. Alternatively, the leading role on the management side may be carried out by the chief executive with the personnel practitioner acting as key advisor. However, line managers and shop stewards may often be involved either individually on local issues or alongside the personnel manager and trade union official on more general issues.

The size and composition of the negotiating team largely depends on the issue for negotiation. It is generally suggested that, with the exception of quite minor issues, a negotiating team should comprise a minimum of two people to facilitate case presentation, record keeping and evaluation of progress (Nierenberg, 1968). Nierenberg argues that using a single negotiator facilitates clarification of responsibility, speedy decision making and prevents differences of opinion. However, he also suggests that increasing the number of representatives ensures greater technical knowledge, improved planning and judgement. This facilitates the allocation of responsibilities in presenting the case, analysis of verbal and non-verbal responses, record keeping and adequate consideration of the consequences of various settlement options and management responses. It also increases objectivity, provides a witness to the event and facilitates conclusion of the final agreement.

Key skills: Negotiators should possess a sound knowledge of the organisation and the issue at hand. They also need to be flexible and articulate in presenting arguments, be good listeners and possess the analytical ability, self-discipline, patience and stamina necessary for prolonged negotiations. A spread of interests and roles facilitates the development of strategy and tactics within the team. It provides a useful source of information and allows for different negotiating styles which may incorporate a 'devil's advocate'. Dealing specifically with the composition of management teams in industrial relations negotiations, Canning (1979) identifies three main tasks which need to be provided for within the management negotiating team:

Spokesman/Team leader: The role of the chief management representative is to present arguments, control strategy and tactics, and take major on-the-spot decisions. This role is often the responsibility of the senior personnel practitioner.

Observer: The role of the observer is to evaluate progress relative to objectives, spot key reactions, identify changes in approach and advise the chief negotiator.

Recorder: This role involves recording key points in negotiations and documenting the final agreement.

As suggested above, a key priority for parties involved in industrial relations negotiations is to ensure they have identified their objectives before entering the bargaining arena. This aspect involves having a clear idea of what they want to achieve from the collective bargaining process in general and each set of negotiations in particular. For managers, the general goals might include the maintenance of a good working relationship with employees and their representatives, maintaining managerial prerogative in certain areas, and the avoidance of industrial conflict. Particular objectives may vary according to the issue at hand and should involve specific targets, trade-off options, and resistance points. Flexible objectives are generally more appropriate than rigid ones since information may be uncovered during negotiations which can alter the substance of the management or trade union case. It is important that each party's objectives are clearly articulated and approved by constituents, particularly top management on the managerial side and trade union members/representatives on the union side. This helps ensure that each negotiating team has a clear mandate. It is also vital that objectives be agreed and communicated within the negotiating team to ensure the commitment of all members of the negotiating team to their achievement.

A central issue in agreeing negotiating objectives is deciding upon the bargaining range including the limits or parameters within which an agreement can be achieved. Negotiating inevitably means compromise and movement. The degree to which this is possible and, consequently, the scope for reaching agreement depends on the bargaining range of both parties and the degree to which these overlap. In practice, this often means establishing an ideal settlement point and also a fall-back position. At preparation stage, it is suggested that each party to the negotiations should establish its ideal settlement point and also its resistance point beyond which each party is not prepared to reach agreement (Hawkins, 1979). This process effectively prescribes the overall bargaining range and the potential area of settlement on the various issues for negotiation. This is demonstrated in the pay bargaining example as outlined in figure 7.3. Here the process of establishing bargaining parameters facilitates the identification of bargaining objectives, deciding on trade-offs and concessions, and provides a benchmark against which to evaluate progress. In this example it is clear that agreement between the management and trade union teams is only possible where resistance points (fall-back positions) overlap, that is in the 2–4 per cent pay range. A settlement is not possible outside this range unless one of the parties alters its position. If this does not happen, then the parties are in conflict over the issue and industrial action may ensue.

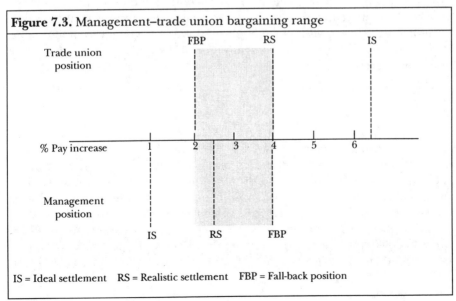

Figure 7.3. Management–trade union bargaining range

IS = Ideal settlement   RS = Realistic settlement   FBP = Fall-back position

Another key factor for parties entering industrial relations negotiations is the issue of *bargaining power*. It is imperative that each party has an accurate evaluation of both their own and the other party's relative bargaining power before entering negotiations. Cole (1988) suggests that bargaining power may be interpreted as the degree to which one party can achieve its negotiating goals despite the opposition of the other side. Relative bargaining power will significantly influence the outcome of industrial relations negotiations since the balance of settlement will normally favour the party with the greatest bargaining power. The amount of bargaining power which a party possesses depends on a range of factors both external and internal to the negotiations process. The general economic and business environment will have a major impact. For example, high levels of unemployment and depressed economic climate may place trade unions in a relatively poor power position in bargaining on pay or related matters. In contrast, a full order book will favour a union claim for bonus payments as management will be keen to meet production targets. Bargaining power will also be influenced by the relative skill and ability of the negotiators and the degree to which they have prepared their case.

While it is not always easy to obtain an accurate picture of another party's resistance point or fall-back position, negotiators need to be aware that this information is important. The extent to which such information is available will often depend on the levels of trust that exist between both parties and the effectiveness of their relationship to date. It is also useful to evaluate the level of commitment of the other party and its constituents to achieving their stated objectives. Much of the negotiations process involves rhetorical arguments indicating the level of feeling on a particular issue. Much of this bluff and rhetoric is aimed at convincing the other side that one's resistance (fall-back position) is higher than it actually is to encourage the other party to make concessions. An accurate perception of actual fall-back positions indicates how far either side can go without risking breakdown in negotiations. It also helps if both parties weigh up the advantages and disadvantages of varying concession levels.

2. THE BARGAINING PHASE

Strategy and Tactics for Industrial Relations Negotiations

The pre-negotiations issues discussed above will help identify and articulate each party's general approach to the subsequent negotiations. In addressing the actual conduct of negotiations a key issue for the parties involves adopting an overall negotiating strategy and selecting complementary negotiating tactics to use during the actual bargaining phase. The development of an overall negotiating strategy incorporates decisions on the general approach to be adopted in the negotiations. For example, one party might adopt an aggressive or defensive approach in the negotiations. Negotiating tactics refer to the various techniques which are implemented to achieve this strategy. For example, if one party wanted to achieve its particular objectives without undue confrontation, the resulting tactics might involve placing issues which are less likely to be disputed at the top of the agenda. These might then be easily agreed during the early stages of bargaining, thereby establishing a conciliatory/friendly tone for the subsequent negotiations for the discussion of subsequent, more contentious issues. Clearly, there is a range of tactics which may be adopted in industrial relations negotiations. Some of the more commonly used approaches are discussed below.

Agenda and timing: At the very outset the structuring of the agenda may allow one side to have an advantage in negotiations. It was suggested above that either party might create a conciliatory atmosphere by placing simple non-contentious issues at the top of the agenda and begin by making concessions on these. When a major issue is subsequently discussed, the party which made the early concessions might then 'throw down the gauntlet', asking the other side to make 'similar' concessions. Alternatively, a crucial issue may be placed first with a stipulation that agreement must be reached on this issue before any discussion can take place on other agenda items. This approach can serve to pressurise the other party, which may be more concerned with subsequent matters on the agenda. The structure of the agenda may also be used to put time pressures on the other party by placing issues crucial to them at the bottom, giving limited time for their discussion and possibly ensuring their deferral. Lastly, it is important to note that management–trade union negotiations are generally expected to be tough, drawn-out affairs, and concessions should not be made too early/easily leading the other party to infer that even better settlement levels can be obtained.

Hard and soft: While the setting of the negotiation agenda is one good way of having control over negotiations, another popular tactic used is to alternate between what are known as 'hard' and 'soft' approaches. This happens when different members of the negotiating team, vary their style of discussion, at one stage being aggressive and at others taking a more conciliatory approach. These roles may often be divided up between members of the negotiating team with one giving no quarter while the other infers that there may be room for compromise. The objective of this tactic is to make any concession offered by the softer partner appear more attractive than they otherwise would to the other party in the negotiations.

Bottom line: This is an approach where, for example, management try to convince the other party of the seriousness of their stance by outlining the implications of the union claim on factors like costs, competitiveness, survival, etc. This may be achieved by using financial information to demonstrate relative ability to pay or by bringing the chief executive into the negotiations to demonstrate the strength of feeling on the issue.

<u>Split the opposition:</u> This is a negotiating technique whereby one party attempts to undermine the apparent unity of the other party by exposing different positions or feelings on issues within the other team. Probing questions may be used to uncover these differences. Any subsequent conflict within a team may result in this party having to withdraw, regroup its forces and reconsider its position.

<u>Probe and question:</u> If a negotiating team is well prepared, it can be in a good position to exploit the benefits that may be derived from probing and actively questioning the other party. Using this tactic, a team can clarify the factual basis of the other side's position, sometimes with very beneficial results. It may be useful to question the validity of comparisons or reliability of data used by the other party. If this questioning points to weaknesses in the other party's case they may be forced to reconsider their position as discussed above. Ideally, such probing should be done sensitively so that the other party does not lose too much face and so that they do not feel 'backed into a corner', an experience that may cause them to react aggressively or irrationally. Keeping in mind that the longer-term relationship must be considered, adjourning negotiations may be useful, and is sometimes necessary in order to allow for changes in position and to give an opportunity to one party to 'save face' on a particular issue. This consideration is often referred to as giving the 'losing' party their 'busfare home'.

<u>Fait accompli:</u> This is a technique sometimes used by management which involves implementing an initiative before it has secured full agreement through the industrial relations process. A common example of this technique is when new technology is introduced, before such changes have been negotiated. Such an approach represents a calculated risk, the implications of which must be carefully evaluated by management in advance.

7.2.2. STAGES IN BARGAINING

The above tactics represent several of the main approaches available to negotiators during the process of bargaining. It is also important, however, to examine the different phases that go to make up this process. It is generally the case that collective bargaining interactions often pass through a number of identifiable phases, namely (1) opening; (2) expectation structuring; (3) offer, concession, movement; (4) agreement/disagreement; and (5) close as outlined in figure 7.4.

When the bargaining process is initiated, both parties are obliged to ensure that negotiations begin and proceed in a business-like way. During this initial period it is traditional for the management team to open the proceedings and then for both parties to articulate their respective positions. This may involve management referring to the subject matter for negotiation, the details of any claim served upon them and their position on such issues. Alternatively, the union/employee team may seek to clarify or substantiate their position/claim. Either way the approach and tone adopted by the management and union/employee teams during this opening period will influence the subsequent bargaining climate. During this opening stage both parties will attempt to establish each other's positions, assess the degree to which movement and concession is possible and predict the likelihood of achieving their respective negotiating objectives.

Figure 7.4. Stages in bargaining

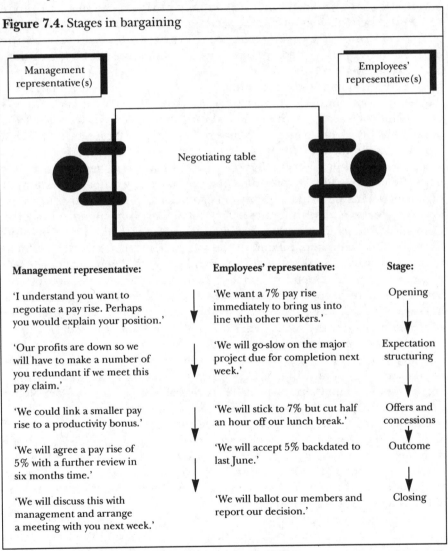

Management representative:	Employees' representative:	Stage:
'I understand you want to negotiate a pay rise. Perhaps you would explain your position.'	'We want a 7% pay rise immediately to bring us into line with other workers.'	Opening
'Our profits are down so we will have to make a number of you redundant if we meet this pay claim.'	'We will go-slow on the major project due for completion next week.'	Expectation structuring
'We could link a smaller pay rise to a productivity bonus.'	'We will stick to 7% but cut half an hour off our lunch break.'	Offers and concessions
'We will agree a pay rise of 5% with a further review in six months time.'	'We will accept 5% backdated to last June.'	Outcome
'We will discuss this with management and arrange a meeting with you next week.'	'We will ballot our members and report our decision.'	Closing

Source: Gunnigle et al., 1992.

After the opening stage of the bargaining process a series of interactions known as 'expectation structuring' often takes place. During this stage both parties attempt to convince the other party as to the logic of their position and the depth of their commitment to that position, while also perhaps attempting to highlight deficiencies in the other party's position. Each party to the negotiations thus attempts to structure or influence the other party's expectations and tries to convince them to accept whatever concessions are offered. For example, the management team in pay negotiations may emphasise factors like the poor economic outlook, the need to retain competitiveness, danger of redundancies, etc. In so doing they attempt to shape the union's expectations by painting a bleak picture of the organisation's operating conditions, thus increasing the likelihood of their accepting a lower level of increase.

The 'offer, concession, movement' phase generally begins after both parties have attempted, at least in some way, to structure each other's expectations. This stage is where the real bargaining actually takes place. Here some initial offers and concessions may be proffered by either party. This is a critical phase in the overall negotiating process. It is felt that correct timing is absolutely crucial in making offers/concessions and, as suggested above, it is normally advisable to take some time before making any major concessions. If such concessions are made too early in negotiations, the other party may press for even greater ones during subsequent bargaining. Any movement or offer from a team's opening position should be carefully weighed up in terms of its long- and short-term implications. At this stage adjournments may be useful in order to allow both parties to evaluate progress to date. After some time it will become clear if agreement is possible, whether the parties will have to refer back to their respective constituents, or if a breakdown in negotiations is imminent. In any case, the details of the issues discussed, the offers and concessions made, the agreement reached or reasons for breakdown in negotiations should be carefully recorded.

If negotiations do break down, then some channel of communication between parties should be kept open, if at all possible. In the event of a breakdown, it is important that neither party walks away from the bargaining table without at least some agreement as to how communication will be reinitiated and by whom. Again, the idea that long-term relations may be more important than the issues at hand during a particular set of negotiations is an important principle for both parties to keep in mind. For this reason the parties to negotiations should be keen to avoid damaging conflict or breakdowns and be prepared to compromise on certain issues for the benefit of that longer-term perspective.

Both parties are likely to recognise when negotiations are beginning to draw to a close. This stage will generally involve finalising the agreement, issues for further negotiation, or details of breakdown. It is important that adequate time should be set aside for this stage in negotiations, as there is a common tendency to rush through this closing stage in negotiations. Each party should be clear on the substance and interpretation of the agreements and on their various commitments during subsequent implementation of what was agreed during negotiations. Details of future meetings or review procedures should be clearly specified and agreed before the parties leave the negotiating table.

3. THE POST–NEGOTIATION PHASE

Once the negotiations have reached an end, the parties involved will normally report back on the outcome: the union reporting back to its members and the management team reporting back to senior and, possibly, line management. This post-negotiation stage will normally review the implementation of the agreement(s) and the overall implications of the outcome of the negotiations for industrial relations and future negotiations. The way in which the agreement is communicated to employees should also be agreed upon as well as deciding on how any administrative obligations should be carried out. It is useful to document all aspects of the negotiations carefully for further reference. Details of implementation should be worked out and responsibilities allocated. Equally, both parties may be keen to review and assess the lessons learned from the negotiations experience.

7.3. TOWARDS EFFECTIVE NEGOTIATION

The negotiations process involves interactions between people of varying personalities in different organisational contexts. Therefore, it is often impossible to predict the ways in which such negotiations will be carried out or, indeed, the kinds of outcomes to which they will give rise. Persistent problems in negotiations may arise for numerous reasons, such as inflexibility and unwillingness to compromise, abrasive style and language, or poor preparation and knowledge. Such problems may be tackled by improving the competence of the negotiating team. It is always worthwhile to ensure that the members of the negotiating team have been selected carefully, are experienced and are appropriately trained. Writers have consistently emphasised the importance of negotiating skills as a means of achieving success in negotiations (Atkinson, 1977; Nierenberg, 1968; Scott, 1981). Other theorists would suggest, however, that problems in negotiation are not caused by incompetent negotiators so much as by inherent flaws in the process itself. It has been suggested that the entire negotiation process needs to undergo re-evaluation (Fisher and Ury, 1986). A general criticism has been the perceived dominance of distributive bargaining with its emphasis on dividing limited resources. It is sometimes felt that this approach encourages both parties to develop adversary positions believing that any gains can only be made by inflicting losses on the other party. Distributive bargaining reflects the very essence of the traditional pluralist industrial relations model: claims, offers, bluff, threats, compromise, movement, agreement or conflict. Approaches based on a more integrative/co-operative bargaining (also known as the joint problem-solving approach) are often seen as a more attractive alternative

211

(particularly from a managerial perspective) with their emphasis on a collaborative approach, exploring common ground and seeking solutions of mutual benefit to both parties.

The work by Fisher and Ury (1986) on developing an alternative approach to negotiations has been one of the most influential in critically evaluating the negotiations process. They suggest that traditional haggling approaches force the parties to take opposing positions and adopt bargaining stances designed to justify and achieve that position. They feel that such 'positional bargaining' produces unwise agreements, is ineffecient, and endangers the ongoing relationship. Alternatively, Fisher and Ury prefer a 'principled' approach to negotiations based on the merits of the case. They suggest that a move away from positional bargaining will help reduce traditional barriers to agreement and bring both parties closer to the joint solution-seeking approach.

It is doubtful, however, that the traditional bargaining aproaches will disappear, despite the criticism they have received. Both the conventional, adversarial approach and the more co-operative alternative tend to be appropriate in different circumstances. Given the structure of organisations and their inherent potential for the emergence of conflicts of interest, it seems inevitable that distributive bargaining will continue to be a common feature of workplace negotiations. In fact, recent research evidence suggests that the pluralist industrial relations tradition continues to characterise industrial relations practice in many Irish organisations (Gunnigle, 1992; Gunnigle and Morley, 1993; Roche, 1990a; Turner, 1993).

7.3.1. INDUSTRIAL CONFLICT

There are several explanations as to why industrial conflict occurs. In the introductory chapter to this text it was suggested that the pluralist and unitarist frameworks are useful models for explaining industrial relations interactions and industrial conflict.[2] The pluralist model suggests that organisations comprise of a range of individuals and interest groups, each of whom have different interests and priorities. The interaction of these competing interests and groups require the establishment of institutional arrangements which manage these competing interests to achieve a level of bargained compromise, which allows the organisation to conduct its normal business. This pluralist model accepts that conflict will occur because the needs and objectives of various interest groups will clash on occasion (Fox, 1966, 1974a). Allen (1971) suggests that the structure of the employment relationship which emphasises management's need for productivity, cost effectiveness and change, is often at odds with employee needs for security and attractive rewards, thus causing inevitable conflict of interests. The Marxist explanation goes further suggesting that alienation caused by the organisation of work within the capitalist framework, involving divisions along labour, ownership and hierarchical lines, makes conflict between labour and management endemic to industrial organisations (Hyman, 1976).

The unitarist framework represents a very different approach. It is based on the premise that organisations are cohesive and harmonious units, and that all members of the organisation (management and employees) share common goals. Also according to this perspective, there is one source of authority, namely management (Fox, 1966, 1974a). Management and employees are seen as having the same interests with conflict occurring only as a result of misunderstandings or due to the efforts of troublemakers. This model does not accept the enduring inevitability of industrial conflict as a structural feature of organisations, since all parties in the organisation are assumed to have one set of key mutual interests and are expected to accept managerial authority for the 'common good' of the organisation. Unitarism is predominantly managerial in perspective and has been used to explain features on industrial relations practice such as opposition to trade union recognition (Gunnigle, 1992c; Marchington, 1982).

It would appear that, in practice, some degree of conflict is inherent in industrial relations and that difficulties will arise between management and workers. Such difficulties are not always harmful and need not necessarily lead to industrial conflict. Indeed, in many instances conflict can have decidedly positive effects by, for example, leading to positive changes in management practice (e.g. better training opportunities) or ensuring the scrapping of an out-of-date work rule. Although much of the conflict that occurs between management and employees may not become manifest, it is a source of ongoing concern to all groups within an organisation. In particular, much of the management focus in industrial relations will be concerned with eliminating or reducing sources of conflict and creating mechanisms through which issues can be resolved amicably without resort to industrial action.

7.3.2. Forms of Industrial Conflict

There are two broad categories of industrial conflict: (1) explicit and organised industrial conflict and (2) unorganised and more implicit industrial conflict (Bean, 1976). Explicit, overt forms of industrial conflict include strikes, go-slows, withdrawal of co-operation and overtime bans. These represent organised and systematic responses by employees and representative associations. Implicit reactions include absenteeism, labour turnover, high accident levels and poor performance, and may often reflect low levels of employee satisfaction and morale.

The most visible way in which workers can demonstrate industrial conflict is to go on strike. Withdrawal of labour (or the threat of withdrawal) by employees is a powerful tool through which trade unions have sought and secured improvements in terms and conditions of employment.[3] Strikes may take different forms and arise for a variety of reasons. Official strikes are those which have been approved by the union executive. Such strikes normally take place after a series of negotiations and meetings have failed to resolve the issue and it has exhausted all stages in a dispute procedure. Such strikes, once approved, may involve large numbers of workers and last for a prolonged period. On the other hand, unofficial strikes lack official union approval and are often sparked off by a particular event or incident at workplace level. Unless subsequently granted official approval by the trade union, unofficial strikes normally last for a shorter time and involve fewer workers (Wallace, 1988a; Wallace and O'Shea, 1987).

A decision to take strike action will be based on a combination of factors. Particularly significant will be the issue at hand and the commitment of employees to using the strike weapon to achieve their particular goals. Related factors include the perceived chances of success and the power balance between the parties. Decisions on strike action will be significantly influenced by contextual factors such as the business cycle, unemployment levels and inflation. It should be noted that a decision to take strike action may involve considerable hardship for strikers through lost income and the risk of job loss. Consequently, such action is rarely taken lightly. For the union too, strike action represents a major dilemma: the prospects of success/failure must be weighed up together with implications for union membership, status and finances. Despite their headline-grabbing status, it is important to remember that strikes are relatively rare and many organisations have never experienced strike action.

7.3.3. AN OVERVIEW OF IRISH STRIKE PATTERNS

There are three central indicators used when strike activity is being analysed: (1) strike frequency (number of strikes), (2) workers involved (number of workers participating in strikes) and (3) working days lost (number of working days lost due to strike activity).[4]

Strike frequency is generally seen as a valuable indicator of strike activity, although it is perceived to have some deficiencies particularly because the use of this measure on its own forces analysts to attribute equal weight to large and small strikes (Turner, 1962). The number of workers participating in a strike is referred to as strike breadth (Kelly and Brannick, 1989). Again, while seen to be a useful indicator, this index is also felt to suffer from some deficiencies, particularly the fact that it is possible to have a drop in the number of workers involved in strikes but still have an overall increase in the number of working days lost (Kelly and Brannick, 1989; Silverman, 1970). The number of working days lost due to strike activity is generally felt to be the most informative index on strike activity. However, analyses of strike activity are most useful where all three indices of strike activity are used. The analysis of strike activity in Ireland discussed below uses these three indices of strike activity but particularly focuses on working days lost in discussing levels of strike activity in Ireland in the period 1970–90. This analysis of strike activity in Ireland relies heavily on data from University College Dublin (Kelly and Brannick) and the Department of Enterprise and Employment.

If the traditional indices of strike activity are examined (i.e. working-days lost, strike frequency and workers involved), there is clear evidence in Ireland of an upward trend in strike activity in the 1960s and 1970s, followed by a significant decline in strike activity for much of the 1980s. Towards the very end of the 1980s, however, a reversal of this trend is in evidence, with increases in strike activity being recorded in 1989 and 1990. Irish strike figures for the period from 1922 to 1991 as compiled from the UCD database on strike activity in Ireland are given in table 7.1, and the trend according to each key index is represented in figures 7.5a, 7.5b and 7.5c (Kelly and Brannick, 1989).

Figure 7.5.a, b, c Strike activities in Ireland, 1922–91

(a) Strike frequency, 1922–91

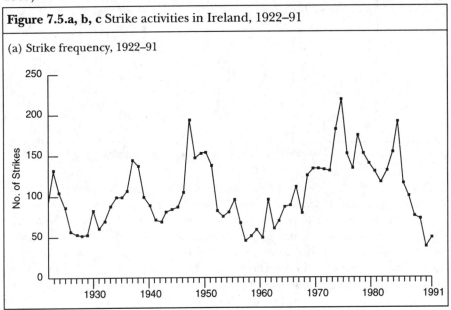

(b) Workers involved in strike activity, 1922–91

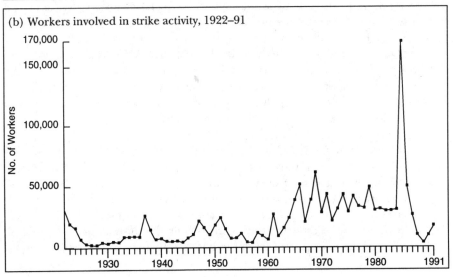

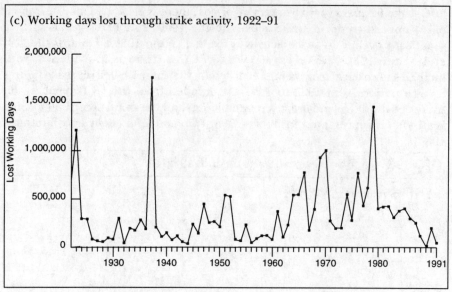

(c) Working days lost through strike activity, 1922–91

Source: UCD Database of Strike Statistics; Kelly and Brannick, 1990.

There are several factors which influence the level and pattern of strike activity. Particularly influential are: the level of economic activity (business cycle), unemployment (tightness/looseness of the labour market), industrial development, inflation (earnings) and unionisation. It will also be influenced by sectoral changes in employment (shifts in the employment share of agriculture, industry and services), and the nature and level of collective bargaining (particularly the existence of centrally agreed incomes policies).

There are two important factors which have been uncovered in an analysis of the changing patterns of strike activity in Ireland. Firstly, as Kelly and Brannick (1983) have pointed out, small numbers of large strikes have traditionally had a disproportionate effect on our aggregate strike statistics. Secondly, the same analysis by Kelly and Brannick identifies significant differences between strike patterns in the public sector and those in the private sector. On the impact of large strikes (which they define as strikes resulting in the loss of 30,000 or more days) over the twenty-year period 1960–79, Kelly and Brannick (1989) comment thus:

> Forty-three such strikes took place during the past twenty years. . . . While these strikes represent only 2 per cent of the total for the period, they involved a loss of over 5.7 million man-days or 57 per cent of all days lost due to strikes over this time. Clearly, the Irish strike pattern is extremely sensitive to this comparatively small number of large strikes and it has been an enduring feature over the 20-year period. Indeed, should these be removed from the Irish strike quantum, the result would

be a record which would show a comparatively strike-free nation in terms of workers involved and total man-days lost.

The study by Kelly and Brannick also showed that the private sector was the source of most strike activity in the 1960–86 period. However, the proportion of strike activity accounted for by the private sector was greatest during the 1960s and has been falling since with a marked increase in the proportion of strike activity accounted for by the public sector over the period (see table 7.1). In the private sector Kelly and Brannick found that manufacturing was by far the most strike-prone sector. Within this sector they identified significant changes in strike activity which reflected structural changes in Irish industry. Certain industrial sectors, particularly printing and paper, and metals and engineering became increasingly strike prone while others, notably textiles and furniture and woodwork, experienced less strike activity. In the public sector Kelly and Brannick found that much of the strike activity has been concentrated among a relatively small number of organisations. They identified nine organisations that accounted for 62 per cent of all strikes, 85 per cent of workers involved and 86 per cent of working days lost in the public sector during the 1960–84 period.

Table 7.1. Public and private sector strike activity, 1960–92 (in %)

	Strike frequency		Workers involved		Working days lost	
	Public sector	Private sector	Public sector	Private sector	Public sector	Private sector
1960–69	17.9	82.1	36.5	63.5	24.2	75.8
1970–79	18.3	81.7	22.6	67.4	37.9	62.1
1980–89	29.1	70.9	68.9	31.1	37.7	62.3
1990–92	47.5	52.5	67.1	32.9	31.9	68.1

Source: Brannick and Doyle, 1994.

Table 7.2. Working days lost—strikes, 1946–92

Year	Working days lost
1946	150,018
1956	48,089
1966	783,635
1970	1,007,714
1975	295,716
1980	412,118
1982	434,253
1984	386,421
1986	315,500
1988	130,000
1990	204,000
1991	82,960
1992	189,623

Source: Department of Labour/UCD.

Recession, product market difficulties and unemployment are seen as the major influences on the extent to which strike activity becomes likely. In the Irish context, the 1980s' decline in strike activity is generally explained in this way. However, management interventions at the workplace level also have some impact. In contrasting the strike records of the two major sources of foreign investment, British and US companies, Kelly and Brannick (1985, 1988) found that US companies were the more strike-prone MNC sector in the 1960s, but that their record improved dramatically since the 1970s to a stage where US MNCs now have low levels of strike activity. In contrast, the strike record of British companies has deteriorated dramatically. The reasons for this deterioration are largely attributed to product market difficulties. In relation to the contrasting improvement of the strike record of US companies, Kelly and Brannick offer two reasons: (1) the changed industrial composition of US MNCs (most are now high-technology companies in the 'newer' industrial sectors, particularly electronics and chemicals, as opposed to labour-intensive companies producing standardised products in the 1960s); (2) US MNCs are predominantly based in the electronics sector, which has been to the forefront in developing innovative and proactive employee relations and HR strategies and policies.

The relative impact of official and unofficial strikes is another important issue relating to strike action. In their study of unofficial strikes in Ireland Wallace and O' Shea (1987) found that there has been a dramatic reduction in unofficial strikes since the mid-1970s (see table 7.3). Since 1982 approximately 40 per cent of strikes have been unofficial (29 per cent in 1987), comparing with an average of 66 per cent in the mid–1970s. Since unofficial strikes are normally of shorter duration and involve less employees, this has meant that unofficial strikes now account for a very small proportion of working days lost due to strike activity. In the years 1985 and 1986 the figures were 10 per cent and 6 per cent respectively (Wallace, 1988a; Wallace and O'Shea, 1987).

Table 7.3. Official and unofficial strikes: frequency and working days lost, 1980–91

Year	No. of unofficial strikes	No. of official strikes	Working days lost in unofficial strikes	Working days lost in official strikes
1980	81	51	184,000	219,500
1981	61	56	131,000	305,000
1982	55	76	74,000	363,000
1983	58	93	58,000	253,000
1984	75	116	51,000	313,000
1985	45	70	43,000	394,000
1986	38	62	20,500	295,500
1987	22	54	25,000	235,000
1988	26	46	6,500	123,500
1989	13	28	11,600	29,800
1990	16	35	6,800	196,900
1991	13	39	9,300	73,600

Source: Department of Labour, 1992.

7.3.4. OTHER FORMS OF INDUSTRIAL ACTION

Though less dramatic, other forms of overt action can be equally successful while at the same time not involving the hardships of strike action. For example, go-slows, overtime bans and withdrawal of co-operation can be used effectively by employees. These actions can put considerable pressure on management to move towards resolution while protecting employee income and not jeopardising their job security to the same extent as in undertaking strike action. Again, the effectiveness of such measures depends on organisational context (e.g. an overtime ban is unlikely to meet with much success when order-books are empty and production requirements are low). Another form of industrial conflict is industrial sabotage. However, there is a dearth of information on the incidence of industrial sabotage as a form of industrial conflict. Nevertheless, it would appear that industrial sabotage has been and remains an important form of industrial conflict. A lock-out by management involves preventing the workforce from attending at work. It represents the equivalent of strike action by employers.

There is also little information on more implicit forms of industrial action. A particular problem with implicit forms of action is the difficulty in differentiating between implicit action taken as a form of industrial conflict from implicit action which may occur for some other reason. Particular cases in point are absenteeism and labour turnover. Absenteeism has been defined by the Irish Business and Employers' Confederation (IBEC) as 'all absences from work other than paid holidays'. It affects the internal supply of labour to the firm in the sense that an organisation which has an absenteeism problem finds itself understaffed and unable to cope with demands made upon it. Absenteeism is a serious cost factor in Irish industry. Data from the Irish Management Institute (IMI) estimates that average absenteeism rates range from 7 to 13 per cent across industry sectors, and its cost in terms of money lost is higher than for total time lost due to official and unofficial strikes. Absenteeism derives from a range of factors which include (a) ability to attend work (affected by illness, sex role responsibilities, age and transportation difficulties) and (b) the motivation to attend. The motivation to attend is a function of satisfaction with the job situation (job content, variety, autonomy and discretion inherent in the tasks performed), internal and external pressures to attend. Internal pressures to attend include a 'sense of duty' to always attend wherever possible (despite sickness in some cases). External pressures to attend include the organisation's incentive system, the extent to which discipline or dismissal is likely to follow repeated absences and the extent to which there are other job opportunities available in the local labour market. It has been noted that aggregate level absences fall in a period of recession and rise in periods of business prosperity.

Labour wastage/turnover refers to the number of persons who leave an organisation within a specified time period. Reasons for leaving may include resignation, redundancy, retirement and dismissal. Bowey classifies the factors generating wastage into 'pull' and 'push' factors. 'Pull' factors are those factors which attract employees to another organisation while 'push' factors cause employees to leave involuntarily. 'Pull' factors identified include moving for higher earnings, moving to further one's career and the attraction of alternative job opportunities. 'Push' factors identified include leaving to avoid strains arising from interpersonal conflict, 'running down' (reducing headcount) of an organisation and poor socialisation induction.

7.3.5. CONFLICT RESOLUTION

While industrial conflict can be seen as a useful catalyst for solving organisational problems, it is important that such conflict remains within acceptable limits so that damage to organisational and national performance does not occur. All parties involved in industrial relations have an important role to play in conflict handling and resolution. For example, an integral part of the role of line managers and shop-stewards is to effectively handle disputes and grievances which arise at shop-floor level. Top management will generally have responsibility for the establishment of an organisational climate which fosters and values good management–employee relations. This role will incorporate the development of effective policies and procedures to handle conflict issues which arise in association with employees and their representative organisations. The specialist personnel function will normally be responsible for advising top management on optimal industrial relations strategies and developing appropriate procedures and practices. It may also provide training, advice and guidance to line management in handling workplace issues. Trade unions undertake a similar role on the employee side.

As mentioned above, industrial conflict should not be viewed as having a necessarily negative impact on industrial relations. Industrial conflict can have certain positive effects. It allows employees to highlight issues of concern and facilitates change and development in the employment relationship. Possibly the most widespread response to conflict in the workplace has been the development of joint mechanisms to discuss and resolve issues of difference. Such institutionalisation of conflict involves the development of agreed practices and procedures for handling issues and is most clearly manifested in the significance of collective bargaining and trade union organisation (Jackson, 1982).

The institutionalisation of conflict through the development of appropriate procedures reflects an implicit acceptance that issues of conflict will arise, and is characteristic of the pluralist model discussed in chapter 1. In creating institutions (such as collective bargaining) and procedures for handling industrial relations and industrial conflict the parties involved seek to create a framework through which the parties can interact, argue, disagree and agree while allowing for the ongoing operation of the business. Industrial relations procedures of various kinds have, over the last two decades, become a pervasive feature of workplace industrial relations in Ireland (Wallace, 1989). These can vary between organisations but will generally provide for the orderly resolution of grievances, disputes and disciplinary issues, and provide an operating framework for management–union negotiations.

7.4. THE HANDLING OF GRIEVANCES AND DISPUTES

'Grievance' is usually used to describe individual employee complaints whereas 'disputes' generally refers to collective grievances based on claims of a group of workers. In practice both terms are used interchangeably with any differences only applying to the level at which an issue enters the procedure (Wallace, 1989). Generally speaking, in an industrial relations context a grievance is defined as a formal expression of employee dissatisfaction.

It is almost inevitable, given the nature of organisations, that grievances will arise from time to time. Employees will, at some stage encounter issues which cause them concern and which, as a result, may be voiced as a grievance. The vast majority of workplace grievances and disputes are handled at shop-floor level by line management and employees/employee representatives. It is particularly important that managers are aware of the importance of good grievance handling and of the positive contribution that this can make to the promotion of good industrial relations. Should employees have problems which they wish to raise with management, these should be handled as promptly and actively as possible. The non-handling of grievances may give rise to frustration which can permeate through to other employees and promote an uneasy working environment in which disputes and poor industrial relations can arise.

It is difficult for managers to anticipate all potential disputes and grievances. The number and range of potential sources of grievances and disputes is infinite. However, while it is impossible to legislate for all grievances that may arise in the workplace, there are some issues management can be actively aware of in order to ensure effective grievance handling. Of particular importance are the following:

Management checklist for grievance handling

- Management should make every effort to understand the nature of and the reasons for disputes and grievances.
- Management should establish a policy which sets out an orderly and effective framework for handling disputes/grievances.
- All levels of management should be aware of the key influence which grievance handling has on industrial and company performance generally.
- Line management, particularly first-level supervision, must be aware of their key role in effective grievance handling.

An initial step is for management to try and understand the nature of disputes and grievances. This facilitates an appreciation of the wide variety of issues which can cause disputes/grievances and highlights the importance of prevention. A useful approach is to analyse the conditions which are most likely to give rise to serious disputes/grievances. These might include poor working conditions, unsafe work practices, discrimination, job insecurity, inadequate wages, and unrealistic rules and regulations. Of course the list is endless and the types of issues that do arise tend to depend on the nature of the organisation. However, a primary concern of management and employees in dealing with disputes and grievances at organisation level is the issue of developing and operating policies and procedures in the area of dispute and grievance handling.

7.4.1. GRIEVANCE AND DISPUTES PROCEDURES

It is considered important that organisations have a formal procedure outlining the stages through which grievances and disputes should be processed. Of course, many of the less serious grievances are best handled in an informal setting. Nevertheless, it is always useful to have formal procedures in place in case a serious grievance does arise. Such procedures are characteristic of large, mostly unionised, companies and often form part of a procedural agreement. These procedures have also found their way into non-unionised companies in the form of 'parallel procedures'. Parallel procedures usually incorporate the main features of grievance procedures in unionised companies but are unilaterally determined by management.

Developing formal procedures in any area of industrial relations involves establishing a framework for handling particular issues and inevitably involves some potential drawbacks. However, it is suggested that a degree of procedural formalisation is necessary if key industrial relations issues are to be effectively and consistently handled (Wallace, 1989). Hawkins (1979) highlights a number of benefits of procedural formality in industrial relations, namely (1) increased clarity in industrial relations interactions; (2) prevention of misunderstandings and arguments over interpretation; (3) ease of communication and (4) increased fairness and consistency in application. Grievance and disputes procedures in industrial relations usually incorporate a number of common features of which the following are important:

– The procedure should be in writing to avoid ambiguity.
– The grievance should be raised at the appropriate level. Usually the grievance is first discussed between the employee and his immediate superior.
– An appeal mechanism should be provided so that decisions can be appealed if agreement is not reached at a particular level.
– Time limits on each stage of the procedure should be specified. If an issue has not been dealt with, the next stage of the procedure may be invoked. The procedure should be simple and rapid in operation.
– An employee must have the right to be represented by his union or by an

employee of his choice at the various stages of the procedure.

– The decision should be deferred to a third party if agreement cannot be reached in-house.

– A 'peace clause' restraining the use of industrial action prior to the agreed procedures being exhausted should also be incorporated.

The main aim of a grievance procedure should be to settle the grievance fairly and as near as possible to the point of origin, emphasising the preventive nature of the grievance procedure in stopping the escalation of the matter into a serious industrial dispute (see figure 7.6).

Figure 7.6. Grievance procedure

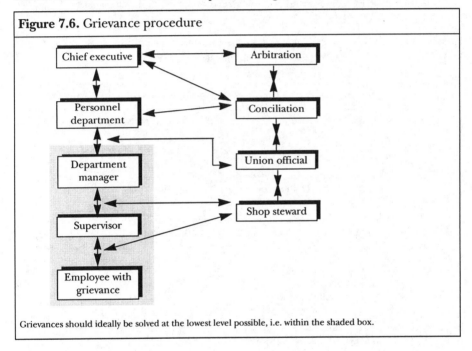

Grievances should ideally be solved at the lowest level possible, i.e. within the shaded box.

Obviously it is beneficial to all parties if grievance and dispute procedures operate effectively. In order for this to happen, both management and employees (including trade unions) should be fully committed to the procedure and know how to operate and enforce it. Line managers may avail of the services of the specialist personnel function in establishing effective procedures and monitoring their operation while employees may rely on the guidance of their shop-steward or trade union official. Clearly, the approaches adopted in handling grievances and disputes will vary considerably between organisations. An example of one company's policy is outlined in box 7.1.

Most problems or complaints raised by employees should, ideally, be handled by the immediate supervisor without recourse to a formal disputes/grievance procedure. However, any issues that do warrant greater consideration may be handled through a more formal written and agreed

223

Box 7.1. Sample company policy on disputes/grievances (pharmaceutical company)

The company recognises that employees have a legitimate interest in the affairs of the enterprise and thus have a right to be concerned and informed about issues which affect them.

Employees have a right to bring matters which concern them to the attention of management.

Management and employee opinions may be at variance on occasion. In such instances management will strive to understand the employee(s) viewpoint, explain the management position and seek a mutually acceptable solution.

Management will give consideration to matters brought to their attention by employees and action these matters in an appropriate, effective and equitable manner.

Box 7.2. Sample grievance and disputes procedure (engineering company)

Stage	Nature of grievance	Procedural level	
		Management	**Employees/ Trade union**
1	Grievance concerning local work rules or employment conditions affecting an individual or small work group	Immediate superior	employee(s)/ concerned
2	(a) Any issue which has remained unresolved at stage 1 (b) Grievance or claim where the issue has direct implications for a group of workers on a departmental or section basis	Department/ section manager	Employee(s) concerned and employee representation
3	(a) Any issue which has gone through the appropriate lower stages unresolved (b) Grievance or claim with company-wide implications	Personnel manager and/or line manager(s)	Employee(s) concerned and/or shop employee representatives (incl. union official)
4	An unresolved issue which has been through the appropriate lower stages	Third-party investigation: Rights Commissioner; Labour Relations Commission	
5	Any issue which remains unresolved after stage 4	Labour Court Investigation: Employment Appeals Tribunal	

procedure. A grievance/disputes procedure will normally be in writing. It should be simple and easy to operate, and aim to handle disputes and grievances fairly and consistently.

Formal procedures generally follow an upward path from one level to the next and, ultimately, if agreement cannot be reached, to external conciliation or arbitration. A sample grievance and disputes procedure in a unionised organisation is given in box 7.2. The same principles apply in non-union organisations. Indeed, it is possibly more important that non-unionised firms have effective grievance and disputes procedures, since employees in these organisations may have less internal support in the processing of issues. Many of the larger non-unionised companies also place considerable emphasis on the rapid and effective handling of employee grievances (Foulkes, 1980; Toner, 1987).

When such procedures are put into operation it is generally desirable that grievance and dispute issues are handled as near their source as possible with the major responsibility resting with line management. Delays in handling issues can become an additional source of agitation. It is generally advisable to operate time limits which are both realistic (allowing reasonable time and opportunity to handle the issues adequately) and fair (avoiding unnecessary delay and frustration).

The specialist personnel function has an important role to play in establishing effective procedures, monitoring their operation, dealing with more serious issues and helping line management handle issues in their area. This involves ensuring that line managers have adequate skills and knowledge to carry out their role effectively.

7.4.2. THE GRIEVANCE INTERVIEW

The vast majority of grievance and disputes issues arise at employee/supervisor level. It is therefore important that senior management delegate adequate authority to enable supervisors to handle issues raised at this level. Equally, supervisors must be willing and able to make decisions and act upon them at this level, thus preventing their further progression through the procedure. When an issue is raised, the initial managerial task is to listen carefully and attempt to understand the dimensions of a problem in a considered way. Responding impulsively or prejudging the issue without having the full facts is potentially a very damaging reaction and should be avoided. Although managers may not attach as much importance to the issue as the employee(s) concerned, they should appreciate that if employees feel strongly enough to raise issues in the first place then they equally merit that management listen, understand and take appropriate action as necessary.

Having taken the time to consider the issue, the manager concerned should take time to consider the issue, consult other people as necessary and respond to the employee within a reasonable period of time. Responses to employee grievances should take account of whatever implications may arise for other employees, the extent to which a precedent is being created and consistency with company policy. If the response is negative (i.e. if the manager decides that the employee has no grounds for feeling aggrieved, or that for some reason it is impossible to solve the problem at this level) the further stages in the procedure should be outlined. The manager involved should ensure that any responses are correct in the circumstances and explain these to employees.

Procedures are an aid to management and employees in dealing with contentious issues, but the importance of informality should not be overlooked and even where procedures exist it plays an important role in workplace industrial relations. Issues will sometimes arise which need a different approach to that set down by formal procedure. For example, an employee may be reluctant to raise a personal problem with his supervisor, and may bring the matter to the attention of a more senior manager. Procedures should not prohibit these informal but useful interactions. Informality is an inherent part of workplace industrial relations and will continue to play a key role. However, such departures from procedure should be an exception and the role of the supervisor should be maintained in handling the great majority of workplace issues.

Another important aspect in the effective handling of disputes and grievances is the need to document each case carefully. Some written records need to be maintained in relation to grievances or disputes which progress above the first stage in a procedure. Some organisations require that issues entering the procedure above the first stage must be served in writing with details of the issue and the employee(s) concerned. This helps clarify the exact nature of the claim or grievance and helps avoid misunderstandings. Such records also provide management with useful information on trends and the effectiveness of procedures. Documentation is therefore important, but should not be excessive, leading to unneccessary red tape.

7.4.3. EXTERNAL REFERRAL

It is not always possible to find a solution at the level of the company, and in some cases the issue at hand may be referred to the offices of an independent third party. The various third-party institutions were outlined in our discussion on the role of the State in chapter 3 of this text. Conciliation normally refers to the introduction of a third party that tries to guide the parties towards a solution but does not make a final decision. Arbitration involves referral to a third party, which makes a final decision on the merits of the case (Kelly, 1989b). In Ireland most arbitration decisions are non-binding, though there are exceptions (e.g. certain Labour Court decisions [such as an Equality Officer's decision] and in areas of the public sector). Arbitration involves the evaluation of both parties' positions and the issuing of a decision based on their respective merits. More recently, there seems to be some interest in pendulum-type arbitration, which involves choosing either of the final positions of the parties. This approach is based on the rationale that traditional arbitration does not encourage the conflicting parties to compromise prior to third-party referral, whereas the pendulum variety encourages them to take more reasonable positions which give the greatest chance of winning the arbitrator's approval.

The accepted practice has traditionally been that organisations only refer cases externally when all internal efforts have been unsuccessful. However, as we saw in chapter 3, John Horgan, a former Chairman of the Labour Court, feels that increases in the number of cases being referred externally (particularly to the Labour Court) reflect a greater reluctance on behalf of managements and unions to compromise at local level. He feels that this has resulted in an over-reliance on third parties which, he suggests, is bad for industrial relations (Horgan, 1985).

Grievance and disputes procedures normally contain a provision that no form of industrial action be taken by either party until all stages of the procedure have been exhausted and that even then a period of notice be given before such action is initiated. Effectively operated, this ensures that both parties have ample opportunity to settle issues either through direct discussion or by opting for third-party referral. Such terms should not be used unreasonably to delay the processing of claims and grievances, as this may give rise to employee frustration resulting in breaches of procedure and, possibly, unofficial action (Wallace, 1989). Lastly, it should be emphasised that workplace procedures are merely a facilitator of good industrial relations and will be of little use where the basic industrial relations climate is poor.

7.5. DISCIPLINE ADMINISTRATION

Clearly, organisations will seek to establish and maintain what they consider acceptable standards or norms in areas like employee performance, conduct, etc. When employees breach such standards management will, ultimately, seek to take some form of disciplinary action. Discipline in the workplace setting may be defined as any action taken by management against an employee or group of employees who have failed to conform to the rules established by management or jointly agreed within the organisation. As with disputes and grievances, the issue of disciplinary procedures and their administration is an inherent aspect of workplace industrial relations. However, discipline should not just be looked upon in the narrow punitive context of the need to discipline transgressors. The wider organisational and legal context should also be taken into account.

At a formal level, the administration of discipline in most larger organisations is facilitated by codification of a set of disciplinary rules and the establishment of disciplinary procedures to deal with breaches of such rules. As is the case in handling disputes and grievances, these disciplinary rules and procedures are commonly agreed through the process of collective bargaining between management and employee representatives, and are often included in the collective or procedural agreement. *Disciplinary rules* set out the standards of acceptable behaviour expected from employees within an organisation and, importantly, the consequences of not meeting these standards. *Disciplinary procedures*, on the other hand, are the administrative machinery for applying these rules and executing any resulting action.

7.5.1. LEGAL CONTEXT FOR DISCIPLINE ADMINISTRATION[5]

From a legal perspective, there are various constraints on how discipline should be administered in organisations. The fundamental principles of natural justice constrain the behaviour of management in instigating discipline. The principles of natural justice, to which the Employment Appeals Tribunal (EAT) often makes reference, require that organisations must have some form of disciplinary procedure in operation, ensure that employees are familiar with its contents and apply this procedure in a reasonable way. The principles of natural justice are a common law concept and, even though never mentioned in the Unfair Dismissals legislation, have become incorporated in the application of this legislation.

Major Principles of Natural Justice

• There should be a basic understanding of what constitutes a transgression: therefore company rules/standards should be clearly outlined and communicated.
• The consequences of breaching such rules/standards should be clear.
• Employees not achieving the required standards should be so informed and given the opportunity to improve where possible.
• Employees who are alleged to have breached discipline are entitled to fair and consistent treatment including opportunity to state their case, access to representation, and a right to appeal to a higher authority.

* *The principles of natural justice allied to legislative change require that organisations must have some formal disciplinary procedure in operation, ensure that employees are familiar with its contents and apply this procedure in a reasonable way.*

Apart from the above principles, changes in employment law have substantially altered the area of discipline administration. Along with the extension of collective bargaining, the legal framework now ensures that employees and trade unions play an important role in discipline administration at work (Von Prondzynski, 1982). In relation to legislative change the Unfair Dismissals Act 1977 and the Unfair Dismissals (Amendment) Act 1993 [henceforth referred to as the 'Unfair Dismissals legislation'] have been the major influencing factors. It requires that employers have a formal disciplinary procedure, lays down guidelines as to what constitutes fair and unfair dismissal, provides a mechanism for dealing with claims of unfair dismissal and decides upon redress for those found to be unfairly dismissed.

For a particular dismissal to be held as fair, case law evidence suggests that it must normally be preceded by the application of an acceptable disciplinary procedure, particularly where the offence was one which would not warrant instant or summary dismissal.[6]

7.5.2. DISCIPLINARY PROCEDURES

There is no specific requirement in the Unfair Dismissals legislation for employers to have a disciplinary procedure, but it does state that each employee is entitled to receive from his employer the company's dismissal procedures. This must be received by the employee within twenty-eight days of starting employment. Furthermore, the lack of such procedures may often be viewed by the Employment Appeals Tribunal as rendering a dismissal unfair.

Leaving aside legislation, there are good practical reasons to justify attention to fair disciplinary procedures including the promotion of order, fairness, consistency and control within the organisation. Disciplinary procedures should adhere to the following general objectives:
(1) to inform employees of offences which may lead to discipline;
(2) to establish a set procedure for bringing alleged offences to an employee's notice;
(3) to allow employees to respond to such charges;
(4) to discover the reason why offences occurred or why performance is inadequate;
(5) to impose or apply sanctions if appropriate.
Rules and standards: For management, the first area of concern in the development of a disciplinary procedure is to outline company rules and standards. The Advisory Conciliation and Arbitration Service (ACAS) Code of Practice (UK) suggests that workplace rules are necessary to ensure consistency in the treatment of employees and to help the firm to operate effectively (ACAS, 1977, 1987). Their major contribution is in establishing standards of conduct at work which employees are expected to adhere to, and in helping to ensure equity in dealing with employees who fail to achieve these standards. The central responsibility for discipline administration lies with management. It is their task to establish workplace rules and standards. Employees and their representative organisations should be consulted in this process.

Exactly how far can an organisation go in outlining rules and standards? This is not an easy question to answer. The primary consideration must be the nature of the enterprise. It would be impossible to cover all the possible transgressions that might occur so that stated rules and standards can only outline general areas or deal with specific transgessions which occur frequently. This is clearly acceptable as very often rules can only be indicative of the type of offences which will lead to discipline. However, management should be as precise as possible—as the ACAS code (1977) states: 'Rules should not be so general as to be meaningless.'

A first and important step is to spell out those rules and standards where breaches may lead to dismissal in the first instance (summary dismissal). Again, every possible offence cannot be forecast but examples might include theft, violence, or criminal offences. The offences which warrant dismissal in one organisation may be entirely different to those in another. Offences which might warrant summary dismissal in a particular organisation but might not do so elsewhere should be clearly highlighted, e.g. hygiene rules in a food-processing firm, confidentiality where research and development is carried out. Case law indicates that instant dismissal (i.e. without a hearing or investigation) is extremely difficult to initiate fairly. Where a serious offence occurs, it is generally recommended that the employee be suspended pending a thorough investigation and hearing. After this investigation appropriate disciplinary action may be initiated.

Secondly, management should also outline those rules and standards where breaches would lead to the operation of a standard disciplinary procedure (e.g. lateness, absenteeism, inadequate work performance). The details of such procedures should be given to all employees. Apart from serious misconduct, most breaches of discipline will lead to the application of a standard disciplinary procedure, an example of which is given in box 7.3.

In the administration of disciplinary procedures the golden rule would seem to suggest that such procedures should be (1) agreed between management and employees, (2) fair, (3) understood by management and employees, and (4) applied consistently. These and other operational aspects of discipline administration are discussed below.

WARNINGS

The daily supervisory role of management includes ongoing coaching and counselling of employees. This may occasionally involve verbally reprimanding employees. However, in the event of the facts of a case pointing to the need for formal disciplinary action management should adhere to the disciplinary procedure and, where appropriate, issue a disciplinary warning. In issuing warnings the managerial approach should be remedial rather than penal, except in the most extreme circumstances. Thus, managers should encourage improvements in individual conduct rather than simply imposing sanctions. Again, clarity of warnings is very important. Therefore, the warning should clearly specify the way in which the employee's behaviour or performance was unsatisfactory, how performance can be improved, what the expected standard is and what the consequences are of not improving. Management should take any reasonable measures which might facilitate improvement. Warnings should normally be in writing and be given to the employee and, if appropriate, his/her representative(s).

Box 7.3. Sample disciplinary procedure (Manufacturing Company)

Preamble: The following disciplinary procedure will be used to deal with all breaches of company rules and standards except where the offences or transgression constitute gross misconduct.

The primary aim of this procedure is to help employees whose conduct or performance falls below company requirements to achieve the necessary improvements. It is desirable both in contributing to company success and the fair treatment of employees. It is company policy to apply this procedure as reasonably as possible and to ensure consistency and order in its application. It will apply to all breaches of company rules or standards not constituting gross misconduct, which may typically include, but are not limited to the following:

(a) bad time-keeping   (b) unauthorised absence
(c) lack of co-operation   (d) unacceptable work performance
(e) poor attendance   (f) breaches of safety regulations

Disciplinary procedure:

(a) In the first instance the individual will be asked to attend a *counselling interview* by his supervisor where the employee's transgression will be made clear, the standard of performance required outlined and the employee verbally reprimanded.

(b) In the second instance the employee will receive a *verbal warning* at a formal meeting with his supervisor and department manager where details of the misdemeanour and the consequences of further offences will be outlined.

(c) In the third instance the employee will receive a *final written warning* from the personnel manager at a meeting with the personnel manager, the department manager and, if appropriate, the supervisor where the employee will be informed of the details of the offence, future performance standards required and the fact that further offences will lead to suspension or dismissal.

(d) In the last instance the employee will either be *suspended without pay or dismissed* (depending on the offence), notice of which will be given to the employee at a meeting with the general manager where the offence will be outlined both verbally and in writing, and the employee advised of his right of appeal.

Gross misconduct: Gross misconduct is conduct of such a serious nature that the company could not tolerate keeping the employee in employment, and it is hoped that such instances will not occur. However, for the mutual protection of the company and its workforce, any employee found guilty of gross misconduct may be dismissed summarily. Examples of gross misconduct include:

(a) violation of a criminal law   (b) consumption or possession of alcohol or illegal drugs
(c) threats or acts of physical violence   (d) theft from another employee or from the company
(e) malicious damage to company property   (f) falsifying company records (including clock cards)

Before any action is taken the company will thoroughly investigate the case, during which time the employee will be suspended. After such investigation the employee will attend a meeting with company management, where he will have an opportunity to state his case and be advised of his right of appeal. Should the company still feel the employee was guilty of gross misconduct he will be dismissed and given a letter outlining the nature of the offence and reasons for dismissal.

For minor offences the immediate supervisor of the employee concerned should give an *oral warning* for the purpose of improving future performance. If further action is necessary or if the issue is more serious, the employee may be given a *written warning* setting out the circumstances and clearly indicating the improvement required. Further misconduct might warrant a *final written warning*, which should contain an unambiguous statement that any recurrence (or unsatisfactory behaviour of another kind) would lead to a specific penalty, e.g. suspension, demotion, loss of seniority or dismissal, as the case may be. Again, a copy of any written warning (final or otherwise) should be given to the employee and, if appropriate, to the employee's representative. The final step in a disciplinary procedure would be the formal imposition of a disciplinary penalty, notified in writing to the employee and, as we have already mentioned, to his representative(s). The range of penalties available to management is broader than the ones usually thought of—dismissal and suspension—and include transfer, loss of privileges, demotion and loss of seniority.

Warnings should remain on an employee's record for as long as is consistent with the nature of the offence in accordance with company rules and practice. Minor warnings will obviously have a shorter time scale than those relating to more serious issues, but defining specific guidelines poses difficulties. The ACAS Code of Practice suggests that warnings should be 'disregarded after a specific period of satisfactory conduct' but does not suggest how long these time scales should be (ACAS, 1987). Hawkins (1979) is more specific in suggesting that verbal warnings remain on an employee's record for six months, written warnings for twelve months and for very serious offences a period of two years or more. Many organisations do not specify limits but, in practice, allow warnings to lapse after a reasonable period of satisfactory performance.

REPRESENTATION

A basic ingredient of procedural fairness and equity in discipline administration is the employee's right to adequate representation (by either a fellow employee or trade union representative, as appropriate). Management should also be aware of the need for independence in discipline administration. Where issues reach a serious stage, at least two management representatives should be present to ensure correct and consistent application of rules and procedures. The personnel practitioner can play an important role here.

RECORD KEEPING

Accurate records should be kept of all disciplinary issues. A major onus in this area falls on management. At counselling interview stage a brief note of the issue, the individual concerned, the date and the nature of the discussion would suffice. At verbal, written and all subsequent stages records should be more elaborate. This is particularly important at and above final warning stage, where it should be clearly documented that the employee was informed of the seriousness of the issue and the fact that future offences may lead to dismissal.

At each stage a written record of the nature of the issue, the date, the action taken and the reasons should be given to the employee for his retention. A copy which has been signed by the employee (as evidence that he received and understood the letter) should be placed on his personal file. A copy should also be given to the employee's representative, the trade union (if appropriate) and to the manager(s) involved.

Much of this work will be the responsibility of the specialist personnel function. The importance of accurate record keeping in the administration of discipline cannot be overemphasised. Since the Unfair Dismissals legislation places the burden of proof primarily on the employer, companies must be able to back up reasons for discipline with substantial documentary evidence.

RIGHT OF APPEAL

Another basic principle of natural justice is that employees subject to discipline have the right of appeal to somebody not directly involved.[7] Management is obliged to investigate the case thoroughly and make a fair decision based on the facts. If an employee or his representative is not satisfied with a decision, they should have the right of appeal to a higher level of management or external arbitration. Indeed, management should remind employees both of their right of appeal during disciplinary meetings and of the appropriate procedures for lodging such an appeal. The first level of appeal should be to the manager above the level at which the penalty was imposed, the second appeal to the highest company level, the managing director, and the third appeal to an agreed independent arbitrator.

DISCIPLINARY INTERVIEWS

When a disciplinary matter arises management should thoroughly investigate the circumstances and establish the facts of the incident. This means that where an employee is observed or reported to have broken rules that warrant some disciplinary action, the supervisor or manager should first establish the facts before recollections fade. When dealing with a disciplinary matter managers need reliable information which may be derived from several sources, e.g. production records, time sheets, clock cards, personal file of the employee and, obviously, talking to people who have knowledge of the situation. If, after a thorough investigation management decide that disciplinary action is merited, a meeting should be arranged with the employee(s) concerned. Alternatively, if the offence is sufficiently serious but all the facts cannot be established there and then, the employee may be taken off the job or suspended (with or without pay) pending the outcome of the investigation.

The purpose of a disciplinary interview is to assess culpability, to decide on appropriate action and to attempt to effect the desired change in the employee's behaviour. It allows the employee to present his/her point of view, which helps give a comprehensive picture of the case and facilitates constructive discussion of the issue. In conducting disciplinary interviews management must decide who is to carry out the interview, where the interview is to take place and establish all relevant facts about the case before the interview (see box 7.4).

Box 7.4. Key managerial considerations in preparing for disciplinary interviews

(a) *Who?* Management should decide who carries out the interview (e.g. supervisor at initial levels; senior management involvement later) and consider the role of employee representatives.

(b) *Where?* Interviews should generally be conducted away from the shop floor, at an appropriate time, with sufficient notice.

(c) *What?* The person responsible for conducting the interview should ensure that management have established the relevant facts before the interview and have available any information pertinent to the case. Such information might include details of the employee's job and the incident, information on the employee(s) concerned (background, records, etc.).

In keeping with the rules of natural justice, the employee must be given a reasonable opportunity to explain his or her position. The disciplinary interview should be treated as a problem-solving exercise with the objective of positively influencing employee behaviour. It is particularly important that management approach disciplinary procedure with an open mind. Only after establishing the facts and discussing the issue with the employee are management in a position to decide on appropriate action. The employee's perspective may throw new light on the incident, and management may need to get additional information or call for an adjournment.

Should the meeting point towards disciplinary action, management's position should be explained to the employee, who should be made fully aware of his shortcomings and management's concern. The nature of improvement and the means for its achievement should be outlined, as should the consequences of future transgressions. Management must ensure that the employee fully understands the discipline imposed and the right of appeal.

After the interview the details should be accurately recorded and a copy given to the employee concerned (and his/her representative, as necessary). Any commitments entered into should be carried out promptly. In the longer term the total process should be monitored from a number of viewpoints (e.g. impact on employee behaviour, trends in disciplinary incidents, effectiveness of various forms of discipline).

MANAGEMENT APPROACHES TO DISCIPLINE ADMINISTRATION

The area of discipline administration should be approached by management in a positive vein, with the overall objective being to change employee behaviour. The personnel function has an important role to play in establishing disciplinary policy and related procedures, and in monitoring their application throughout the organisation. Two key factors which need to be kept in mind are the need for reasonableness and consistency. In his study of unofficial strikes, Wallace notes that employees often have expectations that management will act leniently in disciplinary matters so that the introduction of a more strict managerial approach often causes problems (Wallace, 1988a; Wallace and O'Shea, 1987). This highlights the need to take consistently similar approaches in disciplinary matters so that accusations of favouritism or purges cannot be forwarded with any justification.

Where recognised rules or standards have not been observed, the action taken will depend on the circumstances and the seriousness of the offence. When determining the action to be taken management must bear in mind the test of reasonableness at all times and should, as far as possible, take into account any mitigating factors. This infers that every disciplinary situation be carefully evaluated, taking account of any special considerations or mitigating circumstances. Every issue is different; an employee may have developed a bad time-keeping record for a very legitimate reason (e.g. difficult family circumstances) and managerial decisions should reflect such considerations.

In general, it seems that the impact of unfair dismissals legislation on employers has been largely favourable. There has been a fall-off in levels of strike activity resulting from dismissals since the introduction of the 1977 Act (Murphy, 1986, 1989). It would also seem to have encouraged management to adopt appropriate disciplinary procedures and practices. O'Connor (1982) found that managements were now exercising greater care when recruiting, evaluating employee performance more closely and generally adopting a more systematic approach to handling discipline. This 'learning effect' may be partially reflected in the increased number of Employment Appeals Tribunal decisions favouring employers.

Another factor is the continued significance of establishment-level collective bargaining as a mechanism for processing dismissal issues outside of an explicitly legal context (Lennon, 1983; Murphy, 1989; Murphy and Roche, 1994). Trade unions may be particularly keen to rely on collective bargaining fora where the union case is a strong one. This may imply also that cases allowed to proceed to the Tribunal are often weak (from the union standpoint) or deal with non-unionised employees (e.g. many professional and managerial grades; Meenan, 1985). Indeed, it seems that the legislation has not greatly increased the job security of employees since reinstatement/ re-engagement is awarded in only a minority of cases (Lennon, 1983).

NOTES

1. For detailed treatments of the theoretical and applied aspects of industrial relations negotiations see, for example, Atkinson, 1977; Fisher and Ury, 1986; Hawkins, 1979; Scott, 1981; Sisson, 1977; Walton and McKersie, 1965; Warr, 1973.

2. For a concise review of explanations of industrial conflict see P. Worsley, (ed.), *Introducing Sociology*, Penguin, London, 1977.

3. For an in-depth analysis of strike action see, for example, C. Crouch, *Trade Unions: The Logic of Collective Action*, Fontana, London, 1982; R. Hyman, *Strikes*, Fontana, London, 1972.

4. For a more in-depth analysis of strike indices and a compilation of strike statistics see, for example, R. Stern, 'Methodological Issues in Quantative Strike Series', *Industrial Relations*, Vol. 17, No. 1, February 1978. The most comprehensive analysis of strike activity in Ireland has been undertaken by Professor Aidan Kelly and Teresa Brannick of University College Dublin; see, for example, 'Strikes in Ireland: Measurement, Incidence and Trends', in *Industrial Relations in Ireland: Contemporary Issues and Developments*, University College Dublin, 1989.

5. This textbook provides a summary overview of the legal context of discipline administration and is not a legal interpretation thereof. For a comprehensive review see, for example, F. von Prondzynski, *Employment Law in Ireland*, Sweet and Maxwell, London, 1989; C. Fennell and I. Lynch, *Labour Law in Ireland*, Gill and Macmillan, Dublin, 1993.

6. Summary dismissal means dismissal in the first instance of an offence. It will normally take place after a thorough investigation of the facts and after the employee has been given a chance to state his/her case and has had access to adequate representation.

7. See National Engineering and Electrical Trade Union (NEETU) v McConnell, ILRM 422 (1983).

CHAPTER EIGHT

Human Resource Management and Industrial Relations: The Current Debate and Irish Context

8.1. INTRODUCTION

At organisation level, possibly the most important development identified in the contemporary literature has been the issue of Human Resource Management (HRM) and the contention that HRM-based approaches are increasingly being adopted by employers and are significantly impacting upon establishment-level industrial relations. This chapter attempts to inform the debate on HRM in Ireland by providing an overview of the nature of HRM, and reviewing its development and potential application in Ireland. The development of HRM is considered by exploring its nature, the reasons for its emergence in recent years and suggested contrasts with more traditional industrial relations approaches. The nature of strategic decision making is then considered with particular emphasis on developing competitive strategy at business-unit level. This chapter also explores the impact of product market conditions on strategic decision making. The idea of linking decisions on business strategy, product market characteristics and personnel policy choice is then analysed with specific reference to industrial relations. These various issues are analysed in terms of their relevance to developments in the Republic of Ireland.

As discussed earlier, industrial relations practice in the great majority of medium and large organisations in the Republic of Ireland has traditionally been associated with a strong collectivist emphasis (Roche, 1990b). In this model industrial relations considerations rarely concerned strategic decision makers, relations between management and employees were grounded in the pluralist tradition with a primary reliance on adversarial collective bargaining. This pluralist tradition is manifested in relatively high levels of union density, highly developed collective bargaining institutions at establishment level, and industrial relations as the key role of the specialist personnel function

(Gunnigle and Flood, 1990). However, the period since the early 1980s has been characterised by considerable change in the operating environment of industrial relations. In particular, the deep recession combined with increased competition in product markets placed considerable cost pressures on organisations and led to some significant developments in industrial relations, particularly the decline in trade union membership. At the same time, many organisations sought to establish competitive advantage through improvements in quality, service and performance.

8.2. HUMAN RESOURCE MANAGEMENT

A notable characteristic of management literature over the past decade has been the marked increase in interest in linkages between business strategy and personnel/industrial relations policies. It is further suggested that this emphasis on a strategic perspective of personnel/industrial relations management will continue because it has been the most neglected area of strategic management, and because of its central role in implementing cultural and political changes in organisations (Beer et al., 1984, 1985; Fombrun et al., 1984).

Human Resource Management (HRM) refers to the development of a strategic corporate approach to workforce management (Armstrong, 1991; Beer, et al., 1984, 1985; Guest, 1987). It has its academic roots in two, primarily distinct, sources of literature, both originating in the US. The first of these is encompassed in the Harvard Business School (HBS) model (Beer et al., 1984, 1985). This model focuses on the individual employee as *the* key organisational resource which management must nurture and develop to maximise its contribution to the organisation. The HBS model suggests that management adopt a coherent range of pro-employee ('soft') personnel policies to ensure the attraction, retention and development of committed, high-performing employees. The second literature source advocating increased strategic consideration of personnel/industrial relations emanates in the broader business strategy literature, specifically the work of Fombrun et al. (1984). This approach suggests that organisational performance can be substantially improved by integrating personnel/industrial relations considerations into strategic decision making to ensure that personnel and industrial relations policies complement business strategy. In contrast to the HBS model, this approach does not prescribe either a hard or soft approach to workforce management; rather it suggests that top management adopt the policies which best suit their particular circumstances and complement their business strategy.

Numerous reasons are given for the upsurge of interest in HRM. One such factor is the quest for *competitive advantage* through improved quality and performance. The idea of competitive advantage has been championed by Porter (1985, 1987), and can be described as any factor(s) which allow an organisation to differentiate its product or service from its competitors to increase market share. Price and quality are common mechanisms by which organisations attempt to achieve competitive advantange. While price is clearly a key factor influencing consumer decisions, it is suggested that increasingly purchasing decisions of both goods and services is being made less on the basis of price alone and more on the basis of quality (Carroll, 1985; Feigenbaum, 1983). For an organisation to achieve competitive advantage it needs to orient and utilise its various resources towards the achievement of this goal. Beer et al. (1984) argue that human resources are often underutilised within organisations by comparison with the attention paid to resource utilisation in the finance and technology areas. They also argue that, by virtue of this underutilisation, organisations which have a coherent strategy to utilise their human resources will often achieve advantage over competitors who do not optimally utilise their human resources. Similarly, if an organisation aims to compete largely on price, the extent to which employees contribute to cost control of raw materials, avoidance of wastage, etc. will again have a major bearing on the competitive position of an organisation.

HRM has also been closely associated with the *'excellence' literature* of the 1980s (Kanter, 1984; Peters and Waterman, 1982). This literature argued that certain organisations demonstrate 'excellent' characteristics. It was suggested that by identifying and copying these characteristics organisations could improve performance via greater innovativeness, flexibility, quality, etc. The excellence literature gave particular prominence to the employment (HRM) practices required to establish and sustain a strong organisation culture.

Another reason for the emergence of HRM is the suggestion that more *traditional approaches to workforce management have failed.* A common criticism of traditional industrial relations practice in organisations is that it increasingly became the responsibility of personnel specialists and has failed to promote a strategic awareness of personnel/industrial relations considerations at top management level (Legge, 1978). Miles and Snow (1984) feel the personnel and industrial relations area has lagged behind developments in management strategy and structure. They suggest that the traditional workforce management approaches have been 'technique oriented', with the emphasis on making incremental improvements on current practice rather than adopting a strategic role in evaluating policy options and subsequent implementation. Traditional industrial relations approaches have been described as essentially reactive, dealing with the repercussions of strategic decision making. In contrast, HRM is felt to adopt a more generalist perspective, which places a strong emphasis upon devolving the practice of personnel and industrial relations to line management. Beer et al. (1984) argue that human resource policy decisions are 'too important' to be left to personnel specialists and need to be incorporated into mainstream management activities with strategic human resource decisions vested in top management.

239

Other reasons for the emergence of HRM include financial market preferences for *decentralised organisational models*, thus devolving greater autonomy to business-unit management, *shifting employment patterns* and *declining trade union power* encompassing a reduction in the traditional industrial relations emphasis within personnel management.

8.2.1. THE EMERGENCE OF HUMAN RESOURCE MANAGEMENT IN IRELAND

Workforce management practice in Ireland has traditionally been associated with a strong industrial relations emphasis. As such, management approaches were seen as essentially reactive, dealing with various problematic aspects of workforce management (Shivanath, 1987). This emphasis reflects a historical preference for a collectivist approach to management–employee relations involving collective bargaining with trade unions. Looking at contemporary developments, it appears that recession and subsequent recovery has led to some change in traditional approaches to industrial relations and personnel management generally, a greater devolution of responsibility to line management and the emergence of a greater strategic role for personnel and industrial relations in some Irish organisations (Gunnigle, 1991). A significant aspect of contemporary developments in industrial relations has been the emergence of HRM.

8.2.2. HRM AND THE NON-UNION PHENOMENON

In the Irish context, increasing attention has been focused on HRM approaches of non-union organisations in the high-technology sector. Many are subsidiaries of US organisations which espouse a particular philosophy towards workforce management which emphasises employee commitment and loyalty, and high levels of quality and performance.

Other factors would appear to have facilitated the emergence of HRM in the Irish context, particularly changes in employment structure and the decline in union membership and power. The Irish trade union movement has experienced a serious decline in membership in the 1980s. This has been due in part to high levels of unemployment and emigration. Particularly significant are the changes which have taken place in employment structure in the past decade. Decline or stagnation has characterised many of the traditionally highly unionised sectors. On the other hand, most employment growth has taken place in sectors more difficult for union penetration (high-technology manufacturing, less unionised areas in the services sector). Like most industrialised economies, Ireland has seen a shift away from industrial employment to service employment. Additionally, organisational employment practices, particularly among large non-union companies have acted to reduce union penetration particularly in the high-technology sectors of the economy.

This latter factor highlights the influence of personnel policy decisions and employment practices. Toner's work (1987) on non-union companies in

Ireland identifies a range of employment practices designed to emphasise the 'mutuality' or shared interests of employees and management in achieving certain organisational goals. These goals include profitability and growth, high-quality production and high performance. A range of employment practices to support the achievement of these goals are identified by Toner, and include lifelong employment, single status, merit pay, regular communications, gain sharing, internal promotion and continuous development of employees. These practices are designed to create greater awareness amongst employees of the mutually dependent relationship between organisational performance and employees' work inputs.

Figure 8.1. HBS model of Human Resource Management

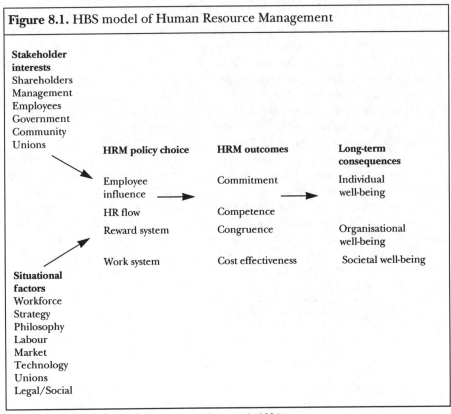

Source: Beer et al., 1984.

8.2.3. The Nature of Human Resource Management

In spite of increasing consensus on the nature of HRM, there remains considerable confusion as to the distinctive characteristics of HRM, its applicability to organisations and contrasts with more 'traditional' approaches to workforce management. Attempts to develop a conceptual model of HRM have drawn heavily from the study of organisation behaviour.

Possibly the most influential work on Human Resource Management has been the Harvard Business School (HBS) model (Beer et al., 1984) mentioned earlier. This model presents a broad causal map of the determinants and consequences of HRM policy choices as outlined in figure 8.1. Beer et al. describe HRM in generic terms as 'involving all management decisions and actions that affect the nature of the relationship between the organisation and its employees—its human resources'. Thus, top management and particularly the chief executive are seen as having the primary responsibility for aligning business strategy and personnel/industrial relations policy choice. Four key components comprise the HBS model, namely (1) stakeholder interests; (2) HRM policy choice; (3) HRM outcomes; and (4) long-term consequences.

A central contention of the HBS model is that personnel and industrial relations outcomes are affected by the policy choices made in four key areas: (1) the reward system (financial and non-financial); (2) human resource flow (recruitment, selection, training, development, deployment, etc.); (3) work system (job/work design, supervisory style, etc.); and (4) employee influence (employee involvement in decision making). Each of these policy areas are seen as key elements of strategic choice which profoundly impact upon employee behaviour and attitude towards the organisation. Strategic choices in these areas are influenced by broader contextual factors: (1) situational constraints (including workforce characteristics, business strategy, management philosophy, labour market, etc.) and (2) stakeholder interests (shareholders, management, employees, government, etc.). Decisions made in these policy areas are seen as affecting personnel and industrial relations outcomes in the area of employee commitment, congruence of employee and management interests, employee competence, and cost effectiveness. These outcomes are also seen as having broader long-term consequences for individual employee well-being, organisational effectiveness and societal well-being.

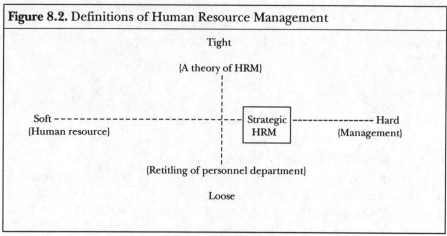

Figure 8.2. Definitions of Human Resource Management

Tight

{A theory of HRM}

Soft — — — — — — — — — — — — — — — — — — — | Strategic | — — — — — — — Hard
{Human resource}   HRM   {Management}

{Retitling of personnel department}

Loose

Source: Guest, 1987.

On this side of the Atlantic, Guest's (1987) 'hard–soft, tight–loose' framework of HRM is possibly the most widely referenced (see figure 8.2). The 'soft–hard' dimension in Guest's framework refers to a continuum ranging from a resource-based ('soft') managerial perspective characterised by benign pro-employee policies to a more calculative ('hard') management perspective where personnel and industrial relations policy choice is driven by the need to complement business strategy and meet financial criteria. The 'tight–loose' dimension refers to a continuum ranging from HRM, merely involving a retitling of traditional industrial relations/personnel management ('loose'), with no real change in practice, to HRM becoming a clearly defined and articulated approach to workforce management with an explicit and strong ('tight') theoretical underpinning (Flood, 1989).

Figure 8.3. A theory of Human Resource Management

HRM policies	HR outcomes	Organisational outcomes
Organisation/job design		High job performance
Management of change	Strategic integration	High problem solving, change and innovation
Recruitment, selection and socialisation	Commitment	
Appraisal, training, development	Flexibility/adaptability	High cost effectiveness
Reward systems	Quality	Low turnover, absence, grievances
Communications		

↑ **Leadership/Culture/Strategy** ↑

Source: Guest, 1988.

Guest proceeds to develop a theory of HRM as outlined in figure 8.3. Guest argues that organisations will be more successful if they pursue four key HRM goals, namely (1) strategic integration; (2) employee commitment; (3) flexibility; and (4) quality. Guest suggests that these HRM goals can be optimally achieved through coherent HRM policy choices in the areas of organisation/job design, management of change, recruitment, selection and socialisation, appraisal, training and development, rewards and communications. Guest identifies five necessary conditions for the effective operation of HRM: (a) corporate leadership (to ensure the values inherent in HRM are championed and implemented); (b) strategic vision (to ensure the integration of HRM as a key component of the corporate strategy); (c) technological/production feasibility (Guest suggests that if heavy investment has taken place in short-cycle, repetitive production assembly line equipment, this mitigates against the job design principles and autonomous team working necessary for HRM); (d) industrial relations feasibility (again Guest suggests

243

that multi-union status, low-trust management–employee relations and adversarial industrial relations orientations mitigate against the implementation of HRM); and (e) the ability of personnel specialists to implement appropriate HRM policies with the assistance of top and line management.

8.2.4. HRM VERSUS TRADITIONAL PERSONNEL MANAGEMENT

When HRM is contrasted with more traditional personnel management, as in table 8.1, a number of key differences emerge. Firstly, it is argued that personnel/industrial relations considerations are fully integrated with strategic decision making in the HRM model, whereas in the traditional personnel management model the personnel input is less pronounced and issue specific. A second contrast is that HRM is seen as essentially proactive and long term, while traditional personnel management/industrial relations is more reactive and adopts a shorter-term perspective. In terms of the desired mode of psychological contract, HRM is seen as facilitating employee commitment while personnel management is seen as a mode of managerial control over employees (Walton, 1985). A specific contrast in the industrial relations sphere is that HRM is seen as essentially unitarist in perspective, involving no apparent conflict of interests between employers and employees. In contrast, traditional personnel management/industrial relations is seen as grounded in the pluralist tradition and essentially concerned with the adversarial relationship between employers and workers. A related factor is that HRM is seen as focusing on the individual and relations between (line) management and the individual worker, while traditional personnel management/industrial relations is seen to operate through collectivist relations between employer and employee representatives. Another area of contrast is that HRM is seen as operating most effectively in organic, fluid organisation structures, while traditional personnel management/industrial relations is felt to characterise more bureaucratic and rigid organisational structures. As we have seen, HRM is seen to operate primarily through line management, while in the personnel management model primary responsibility for workforce management is vested in the specialist personnel function. The final perceived difference between HRM and personnel management relates to the criteria utilised to evaluate effectiveness. HRM is seen as being essentially focused on the maximum utilisation of human resources through policies which seek to release the individual potential of employees to make the optimal contribution to organisational effectiveness. In contrast, personnel management is seen as having somewhat more pragmatic objectives—the maximisation of cost effectiveness. Despite these argued contrasts between HRM and personnel management, Guest (1987, 1989a,b) cautions that this does not necessarily infer that HRM is better than 'traditional' personnel/industrial relations management and should be adopted by organisations in general (as might be inferred from some of the 'excellence' literature). Rather, Guest suggests that traditional approaches may be more appropriate in certain organisational contexts such as large bureaucratic organisations or heavily unionised organisations with adversarial collective bargaining traditions, while HRM may be appropriate in organisations with more organic structures, and characterised by more individualist high-trust management–employee relations.

Table 8.1. Personnel management and Human Resource Management compared

	Personnel management	HRM
Input into corporate planning	Issue-specific	Integrated
Time and planning perspective	Short-term; reactive; marginal	Long-term; proactive; strategic
Psychological contract	Compliance	Commitment
Industrial relations	Pluralist; collective; low-trust; adversarial	Unitarist; individual; high-trust
Organisation structures/ systems	Bureaucratic, mechanistic; centralised; formal, defined roles	Organic, fluid; devolved; flexible roles
Principal delivery mechanism	Specialist personnel management function	Line management
Aims	Maximise cost effectiveness	Maximise HR utilisation

Source: Adapted from Guest, 1987.

As discussed above, a significant aspect of the HRM approach is an accent on greater individualism in management–employee relations. This is generally manifested in a managerial preference for dealing with employees directly rather than via representative mechanisms, particularly trade unions. This development is seen to contrast with the traditional pluralist model characterised by union recognition and extensive reliance on collective bargaining. Under this mode management/union relations are often formalised in a procedural agreement which regulates relations between the parties and covers issues like union recognition, disciplinary, grievance and disputes procedures. Where a personnel function exists, its primary role lies in co-ordinating collective bargaining with trade unions. As indicated above, this emphasis on collective bargaining, often termed the 'adversarial' model of industrial relations, forms the basis for traditional approaches to workforce management in many Irish organisations (Roche, 1990).

8.2.5. CONTRADICTIONS AND INCONSISTENCIES IN HRM
Several authors have identified a number of inherent contradictions and inconsistencies in HRM, particularly the 'soft variant' advocated by the

Harvard Business School model (Blyton and Turnbull, 1992; Cradden, 1992; Keenoy, 1990; Legge, 1988). For example, Legge (1988) highlights the apparent paradox between the traditional commodity status of labour under the capitalist framework and the essentially unitarist perspective of HRM, which sees no inherent conflict of interests between management and employees. It has generally been accepted that in the capitalist framework there is an inherent conflict of interest between management and employees over the price of labour. Indeed, this conflict of interest is the very basis for the existence of industrial relations as a key concern of workers and management. However, the HRM perspective appears to ignore the 'inherency' of a conflict of interests but rather focuses on the achievement of congruence of management and employee interests.

HRM focuses on achieving high levels of employee commitment. For example, Flood (1989) suggests that HRM emphasises the need for organisations to focus on the extrinsic and intrinsic needs of employees, and to develop employment practices which increase employee commitment. In a similar vein Walton (1985), advocates that organisations adopt employment policies which emphasise the mutuality of employer and employee interests to ensure employee commitment to achieve organisational goals. This focus on employee commitment would not only seem to be incongruent with the pluralist perspective of the organisation (discussed above), but also appears to conflict with another basic tenet of HRM, namely that personnel policies should be integrated with, and complement, business strategy. Clearly, many decisions which complement business strategy may not develop employee commitment. If, for example, an organisation's business strategy is to maximise short-term returns to owners/shareholders, this may well involve decisions which do not develop employee commitment such as replacing labour with technology, contracting out certain tasks and/or making employees redundant. A related issue on this theme is the suggestion that HRM involves the simultaneous achievement of higher levels of individualism and teamwork. These twin goals clearly have tremendous potential for conflict. For example, performance-related pay based on individual employee performance may indeed prohibit teamwork, as can individual communications/negotiations.

High levels of flexibility are seen as a core objective of HRM. Guest (1988) suggests that increased flexibility involves the creation of structural mechanisms in organisations to ensure responsiveness to changing environmental conditions. Guest suggests that such flexibility should encompass both functional and numerical flexibility. However, several authors have noted the difficulties in achieving congruence in different flexibility forms, namely numerical, functional and financial flexibility. It is clearly difficult to achieve high levels of functional flexibility (e.g. multi-skilling) where employees have a tenuous relationship with the organisation as may result from attempts to improve numerical flexibility through, for example, temporary working (Blyton and Morris, 1992; Gunnigle, 1992b). The issue of flexibility is considered in greater detail in the final chapter of this text.

Another contradiction in the HRM argument, that personnel HRM policies must be internally consistent, arises in relation to job security. A prominent theme in the extant literature is that for HRM to be effective management must provide implicit job tenure guarantees for employees (Beer et al., 1984; Guest, 1987, 1989a,b; Walton, 1985). Guest (1989a,b) identifies high levels of employee commitment involving a move to achieve a 'mutuality of management and employee interests' as a key policy goal of HRM. In achieving this policy goal a commitment to job tenure is seen as a necessary precondition. However, it is patently evident that high levels of competition and volatility in product markets have made job security ever increasingly difficult to achieve. Indeed, job security may itself be incompatible with broader business goals attributed to HRM, such as increased flexibility in responding to rapid changes in demand. In practice, it would appear that some organisations seek to achieve such flexibility by policies which actually reduce the likelihood of job tenure commitments—for example, using atypical employment forms. On the issue of the practicability of job tenure commitments Blyton and Turnbull (1992) comment:

> This [job security] is particularly problematic in highly competitive or recessionary conditions where the 'needs of the business' are likely to undermine any internal 'fit' with ('soft') HRM values: shedding labour, for example, will severely challenge, if not destroy, an organisation's HRM image of caring for the needs and security of its employees.

Another apparent inconsistency in HRM is the focus on achieving greater individualism in management–employee interactions. As we have seen, industrial relations in the Republic of Ireland have been characterised by extensive reliance on collectivist approaches as manifested in, for example, a high level of trade union density and low-trust management–employee relations (Whelan, 1982). The 'soft' HRM approach as outlined by the HBS model and Guest places the managerial emphasis on achieving high-trust relations between management and employees, and appears to have a preference for pursuing this goal in a non-union environment. Within the 'soft' HRM model high-trust relations are pursued through managerial initiatives to increase individual employee involvement and motivation, and the adoption of techniques such as performance appraisal and performance-related pay. Thus, such organisations attempt to create close management–employee ties and break down the traditional management–worker dichotomy of which collective bargaining is seen as the principal manifestation. Such initiatives are indicative of a unitarist management perspective, albeit a very sophisticated variant, and have potential for significant conflict with the pluralist perspective and collectivist approach characteristic of workplace industrial relations practice in Ireland. This unitarist perspective is described by Guest (1989a,b) thus:

> HRM values are unitarist to the extent that they assume no underlying and inevitable differences of interest between management and workers. . . . HRM values are essentially individualistic in that they emphasize the individual–organization linkage in preference to operating through group and representative mechanisms. . . . These values . . . leave little scope for collective arrangements and assume little need for collective bargaining. HRM therefore poses a considerable threat to traditional industrial relations and, more particularly, trade-unionism.

8.3. BUSINESS STRATEGY AND PERSONNEL POLICY CHOICE

The previous discussion serves to highlight the increased emphasis on personnel policy choice as an important component of strategic decision making. A particular characteristic of the HRM debate is the suggestion that organisations need to tailor their personnel and industrial relations policies to complement overall business strategy. It is suggested that top management in organisations need to develop a 'fit' between competitive strategy and personnel policies.

However, this literature sheds little light on what are the appropriate conditions for different personnel/industrial relations policy choices, how these fit with different business strategies and product market conditions, and what the different personnel/industrial relations policy menus are from which organisations might choose 'best-fit' policy combinations. Equally, there is a dearth of empirical evidence to demonstrate particular linkages in strategy–product market–personnel policy fit, or the impact of such linkages on organisational performance.

This section considers the nature of strategic decision making with particular emphasis on competitive strategy at the level of the business unit, and the linkages with personnel/industrial relations policy choice.

The study of strategic management has achieved increasing prominence as organisations seek to adapt to a changing business environment. Strategic management is concerned with policy decisions affecting the entire organisation with the overall objective being to optimally position the organisation to deal effectively with its environment, and is a vital ingredient in achieving and maintaining effective performance in a changing environment. Fombrun et al. (1984) define *strategy* as both the process by which the objectives of the organisation are chosen from a set of all feasible objectives available, as well as the process by which the organisation uses its resources to achieve those objectives. Strategic decisions are long-term in nature, affect the future of the organisation and serve to guide subsequent decision making at lower levels. Strategic decision making incorporates strategy formulation, strategy implementation and evaluation, and control; it emphasises the monitoring and evaluation of environmental opportunities and constraints as well as the strengths and weaknesses of the organisation. Therefore knowledge of strategic management and planning and the range of policy choices available, are vital apects of the top management role.

8.3.1. LEVELS OF STRATEGIC DECISION MAKING

In large, multi-business organisations three levels of strategic decision making may be identified: (a) corporate, (b) business and (c) functional (see figure 8.4). For the single-business organisations corporate- and business-level strategies become synonomous. However, for multi-business organisations it is important to differentiate between business-unit ('competitive') strategy and organisation-wide ('corporate') strategy.

Figure 8.4. Levels of strategic decision making

Corporate strategy *Multi-business*
(What business should we be in?)

Business/competitive strategy
(How to establish competitive advantage?) *Single/related business(es)*

Functional strategy
(Role of component parts)

Production/operations Marketing Finance Personnel/HRM

Corporate strategy incorporates the overall strategic plan for the diversified company. It involves identifying the role and mission of the component groups in the organisation, is concerned with the relationship between corporate headquarters and its constituent business groups and the distribution of resources between groups. Wheelen and Hunger (1990) identify three optional corporate strategies: stability, growth and retrenchment.

Business strategy occurs at the level of the individual business unit, is concerned with maintaining/improving a competitive position in a particular industry or industry segment. It is concerned with securing and allocating the necessary resources to achieve strategic purpose.

Functional strategy is designed to achieve the optimal utilisation of the constituent resources within the organisation. It is concerned with developing effective and coherent strategies for the various component sections of the organisation within the context of business and corporate strategy.

Corporate, business and functional strategies represent different levels of strategic decision making in an organisation. Each level involves decisions which are strategic in nature. However, decisions at higher levels, such as those at corporate or business unit level will guide subsequent decisions on functional strategy. Purcell (1989) emphasises this point by differentiating between *upstream* (first-order) and *downstream* (second-/third-order) strategic decisions (see figure 8.5). Upstream decisions concern the long-term direction and nature of the organisation. Downstream decisions deal with the implications of first-order decisions. Purcell argues that personnel and industrial relations policy choices are made in the context of downstream strategic decisions on organisation structure. Such choices are strategic in nature since they establish the basic approach to workforce management. However, they will be heavily influenced by first- and second-order decisions and by broader environmental factors. Thus, it is suggested that personnel and industrial relations policy choices are third-order strategic decisions.

Figure 8.5. Upstream and downstream strategic decisions

	Upstream	E
		N
First order	Long-term direction of the firm	V
	Scope of activities, markets, location	I
		R
Second order	Internal operating procedures	O
	Relationships between parts of the organisation	N
		M
Third order	Strategic choice in human resource management	E
		N
		T
	Downstream	

Source: Purcell, 1989.

Using British data, Purcell examines how trends in first- and second-order strategy, particularly diversification and decentralisation, affect management decision making. Purcell highlights the growth in size and influence of the diversified firm, giving greater prominence to decision making at the corporate level. Within this business form portfolio planning is commonly used to evaluate the performance of constituent business units and to aid resource allocation and investment/divestment decisions. A commonly used portfolio planning approach classifies business units on two criteria: current market share (profit generation capacity) and rate of market growth (demand for investment), and leads to a categorisation into four business units: star, cash cow, wild cat, and dog (Abell and Hammond, 1979). Purcell argues that organisations in each of these categories need to develop different product and marketing strategies to meet their particular needs and circumstances. This equally applies to personnel and industrial relations policy choice.

Within the portfolio planning approach to corporate strategy, the organisation is seen as a collection of different businesses which should pursue different strategies to suit particular market conditions. This implies that different functional strategies, including personnel/industrial relations, need to be applied at the business-unit level to suit particular business strategies, which in turn have been determined at corporate level. Key decisions on resource allocation (first-order decisions) are taken at corporate level and it is the responsibility of business-unit managers to deal with the implications of such decisions and take appropriate operational decisions to satisfy corporate requirements. Thus, first-order decisions, while not necessarily incorporating personnel/industrial relations considerations, exert considerable influence on industrial relations practice within a particular business unit.

Second-order decisions concern decisions on organisation structure, operating procedures and control of business-unit performance. Purcell notes that diversified organisations tend to prefer decentralised structures with a clear differentiation between strategic and operational responsibilities. He also notes that such organisations normally view decisions on personnel and industrial relations as an operational responsibility at business-unit level. An important consideration in examining second-order strategy is the approach of the corporate head office to managing its constituent business units. Goold and Campbell (1987) identify three categories of corporate approach: strategic planning, financial control and strategic control. *Strategic planning organisations* place a major emphasis on achieving maximum competitive advantage from a small number of core businesses using co-ordinated global strategies. Ambitious long-term goals are pursued, and financial performance is normally strong with fast organic growth despite occasional setbacks. There is normally less strategy ownership by the business unit. *Financial control organisations* are more concerned with financial performance than with competitive position. Expansion is achieved through acquisition and merger. Profit is the key success criterion at business-unit level which, though creating a strong incentive to succeed, can prohibit consideration of long-term initiatives. *Strategic control organisations* attempt to balance competitive and financial considerations. Growth in strategically sound businesses is encouraged but there may be divestment from other areas. The focus is long-term and there is considerable emphasis on the motivation of business-unit managers.

Purcell suggests that a critical issue in considering second-order strategies is the time period over which profits are expected and who stands to gain from profit generation. It is suggested that strategic planning organisations are most likely to have a defined sense of purpose which includes broader concerns than solely financial considerations. Consequently, they are felt to be more likely to adopt a more 'benign' approach to business-unit management and have a greater capactity to develop a co-ordinated culture and management style. Guest (1987) suggests that only strategic planning organisations have the capacity and commitment to develop HRM approaches along the lines of his model outlined earlier in this chapter. On the other hand, Purcell feels that tight financial control approaches and a short-term financial return ethos prohibit the long-term consideration of industrial relations issues and destroy the basis for personnel/industrial relations policy as an issue of strategic concern. He feels that financial control organisations produce good results for shareholders but do not substantially contribute to job creation and, indeed, are quick to divest from unprofitable businesses. In contrast, strategic planning organisations are more likely to create jobs and retain business interests through long-term investment and subsidisation.

Purcell feels that in Britain and the US a short-term stock-market emphasis is a primary characteristic of first-order strategies. Economic values are the key yardstick rendering less concrete values, like personnel/industrial relations policy, unsuitable. He suggests that examples of strategic planning companies with integrated HRM policies (such as IBM, Hewlett–Packard and Marks & Spencer) are the exceptions that prove the rule. These organisations are characterised by reliance on a core business, and a culture and value system which strongly reflects the founders' ideology.

This raises an important contrast between highly diversified organisations operating in a variety of business sectors and 'critical function' organisations, whose main activities are restricted to a core industry/sector. Purcell argues that a strategic planning style conducive to strategic HRM is more likely to develop where there is a high level of vertical integration (interdependence between business units). Porter (1987) also argues for a more integrative aproach. He feels that portfolio management, which tends to view business units as independent entities, is an inappropriate basis for the development of corporate strategy in the diversified organisation. However, Purcell feels that organisations which emphasise long-term strategic objectives, core values and vertical linkages are becoming less common as the trend towards diversification into geographically and industrially unrelated areas gathers momentum. He feels that this trend will increasingly place the corporate focus on performance control and financial return and less weight will come to be placed on long-term strategic planning. This type of first-order strategies (on business priorities) and second-order strategies (on organisation structure and operational control) will heavily influence third-order personnel/industrial relations policy choices. Where the corporate value system emphasises short-term financial return and tight performance control it is more difficult to develop an integrated approach to personnel/industrial relations policy and related culture and style.

Purcell concludes that current trends in corporate strategy in many diversified organisations prohibit the development of strategic HRM. Consequently, he is pessimistic that many of the ingredients of new patterns of HRM will find favour with the majority of diversified organisations, whose corporate strategy is dominated by a concern for short-term financial criteria.

8.3.2. THE IMPORTANCE OF COMPETITIVE STRATEGY

In contrast to the prominence given by Purcell to the corporate level and, particularly, to portfolio planning, Porter (1985, 1987) argues that corporate strategy has failed 'dismally'. Using evidence from the diversification and subsequent divestments of thirty-three large, prestigious US organisations, Porter argues that the emphasis should be placed on developing competitive strategy at the business-unit level, since it is here that competition occurs. *Competitive strategy* is concerned with achieving sustainable competitive advantage. Porter identifies three generic strategies for achieving competitive advantage: (a) cost leadership, (b) product differentiation, and (c) focus/nichemanship. He feels that organisations must choose which of these types of competitive advantage they wish to achieve.

Cost leadership involves positioning the organisation as a low-cost producer of a standard 'no frills' product for a broad market. To succeed with a cost-leadership strategy Porter argues that the firm must become *the* cost leader and not one of several firms pursuing this strategy. Cost leadership requires an emphasis on tight managerial controls, low overheads, economies of scale and a dedication to the learning curve. Such characteristics would be unsuitable to the second generic strategy, *differentiation*. This strategy requires that an organisation's product or service becomes unique on some dimension which is valued by the buyer, thus ensuring a premium price. The basis for a differentiation may be the product or service itself, or other aspects such as delivery or after-sales service. Unlike cost leadership, Porter suggests that several firms can successfully pursue a differentiation strategy in an industry. Cost leadership and differentiation strategies involve a broad focus which serves all or a major portion of the target market. In contrast, the third generic competitive strategy, *focus*, involves choosing a narrow market segment and serving this either through a low-cost or a differentiation focus.

Porter feels that in order to achieve sustainable competitive advantage, organisations must successfully pursue one of these three competitive strategies. An organisation's choice of generic strategy specifies the fundamental approach to competitive advantage that the firm seeks to achieve, and provides the context for policies and actions in each key functional area, such as personnel/industrial relations management.

8.3.3. LINKING BUSINESS/COMPETITIVE STRATEGY AND PERSONNEL/INDUSTRIAL RELATIONS POLICY CHOICE

Porter suggests that each generic competitive strategy (low-cost, differentiation and focus) warrants different skills and requirements for success. Of particular significance is the need to match personnel selection, workforce profile and employment practices with the desired generic strategy. Porter further contends that different organisation cultures are implied in each strategy, and that personnel/industrial relations policy choice is a key influence in establishing and maintaining 'appropriate' corporate cultures. In the differentiation strategy, it is suggested that culture might serve to encourage innovation, individuality and risk taking; in cost leadership, culture might encourage frugality, discipline and attention to detail. Porter suggests there is no such thing as a good or bad culture. Culture is a means of achieving competitive advantage, and should match the organisation's business strategy. Culture is a means to an end, not an end in itself: 'Culture can powerfully reinforce the competitive advantage a generic strategy seeks to achieve, if the culture is an appropriate one' (Porter, 1987).

Another important aspect of the link between business strategy and personnel/industrial relations policy choice is the impact on organisation structure. At the formal level, *organisation structure* refers to the way an organisation is designed to achieve its objectives, and incorporates decisions on divisions of labour, job design, grouping of jobs/tasks, grouping of functions or businesses, and the degree of control exercised by senior management over operating units/sections. Chandler (1962) argues that an organisation's structure will largely be determined by its business strategy. He identifies four growth strategies that result in different organisation structures: (a) volume expansion, (b) geographic dispersion, (c) vertical integration and (d) product diversification. Chandler contends that, as organisations grow, their structures change from functional through product to multidivisional structures. Chandler's analysis indicates that organisations need to modify their structures and management practices to meet the requirements of different strategies.

Turning to the specific links between business strategy and personnel/industrial relations policies, it has been argued that organisations will experience severe problems in strategy implementation if it is not effectively linked with appropriate personnel/industrial relations policy choices (Fombrun, 1986; Fombrun et al., 1984). Fombrun et al. (1984) suggest that strategic management involves the consideration of three key issues:

(1) mission and strategy: identification of an organisation's purpose and plan on how this can be achieved;

(2) formal structure: for the organisation of people and tasks to achieve mission and strategy;

(3) personnel/industrial relations systems: recruitment, development, evaluation and reward of employees.

This framework is seen to differ from traditional approaches to strategic management by incorporating personnel/industrial relations (human resource) considerations as an integral component of strategic decision making. Fombrun et al. (1984) suggest that an organisation's personnel policies and practices symptomise managerial assumptions about employees and 'appropriate' workforce management practices. Fombrun (1986) identifies four key aspects of organisational approaches to workforce management, which give valuable insights into the managerial approach to employees:

(a) the nature of the psychological contract: This may vary from, at one extreme, a managerial perspective which views employees in instrumental terms and emphasises high levels of control of both employees and the work environment to, at the other extreme, an approach which sees employees as intelligent and committed beings who should be afforded challenging and meaningful work in a more benign work environment;

(b) level of employee involvement: Here organisational approaches may vary from those with high levels of employee involvement in decision making to those where decisions are solely a management prerogative;

(c) internal/external labour market: This addresses the relative emphasis on internal versus external recruitment and related differences in emphasis on employee development;

(d) performance evaluation: This factor addresses the relevant managerial emphasis on group versus individual performance.

8.3.4. MODELS OF BUSINESS STRATEGY—PERSONNEL POLICY LINKAGES

Numerous authors have identified models of suggested *business strategy –personnel/industrial relations policy linkages* (Fombrun et al., 1984; Miles and Snow, 1984; Porter, 1987; Schuler et al., 1987). These models are predominantly US based and some of the more prominent examples are reviewed below.

'DEFENDERS, PROSPECTORS, ANALYSERS' MODEL

Miles and Snow (1984) develop a conceptual framework linking business strategy and personnel/industrial relations policy choice by identifying three 'viable' organisation types characterised by the organisation's product market strategy. *Defenders* operate in relatively stable product markets, offer a narrow product range, use capital-intensive technology, adopt a functional structure, possess centralised planning and control systems, and emphasise skills in production efficiency, process engineering and cost control. Such organisations stick to established product lines and are characterised by stability in structure and a primary emphasis is on improving cost efficiency. *Prospectors* operate in broad product markets, offering diverse product lines, and continually pursue new product/market opportunities. These organisations adopt multiple and changing technology, a divisionalised and decentralised structure, and emphasise skills in product development and marketing. *Analysers* operate in both changing and stable product markets. They tend to combine the functional structure of defender organisations and the divisionalised structure of prospectors. In the stable areas, production efficiency is the key goal. In other areas, analysers closely evaluate competitors' initiatives and attempt to exploit these through a 'second-to-market' approach. Analysers are characterised by a limited product line, ongoing search for related product/market opportunities and a mixed organisation structure.

Miles and Snow suggest that successful organisations possess a consistent strategy which is aligned with and supported by complementary organisation structures and management practices. They also suggest that organisations which do not possess this environment–strategy–structure alignment (*reactors*) are not as successful as the other three categories. Miles and Snow also feel that these three strategies are similar to other strategic categorisations (such as Porter's three generic strategies); likening defenders to low-cost producers, prospectors to product differentiators and analysers to focused operations or 'nichemanship'. Difficulties in developing appropriate personnel/industrial relations policies are seen as a major barrier to the effective implementation of appropriate business strategies and structures. To emphasise the need to align personnel/industrial relations policy choice and business strategy, Miles and Snow identify organisations in each of the three strategic categorisations, namely defenders (Lincoln Electric), prospectors (Hewlett–Packard) and analysers (Texas Instruments), and suggest relevant personnel/industrial

Table 8.2. Linking business strategy and personnel/IR policy

	Strategic type		
	Defender	**Prospector**	**Analyser**
Product and market strategy	Limited, stable product line; predictable markets	Broad, changing product line; changing markets	Stable and changing product line; predictable and changing markets
Research and development	Narrow; product improvement	Broad; new product development	Focused; 'second to market'
Marketing	Sales emphasis	Market research emphasis	Extensive marketing campaigns
Personnel strategy	Maintenance	Entrepreneurial	Co-ordination
Recruitment and selection	'Make'; internal	'Buy'; external	'Make and Buy'; mixed
Manpower planning	Formal, extensive	Informal, limited	Formal, extensive
Training and development	Extensive; skill building	Limited; skill acquisition	Extensive; skill building
Appraisal	Process oriented; identify training needs	Result oriented; identify staffing needs	Process oriented; identify training and staffing needs
	Individual/group performance evaluation	Corporate/division performance evaluation	Individual/group/ divisional evaluation
Rewards	Based on level in hierarchy; internal equity	Based on performance; external equity	Mostly based on level in hierarchy; internal and external equity
	Pay oriented	Incentive oriented	Pay and incentive oriented

Source: Adapted from Miles and Snow, 1984.

relations approaches for each strategy (see table 8.2). In defender organisations the emphasis is on *building* their own human resources through recruitment at entry levels and promotion through the ranks. Selection, placement, training/development, appraisal and ensuring a fit between the reward system and job design are the key personnel activities. Defender organisations are characterised as lean and hard working, and demand predictable, planned personnel/industrial relations policies and regular maintenance of these policies. Prospector organisations experience rapid change demanding considerable human resource redeployment. The major personnel emphasis is on sourcing and deploying high-quality human resources. The personnel objective is entrepreneurial, acquiring and developing critical staff. There is little opportunity for long-term planning or sophisticated personnel techniques. In analyser organisations the emphasis is on developing appropriate organisational structures and management practices. A key skill is the allocation of human resources across business units operating in different strategic modes. Thus, the personnel emphasis is on *co-ordinating personnel/industrial relations policies* and allocating human resources across the organisation.

Table 8.3. Linking business strategy, employee characteristics and personnel/IR policy choice

Strategic type

1 Entrepreneurial	2 Dynamic growth	3 Extract profit	4 Divestiture	5 Turnaround

Employee characteristics

Short- v Long-term focus
Repetitive, predictable v Creative, innovative behaviour
High v Low organisational identification
Co-operative, interdependent v Independent autonomous behaviour
High v Low concern for quality
High v Low concern for quantity
High v Low risk taking
High concern for process v High concern for results
High v Low preference for responsibility
Flexible v Inflexible attitude to change
Comfortable with stability v Tolerant of ambiguity/instability
Narrow skill application v Broad skill application

Personnel policy menu

Manpower planning
Staffing
Rewards
Appraisal
Training and development
Labour–management relations

Source: Adapted from Schuler and Jackson, 1987.

'LIFE CYCLE–EMPLOYEE CHARACTERISTICS' MODEL

Possibly the most extensive work on linking business strategy and personnel/industrial relations has been conducted by Randall Schuler in the US. Schuler et al. (1987) suggest that business strategies are most effective when '. . . systematically co-ordinated with human resources management practices'. Schuler further suggests a key objective in personnel and industrial relations policy choice is to develop employee characteristics which 'fit' the organisation's particular strategy. Schuler et al. identify five possible strategic types and indicate the optional employee characteristics which organisations may seek to develop via choices from key personnel/industrial relations policy menus (see table 8.3). In matching business strategy and personnel/industrial relations policy, Schuler (1987a,b) suggests that correct policy choices depend on what the organisation, and particularly its business strategy, demands from employees. Choices may be made from six personnel/HR policy menus: manpower planning, staffing, rewards, appraisal, training and development, and labour–management relations. Optional policy choices are identified for each policy 'menu', as outlined in table 8.4. The overriding objective is to achieve a match between business strategy and complementary employee characteristics: 'The strategically driven company must instil in and elicit from its employees the characteristics that best support its chosen strategy' (Schuler and Jackson, 1987).

Schuler and Jackson (1987) also suggest that different market and cost considerations influence the appropriateness of different personnel/industrial relations policy choices. They use product-life-cycle phases to evaluate product market influences on both business strategy and personnel policy choice. In the *growth phase*, the attraction of high-calibre employees is seen as the main priority. The key organisational need is for technical talent to transform ideas into saleable products or services. The major source of human resources is the external labour market. The organisation attracts employees by differentiating itself using innovative personnel policies such as employment tenure and high levels of employee participation. Various categories of part-time, temporary or subcontract labour may be used to buffer full-time employees during economic downturns. Industrial relations issues are handled via various communications/participative mechanisms. Wages are normally high and tied to profitability and/or employee skills. This phase is felt to parallel closely the dynamic growth strategy.

In the *maturity phase*, the organisation has a large internal labour market and the emphasis is on manpower retention. Jobs tend to be more narrowly defined and wages tend to be based more on grade definitions than profitability or skills. There is less employee participation, and downturns in profitability may result in layoffs. Industrial relations issues are handled through collective bargaining. This phase is felt to parallel closely the extract profit strategy.

Table 8.4. Personnel policy menus

1. Manpower planning

Formal	v	Informal
Loose	v	Tight
Short-term	v	Long-term
Explicit job analysis	v	Implicit job analysis
Narrowly defined jobs	v	Broadly defined jobs
Segmented organisational design	v	Integrated organisational design

2. Staffing

Internal	v	External sources
Narrow career paths	v	Broad career paths
Single	v	Multiple promotion ladder
Explicit	v	Implicit promotion criteria
Limited	v	Extensive socialisation
Closed	v	Open selection procedures

3. Appraisal

High	v	Low integration with other personnel activities
Behavioural	v	Results criteria
Concern for current	v	Future performance
High	v	Low employee participation
Long-term	v	Short-term criteria
Individual	v	Group criteria

4. Rewards

High	v	Low basic salary
Internal	v	External equity
Many	v	Few benefits
Flexible	v	Fixed reward package
Many	v	Few incentives
Long-term	v	Short-term incentives
High	v	Low employment security

5. Training and development

Long-term	v	Short-term emphasis
Broad	v	Narrow emphasis
Productivity	v	Quality of worklife emphasis
Planned, systematic	v	Unplanned, unsystematic
Individual	v	Group orientation
High	v	Low employee participation

6. Labour–management relations

Traditional	v	Non-traditional orientation

Source: Adapted from Schuler and Jackson, 1987.

In the *decline phase* the organisation must cut both costs and employee numbers. There is downward pressure on wages and a need to agree criteria on which to base redundancy decisions. While this phase is not seen as a parallel to a turnaround strategy, it is clearly a precipitating factor. In such a crisis situation the future direction of the organisation is uncertain.

Schuler and Jackson (1987) then examined personnel policy choice decisions in four specific areas (job design, performance appraisal, rewards, and training and development) in organisations pursuing three distinct business strategies (namely dynamic growth, extract profit and turnaround) They concluded that there are predictable relationships between business strategy and personnel/industrial relations policy choice. However, they found no proof that these choices were systematically selected to fit particular strategies. They also found no conclusive evidence that personnel/industrial relations policies which fit business strategies contribute to greater organisational effectiveness. They suggest that fitting personnel/industrial relations policies is an important variable in contributing to effectiveness, but that other factors such as leadership and culture must also be taken into consideration. Schuler and Jackson feel that as organisations strive to achieve greater fit between business strategy and personnel/industrial relations policies, this will lead to continuous change in personnel and industrial relations management practices with employees being exposed to a range of different practices in the course of employment. Thus, employees may be expected to exhibit different characteristics and work under different sets of employment conditions at different stages in their working lives. This implies that multi-business (diversified) organisations are likely to have considerable variation in personnel/industrial relations policies to fit with their different business conditions and strategies. This conclusion is similar to that of Purcell (1989) and Armstrong (1988), who suggest that in diversified organisations strategic decision making will primarily concern financial issues with decisions on personnel and industrial relations policy devolved to business-unit management.

'STRATEGY IMPLEMENTATION' MODEL

A similar model linking business strategy, organisation structure and personnel/industrial relations policies is developed by Fombrun et al. (1984). They contend that integrating human resource considerations into strategic decision making represents 'a true frontier' for personnel and industrial relations management but suggest that, while many organisations wish to include human resource issues in strategic decision making, the traditional approach has been to consider these issues only after strategic decisions have been taken. Fombrun et al. suggest that very often the major emphasis in strategic planning has been on strategy formulation, with very little thought being given to strategy implementation. They feel that this has resulted in the failure of strategic planning at the operational level. This lack of attention to strategy implementation is seen as a major challenge to organisations and serves to give a central role to personnel/industrial relations policies in ensuring employees work to make strategies happen. It is suggested that personnel/industrial relations policies have a key role to play in effective strategy implementation since they are the key to implementing strategic choice and to achieving better alignment between strategic direction and workforce management practices. This view is echoed in the work of Butler (1988) and Purcell (1989). Purcell sees personnel/industrial relations policy choice as important 'downstream' strategic choice, which serves to effectively implement 'upstream' strategic decisions on competitive strategy.

Fombrun et al. suggest that personnel and industrial relations systems need to become more flexible so as to 'fit' strategic choice. They identify four key areas of policy choice: selection/promotion/placement, rewards and employee development, appraisal, and evaluate each in relation to their 'fit' with business strategy.

Selection/promotion/placement incorporates the external hiring of employees and all activities related to the internal movement of employees across positions. This policy area has been characterised by Beer et al. (1984) as 'human resource flow', and is seen as a prerequisite of effective performance. The role of an effective *reward system* is to encourage a balance of priorities between the achievement of long- and short-term goals. *Employee development* helps to ensure that the organisation has an adequate supply of human resource talent. An important facilitator of effective employee development is an adequate manpower planning system, which provides an accurate inventory of human resources and makes accurate forecasts of manpower needs. Fombrun (1986) feels that few organisations have effective manpower planning systems. A major reason is that data on employees is often inadequate. This is partially attributed to inadequate *appraisal*, which is seen as the weakest of all personnel activities. It is suggested that the key to effective appraisal at a strategic level is the commitment of 'quality managerial time to systematic examination and evaluation of executive talent' (Schuler et al., 1987).

COMMENTARY

It would, therefore, appear that personnel and industrial relations policy choice represents an important strategic decision for organisations. It is felt to have a major impact on competitive advantage (Porter, 1987), organisation structure (Chandler, 1962) and culture (Peters and Waterman, 1982). While much of the prescriptive literature suggests that organisations should adapt particular 'best-practice' modes in each specialist personnel/industrial relations area, it is increasingly argued that optimal policy choice is linked to the unique characteristics of the individual organisation. Consequently, it is suggested that organisations need to achieve a fit between personnel and industrial relations policy choice and broader strategic considerations, particularly business/competitive strategy and product market conditions.

This latter issue concerning product market conditions is clearly a key contextual concern for organisations in taking strategic and operational decisions, and is discussed in the next section.

8.4. THE INFLUENCE OF THE PRODUCT MARKET

An organisation's business strategy will be developed within the context of a particular product market. The characteristics of a particular product market will be influenced by a variety of factors such as the cost of entry, nature of competition, technology and the customer base. Thurley and Wood (1983) argue that broad strategy objectives can be linked to the product market objectives, the enterprise's position in that market, the organisational characteristics and the political, social and economic influences in the community where the enterprise operates (expressed through government policy and legislation, and interest-group pressures). These factors will impact upon the industrial relations strategies adopted in the organisation. This can be seen from figure 8.6, where a product market change may lead to a variety of business decisions which may profoundly affect industrial relations, such as the decision to relocate to a greenfield site.

Figure 8.6. Product market change, business strategy and industrial relations

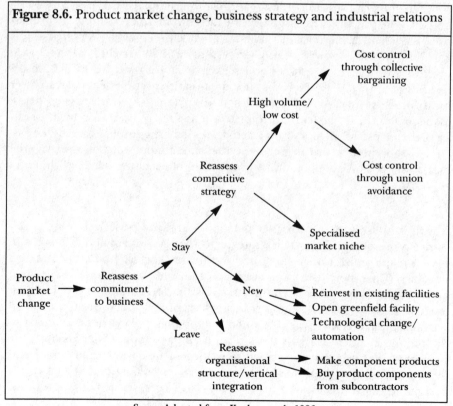

Source: Adapted from Kochan et al., 1986.

There are some obvious key economic factors which influence the employment relationship. These include the nature of labour markets, profit levels and inflation. Thurley and Wood (1983) argue that the following seven examples of businesses provide a typical overview of the business strategy types, and the likely product market conditions of each strategy type:

– economic mission based (founder organisations);
– public sector—service based;
– key private and public companies and other public sector companies;
– multinational conglomerates;
– small businesses and contractors;
– market entry companies;
– established firm in decline.

The strategy type and product market conditions are felt to have a knock-on effect on personnel/industrial relations strategies, policies and practices, e.g. recruitment, remuneration and industrial relations strategies. Thurley and Wood (1983) outline the 'appropriate' conditions for different types of strategies. It is argued that managements are increasingly recognising that improved utilisation of employees is linked to competitive advantage (Guest, 1987). This leads them to search for the appropriate style to suit their particular circumstances. This is particularly necessary where the organisation faces increased competition in its product market(s).

The impact of product market conditions on management approaches to industrial relations is discussed in detail in chapter 9.

8.5. SUMMARY AND CONCLUSIONS

This chapter has attempted to critically review the emergence of Human Resource Management in general and in the Irish context. It has also considered the issues of corporate and competitive strategies, the impact of product markets and the increased emphasis on more closely aligning business strategies and personnel/industrial relations policy choice. In focusing on change in industrial relations practice an area of particular significance to both researchers and practitioners is the degree to which HRM-type approaches are being adopted and are replacing the traditional pluralist industrial relations model. In Ireland, as elsewhere, it has been argued that competitive pressures, reduced trade union power and new models of management practice have encouraged organisations to adopt more innovative industrial relations practices (Flood, 1989).

This basis for integrating personnel and industrial relations considerations into strategic decision making seems to stem from two contrasting sources in the literature. The first source emanates from the 'personnel/industrial relations' literature and is based on the 'human capital approach' of the Harvard Business School model (Beer et al., 1984, 1985). This model is the

263

basis for the 'soft' or benign approach to industrial relations management, whereby senior management acknowledge that people are the organisation's 'most valuable' resource and consequently seek to implement strategic decisions to optimally utilise this resource by implementing a range of personnel policies designed to increase employee commitment and involvement (Blyton and Turnbull, 1992; Guest, 1989a,b; Storey, 1989). The second source emanates from the business strategy literature (specifically Fombrun et al., 1984) and equates to what has been termed '*hard HRM*' (Keenoy, 1990; Storey, 1989, 1992). This approach rationalises the strategic importance of HRM on colder economic criteria by suggesting that economic returns from human resources can be substantially improved by integrating personnel and industrial relations considerations into business strategy. Blyton and Turnbull (1992) suggest that this approach is 'avowedly unitarist in outlook: a form of "utilitarian-instrumentalism" which provides a singular endorsement of managerialist views'. This view would seem to be confirmed by the proliferation of somewhat prescriptive *product market–strategy–personnel/IR policy choice* configurations, briefly discussed in this chapter. These seem to imply that there is a 'best-policy' menu to suit an organisation's particular business strategy and product market conditions, and it is up to senior management to find and implement this personnel and industrial relations policy menu.

In the Irish context there has been little investigation of the linkages between business strategy, product market conditions and developments in industrial relations. In evaluating current developments in industrial relations in Ireland, there is a danger of confusing prominent examples of 'soft' HRM with the widespread pervasiveness of such approaches. In the UK context Blyton and Turnbull (1992) note that empirically it is difficult to find examples of organisations that adopt coherent HRM approaches and that, when firms attempt to implement HRM, they run up against its inherent contradictions and inconsistencies. Indeed, much of the evidence and support for HRM approaches emanates from the US. However, the context of such developments in the US is considerably different from Ireland, and it seems inappropriate to simply extrapolate from the US experience and infer similar trends here. Differences in industrial and employment structure and trade union density are some of the unique factors influencing organisational approaches to industrial relations in the Republic of Ireland.

In the Irish context it has been suggested that organisations will increasingly examine alternative personnel/industrial relations policy choices which might be used to complement different product market conditions and business strategies (Hannaway, 1987, 1992; Murray, 1984). If this were indeed the case and HRM-type approaches were being adopted on a large scale, it is probable that these developments would be most evident in two areas of workforce management, namely manpower planning and industrial relations. Firstly, manpower planning is identified as an important indicator of the strategic significance of workforce management considerations. Organisations which place a strong emphasis on personnel/industrial relations policy choice would be expected to adopt a sophisticated approach to manpower planning, particularly in relation to profiling current manpower resources, identifying manpower needs and developing appropriate workforce competencies. Secondly, industrial relations is identified as a key issue. Industrial relations has traditionally been the mechanism through which employers and workers have attempted to resolve conflicting interests. For most larger organisations in the Republic of Ireland this has traditionally been achieved via the 'pluralist' model, incorporating adversarial collective bargaining between organised employees and management. The objective of management in industrial relations was to establish and sustain adequate control and co-operation in industrial relations, and to ensure a stable working environment which allowed the organisation to meet its primary production/service goals. If, as some of the literature suggests, organisations are moving away from the pluralist–adversarial model, this would involve significant change in managerial approaches to industrial relations in the Republic of Ireland. Specifically, it would involve change in areas such as management–employee communications, employee involvement and collective bargaining. This development is considered in the next chapter on management styles in industrial relations.

CHAPTER NINE

Changing Patterns of Industrial Relations: The Significance of Management Styles in Industrial Relations

9.1. INTRODUCTION

The previous chapter has highlighted the marked increase in emphasis in the literature in developing linkages between business strategy and personnel/ industrial relations policy choice. This literature places considerable emphasis on the strategic significance of personnel and industrial relations considerations. Despite this persuasive literature, there remains considerable confusion, and indeed doubt, about the degree to which managements consider personnel and industrial relations issues in strategic decision making and choose complementary policies. Beyond some prominent examples of strategic approaches to workforce management, there remains a reservation that the great majority of organisations do not exercise any degree of strategic choice in personnel or industrial relations management and, consequently, their approach may be variously characterised as pragmatic, opportunist, reactive or, to use the old cliché, 'fire-fighting'.

This chapter considers the issue of management styles in industrial relations in the context of changing patterns of industrial relations. It examines the nature of management styles in industrial relations, the possible determinants of style, the dimensions along which management styles in industrial relations may differ and the alternative styles that may be adopted in organisations. The final section reviews contemporary developments in industrial relations style in the context of changing patterns of industrial relations in Ireland, and presents a typology of management styles considered appropriate in the Irish context.

9.2. MANAGEMENT STYLES IN INDUSTRIAL RELATIONS

9.2.1. THE MEANING OF MANAGEMENT STYLE

The concept of style is defined as 'the distinctive manner, pattern or approach of individuals or entities in doing something' (Oxford Dictionary, 1986). In industrial relations the concept of management style has been principally used to explain variations in organisational policies and practices in industrial relations (Fox, 1966, 1974a,b; Marchington and Parker, 1990; Poole, 1986; Purcell, 1987; Purcell and Sisson, 1983). The idea of management style in industrial relations has been inextricably linked to the notion of strategic choice (Kochan et al., 1986; Purcell, 1987). Thus, differences in management styles are related to managerial choice in employment policies and practices patterned according to general categories of action and wider values/ideologies, and constrained and modified by external and internal variables (Poole, 1986; Purcell, 1987). This patterning has led to the development of typologies of identifiable and different 'ideal-typical' management styles (Poole, 1986; Purcell, 1987; Purcell and Sisson, 1983; Salamon, 1992). However, beyond this general understanding, the notion of management style in industrial relations is a problematic concept and there appears to be little broad agreement on precisely what is meant by the term 'style' in industrial relations.

The most influential contemporary writer on the area of management style is John Purcell (see Purcell, 1983, 1987; Purcell and Gray, 1986; Purcell and Sisson, 1983). Purcell (1987) conceives of management style in quite narrow terms as implying '. . . the existence of a distinctive set of guiding principles, written or otherwise, which set parameters to and signposts for, management action in the ways employees are treated and particular events handled'.

Thus, for Purcell it would appear that management style can only exist where senior management have made explicit choices about their desired approach to industrial relations and have translated these choices into particular industrial relations policies and practices. Purcell's definition of management style thus excludes implicit reactive patterns of industrial relations management stating that 'pragmatic, reactive responses to labour problems cannot be classified as management style'. Purcell goes on to suggest that the study of management style should be restricted to those organisations 'which, for whatever reason, but often related to the unique contribution of the founding fathers . . . have a guiding set of principles which delineate the boundaries and direction of acceptable management action in dealing with employees' (Purcell and Sisson, 1983).

While Purcell's observations are useful and have made a significant contribution to the academic debate, there are a number of inherent difficulties with his interpretation. A particular difficulty arises in relation to Purcell's definition of management style as only existing where management have made explicit choices in relation to its desired style and translated these into specific policy manifestations. While a large number of organisations have a philosophy towards workforce management, this may not be written down or indeed espoused but must be inferred from how employees and trade unions are managed and treated within the organisation. Thus, what may seem pragmatic or reactive responses to industrial relations issues are often guided by an implicit philosophy on workforce management. To say that such implicit patterns do not constitute a style of industrial relations management appears excessively restrictive (see also Marchington and Parker, 1990). It is therefore suggested that Purcell's interpretation of management style is somewhat narrow and that management style should be conceived of in more generic terms as '*the distinctive approaches, policies and practices which organisations may adopt in the management of industrial relations issues in an organisation*'. This conception of management style is illustrated in figure 9.1. Thus, it is not necessary for management style to lead to a desired outcome, and, as Purcell (1987) acknowledges, there may well be 'a frequent shortfall between aspiration and outcome' given the power relations between management and employees. It is therefore the approach, policies and practices (action) which lead to the development of distinctive industrial relations styles rather than the outcomes of policies and practice (results). Equally, management style is a dynamic concept which may be refined and changed over time in the light of changing needs and circumstances. The influence and mediating effect of environmental variables on industrial relations styles is considered later in this chapter.

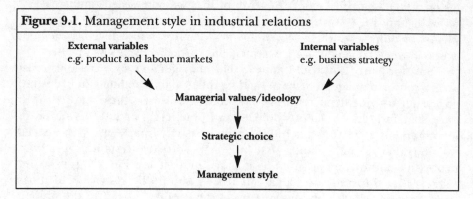

Figure 9.1. Management style in industrial relations

External variables
e.g. product and labour markets

Internal variables
e.g. business strategy

Managerial values/ideology

Strategic choice

Management style

9.2.2. STRATEGIC DECISION MAKING AND INDUSTRIAL RELATIONS

With the ownership of industry primarily vested in the hands of private enterprise, profitability remains the major yardstick of corporate success and management objectives are primarily identified with owner interests. Since control is associated with ownership, the power to exercise control over work is exercised by the owners of organisations through their representatives in the workplace, namely management. This link between ownership and the legitimacy of management authority is inescapable despite the fact that management must also be responsible to other interest groups such as employees and their trade unions. Consequently, management (and particularly senior management) exercise considerable power and influence by virtue of their scope to take strategic decisions. Often the impact of strategic decisions on industrial relations will be indirect. For example, an organisation may decide to terminate a particular product line because of financial and market considerations. However, this decision may necessitate redundancies and detrimentally affect morale and ultimately industrial relations. Management may also take strategic business decisions which directly influence industrial relations such as those relating to trade union recognition. Whether senior managements actually *do* take strategic industrial relations decisions is a matter for debate. A traditional feeling has been that senior management concentrate their strategic decision making on 'primary' business areas such as investment or production, and any attention devoted to industrial relations was secondary and somewhat 'incidental' to the main thrust of such strategic decision making (Purcell, 1987). On the other hand, there is tentative evidence to suggest that some organisations adopt a particular industrial relations style or approach and take well-thought-out strategic decisions to establish and sustain this style (Beer et al., 1984; Guest, 1987). Indeed, practice would seem to vary widely from a general approach of 'incidentalism' characterised by little or no strategic decision making in industrial relations, to a planned approach involving a series of key strategic decisions taken to effect a particular desired style. This variation is portrayed in figure 9.2 as a continuum ranging from 'incidentalist' to 'planned' approaches to industrial relations management. On this continuum organisations may adopt a variety of positions and it is difficult to ascertain the exact status of industrial relations in strategic decision making. However, it is possible to identify areas where management may take strategic decisions which directly or indirectly impact upon industrial relations as indicated in table 9.1.

Figure 9.2. Continuum of strategic decision making in industrial relations

'Incidentalism'	Planned industrial relations approach
No consideration of employee relations in strategic decision making	Key strategic decisions taken to achieve/advance a particular desired IR approach

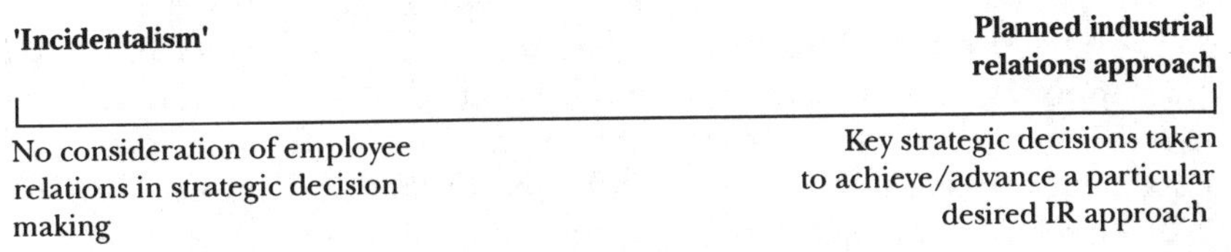

Table 9.1. Indicative strategic decisions impacting on industrial relations

Decisions	Impact on industrial relations
Location of plant	Influences nature of labour force and related issues such as unionisation.
Size of plant	Influences span of managerial control, communications, leadership/managerial style.
Recruitment	By deciding on the nature of the workforce, management may directly and indirectly influence IR (e.g. closed shop).
Training and development	Training and development allows opportunity to influence both management and employee approaches and attitudes to IR.
Unionisation	In a 'greenfield' situation senior management may have the opportunity to decide on unionisation or non-unionisation. This will obviously affect the whole nature of subsequent approaches to IR.
Level of bargaining	In a unionised framework management can influence the nature of IR and particularly the role of trade unions by determining the bargaining level.
Employer association	Deciding whether to join an employer association will influence subsequent IR decisions.
Procedural formalisation	The degree to which IR procedures are adopted and implemented will influence workplace IR.
Use of management techniques	By introducing techniques such as performance appraisal or job evaluation to aid decisions on issues such as pay, management may effectively limit the scope of trade unions in influencing such decisions. Such techniques may also be used to facilitate a move away from distributive collective bargaining to a more consultative approach.

9.2.3. THE IMPACT OF STRATEGIC CHOICE ON INDUSTRIAL RELATIONS STYLE

As discussed above and illustrated in figure 9.1 organisations will clearly differ in their approaches to industrial relations. Purcell (1987) notes the tendency to identify and contrast prominent organisations according to their 'employment policies and practices', and suggests that differences which arise cannot be wholly explained by structural variables such as size, product markets and technology. Rather, Purcell identifies strategic choice (exercised by senior management) as a key factor explaining differences in styles of industrial relations management. Strategic decisions are conscious long-term decisions affecting the future of the organisation, and are integrative and proactive in nature, linking and affecting all business functions (Marchington and Parker, 1990). Several writers have identified the notion of strategy as basic to the analysis of managerial roles in industrial relations (Kochan et al., 1986; Poole, 1986; Purcell, 1987). Strategic choice in industrial relations addresses the degree to which management (a) possess and (b) exercise strategic choice in developing industrial relations policies and practices. The notion of strategic choice infers that senior management possess some room for manoeuvre and, while environmental factors may constrain the range of choice, they retain considerable power in making decisions on 'appropriate' styles and policies. Senior management can therefore use their resources and power to make strategic choices which both influence environmental factors and affect particular management styles. Management styles in industrial relations should therefore be evaluated in terms of the interplay between environmental factors, managerial ideology/values and strategic choice. As Marchington and Parker (1990) state:

> Choice should be viewed as both a cause and a consequence of environmental influences, that is, managements have some influence over the kind of markets in which they choose to operate, and in some cases over the structure of the market itself, as well as having some choice over the way in which they respond to environmental pressures.

The interplay of such factors will clearly lead to different management styles and consequent variations in patterns of industrial relations management. Such variation will become manifest in an infinite range of industrial relations areas. Some generic areas of variation in management styles include the degree to which management adopt explicit desired styles of industrial relations, the levels of strategic consideration of industrial relations issues and the degree of policy sophistication in industrial relations. The impact of managerial ideology/values in interpreting developments in the internal environment and impacting upon strategic choice in industrial relations is discussed later in this chapter.

9.3. THE CONTEXT FOR CHOICE: INFLUENCES ON INDUSTRIAL RELATIONS STYLE

The different industrial relations styles discussed above are illustrative of the range of industrial relations choice confronting organisations. To identify and explain variations in management styles in industrial relations in different organisations requires an examination of the interplay of a diverse range of external and internal factors which influence and constrain managerial choice and practice in industrial relations. Kochan et al. (1986) have developed possibly the most comprehensive theoretical framework to explain

271

changing patterns in industrial relations. Kochan's analysis places particular emphasis on the external environment (such as product and labour markets), management values, business strategy and historical factors as key triggers in stimulating change in industrial relations. It is argued that changes in environmental conditions affect decisions on business strategy and, ultimately, industrial relations. Such decisions will be conditioned by managerial values and constrained by historical factors and current practice in industrial relations.

9.3.1. THE EXTERNAL ENVIRONMENT

The external environment is a major influence on organisational decision making. Trends in the external environment such as levels of *economic performance, public policy* and *cultural/societal values* will impact upon business strategy and management practice. Economic performance and public policy as manifested in areas such as levels of economic activity, state intervention and control, and approaches to organised labour clearly have a general impact on industrial relations style. For example, it may be argued that the anti-union policies of successive Conservative Governments in the UK give legitimacy and support to 'macho' management styles and policies designed to undermine the role of trade unions in the workplace. These factors are particularly important at an aggregate level in explaining variations in national approaches to industrial relations. Poole (1986) identifies the role of Government and centralised control ('challenge from above') as a key constraining influence on managerial prerogative/discretion in decision making. This line of argument suggests that the greater the level of centralised control (corporatism), the more limited the scope of management to develop atypical industrial relations styles and, particularly, non-union approaches. Conversely, it may be argued that a low level of central intervention in industrial relations allows management greater discretion in industrial relations and renders more likely the emergence of industrial relations styles diverging from the traditional pluralist-adversarial model.

Developments in *technology* is another key external environmental factor affecting managerial styles in industrial relations. Technology, seen in generic terms as the equipment used to perform particular tasks in the organisation and the way it is organised, is a major influence on approaches to managing industrial relations (Beer et al., 1984, 1985). Guest (1987) identifies technological/production feasibility as a requisite condition for the successful implementation of HRM-type styles and suggests that large-scale investment in short-cycle, repetitive, assembly-line technology mitigates against the job-design principles and autonomous team-working characteristic of 'soft' HRM. Technology also affects cost structure and consequently impacts upon key aspects of industrial relations such as reward systems. Marchington (1982) suggests that in labour-intensive sectors, where labour costs are high, organisations may be more constrained in developing employee-oriented management styles. However, in capital-intensive sectors where labour constitutes a small proportion of total costs, organisations may have greater scope to adopt 'softer' industrial relations styles, incorporating, for example, attractive rewards and employee development policies.

The *labour market* is a particularly important influence on industrial relations especially in relation to recruitment, employee development and reward systems. Poole (1986) notes the modifying effect of labour market conditions on industrial relations styles. In particular, high unemployment clearly impacts on the power balance in labour–management relations and can facilitate 'directive' forms of decision making. Looking at the Irish labour market the most notable developments include the progressive decline of agricultural employment and the growth of the service sector. Other notable developments in employment structure are the increased feminisation of the workforce and the growth of 'atypical' employment forms. A more unique characteristic of the Irish labour market is its relatively young age profile and exceptionally high level of unemployment. The consequentially 'loose' nature of the Irish labour market means that most categories of labour are in oversupply, with the result that 'dipping' into the external labour market is a ready option for employers. Such labour market conditions tend to reduce the onus on organisations to establish comprehensive employee development policies as might be the case in less buoyant labour markets. These factors clearly affect industrial relations. For example, high unemployment tends to place a premium on job security. It also exerts a downward pressure on wages and affects other aspects of industrial relations such as labour turnover and power relations in collective bargaining.

An organisation's *product market* is seen as possibly the most significant influence on strategic decision making and will exert considerable influence on industrial relations style. It has been suggested that the growth of distinctive managerial styles and strategies in industrial relations may be attributed in part to economic conditions and especially to the nature of product markets (Kochan et al., 1984, 1986; Purcell, 1983). Poole (1986) identifies the existence of a mature market and the will to compete across all segments as leading to a 'shift in emphasis in [industrial] relations away from maintaining labour peace . . . to one of controlling labour costs, streamlining work roles and increasing productivity in order to meet growing price competition'. He suggests that highly competitive product markets lead to more 'directive managerial styles, the abandonment of constitutionalism and the focus on individual employees at the expense of trade union representatives' (Poole, 1986). The characteristics of an organisation's product market will be influenced by a variety of factors such as the cost of entry, nature of competition, technology, and the customer base. Marchington and Parker (1990) evaluate an organisation's product market along two dimensions: (a) monopoly power and (b) monopsony power. Monopoly power refers to the degree the organisation has power to dictate market terms to customers. High monopoly power may exist due to the dominance of a few organisations, high barriers to entry, unique product, etc. Monopsony power refers to the degree to which customers exert power over the organisation. High monopsony power may exist as a result of high levels of competition or because of reliance on powerful customers who can exert considerable control over price and other factors (e.g. credit terms, service); see figure 9.3.

Figure 9.3. Product market conditions and industrial relations style

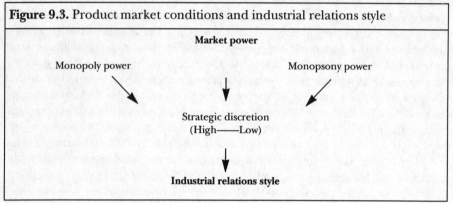

Source: Adapted from Marchington and Parker, 1990.

Marchington and Parker argue that the relative levels of monopoly and monopsony power which an organisation experiences provide a measure of the power of the market over employers and consequently influence the degree of management discretion in making strategic policy decisions in all functional areas including industrial relations. Where market power is low, senior management will have considerable discretion to make broad policy choices. Such favourable market conditions (high market share, growing market, stable demand) allow organisations greater scope to adopt 'investment-oriented styles' and are more conducive to the application of benign industrial relations practices such as comprehensive employee development policies, tenure commitments and gain sharing. This does not imply that employers will always adopt strategic 'resource'-type policies in favourable product market conditions. Rather, such conditions provide management with greater scope to choose from a range of personnel policy choices; actual choice will be further influenced by factors internal to the organisation, particularly management values and competitive strategy. On the other hand, organisations operating under high levels of market pressure may have considerably less scope for choice, and a more traditional cost and labour control approach may be appropriate.

9.3.2. THE INTERNAL ENVIRONMENT

While factors in the external environment will serve to guide management decisions on industrial relations, factors internal to the organisation will determine unique organisational responses to external factors. Such factors include managerial ideology, business strategy and organisation size/structure. *Organisation structure and size* are clearly important factors impacting upon industrial relations style. Numerous British studies have noted that trade union recognition and greater specialisation in personnel management are positively correlated with organisation size. In the Irish context, Gunnigle (1989) has found that managements in smaller organisations veer towards a unitarist frame of reference and adopt less formality in industrial relations than their counterparts in larger organisations. In relation to organisation structure, Purcell (1989) argues that senior (corporate) management in highly diversified organisations are primarily concerned with financial issues with the consequence that human resource considerations (including industrial relations) are not a concern of corporate decision making but rather an operational concern of management at the business-unit level. A corollary of this argument is that 'core business' organisations, whose operation relies on a narrow product range, are more likely to integrate human resource issues into strategic planning whereas highly diversified organisations are more likely to adopt differing personnel and industrial relations policies suited to the needs of different constituent divisions and establishments. Several writers identify the locus of industrial relations strategy formulation as a key issue in influencing the nature of establishment-level industrial relations including the presence or absence of trade unions (Kochan et al., 1984, 1986; Poole, 1986; Purcell and Sisson, 1983). Poole (1986) argues that the growth of conglomerate multinational enterprises presents management with the opportunity to develop industrial relations policies at corporate level 'where they are relatively unrestricted by intervention by Government or plant-level agreements with labour'. Of course, such discretion is dependent both on public policy (e.g. in relation to trade union recognition) and the distribution of power between the various parties, most notably employers, Government and trade unions/employees.

Another major internal factor impacting upon industrial relations style is *business strategy*. This issue was discussed at some length in chapter 8, and is seen as particularly significant in that HRM-based styles suggest that industrial relations considerations are an integral part of an organisation's business strategy, and that industrial relations policies and practices should be developed to complement strategy implementation. Business strategy occurs at the level of the individual business unit and is concerned with achieving sustainable competitive advantage in a particular industry or segment. As outlined earlier, Porter (1985, 1987) identifies generic strategies for achieving competitiveness with particular emphasis on two distinctive routes to competitive advantage: cost leadership and product differentiation. Porter maintains that the organisation's choice of generic strategy specifies the fundamental approach to competitive advantage that the firm seeks to achieve and provides the context for policies and actions in each key functional area including workforce management and employee development. Business strategy is therefore seen as a significant influencing factor on management approaches to industrial relations.

Other important factors which impact on an organisation's industrial relations style include the *characteristics of the current workforce* and *established personnel/industrial relations practices*. These factors will be particularly important in impacting upon the effectiveness of change initiatives in areas such as employee involvement or job redesign. For example, Hackman and Oldham's (1980) job enrichment approach acknowledges that all employees may not react favourably to their suggestions for enriching jobs or quality of work life; only those with a strong desire for achievement, responsibility and autonomy are expected to be motivated by such job redesign initiatives. These traits may in turn have been conditioned by traditional personnel/industrial relations policies and practices. For example, if internal mobility and individual initiative have traditionally been discouraged, it may be difficult to quickly implement a comprehensive employee development and promotion policy. At a more general level industrial relations management practice in Ireland has traditionally been associated with a strong collectivist industrial relations emphasis and consequent reliance on collective bargaining as the main vehicle for managing industrial relations at establishment level. Over time these traditions have led to the institutionalisation of established or accepted personnel/industrial relations practices and systems which reflect both the roles and influence of the major actors and 'custom and practice' on how key issues in industrial relations are handled. The significance of 'established personnel/industrial relations' is clearly a factor whose impact differs significantly between established and new companies. Specifically, newly established 'greenfield' firms are felt to have considerably more scope to choose from a range of alternative approaches to industrial relations, while management approaches to industrial relations in established companies will be circumscribed by past practice and the established industrial relations system. In the absence of severe crisis it is likely that change in industrial relations in established companies will comprise of incremental variations on the established system.

9.3.3. MANAGERIAL VALUES AND IDEOLOGY

Management values and ideology are seen as key variables impacting on managerial styles in industrial relations. Management values and ideology incorporate the deeply held beliefs of senior management which guide decisions on various aspects of workforce management. It is clear from our earlier discussion that managerial values and ideology are critical factors in interpreting developments in the external and internal environment, and in making decisions on the organisation's overall approach to industrial relations (Purcell and Sisson, 1983; Purcell, 1987; Rollinson, 1993). It was also noted earlier that management's desired approach will closely reflect their underlying values but may not necessarily translate into practice or behaviour because of the mediating effect of environmental variables (Poole, 1986; Rollinson, 1993; Salamon, 1992). Thus, a critical issue in the study of management style is the interaction between management values, environmental variables, strategic choice and industrial relations style.

Analyses of change in industrial relations over the past two decades have given ever-increased prominence to the role of management. In evaluating the nature and extent of change in American industrial relations, Kochan et al. (1986) place managerial values and styles at the centre of their analysis and suggest that '. . . since 1960 union behavior and Government policy have been much slower than employers to adapt to changes in their external environment and to changes in managerial strategies and policies'.

In relation to managerial values, Kochan et al. (1986) argue that these have a tremendous impact upon industrial relations styles and strategies, acting as a 'lens' through which 'managerial decision makers weigh their options for responding to cues from the external environment'. Thus, options that are inconsistent with accepted values are discounted or not consciously considered, and organisational responses in industrial relations will conform to managerial choices, which in turn reflect managerial values towards industrial relations. Friedman (1977, 1984) also places the role of management at the centre of his analysis of developments in industrial relations suggesting that the primary 'dynamic influence on the organisation of work is normally exerted through the initiatives of managers'. Friedman relates this dominance to the structure of capitalist societies: '. . . the fundamental structure of property rights in capitalist societies means that those with a primary claim of possession of the means of production will normally take the primary initiatives in the organisation of productive activity.'

Friedman argues for the primary consideration of managerial roles rather than external (such as technology or product markets) or structural factors on the basis that managerial responses to particular environmental contexts 'cannot be predicted simply from a reading of the structural factors' and because different styles and strategies may be chosen in response to particular contexts.

Clearly, all organisations are characterised by particular values and philosophies on workforce management and industrial relations. In some organisations such values/ideology may be explicit as demonstrated in statements of corporate mission or philosophy. In others it may be implicit and inferred from management practice in areas such as supervisory style, reward systems and communications. Guest (1989a) argues that strong leadership and strategic vision which incorporates human resources as a key component of strategic decision making are essential to the effective implementation of 'soft' HRM approaches.

Two cases may be highlighted to emphasise the key role of managerial values in impacting upon industrial relations style. Firstly, in a number of organisations the role of influential founders has had a determining influence on their organisation's corporate values and industrial relations style. Prominent international examples include Marks & Spencer, Hewlett–Packard and Wang. The influence of entrepreneurial founders is also prominent in Irish indigenous firms, and the industrial relations styles adopted in organisations such as Guinness Peat Aviation, Dunnes Stores and SuperQuinn seem to be heavily influenced by the values and philosophy of their respective founding chief executives. A second instance of the impact of managerial values on industrial relations style relates to the notion that managerial ideology is related to broader ethnic and cultural values. Of particular significance is the suggestion that managerial opposition to pluralism, and particularly unionisation, is characteristic of the value system of American managers, whereas certain HRM-type approaches which emphasise individual freedom and initiative, direct communications and merit-based rewards are very much in line with this value system (Bendix, 1956; Kochan et al., 1986). This interpretation is very significant in Ireland where the economy is heavily dependent on foreign investment, and where the bulk of such investment is American. In analysing the broad links between ideology and style Poole (1986) finds support for the suggestion that managerial ideologies differ between countries particularly in relation to the achievement of control over labour, and suggests that these have led to the emergence of different managerial styles in industrial relations. In relation to Japan, Poole (1986) suggests that, while culture is not solely responsible for 'benevolent paternalism' in the Japanese system of industrial relations, the 'modified Confucian world-view which prevailed in the late nineteenth century' was a significant influence in encouraging employers to evoke moral appeals to authority and to stress the efficiency of employees/management in facilitating both the achievement of personal objectives ('the desire of private industrialists and managers to be good moral citizens') and economic objectives ('such as public reputation as well as greater profits and efficiency and faster expansion' (Dore, 1973; Poole, 1986)). Poole (1986) argues that in the US context the effects of values and ideologies are most obviously manifest in union avoidance practices, a pronounced 'unitary' perspective and deployment of sophisticated human resource management approaches. Both Poole (1986) and Kochan et al. (1984, 1986) note that while managerial preferences have fluctuated over time, many US employers have embraced a non-union approach against a more general trend in the developed world towards a tacit acceptance of trade unions. Several writers identify the origins of this approach with the concept of 'individualism' in the wider US culture, coupled with prevalent private enterprise commitments (Foulkes, 1980; Guest, 1989a; Myers, 1976; Poole, 1986; Rothenberg and Silverman, 1973).

9.4. THE NATURE OF CHOICE: DIMENSIONS OF INDUSTRIAL RELATIONS STYLE

Turning to the nature of industrial relations style it is suggested that there are a number of benchmark dimensions along which managerial styles in industrial relations may differ, namely strategic integration, individualism and collectivism, and which may be used as a basis for analysing variations in management styles between organisations (Beer et al., 1984; Kochan et al., 1986; Purcell, 1987; Storey, 1989, 1992).

9.4.1. STRATEGIC INTEGRATION

Strategic integration refers to the degree to which industrial relations issues are part of strategic decision making and the degree to which decisions on industrial relations are linked to business strategy. High strategic integration involves integrating industrial relations issues into strategic planning, integrating personnel/industrial relations (IR) policies with policies in other functional areas (e.g. operations or marketing) and integrating policies across personnel/IR areas (e.g. recruitment, employee involvement, rewards). Low strategic integration is characterised by an absence of industrial relations considerations in strategic planning. A consequence is that industrial relations policies are essentially reactive in nature, are problem oriented and may indeed be incompatible across personnel policy areas. A traditional perception of strategic decision making is that it concerns 'primary' business issues (such as operations or finance) and any attention devoted to industrial relations issues is secondary and somewhat 'incidental'. On the other hand, it is evident that some organisations incorporate human resource issues in strategy creation and take well-thought-out strategic decisions to establish a particular industrial relations style. In practice, the idea of strategic integration as either total or absent does not adequately reflect the complexities of personnel and industrial relations policy choice in organisations. A more useful analysis is provided by Wood and Pecci (1990), who differentiate between *strategic human resource management*, where human resource issues are fully integrated into the strategic planning process, and *business-led human resource management*, where human resource policies are linked to the commercial imperatives of the organisation. Differences between these two approaches lie in the level of strategic consideration of personnel and industrial relations issues. In relation to strategic HRM, personnel and industrial relations issues are integral to strategic planning and form part of the organisation's long-term business strategy. In business-led HRM, personnel/industrial relations policies and practices are 'very much' a lower-order strategic activity but are linked to higher-order strategic decisions in areas such as product development or market penetration. This model differs significantly from the 'traditional' industrial relations model, where human resource considerations are not a significant top management concern but rather a peripheral operational responsibility. Consequently, they are not strategic in nature but rather *ad hoc*, piecemeal responses to immediate issues. These alternative approaches are represented in figure 9.4.

Figure 9.4. Dimension 1: strategic integration

High strategic integration	Strategic HRM	Human resource/IR issues are an integral component of the organisation's long-term strategy and mission.
	Business-led HRM	Human resource/IR issues are dependent upon but linked to higher-order decisions on corporate mission and objectives.
Low strategic integration	'Traditional' industrial relations/ personnel management	Human resource/IR issues are a peripheral management concern and handled in an essentially reactive fashion.

Contextual factors encouraging greater strategic integration include: increased competition and greater emphasis on achieving competitive advantage; organisation restructuring to devolve more responsibility to strategic business units (Flood, 1989; Goold and Campbell, 1987); increasing importance of culture and mission in focusing management effort and guiding decisions on resource allocation (Kelly and Brannick, 1988b; Storey and Sisson, 1990; Toner, 1987); quality rather than price as a dominant route to competitive advantage (Carroll, 1985). However, there is considerable debate on the nature of these developments, and factors mitigating against greater strategic integration include the traditionally low level of consideration of human resource issues in strategic decision making, the persuasiveness of the pluralist industrial relations tradition and probable growth in organisation size and diversity. A further limiting factor is the suggestion that comprehensive 'soft' HRM initiatives are confined to foreign-owned organisations (Storey and Sisson, 1990). In Ireland, the most notable examples of such approaches have been in foreign-owned, particularly US-owned, organisations (Toner, 1987).

9.4.2. INDIVIDUALISM

The second major dimension of industrial relations style is *individualism*. This dimension refers to the degree to which management adopt an essentially individual focus in industrial relations management and relates to factors such as advancement, fulfilment and opportunity for self-expression (Marchington and Parker, 1990; Purcell, 1987; Purcell and Gray, 1986). Purcell (1987) describes individualism as 'the extent to which the firm gives credence to the feelings and sentiments of each employee and seeks to develop and encourage each employee's capacity and role at work'. Purcell goes on to state that: 'Firms which have individualistically centred policies are thus expected to emphasise employees as a resource and be concerned with developing each person's talents and worth.'

High individualism is characterised by management recognising the resource value of employees. It is associated with comprehensive employee development policies and adopts the ideal-typical characteristics of 'soft' HRM, including sophisticated recruitment and socialisation of new employees, internal labour market emphasis, attractive rewards and good employment conditions. In contrast, low individualism sees employees in utilitarian terms within the overriding goal of profit maximisation, with the key managerial focus on labour control. The consequent management emphasis is on tight supervisory control, restrictive job design, minimisation of labour costs and little concern for broader human resource issues such as job satisfaction, employment security or employee commitment. Purcell suggests that paternalism, characterised by managerial values of caring, benevolence and welfare but little emphasis on employee development or internal labour markets, is a middleground between high and low individualism (see figure 9.5). High individualism is seen as a central ingredient of industrial relations styles which incorporates significant elements of human resource management (HRM). Guest (1987) argues that a major objective of strategic HRM is to 'develop in individual employees a feeling of commitment to the organisation', adopting the assumption that increased levels of commitment have substantial benefits for employees (e.g. job satisfaction) and the organisation (e.g. improved performance).

Figure 9.5. Dimension 2: individualism		
High individualism		Employees as a resource; comprehensive employee development emphasis
Paternalism		Caring, benevolence approach; little employee development
Low individualism		Employees as commodities; no employee development

Source: Adapted from Purcell, 1987.

9.4.3. COLLECTIVISM

The third benchmark dimension underpinning industrial relations style is *collectivism* (Purcell, 1987; Purcell and Gray, 1986). This refers to the degree to which management acknowledge the right of employees to collective representation and the involvement of the collective in influencing

management decision making. The collectivism dimension thus addresses both the level of democratic employee representative structures and the extent to which management legitimise their representational and bargaining role. This may primarily occur in a *de facto* fashion through the recognition or otherwise of trade unions for collective bargaining purposes, but also focuses on the extent of industrial democracy incorporating the degree to which employees have a *de jure* say (influence) in decision making. Employee influence is an important concept here. Employee influence implies that employee opinions are not only heard (i.e. employee 'voice') but that institutional arrangements are put in place to ensure such views are acted upon and effectively shape management decision making. Walton and McKersie (1965) provide a range for the extent of legitimacy which may be accorded to the concept of employee influence as follows:
– conflict marked by denial of legitimacy (unitary);
– containment—aggression by grudging acknowledgement;
– accommodation by acceptance of the *status quo*;
– co-operation through fully accepted legitimacy (pluralist).

The collectivist dimension thus spans a continuum from unitarist to co-operative, with adversarial collectivism taking up the middleground (Marchington and Parker, 1990; Purcell, 1987; see figure 9.6).

Figure 9.6. Dimension 3: collectivism

Source: Adapted from Purcell, 1987.

High collectivism is manifested in mechanisms for employee representation such as trade unions or works councils. It incorporates both the existence of such mechanisms and the spirit in which management approaches their operation, particularly the degree to which management actively supports employee involvement or alternatively seeks to minimise its impact on the organisation (Purcell, 1987). The 'soft' HRM approach has been associated with a move from collectivism to individualism via sophisticated recruitment, rewards and employee development policies (Guest, 1987, 1989a). However, Purcell (1987) draws on a number of British studies to demonstrate that individualism need not necessarily counterpoise collectivism so that managements can develop policies to increase individualism whilst retaining established collectivist structures including trade union recognition. Marchington and Parker (1990) comment that this interpretation makes the dimensions of management style more 'dynamic', allowing organisations to alter their positions along these dimensions over time.

9.5. PERSONNEL POLICY CHOICE AND INDUSTRIAL RELATIONS STYLE

Management styles in industrial relations will strongly reflect managerial preferences along the benchmark dimensions of strategic integration, individualism and collectivism. Organisational approaches to workforce management are often seen as operating between two extreme positions: one emphasising managerial control, the other allowing greater employee control and autonomy. Friedman (1977) highlights these contrasting positions in identifying two major types of workforce management strategy: (a) responsible autonomy and (b) direct control. *Responsible autonomy* involves giving employees status and authority and allowing them scope to undertake challenging work which benefits both themselves and the organisation. *Direct control* seeks to reduce employee power and authority via coercive supervisory approaches and minimising employee discretion. Given these optional strategies it is largely a management decision on which approach to adopt, although other factors will influence managerial choice such as product and labour market conditions. Walton (1985) similarly identifies two 'radically different' strategies for managing an organisation's workforce: (1) *control strategy*, whereby employees are controlled via tight supervision, work in narrowly defined jobs, and are afforded little incentives or involvement beyond 'a fair day's pay'; (2) *commitment strategy*, whereby employees are given expansive and challenging jobs, subjected to minimal supervision, afforded considerable influence on employment-related matters, and receive attractive rewards and working conditions.

9.5.1. KEY AREAS OF PERSONNEL POLICY CHOICE
These contrasting approaches are indicative of the range of industrial relations styles and related personnel policy choice combinations. These policy options also serve to underpin the powerful link between management style and personnel policy choice. This hypothesis does not ignore any practical difficulties in implementing particular policies. Rather, it highlights the importance of management preferences which may be modified to suit particular circumstances. These policy options also highlight the influence of the three benchmark dimensions in guiding management choice in each key policy area.

The manifestations of managerial preferences in desired approaches to industrial relations will be evident in key areas of personnel policy choice, particularly the work system, communications, rewards, recruitment/internal flow policies and the role of the personnel function. Personnel policy choice in these areas will both reflect and reinforce preferred industrial relations styles which are seen as the outcomes of personnel policy choice as guided by managerial preferences and conditioned by external and internal environmental factors. These relationships are summarised in figure 9.7 and the key areas of personnel policy choice are discussed below.

Figure 9.7. Management style and personnel policy choice in industrial relations

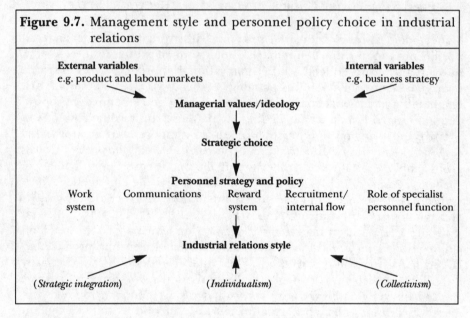

The *work system* incorporates the way in which the various tasks in the organisation are structured and impacts on issues such as organisation structure and job design (Beer et al., 1984, 1985). Decisions on the work system are primarily a management responsibility. The particular approach chosen is a valuable indicator of management beliefs about how employees should be managed. Traditional approaches to the organisation of work have been dominated by a desire to maintain control over the work process and maximise the productive efficiency of the organisation's technical resources. Choices on the organisation of work and the design of jobs were seen as primarily determined by the technical system. Management's role was to ensure other organisational resources, including employees, were organised in such a way as to facilitate the optimal utilisation of the technical system. This approach resulted in bureaucratic organisation structures, elaborate procedures and systems, top-down supervisory control and little employee involvement. It encouraged the fragmentation of jobs into simple, repetitive, measurable tasks, which gave post-holders little autonomy. Over the past decade it is suggested that an increased emphasis on improving quality, service and overall competitiveness has led to work redesign initiatives aimed at restructuring work systems to increase employee autonomy, motivation and performance. Much of the focus of work-system redesign has been on restructuring organisations and jobs to incorporate greater scope for intrinsic motivation, and to facilitate greater employee involvement (Beer et al., 1984). This alternative approach suggested that employees gain most satisfaction from the work itself. The consequent management emphasis was on developing broadly defined, challenging jobs within a more organic, flexible organisation structure. These contrasting approaches to work systems are an important indicator of employer preferences in industrial relations style, and help explain variations in styles between organisations. Alternative organisational approaches will involve different positions on the benchmark dimensions of strategic integration, individualism and collectivism, and serve to establish and reinforce particular management styles. They will particularly impact on personnel policy choice in areas such as employee influence, supervisory style and the nature of work.

A second important aspect of personnel policy choice having a significant impact on industrial relations is the area of *communications*. A notable characteristic of 'soft' HRM-type approaches is an emphasis on direct communications with employees. This involves a strong individual emphasis using a variety of communications devices to promote employee involvement, and instil 'desired' corporate values such as quality and high performance. This approach is sometimes seen to contrast traditional management–employee communications in unionised organisations where collective bargaining is the main communications device. Evidence from the US indicates that supplementary communications mechanisms may be used in addition to traditional collective communications, giving the approach both a collectivist and an individualist dimension (Kochan et al., 1986). The nature of management–employee communications, the presence or absence of particular communications mechanisms, the relative emphasis on collective and individual devices and the extent of mutuality in communications flow will again reflect different positions on the benchmark dimensions of strategic integration, individualism and collectivism.

A third key area of personnel policy choice is the *reward system*. Reward systems are an important aspect of personnel policy choice; they are important to the organisation because they help attract and retain employees, and influence performance and behaviour at work. They are important to employees because they provide the means to satisfy basic needs and may also allow them to satisfy less tangible desires for personal growth and satisfaction. As with the design of the work system, an organisation's reward system is a powerful indicator of organisational philosophy and approach to industrial relations management. High or low pay, the range of fringe benefits and the mechanism for determining reward levels provide valuable insights into the corporate approach to managing human resources. Significant considerations in the design of an organisation's reward system are the relative emphasis on extrinsic versus intrinsic rewards, the role of pay and whether it is contingent upon individual performance and compatible with the organisation's business goals and other personnel policies. Further management considerations and related areas of personnel policy choice include the degree to which variable pay components are based on quantitative or qualitative criteria and the absence/presence of commitments to employment tenure.

A fourth area of personnel policy choice is *recruitment* and, particularly, the relative emphasis placed on *internal or external labour markets*. This concerns the degree to which management seek to fill vacancies from within the organisation via the current pool of employees or, alternatively, rely on the external labour market. Emphasis on internal labour markets is often linked to a range of supportive personnel policies and practices in areas such as employee development, succession planning, appraisal and career counselling. Such policies are designed to facilitate internal mobility. They are also seen as having broader organisational benefits such as improved intrinsic satisfaction and related improvements in morale and motivation. It is argued that an internal labour market emphasis leads to greater employee commitment and loyalty, better performance and lower levels of absenteeism and turnover (Beer et al., 1984). To operate effectively, an internal labour market emphasis demands a strong focus on individualism and high levels of strategic integration. In contrast, a preference for using the external labour market infers less internal mobility, and demands less sophisticated employee development practices.

A final aspect of personnel policy choice concerns the *role of the specialist personnel function*. Organisational approaches to the management of human resources exert a significant influence on the organisational role of the personnel function. For example, it is suggested that a key feature of strategic HRM approaches is that the major responsibility for managing human resources be assumed by senior line managers. However, Guest (1987) notes 'the well-established "professional" structure of personnel management' in Britain whereby 'professional' personnel specialists undertake responsibility for a range of human resource issues, and possess valued expertise in 'core' personnel management areas such as selection, training, pay and industrial relations. It would seem that the issue of whether personnel issues are best managed by the specialist personnel function or by line managers is a matter of emphasis since, in most larger organisations, both will be involved in various aspects of personnel and industrial relations management practice. For example, the 'professional' personnel management model involves a major role for the personnel function in handling personnel activities with a heavy reliance on systems and procedures and a strong emphasis on industrial relations. Guest feels that this approach is most appropriate in stable, bureaucratic organisations. On the other hand, HRM-type approaches emphasise the primary role of line management in personnel activities, high levels of individualism and greater strategic integration.

Recognising such variations in the organisational role of the personnel function, Tyson (1985, 1987) identifies three alternative role models of the personnel function as outlined in table 9.2. These differing role models reflect different positions along the three benchmark dimensions of strategic integration, individualism and collectivism. The *administrative support model* infers an absence of strategic integration, with personnel issues being a low management priority. The *systems reactive model* approximates to the pluralist industrial relations tradition. It incorporates a primary emphasis on systems and procedures, particularly in industrial relations, and is characterised by minimal strategic integration (except on particular issues), low individualism and high collectivism. The *business manager model* is characterised by higher levels of strategic integration, while management preferences on dimensions of individualism and collectivism will be guided by broader issues of management philosophy, as well as by environmental factors such as labour and product markets. However, a key difference from the other models is that human resource issues are a strategic management concern, and personnel policy choice is guided by the conscious strategic preferences of senior management.

Table 9.2. Role models of the specialist personnel function

(a) *Administrative/support role:* Within this role model personnel is a low-level activity operating in a clerical support role to line management. It is responsible for basic administration and welfare provision.

(b) *Systems/reactive role:* Within this role model personnel is a high-level function with a key role in handling industrial relations and developing policies and procedures in other core personnel areas. The role is largely reactive, dealing with the personnel implications of business decisions. This model incorporates a strong 'policing' component where the personnel department are concerned with securing adherence to agreed systems and procedures.

(c) *Business manager role:* Within this role model personnel is a top-level management function involved in establishing and adjusting corporate objectives and developing strategic personnel policies designed to facilitate the achievement of long-term business goals. Personnel considerations are recognised as a key ingredient in corporate success with the personnel practitioner being the management specialist best placed to assess how the organisation's human resources can best contribute to this goal. Routine personnel activities are delegated allowing senior personnel practitioners adopt a broad strategic outlook.

In a similar vein but using a two-dimensional model Storey (1992) categorises the personnel function along (1) strategic/tactical and (2) interventionary/non-interventionary continuums. The *tactical/strategic dimension* measures the level at which the personnel function operates in making decisions or providing support in organisations. This dimension suggests that personnel may act at a strategic level, but in an advisory capacity, and thus may exhibit the strategic input of the business manager model but with the discretion of an administrative/support model (Foley, 1994). The *interventionary/non-interventionary dimension* raises the suggestion that the personnel function is adopting a less 'hands-on' approach in the management of the employment relationship (Clarke and Clarke, 1991; Mackay, 1987). Whether or not this approach has been as a result of a conscious policy decision, there is certainly an evident trend towards reassessing the level of intervention that personnel/HR departments engage in, and thus the level of intervention represents an informative measure of the role of personnel/HR function in organisations. Storey uses this two-dimensional model to produce a categorisation of four personnel function types, namely (1) advisors; (2) handmaidens; (3) regulators and (4) changemakers. In the *advisor* typology, the role of the personnel function is one of providing support to line and general managers. While this function is carried out at a strategic level, it is reactive and non-interventionary providing expertise and specialist skills, but in a consultancy capacity. *Handmaidens* represent a 'subservient, attendant relationship', with personnel operating in a low-level and non-interventionary capacity reacting to the needs of line managers in response to day-to-day operational problems. Storey suggests that this type of personnel function is indicative of a clerical and welfare role, and was characteristic of companies where the personnel presence had been depleted or reduced. *Regulators* operate in an interventionary mode, but rarely at the level of strategy formulation. This approach is representative of a 'traditional' industrial relations orientation with the senior personnel practitioner responsible for devising and negotiating policies and procedures to ensure the smooth operation of the organisation. This bears many similarities with Tyson's systems reactive role. The rationale behind this category is that even where line managers wish to undertake this role many are not competent enough to do so or are not sufficiently trained to undertake many of these roles adequately. In this model the personnel contribution is significant at an operational level (in ensuring the smooth running of the organisation) rather than at a strategic level. In contrast, *changemakers* act as specialists and are highly intervention-alist and strategic in perspective. This represents the highest level of the operation of the personnel function and bears marked similarities to Tyson's business manager typology. In this model senior personnel practitioners are aware of both the 'soft' and 'hard' elements of personnel/industrial relations practice. The two roles may exist in part side by side: the calculated, quantitative rational approach of the business-oriented specialist and the 'softer' approach of realising the full potential of the 'human' side of the organisation.

The choice of model adopted in a particular organisation, like the other key areas of personnel policy choice discussed above, will be influenced by factors in that organisation's internal and external contexts. The particular model adopted then provides a rationale and driving force for the activities and operation of the personnel function.

9.6. THE OUTCOME OF CHOICE: CATEGORISING MANAGEMENT STYLES IN INDUSTRIAL RELATIONS

The earlier sections of this chapter have attempted to chart the main influences on management style in industrial relations, the dimensions along which managerial choice may differ and the manifestations of managerial preferences in key areas of personnel policy choice. The interplay of environmental factors and managerial choice as manifested in key personnel policy areas thus facilitates the development of particular industrial relations styles in organisations. This final section examines alternative typologies of management styles in industrial relations and proposes a typology of managerial styles considered appropriate to the Irish context.

9.6.1. FRAMES OF REFERENCE

In his seminal work on management approaches to industrial relations, Fox (1966) argues that managerial styles in industrial relations are largely determined by the frame of reference adopted by managers. A frame of reference embodies 'the main selective influences at work as the perceiver supplements, omits and structures what he notices' (Thelen and Withall, 1979). Fox suggests that a manager's frame of reference is important because (a) it determines how management expect people to behave and how they think they should behave (i.e. values and beliefs); (b) it determines management reactions to actual behaviour (i.e. management practice); and (c) it shapes the methods management choose when they wish to change the behaviour of people at work (e.g. strategies/policies). Fox identifies two alternative frames of reference which highlight the potentially extreme variations in management approaches to industrial relations: the *unitarist* and *pluralist* perspectives. The key features of both frames of reference were discussed earlier in chapter 1. In practice, managers will not simply adhere to one of these approaches but may adopt different attitudes and behaviour in different situations, and change their attitudes and behaviour over time. However, they represent dominant orientations which may be present in particular managerial approaches and offer a useful framework for evaluating management approaches to industrial relations. In this context it is useful to consider how management approaches might differ depending on the frame of reference adopted. Marchington (1982) suggests that, depending on the frame of reference adopted, management approaches will differ in three key areas of industrial relations, namely: (a) the role of trade unions, (b) managerial prerogative and (c) industrial conflict.

According to Marchington, managers who hold a unitary perspective, would see no role for *trade unions*. They would be seen as 'encroaching on management's territory', making unreasonable demands, prohibiting change, flexibility, and therefore competitiveness. This approach is expressed in attitudes like 'Trade unions were necessary years ago, but there's no need for them now' or 'There is a need for a union in some companies but not here'. Unions are viewed as an externally imposed force which introduce conflict into the organisation and prohibit the development of good industrial relations. Employees associated with the introduction of trade-unionism are seen as disloyal or as agitators. On the other hand, managers who hold a pluralist perspective would see a legitimate role for trade unions in representing and articulating employee views. Unions are not seen as being in competition for employee loyalty but rather as a useful mechanism for handling industrial relations issues in a logical and acceptable fashion.

Managerial prerogative refers to areas of decision making where management see themselves as the sole authority. With the growth of organised labour, employers have had to share some of their decision-making power and come to terms with other forms of authority within the organisation, particularly trade unions. Marchington suggests that the two frames of reference contrast in their approach to the reduction of management prerogative by trade unions. Managers holding a unitary view would be unwilling to accept a reduction of management prerogative as a result of trade union organisation. Management is seen as the legitimate decision-making authority and it is their job to take decisions in the best interests of both the organisation and its employees, deciding which issues to discuss with employees and those where management alone should decide. Those veering towards the pluralist view would recognise other sources of leadership and loyalty in the organisation and accept that management should share some of its decision-making authority with other legitimate interest groups, particularly trade unions. Such a management approach would hold firm views on the specific role the trade union should play and would not like to see it stray beyond this and 'interfere' with all aspects of management decision making. In effect, the pluralist approach, while accepting certain limits on managerial prerogative (e.g. areas of collective interest—wages, hours of work, etc.), would strive to retain authority in areas where it does not see a legitimate role for trade unions (e.g. corporate decisions like investment).

Depending on the frame of reference adopted, attitudes and approaches to *industrial conflict* may vary considerably. Managers holding a unitary perspective would see their firm very much in the 'team/family' mould with everyone working together to achieve company objectives. Within this model conflict is not seen as inherent in workplace industrial relations but rather as a symptom of either a breakdown in the industrial relations framework or introduced by people who do not have the company's interests at heart. Managers holding a pluralist perspective would see a certain degree of conflict as inevitable due to the differing objectives held by different interest groups in the organisation. They will not tend to look for immediate causes such as bad communications or 'troublemakers', but will examine the sources and nature of such conflict and try to find mutually acceptable solutions with the aid of the other party. Such managers, because they see employer and employee interests as inevitably coming into conflict, will seek to plan for such occurrences and create institutional arrangements to ensure such conflict is handled in a reasonable fashion and does not have a detrimental impact on the overall industrial relations fabric.

9.6.2. 'IDEAL-TYPICAL' STYLE TYPOLOGIES

This chapter has introduced and explored the issue of identifiable patterns of industrial relations management and has attempted to distinguish between organisations that develop some kind of strategic approach to industrial relations from those that manage industrial relations in a more reactive or *ad hoc* manner. Several writers have attempted to move beyond this crude distinction to develop ideal-typical styles of industrial relations management and to classify them according to specific criteria. While the unitarist/pluralist classification discussed above is useful in evaluating the approach of individual managers to industrial relations, it is of limited benefit in considering different organisational approaches/styles in industrial relations (Purcell and Sisson, 1983). Recognising this, Fox (1974a,b) developed a typology of industrial relations styles, which was subsequently modified by Purcell and Sisson (1983) to produce a fivefold classification of ideal-typical industrial relations styles. This typology is outlined in figure 9.8 and is based on differing management aproaches to trade unions, collective bargaining, consultation and communications.

Despite the numerous attempts to categorise management styles in industrial relations, there is a dearth of empirical investigation in this area. Deaton (1985) attempted the first major empirical study of management styles using evidence from the UK Workplace Industrial Relations Survey (WIRS, 1980). In investigating differences in management styles Deaton (1985) adopted a variation of Purcell and Sisson's (1983) classification, using five ideal-typical styles which distinguished between traditionalists who consult employees (paternalists) and those who do not (anti-union), and identified only one type of sophisticated modern style suggesting that constitutionalists were virtually non-existent. In initially looking at organisations which recognised trade unions, Deaton attempted to classify employer styles as either sophisticated or standard moderns. Using data from over 1,000 organisations he found it difficult to distinguish between these two types of management styles, suggesting that it is rather tenuous to classify firms that recognise trade unions into either of these groupings. Looking at management styles where there was no trade union recognition he attempted to classify firms into paternalist, anti-union and sophisticated paternalists. Here Deaton found much greater evidence of organisations having particular styles. Sophisticated paternalists and anti-union organisations were seen as 'polar opposites', with paternalist organisations taking up a middle position having some characteristics common to both anti-union and sophisticated paternalist organisations. Deaton concluded that attempts to classify firms into

Figure 9.8. Management styles in industrial relations	
Management style	**Characteristics**
Traditionalist	'Orthodox unitarism': oppose role for unions; little attention to employee needs
Sophisticated paternalist	Emphasise employee needs (training, pay, conditions, etc.); discourage unionisation; demand employee loyalty and commitment
Sophisticated modern	Accept trade unions' role in specific areas; emphasise procedures and consultative mechanisms; two variations: (a) constitutionalist: emphasise codification of management–union relations through collective agreements;
	(b) consultors: collective bargaining established but management emphasise personal contact and problem solving, playing down formal union role at workplace level
Standard modern	Pragmatic approach; unions' role accepted but no overall philosophy or strategy developed: 'fire-fighting' approach

Source: Purcell and Sisson, 1983.

a small number of ideal styles was problematic and that, while the distinction between organisations which recognised trade unions and those that do not is crucial, it may not be possible to further subdivide styles in organisations where unions are recognised. However, Deaton felt there was a greater tendency in organisations which do not recognise trade unions to adopt the 'identikit' styles suggested above.

Using more anecdotal evidence to examine variations in managerial styles in industrial relations, Poole (1986) does not focus on particular identikit styles but rather suggests that the evidence points to the emergence of 'a progressively rich array' of hybrid styles rather than any convergence towards particular predominant styles or patterns. Other research studies have also identified the development of particular management styles in industrial relations. A number of studies have noted the significance of styles designed to develop and sustain employee commitment (Edwardes, 1985, 1987; Walton, 1985) while others have identified the development of neo-pluralist styles (Batstone, 1984; Edwardes, 1985) and 'sophisticated' non-union styles (Foulkes, 1980).

9.7. CHANGING PATTERNS OF INDUSTRIAL RELATIONS: EXPLAINING DEVELOPMENTS IN MANAGEMENT STYLES IN THE REPUBLIC OF IRELAND

Possibly the most widely debated aspect of contemporary developments in the management of industrial relations has centred on the development of management styles which incorporate human resource management (HRM) approaches. This debate was considered in the previous chapter. Assessments of management styles in industrial relations often contrast those styles which incorporate characteristics of HRM with the 'traditional pluralist-adversarial model'. In Ireland, as elsewhere, it has been argued that competitive pressures, reduced trade union power and new models of management practice have encouraged organisations to adopt more innovative industrial relations practices (Flood, 1989). However, the nature of change, if any, remains unclear. It is suggested that much of this confusion seems to stem from the tendency to view HRM as an essentially distinct and homogenous approach, designed to increase employee commitment and performance through the coherent adoption of a combination of 'soft' personnel policies. However, research evidence in Ireland and abroad points to the existence of variants of HRM incorporating different approaches to industrial relations as discussed in chapter 8, namely (1) 'soft' HRM, (2) 'hard' HRM and (3) neo-pluralism (see Guest, 1989a; Gunnigle, 1992b; Keenoy, 1990; Storey, 1992). While there are differences between the different HRM variants, it is significant that all are characterised by greater integration of industrial relations considerations into strategic decision making and the development of complementary policies to improve human resource utilisation, while the pluralist-adversarial model is more reactive in nature. HRM has therefore been associated with a strategic perspective on personnel/industrial relations management as manifested in the development of coherent and integrated styles of workforce management and adoption of an integrated set of personnel/industrial relations policies designed to achieve a prescribed set of personnel and business objectives (Beer et al., 1984; Fombrun et al., 1984; Guest, 1987, 1989a; Sisson, 1989; Storey, 1989, 1992).

The adoption of HRM strategies and styles clearly reflects developments in the external and internal environment of organisations and, particularly, increased competitive pressures which have stimulated both organisations and nations to seek means of protecting and/or enhancing their competitive position (Porter, 1987). This has led to increased emphasis on seeking improvements in areas such as productivity, costs, quality and customer service. These developments have also led to revisions and change in the internal structures of organisations in areas such as levels of authority and communications (Hendry et al., 1988). HRM approaches and styles are therefore identified with a strategic view of industrial relations which sees policy and practice in this area as significantly impacting upon the fundamental nature and thrust of the business. Thus, the dimension of strategic integration (significance of industrial relations considerations in strategic decision making) seems a valid initial basis for analysing differences in management styles in industrial relations. A second critical basis for evaluating management styles in industrial relations relates to the issue of individualism and collectivism in management approaches to industrial relations as discussed earlier. While a central aspect of the HRM literature is concerned with the creation and reinforcement of desired corporate cultures (Beer et al., 1984; Peters and Waterman, 1982), there is considerable debate on whether the optimal culture required to underpin HRM should be based on a primarily individualist orientation or, alternatively, whether HRM can accommodate collectivist industrial relations structures. One hypothesis suggests that we are witnessing the emergence of a 'sophisticated human resources' style of management, increased 'investment-oriented' individualism and decreased collectivism. For example, Guest (1989a) argues that the values underpinning HRM are 'predominantly individualist and unitarist' and consequently challenge collectivism and the role of trade unions with 'traditional industrial relations' no longer seen as a central management activity. However, this conception of HRM as heralding the death of collectivism is not shared by all commentators with some arguing that HRM merely reflects a development of collectivism involving a shift from an adversarial mode to a co-operative mode (Roche, 1990b; Salamon, 1992; Sisson, 1989; Storey and Sisson, 1990). Indeed, Salamon (1992) suggests that the maintenance of collectivism in HRM strategies implies a move towards the adoption of a sophisticated consultative style of management. It is clear from this debate that the relationship between individualist and collectivist dimensions of management style in industrial relations comprises a complex dynamic of interaction rather than a simple choice between collectivism and individualism. Thus, individualist styles and policies may not necessarily mean a move away from collectivism, so that it is possible to have both high levels of individualism and collectivism as well as approaches which counterpoise collectivism and individualism.

9.7.1. INDUSTRIAL RELATIONS IN IRELAND: TOWARDS A TYPOLOGY OF MANAGEMENT STYLES

Turning to the Irish context this text suggests a typology of industrial relations styles as appropriate to the Irish context, as discussed below. This classification identifies six major management styles with differences deriving from varying positions on the benchmark dimensions of strategic integration, individualism and collectivism, and gauged through personnel policy manifestations in relation to work systems, communications, reward systems, internal/external labour markets and the role of the specialist personnel function. This typology is seen as indicative of the predominant styles that might be adopted by organisations. There will obviously be 'grey' areas where the management approach will have characteristics common to two or more styles categories.

A. *Traditional anti-union:* Organisations in this category are characterised by no strategic integration of HR/IR issues, low collectivism and individualism, with employees seen in commodity status terms. The personnel policy manifestations of this approach include: a preoccupation with retaining managerial prerogative; rejection of any role for trade unions or other modes of collective representation and open hostility to unions; little or no attention to personnel/industrial relations except where absolutely necessary; no, or at best a low-level personnel function; absence of any procedures or mechanisms for communicating or consulting with employees; associated with authoritarian management and other characteristics of Friedman's (1977, 1984) direct control approach; poor rewards and tenure commitments.

B. *Paternalist:* This style differs from the former in so far as top management prioritise a need to 'look after' employees. The characteristics of this approach are a benevolent, welfare-oriented approach to employees. However, as in the 'traditional anti-union' style, the management view of the organisation is essentially unitarist. Little attention is paid to employee representation, involvement or development. Divergent opinions from those of management are seen as indicative of disloyalty, potentially damaging to the whole fabric of employer–employee relations. Indeed, the paternalist style may incorporate a high level of management complacency about the perceived closeness of management and employee interests and expectations. In relation to the benchmark dimensions of management style, the paternalist style is felt to be characterised by little strategic integration, medium individualism (i.e. caring approach to employees but few mechanisms to enhance employee involvement or commitment) and no collectivism. Personnel policy manifestations include a caring supervisory style but a work system which limits employee involvement and discretion, limited communications mechanisms, an external labour market and extrinsic rewards emphasis, and a personnel function whose role is of an administrative support nature. This style equates to what has been termed 'union suppressionists' incorporating low employment standards and contrasts with 'union substitionists' or high-standard non-union firms (Beaumont and Harris, 1991; Foulkes, 1980; Kochan, 1980).

C. *'Soft' Human Resource Management:* This approach emphasises the *human resource* aspect of the term 'human resource management' (Beer et al., 1984; Guest, 1987, 1989a; Keenoy, 1990). It is characterised by a resource perspective of employees incorporating the view that there is an organisational pay-off in performance terms from a combination of policies which emphasise consensualism and mutuality of management and employee interests in terms of high quality, flexibility and commitment leading to increased competitive advantage. This style is grounded in the unitarist perspective and is normally associated with pronounced preference for non-union status. However, in contrast to the traditional and paternalist styles above, management seek to create a positive organisational climate where individual employee needs are satisfied through a combination of positive employee-oriented personnel policies designed (in part) to render collective representation by employees unnecessary (Purcell and Sisson, 1983; Salamon, 1992). This is achieved by providing competitive pay and employment conditions, and establishing participative and communications mechanisms to effectively handle issues which in unionised organisations would normally be the prerogative of trade unions. Further personnel policy manifestations of this style include an internal labour market emphasis, availability of intrinsic and extrinsic rewards (at least partially based on merit), and a highly developed and influential personnel function. The hallmarks of this management style are high individualism (resource perspective of employees), high strategic integration and medium collectivism; the latter, however, is achieved through non-union fora such as consultative committees, quality circles, etc. This style equates to what has been termed 'union substitutionists' whereby such firms, while not claiming to be overtly 'anti-union', would take careful steps to ensure that a need for unionisation does not arise by, for example, extensive line management training in industrial relations, prompt handling of employee grievances, good terms and conditions of employment, attractive fringe benefits and a 'relaxed' supervisory style (Beaumont and Harris, 1991; Foulkes, 1980; Kochan, 1980).

D. *'Hard' Human Resource Management:* This style is characterised by the integration of human resource considerations into strategic decision making so as to ensure that personnel/industrial relations policy decisions are tailored to establish competitive advantage and make the maximum contribution to business performance. This style predominantly focuses on the *management* aspect of the term 'human resource management'. In this approach the management of the organisation's human resources (incorporating not only employees but also subcontracted labour) is largely focused on transaction costs. Thus, the management objective is to source and manage labour in as cheap and cost-effective a fashion as possible to ensure achievement of the organisation's 'bottom-line' objectives. On the benchmark dimensions this style is characterised by high strategic integration, low/medium collectivism and low individualism. Examples of this approach are most obvious in the adoption of 'atypical' employment forms, particularly extensive use of subcontracting and temporary/part-time employees, to improve cost effectiveness while meeting required performance standards, and in the use of performance management techniques designed to achieve maximum return on the organisation's investment in human resources. Storey (1992) describes this approach as follows: '. . . calculative, business-like treatment of labour with the accent upon it as a resource like any other to be deployed and disposed of in an economically rational way and with impatience towards institutional arrangements or procedures which interfere in that process.'

E. *Neo-pluralism:* This style is characterised by an acceptance of the role of trade unions but supplemented by an individualist employee emphasis

296

designed to reduce trade union activity and influence at shop-floor level. Organisations adopting this style would differ from sophisticated paternalists on the union issue but otherwise would pursue broadly similar policies. Union recognition would generally be formalised in a procedural agreement specifying management and union rights, and collective bargaining arrangements. At shop-floor level management will seek to keep formality to a minimum. The management focus is placed on minimising the extent of collective bargaining, especially that of an adversarial/distributive nature, and on emphasising more integrative/co-operative bargaining and on direct dealings with employees. On the benchmark dimensions, this style is characterised by high strategic integration, high individualism and high collectivism. The personnel policy manifestations include a more organic organisation structure, broadly defined jobs, sophisticated communications devices, internal labour market emphasis, extrinsic and intrinsic rewards and a well-developed and influential personnel function. Further characteristics may include careful selection and good employee development opportunities; employees encouraged to deal directly with management on any issues that concern them; line management trained in industrial relations and backed up by a developed personnel department which, on the one hand, co-ordinates collective bargaining with the trade unions and, on the other, oversees various 'employee-oriented' policies. This style might be termed a 'dualist' approach, involving the use of HRM techniques such as direct communications with employees and performance-related pay systems alongside established collective bargaining procedures, and involves moves towards greater consensualism and commitment in unionised companies (see Kochan et al., 1986).

F. Traditional unionised: Industrial relations in Ireland has traditionally been characterised by an essentially pluralist orientation using collective bargaining as the main device for handling management–employee interactions. This model equates to the traditional pluralist perspective characterised by adversarial industrial relations often incorporating multi-unionism and employer association membership. The traditional unionised approach is seen as typical of this 'bargained pluralism' incorporating traditionalist values and a desire to minimise the impact of trade union recognition. It is characterised by low strategic integration, low/medium individualism and medium to high collectivism (of an adversarial nature). This style has many of the characteristics of Purcell and Sisson's 'sophisticated modern— constitutionalist' style, particularly in the conception of industrial relations in terms of 'conflictual terms and conditions of employment', and the 'codification and limiting of collective bargaining arrangements' (Purcell and Sisson, 1983; Salamon, 1992). The personnel policy manifestations are union recognition and reliance on collective bargaining (however, the role of trade unions is not actively supported and management prerogative is stoutly defended in all areas of decision making). Management–union relations may sometimes be formalised in a procedural agreement regulating relations between the parties and encompassing issues such as union recognition (including closed shop), disciplinary, grievance and disputes procedures. However, other organisational arrangements may not be formalised in a comprehensive written agreement and are largely a product of custom and practice. Other personnel policy manifestations include a bureaucratic organisation structure, tightly defined jobs, limited and top-down communications, extrinsic rewards and a 'systems-reactive' type of personnel function whose primary role is to handle industrial relations. Information sharing and consultation are not common in these companies.

9.7.2. ANALYSING MANAGEMENT STYLES

It is important to acknowledge the limitations of categorisations of management styles such as the above taxonomy. In particular it is important to differentiate between management style and outcomes or results in industrial relations. As Purcell (1987) notes there is a 'distinction between the outcomes of interaction of management and labour and the attitudes, beliefs and frames of reference of the parties'. The assumption that management attitudes will translate into practice may on occasion be erroneous, as there may be discrepancies between what is prescribed and what is practised. At a more general level, it should also be noted that the majority of organisations will not fit neatly into one particular ideal-typical style. Salamon (1992) suggests that some organisations are hybrids seeking to combine aspects of different styles, or may be in transition from one style to another (Kochan et al., 1986; Walton, 1985) and that the degree to which a particular organisation fits into an ideal-typical category depends on 'the extent to which management (in particular senior management) is committed to a particular and defined long-term industrial relations policy, philosophy or style' (Salamon, 1992).

9.7.3. EMERGENT MANAGEMENT STYLES IN IRELAND

Given the above caveats and reflecting on the Irish situation, the most striking feature of the typologies outlined above relates to the human resource management (HRM) and 'neo-pluralist' groupings. These styles are significant because they indicate a planned and co-ordinated approach to industrial relations management in contrast to the other styles which are indicative of a more 'incidentalist' approach. The 'traditional unionised' style equates to the basic pluralist-adversarial model and has been the most pervasive style in the majority of medium and large organisations in Ireland (Roche, 1990b). On the other hand, the 'traditional anti-union' and 'paternalist' styles indicate opposition to the pluralist tradition either through forthright attempts to curb or eliminate any moves towards collective representation or more subtle policies to demonstrate to employees that their best interests lie in accepting managerial prerogative. It has traditionally been argued that these styles were confined to smaller organisations and that in the event of growth they would 'succumb' to the pluralist-adversarial model over time (Gunnigle, 1989; Roche, 1990b). However, recent Irish evidence points to greater opposition to unionisation in the 1980s and a growth of larger non-union organisations adopting 'soft' HRM styles and also the increased use of such approaches in unionised organisations (Gunnigle and Flood, 1990; Kelly and Brannick, 1988b; McGovern, 1989a,b). These developments, if pervasive, would indicate a significant change in Irish industrial relations. In terms of management styles, such developments would be characterised by the increased adoption of either human resource management ('hard' or 'soft') variants or neo-pluralist styles. Unlike the 'neo-pluralist' style (which is essentially a variant of traditional pluralism), HRM-based styles contrast significantly with the traditional pluralist-adversarial model and are essentially unitarist in character. Of particular interest is the 'soft' HRM style, where related personnel policies are individualistic in orientation and seek to develop total employee identification with the organisation. This style is generally associated with practices designed to entice employees away from collective representation towards more individual, consensual forms of direct involvement. Such styles are indicative of a neo-unitarist approach to industrial relations management which leave little role for collective representation and collective bargaining (Horwitz, 1990). It would seem that recent developments suggest a strengthening of the unitarist ideology among Irish organisations and, particularly, greater opposition to union recognition, the emergence of a strong non-union sector and a fall in union membership (Flood, 1989; Hannaway, 1987, 1992; Kelly and Brannick, 1988b). However, this case is yet unproven in the absence of substantial empirical evidence to indicate a major change in management styles in industrial relations in Irish organisations. If such a trend is in fact developing, one would expect to see it most in evidence in greenfield sites where management are not constrained by established practice and have the opportunity to develop personnel policies to establish their desired industrial relations style. In evaluating current developments in industrial relations styles in Ireland, there is a danger of confusing prominent examples of 'soft' HRM with the widespread persuasiveness of such approaches. Indeed, much of the evidence and support for HRM approaches emanates from the US. However, the context of such developments in the US is considerably different from that in Ireland, and it seems inappropriate to simply extrapolate from the US experience and infer similar trends here.

9.8. CONCLUSIONS

This chapter has attempted to explore managerial styles in industrial relations. It has examined the nature of managerial choice in industrial relations and specifically the context, dimensions and key areas of choice affecting industrial relations styles. It has also presented a typology of managerial styles in industrial relations considered most relevant to the Irish context. The different approaches to workforce management discussed above are illustrative of the range of managerial choice confronting organisations. Thus, management style in industrial relations may be either unitarist or pluralist, co-operative or conflictual. HRM-based styles incorporate a greater strategic perspective on human resource issues and closer linkages with broader business policy while styles reflecting traditional industrial relations approaches are more reactive and adversarial in nature.

CHAPTER TEN

Contemporary Developments in Industrial Relations

10.1. Introduction

This chapter considers contemporary developments in industrial relations in Ireland. The objective of this chapter is to place industrial relations practice in the Republic of Ireland within a national and an international context, and thus enable us to analyse developments in Irish industrial relations in the context of broader contemporary developments in the field. Using recent research data the chapter then considers current developments in industrial relations with particular emphasis on labour market developments, flexibility initiatives, employee participation and communications, developments in technology, quality enhancement inititiatives and the impact of European Union developments on industrial relations.

10.2. The Context for Developments in Irish Industrial Relations

As we have seen, industrial relations practice in most larger Irish organisations in the Republic of Ireland has traditionally been associated with a strong collectivist emphasis (Roche, 1990b). In this model, relations between management and employees were grounded in the pluralist tradition with a primary reliance on adversarial collective bargaining, aptly described by Bill Roche (1990b) thus: 'Over a wide range of industries and services, employers and unions have conducted their relations on the basis of the premise that their interests were in significant respects different and in opposition. . . . These differences of interest were reconciled on an ongoing basis through collective bargaining pure and simple.'

It was suggested earlier in chapter 8 that the period since the early 1980s has witnessed considerable change in both the environment and practice of industrial relations in Ireland. From an employer perspective, the onset of recession lessened the emphasis on hitherto core workforce management activities such as recruitment and, particularly, industrial relations. Trade union membership fell significantly in the period 1980–87, and industrial unrest also declined significantly over the decade (Roche and Larragy, 1989a). At the same time many organisations responded to increasing competitive pressures by instigating improvements in areas such as quality, costs and performance. Consequently, it has been argued that there has been greater innovation in industrial relations practice, particularly in areas such as work systems, rewards, management–employee communications and employee development (Flood, 1989; Garavan, 1990; Hannaway, 1987, 1992; Murray, 1984).

10.2.1. PUBLIC POLICY

In terms of Government approaches to industrial relations a number of significant issues emerge. At a general level, Irish Governments have had a largely benign approach to organised labour. The traditional approach of successive Governments to industrial relations in the Republic of Ireland has been grounded in the 'voluntarist' tradition. This meant that employers and employees or their representative bodies were largely free to regulate the substantive and procedural terms of their relationship and that there was a minimum of intervention from Government or its agencies (Breen et al., 1990; Hillery, 1989). This approach was largely a historical legacy of the British voluntarist tradition, and endured up to the end of the 1970s. In general, Irish Governments have been supportive of trade unions and a consensus approach to labour relations.

However, since the early 1980s it would appear that the approaches of British and Irish Governments have taken markedly contrasting directions in the areas of pay and industrial relations. In the UK, the Conservative Governments have taken progressive steps, both legislative and otherwise, to reduce union power and to ensure that wage levels and other industrial relations outcomes are determined by market forces. In Ireland, the voluntarist tradition has been considerably diluted in recent years. In contrast to the UK, however, this change has taken the form of emerging corporatist structures involving a consensus approach to pay and greater centralisation and State intervention in industrial relations (Roche, 1989). In the period 1970–82, as discussed in detail in chapter 6, Ireland had a series of National Agreements on pay and related employment issues. These were initially heralded as important vehicles in delivering wage restraint, reduced industrial conflict and low inflation. However, these agreements failed to deliver, and the period was characterised by high levels of inflation, wage drift and industrial conflict. Central agreements were abandoned by the somewhat disillusioned social partners (particularly employers) and there was a brief return to decentralised bargaining in the 1982–86 period.

In a period of severe fiscal rectitude the Fianna Fail administration revived central agreements through the Programme for National Recovery (1987–90). This period was characterised by very moderate wage increases and high GDP growth. Much of the credit for such success has been given to centralised agreements, although it is plausible to argue that this period would have been characterised by low pay increases and low levels of industrial conflict regardless of whether pay was negotiated centrally or locally. The process of centralised bargaining continued with the Programme for Economic and Social Progress (1990–93), which was succeeded by the present Programme for Competitiveness and Work. Recent Governments have been strong advocates of centralised agreements on pay and other aspects of economic and social policy involving negotiations with the main social partners (viz. Government, employer, trade union and farming federations). In the area of industrial relations the achievement of a high level of national consensus has possibly been the most significant development.

A more established aspect of public policy is the constitutional guarantee of freedom of association. This constitutional guarantee of freedom of association, embodied in article 40.6.1. of the Constitution, confers the right on workers to form or join associations or unions. However, while the Constitution supports the freedom of workers to organise, there is no statutory provision for trade union recognition with the consequence that there is no obligation on employers to recognise or bargain with trade unions (see chapter 4). Historically, this lack of a statutory mechanism for securing trade union recognition did not seem to cause much difficulty, as most larger employers seemed happy to recognise and conclude collective agreements with trade unions. However, with the declining membership and power of Irish trade unions the issue of recognition appears to have become contentious with some evidence of increased opposition to unionisation in recent years (Gunnigle, 1992c, 1994; Gunnigle and Brady, 1984; McGovern, 1989a,b).

A final important aspect of public policy relates to approaches to industrial development. Since the mid-1960s Irish Government policy has actively encouraged direct foreign investment in Ireland. There are now over 950 overseas companies operating in Ireland with particular focus on the engineering (including electronics) and chemicals sectors. These foreign-owned companies employ some 80,000 employees. The US and UK have been the major source of overseas investment. Ireland has been the most profitable location for US firms in the EU, achieving an average return on investment of 23 per cent in the period 1982–87, or three times the EU average. On the industrial relations front it certainly appears that multinational companies (MNCs) have been a source of innovation in management practices, particularly in the application of new personnel approaches and in expanding the role of the specialist personnel/human resources (HR) function (Gunnigle and Flood, 1990). However, it would also seem that MNCs pose particular and unique challenges in the industrial relations sphere, particularly in their ability to switch the locus of production and in the recent and increasing trend of union avoidance (Kelly and Brannick, 1988b; McGovern, 1989a,b; Gunnigle, 1992c).

10.3. CHANGE IN INDUSTRIAL RELATIONS

Analyses of change in industrial relations are fraught with danger. A particular problem is the tendency to focus on evidence of change while failing to highlight areas of stability (Dastmalachian et al., 1991). In the Irish context there is a widespread view that industrial relations practice in Ireland has undergone significant change over the past decade and that the pluralist model is being replaced by approaches incorporating either a variant of traditional pluralism (neo-pluralism) or a unitarist perspective involving a range of HRM policies designed to eliminate employee needs for collective representation (neo-unitarism) (Flood, 1989; Hannaway, 1987, 1992; Kelly and Brannick, 1988b). This section briefly considers the context and some manifestations of change in key aspects of industrial relations in the Republic of Ireland.

10.3.1. LABOUR MARKET DEVELOPMENTS
The most notable changes in the Irish labour market over the past twenty years have been the dramatic fall in numbers employed in agriculture and the consistent growth in employment in the services sector, which now accounts for almost 60 per cent of all employees (see table 10.1). Much of this services sector growth in recent years has been concentrated in private services. In the period 1975–89 there was a significant increase in employment in financial and business services (42 per cent), professional services (21 per cent) and personal services (16 per cent) (Dineen, 1992). In contrast, the fiscal rectitude policies of successive Governments since the early 1980s have seen a contraction of employment in the public sector.

Table 10.1. Employment changes by sector, 1961–89 (in thousands, % in parentheses)

	1961	1975	1979	1985	1989
Agriculture	380 (36)	238 (22)	221 (19)	171 (16)	163 (15)
Industry	257 (25)	337 (31)	365 (32)	306 (28)	306 (28)
Services	415 (39)	498 (47)	559 (49)	602 (56)	621 (57)

Source: Labour Force Surveys/CSO, 1961–89.

While employment has remained relatively constant in industry as a whole, there has been significant change in the sectoral distribution of industrial employment. In particular the period since the 1970s has seen a substantial fall in the numbers employed in older indigenous manufacturing, involving a large reduction in the numbers employed in the textiles, clothing and footwear sectors. In the same period there were substantial increases in employment in foreign-owned firms, particularly in chemicals and engineering. Generally, job losses in the manufacturing sector tended to be concentrated in lower-paid, labour-intensive industries catering for the home market while companies (largely foreign-owned) in more capital-intensive export-oriented sectors fared much better.

Unemployment has increased dramatically during the 1980s, and in early 1993 reached over 300,000, or almost 20 per cent of the workforce. The onset of the second economic recession in the early 1980s, combined with the rapid growth in numbers joining the labour force, caused major problems for employment creation. Total numbers at work fell by 6.6 per cent in the 1979–85 period, and unemployment increased by almost 230 per cent since 1979. Dineen (1992) suggests that the reasons for this dramatic growth in unemployment are partly supply driven (population growth and increased labour force participation rates) and partly demand driven (weak international demand abroad and fiscal rectitude at home).

Other important developments in employment structure over the past decade have been the growth in long-term unemployment, a lowering of the retirement age and the return of widespread emigration up to the late 1980s. Within this overall pattern it is interesting that participation rates of women in employment have increased. The sectoral shifts in employment are favourably biased towards greater female employment, with women proportionately over-represented in the expanding sectors. Much of the growth in female participation rates have been in the areas of retail distribution, insurance, financial/business, professional and personal services.

Table 10.2. Ireland, some basic facts (1991)

Population: 3.5 million   GDP per head: $11,900
Inflation: 3.3% p.a. (1986–90)   GDP growth rate: 3.5% (1986-90)
Exports as a % of GNP: 62%

Labour force: 1.3 million

Age structure:		Sectoral employment distribution:	
0–19 years	38%	Agriculture	15%
20–28 years	15%	Industry	28%
29–45 years	24%	Services	57%
46–75 years	23%		

– % of school leavers progressing to further education: 30% (1989)
– No statutory minimum wage
– Trade union membership: constitutional guarantee of freedom of association
– Trade union density (% of workforce unionised): approx. 44%

At the macro-level the single greatest challenge facing the Irish economy is the need to effectively tackle the persistently high level of unemployment. Despite a pervasive feeling that the fundamentals of the Irish economy are sound (low inflation, balance of payment surpluses, good industrial relations, solid GNP growth), the country has increasingly struggled to provide jobs for its young, well-educated workforce (see table 10.2). The openness of the Irish economy also means that any downturn in the world economy significantly impacts upon domestic economic performance, particularly in relation to export growth and emigration opportunities.

10.3.2. THE GROWTH OF 'ATYPICAL' EMPLOYMENT

It would appear that shifts in employment structure and the depressed economic environment have led to greater variation in forms of employment, with a trend away from traditional employment arrangements to more 'atypical' forms of employment. Indeed, one of the most visible changes in employment practices in Ireland has been the growth of atypical employment forms (see tables 10.3–10.6). Atypical employment is defined as any form of employment which deviates from the full-time, permanent format. Analyses of atypical employment have primarily focused on part-time, temporary and self-employment, although broader definitions include areas such as the black economy and teleworking (Cordova, 1988; Dineen, 1992).

Table 10.3. Part-time employment, 1979–89 (in thousands)

	1979	1987	1989
Regular part-time	35.5	65.6	70.3
Occasional part-time	22.1	12.8	12.1
All part-time	57.6	78.4	82.4
Part-time as % of total employment	5.4	7.1	7.6

Source: Labour Force Surveys/CSO, 1961–89.

Table 10.4. Temporary employment, 1983–89 (in thousands)

	Males	Females	Total	Temporary as % of total
1983	25.5	26.4	51.9	6.0
1985	28.5	33.0	61.5	7.4
1987	32.8	38.9	71.7	8.5
1989	32.9	38.8	71.7	8.5

Source: Labour Force Surveys/CSO, 1961–89; Dineen, 1992.

Table 10.5. Self-employment, 1979–89 (in thousands)

	1979	1983	1987	1989	% Change 1979–89
Agriculture	160.7	137.3	123.9	124.3	-22.7
Non-agriculture	94.9	100.5	112	119.3	+25.7
Total	255.6	237.8	235.9	243.6	-4.7

Source: Labour Force Surveys/CSO, 1961–89; Dineen, 1992.

Table 10.6. Atypical/typical employment, 1983–89 (in thousands)

	Total employment	Atypical employment*	Atypical as % of total
1983	859.1	180.7	21.0
1985	830.1	195.6	23.5
1987	841.0	215.4	25.6
1989	840.8	226.3	26.9

* These figures are adjusted to allow for overlaps in atypical employment forms (see Dineen, 1992).

Source: Labour Force Surveys/CSO, 1961–89.

The increased incidence of atypical employment forms must be viewed in the context of broader changes in employment patterns: particularly (a) the expansion in unemployment and (b) shifting employment patterns characterised by a fall in agriculture and manufacturing industry and a growth in the services sector. We have already seen that growth in the services sector has been primarily restricted to private (professional and personal) services—areas traditionally associated with atypical employment forms. In contrast, the public sector, which is traditionally associated with typical employment forms, has not experienced the same level of growth. Consequently, changes in the sectoral employment distribution have been biased towards an increase in atypical employment. It has also facilitated a rise in female employment. However, the nature of the jobs lost and those created differ substantially. Areas of job loss, particularly the manufacturing industry and the public sector, are traditionally associated with providing relatively secure, well-paid employment. In contrast, areas of employment growth, particularly personal services (e.g. contract cleaning, catering) are associated with more insecure, poorly paid jobs.

A second important issue is that, despite the growth in atypical employment, the majority of workers in the non-agricultural sector (almost 80 per cent) still work in typical employment. Thus, while there is a definite trend towards atypical employment, the change is a gradual one and must be viewed in the context of broader economic and, particularly, labour market change. It would also seem that the apparent substitution of atypical for typical employment forms, particularly in the public sector, is largely expedient and reactionary in face of the difficult economic environment in which many organisations now find themselves. However, it is also likely that these changes will pertain in the longer term, at least in part, due to the financial attractions to employers of lower wage levels, reduced employment-related overheads (such as pensions, holidays) and increased numerical flexiblility (Hakim, 1991). This latter issue is discussed below.

10.3.3. THE FLEXIBILITY DEBATE

An associated issue is the contention that the flexible firm model as advocated by Atkinson (1984a) and characterised by the planned development of a core/periphery employment model is emerging in Irish organisations (Flood, 1990). Within this scenario the 'core' is composed of full-time staff enjoying relatively secure, challenging jobs with good pay and employment conditions, while the 'periphery' is composed of an amalgam of temporary, part-time and contract groups enjoying much less favourable pay and employment conditions and less job security or training and promotion opportunities. The flexible firm scenario is based on the planned development of this core/periphery employment model incorporating increased flexibility in three key areas, notably (1) *numerical flexibility*, incorporating extensive use of atypical employment forms which allow the organisation to take on and shed labour flexibly in line with business needs; (2) *functional flexibility*, incorporating multi-skilling; and (3) *financial flexibility*, whereby pay rates are linked to labour and product market conditions, and pay increases for individual employees are variable and contingent on performance.

Current Irish evidence indicates a definite trend towards greater flexibility (Flood, 1990a; Suttle, 1988). However, this development appears to be largely confined to *numerical flexibility* in the services sector. This trend may in part be explained by the 'looseness' of the Irish labour market (characterised by unemployment levels of *circa* 20 per cent) and the consequent ready availability of people willing to work in temporary or part-time jobs. Developments in numerical flexibility were discussed above in the context of growth in 'atypical' employment forms. However, a particular and more contentious issue in the area of numerical flexibility relates to the multinational (MNC) sector. In a recent study of 'greenfield' companies undertaken by Gunnigle (1992c; 1994) it was found that numerical flexibility is endemic in many Irish subsidiaries of MNCs. In many cases the Irish subsidiary carries out direct manufacturing/service activities only and is not involved in areas such as product development. MNC headquarters use the subsidiary to deal with immediate business demands and thus that subsidiary needs to be able to add or shed labour quickly in line with fluctuations in demand. It is therefore argued that Atkinson's model may be modified to explain the operation of MNCs, whereby core activites such as product development are retained at corporate level while direct production is located at peripheral locations (such as Irish subsidiaries), which in effect operate as the (numerically) flexible component of the MNC's operations.

Functional flexibility is defined as the expansion of skills within a workforce or the ability of firms to reorganise the competencies associated with jobs, so that the job holder is able and willing to deploy such competencies across a broader range of tasks. This process can mean employees moving into either higher or lower skill areas or a combination of both. It is often referred to as 'multi-skilling'. The evidence on functional flexibility suggests that this form of flexibility is extremely rare and largely confined to tentative initiatives in the manufacturing sector (Gunnigle and Daly, 1992; Suttle, 1988). Some larger organisations have taken a number of initiatives in the area of multi-skilling, such as the Electricity Supply Board in the semi-state sector, and Krups Engineering and Auginish Alumina in the private sector. Early case evidence suggests that 'add-skilling' or 'extra-skilling' are more accurate descriptions of these developments than multi-skilling. This conclusion is based on the evidence that functional flexibility among skilled workers largely involves those categories receiving training in and agreeing to undertake a quite limited range of extra tasks in addition to their traditional trade (for example fitters undertaking some electrical/instrumentation work (see Gunnigle and Daly, 1992)). There is, of course, evidence of organisations claiming to have total functional flexibility in their operations. However, such flexibility would appear to only pertain in unskilled assembly-type work where there is a minimal training requirement and it is thus relatively easy to deploy workers across a large range of (simple) tasks as required (Gunnigle, 1992b).

Financial flexibility consists of two elements. Firstly, it incorporates the ability of organisations to adjust pay rates to reflect market conditions (particularly the labour market). Secondly, it encourages the introduction of merit-/performance-related (PRP) reward systems whereby employees are paid at a rate dependent on their performance, using an assessment-based system or payment related to their level of skills acquisition. One may often find that financial flexibility is used to encourage functional flexibility (Keenan and Thom, 1984). It is difficult to identify a clear picture in the area of financial flexibility. Findings from the Price Waterhouse Cranfield (PWC) Project suggest an evident trend towards greater financial flexibility particularly in the increased incidence of variable pay systems (Brewster and Hegewich, 1993; Gunnigle et al., 1994) (see table 10.7). However, in examining the application of PRP systems to different employee categories, we find a much more traditional picture. Here, the survey evidence points to merit- or performance-related pay being largely confined to managerial and professional categories with a low level of utilisation among manual grades (see table 10.8). In relation to the second aspect of financial flexibility, viz. basing pay level to market conditions, there have been two prominent examples of 'two-tier' pay systems in Bank of Ireland and Aer Lingus (Flood, 1989). Both of these involved the introduction of a new entry grade at pay levels considerably below that pertaining to those who traditionally carried out such work. There is little empirical evidence of a widespread incidence of this form of flexibility, although the current state of the Irish labour market clearly facilitates such initiatives.

Table 10.7. Change in reward systems (in %, N = 269)

	Increased	Decreased	Same	Don't know/missing
Variable pay	32	4	56	8
Non-money benefits	21	1	66	12

Source: Price Waterhouse Cranfield Project (Ireland), 1992.

Table 10.8. Utilisation of merit-/performance-related pay (in %, N = 269)

	Level of utilisation of merit-/performance-related pay
1. Among managerial grades	46
2. Among professional grades	39
3. Among clerical grades	29
4. Among manual grades	13

Source: Price Waterhouse Cranfield Project (Ireland), 1992.

Overall it appears that, while there have been increases in all forms of flexibility, the aggregate picture does not point to a widespread emergence of the flexible firm model. Suttle's (1988) examination of ninety-six companies that had introduced some form of flexibility found that none of these firms had attempted to combine numerical, functional and financial flexibility. Indeed it seems that, while flexibility is on the increase, this is occurring in a somewhat piecemeal form in reaction to depressed labour and product market conditions rather than as a planned emergence of the totally flexible firm. However, such apparently expedient responses to environmental conditions may well be sustained when the environment changes as organisations wish to retain the advantages of certain flexibility forms (see Hakim, 1991).

10.4. EMPLOYEE PARTICIPATION [1]

Employee participation may be broadly interpreted as incorporating any mechanisms designed to increase employee input into managerial decision making. It is based on the concept that those who are involved in an organisation are entitled to share in decisions which affect them. It is sometimes seen as the political democratisation of the workplace in so far as it facilitates the redistribution of decision-making power within organisations (Chamberlain, 1948; Schregle, 1974; Thomason, 1984).

It was suggested earlier in chapter 5 that the structure of industrial organisations, with the support of our legal and business system, has traditionally placed decision-making power in the hands of employers. Since the foundation of this system, various initiatives have been taken to increase employee involvement in managerial decision making. Such involvement may range from the relatively superficial level of management informing employees of decisions which affect them to consultation with employees on certain decisions or joint participation in the actual decision-making process. Such initiatives may result in a variety of institutional arrangements to facilitate employee participation at workplace level such as suggestion schemes, joint consultative committees, works councils, quality circles, and board-level participation. Employee participation can also be facilitated through the collective bargaining process, which attempts to lessen the sphere of managerial prerogative and makes more issues subject to joint negotiation and agreement.

The movement for increased employee participation has its roots in early attempts to achieve worker control dating from the Industrial Revolution period in the UK (Coates and Topham, 1968). These initiatives were based on a rejection of a new economic order based on capitalism and wage labour (which from the Marxist perspective created worker alienation and frustration as a result of divisions of labour, the removal of discretion and responsibility from the individual worker and the creation of hostile social classes). The movement for worker control and self-management highlight an important element in the worker participation debate: whether it should aim at achieving a new economic order through redrawing the decision-making mechanisms within organisations or try to bring about greater employee participation within the current structure of industrial organisations. It now seems that most developments in employee participation are along the latter route (see IPM/IPA Code of Practice on Employee Participation, 1983).

Developments in employee participation have taken varying directions and proceeded at different paces in different countries. With the demise of the early movements for worker control, participation achieved its most concrete form through the extension of collective bargaining as evidenced, for example, by the establishment of joint councils for collective bargaining and consultation in Britain after the first World War. More extensive developments took place in the post-second World War era, with various institutional arrangements developed to further employee participation in a number of European countries. Mulvey (n.d.) distinguishes between those countries where such arrangements were given statutory support (the former West Germany, Yugoslavia) and those where they were based on collective agreements (Norway, Sweden, Denmark).

Most of the recent focus of the employee participation debate has taken place at European Union (EU) level, where various policy documents have concentrated on board-level participation and disclosure of financial information. Initial proposals through the first draft of the European Company Statute proposed a two-tier board system along West-German lines, with the senior supervisory board having one-third employee representatives. It also dealt with the role of works councils and information disclosure. The Draft Fifth Directive also favoured the two-tier board system, with employee participation on the supervisory board. The European Community Green Paper on Employee Participation and Company Structure represented a more flexible approach, and reflected widespread opposition to the imposition of structures deemed contrary to some traditional national systems. It suggested that the worker–director route was only one option in extending employee participation and, while believing that the two-tier approach of the Fifth Directive represented the optimal solution, proposed flexibility in developing transitional arrangements. At the same time, the Vredeling Directive on employee rights to information disclosure recommended that multinational companies (MNCs) must consult and inform employees in subsidiaries of their plans and decisions. Additionally, other proposals have demanded the provision of financial information through consolidated accounts.

The employee participation debate really only took off in Ireland after our entry into the European Community. This resulted in much discussion and activity throughout the 1970s and early 1980s. This surge of interest was manifested in the passing of the Worker Participation (State Enterprises) Act 1977, which introduced board-level participation to seven semi-state companies. These provisions were extended to a number of other State organisations under the terms of the Worker Participation (State Enterprises) Act 1988. Board-level representation in Ireland has been largely restricted to the semi-state companies covered by the 1977 and 1988 Acts.

10.4.1. OPTIONS IN PARTICIPATION

At a generic level it is possible to identify four differing forms of participation, each varying in both level and nature of participation: (1) representative participation; (2) equity participation; (3) job/work participation; and (4) participation through collective bargaining (Gunnigle and Flood, 1990). These various forms of participation are discussed below, together with some smaller-scale initiatives in participation. Variations in approaches to employee participation may stem from a variety of reasons, such as the structure and development of collective bargaining, the attitude of trade unions, or the political philosophy of government. The variety of institutional arrangements adopted in different countries and by different organisations may also reflect different philosophies and approaches to employee participation. Participation may be supported by the law or may be established through collective agreements, and may be minimal or extensive.

REPRESENTATIVE PARTICIPATION

This form of participation has been the focus of most attention and applies to institutionalised arrangements which give employees an input into management decision making, sometimes with statutory support. The most obvious example is provision for the election of worker directors to the board of management. It also applies to lower-level participation such as joint consultative committees and works councils. Board-level representation in Ireland has been largely restricted to the semi-state bodies. In evaluating the operation of worker directors under the terms of the 1977 Act, Kelly (1989) suggests that the experience has been 'broadly successful'. Using the findings of some preliminary research on board-level participation, he concludes that employees have positive attitudes to board-level participation and management, though harbouring some reservations about the role and contribution of worker directors, have now largely accepted their role in the senior decision-making process (IPC, 1980; see also Galvin, 1980). On the issues of conflict with traditional collective bargaining and trade union structures, Kelly found this was a non-runner. He found that trade unions had largely dominated the participatory process in the organisations concerned. Consequently, the likelihood of an alternative representative mechanism to the trade union developing 'dissolved into insignificance' (Kelly, 1989a).

Apart from these developments in the State sector, the prospects for the extension of board-level participation in other areas seem dim in the absence of statutory compulsion. Employer bodies have generally favoured the extension of participation at sub-board level, particularly through works councils, and have advocated flexibility in allowing organisations to develop their own participative arrangements. The Institute of Personnel Management (IPM/IPA, 1983) adopted a similar approach suggesting that: 'Participation may be attained through a wide variety of means depending on the characteristics of the organisation and the nature of its activities, structure, technology and history.'

Morrissey (1989) notes some renewed interest in extending participative arrangements at sub-board level while acknowledging that the 'absence of a sustained commitment' from employers and trade unions has been a major stumbling block to more extensive developments. He notes the difficulties which mechanisms such as works councils pose for trade unions, and the reluctance of both parties to move from the 'tried and trusted' ground of collective bargaining. A number of other writers have warned against the blanket adoption of European models. In particular, Kelly (1979) suggests that the 'European format' may not suit our collective bargaining or trade union structures and that initiatives in expanding worker participation here should be focused at shop-floor level.

EQUITY PARTICIPATION

This approach to employee participation involves the adoption of mechanisms through which employees can gain an equity share in their organisations through various profit-sharing and share-ownership schemes. Most such schemes have the broad-based objective of increasing employee loyalty, commitment and morale through the closer identification of employee interests with those of the organisation. Such schemes may often be accompanied by some form of consultative or participative machinery, which allows for greater employee participation in certain management decisions. However, equity participation by itself will not normally allow for a substantial increase in employee influence, as employees will generally represent a minority of the shareholders. Organisations such as the John Lewis Partnership in the UK and Donnelly Mirrors in Ireland have long been known for their policy of sharing profits with employees, and many companies now offer share options or some other form of profit sharing.

JOB/WORK PARTICIPATION

Ever since some of the less attractive aspects of industrial work became evident, various initiatives have been undertaken to increase employee satisfaction and motivation by designing jobs in a way which offers employees greater opportunities for expression, responsibility and achievement. Many of these initiatives involve devolving greater discretion to employees in deciding how jobs should be carried out and giving them a greater decision-making role in their immediate work environment.

Job or work participation is a most practical type of employee participation but can be difficult to effect successfully. It is suggested that increased employee participation in workplace decision making requires effective, trusting two-way communications between management and employees, where workers feel they have a valuable input to make and where that input is recognised and valued by the organisation's management (Beer et al., 1984). It is also felt to demand a more flexible and open approach to the management process with less emphasis on direction and supervision and more on co-ordination and communication (Walton, 1985). This form of employee participation also involves an element of role reversal with superiors listening to employee comments, discussing these with top management and consulting employees on decisions (Lawler, 1978, 1982; Walton, 1985). Such approaches may take a variety of forms ranging from some type of Management by Objectives (MBO), to job enlargement, autonomous work groups, quality circles, suggestion schemes and consultative meetings. An important facilitator of increased job/work participation is a high level of informality, trust and openness in the manager–employee relationship, and the adoption of a managerial style which makes employees feel that their participation is both valued and worthwhile. A broader development relying on various forms of direct job participation is the Quality of Working Life movement (QWL), which attempts to encourage an organisational culture that promotes employee feelings of control, responsibility and involvement (see Schuler, 1987a,b).

Trade unions have traditionally been suspicious of such managerial initiatives believing them to stem from attempts to undermine the union's role, particularly the predominance of collective bargaining. Such suspicions are undoubtedly fuelled by the extensive use of such techniques by non-union firms (Morrissey, 1989).

PARTICIPATION THROUGH COLLECTIVE BARGAINING

Despite some success with the above options, many would argue that the most notable improvements in extending employee participation have been achieved through collective bargaining and that it should remain the major vehicle for further developments. The growth of workplace bargaining in Ireland has greatly facilitated this process, with trade unions being the key mechanism for representing and extending employee rights at workplace level. While there may be some tentative evidence of a demise in trade union influence and consequent reliance on the collective bargaining process, it still seems that union representations through collective bargaining offer a most pragmatic route to greater employee participation. Indeed, the trade union role in employee participation is particularly significant and is discussed below in some detail.

SMALLER-SCALE INITIATIVES

Before considering the role of trade unions in employee participation it is worth mentioning some smaller-scale initiatives which may be used to facilitate employee participation. One particular intitiative which has been around for some time is the Suggestion Scheme. Many Irish organisations have operated suggestion schemes with, apparently, varying degrees of success. It has been argued that suggestion schemes can be a useful mechanism for involving employees and increasing their commitment to the organisation. However, it is unlikely that such results can be achieved without suggestion schemes being accompanied by other participation initiatives. An initiative which appears to be increasing in popularity is the Attitude Survey. Opinion or attitude surveys normally involve management seeking to ascertain employees' views on the organisation, the effectiveness of communications, areas for improvement, employee benefits, etc., using structured questionnaires and/or interviews. Such surveys may often be independently administered and/or validated by external consultants or institutions (such as universities). In a recent research project on industrial relations in newly established (greenfield) companies it was found that a number of non-union organisations periodically administered attitude surveys to employees to elicit information on the general industrial relations climate in the organisation (Gunnigle, 1992c, 1994).

10.4.2. TRADE UNIONS AND EMPLOYEE PARTICIPATION

A particularly significant aspect of the debate on employee participation is the role and approach of trade unions. Despite occasional pronouncements, the trade union movement has not seemed particularly committed to representative forms of employee participation such as worker directors or works councils. Reactions to participation through equity participation have been mixed and no discernable trend is evident. Indeed, apart from support for greater disclosure of information, the traditional trade union approach to employee participation has been marked by a considerable degree of apathy. Such apathy has strong links with the doubts many trade-unionists harbour about the implications of representative participation for the union's role in collective bargaining.

While some models have suggested that representative participative mechanisms would operate concurrently with, but separate to, established collective bargaining arrangements, it is difficult to see how such approaches would operate effectively in practice. It is equally difficult to imagine trade unions allowing an alternative method of employee representation to be established at workplace level. In countries where worker directors and works councils are extensively used (e.g. the former West Germany) the trade union's role primarily involves industry-level negotiations. At workplace level most industrial relations issues are handled through the works council. In Ireland, trade unions have traditionally played a key role in workplace bargaining and would therefore be keen to retain a significant role in any representative participative mechanisms.

However, although collective bargaining has been a successful mechanism for extending employee participation, it has limitations. Firstly, collective bargaining depends on employee organisation and a degree of power balance between the parties. These ingredients may not be present in a large number of organisations, and thus collective bargaining may not be a viable route to employee participation. Secondly, collective bargaining operates best at workplace level. Where the locus of management decision making is removed to a higher level, such as in many multinational organisations, the effectiveness of collective bargaining in achieving employee participation may be severely limited.

Despite the suggestions above that the traditional trade union approach to employee participation has been characterised by some indifference, this position seems to have altered considerably in the recent past. A recent report by the Irish Congress of Trade Unions on the trade union response to new forms of work organisation suggests that trade unions need to take a more proactive role in influencing the planning and implementation of new workforce management strategies (ICTU, 1993). In the area of employee participation, the report appears to encourage a particular focus on developing and influencing employee involvement intitiatives at workplace level. On the issue of employee participation, the ICTU report suggests the following: 'Involvement with management in the implementation of . . . initiatives will be the key to ensuring that the interests of . . . members are met.'

316

This report also identifies key aspects of employee participation which trade unions need to address, particularly the joint monitoring of participation initiatives at organisation/workplace level, involvement of trade unions in the internal communications processes of organisations, access to and understanding of business information, and involvement in high-level business decision making. The issue of management–employee communications is seen as particularly important and is considered in detail later in this chapter.

10.4.3. ACHIEVING PARTICIPATION

From a normative perspective it is suggested that all parties involved in industrial relations can benefit from increased employee participation (Beer et al., 1984, 1985). For example, it is suggested that employers need a flexible and committed workforce, who will respond to change and perform at high levels of productivity with minimum levels of supervision, and that this can be achieved through employee involvement/participation initiatives (Beer et al., 1984; Lawler, 1978, 1982). From an employee perspective it is suggested that the achievement of an input into decisions which affect their working lives is a very legitimate goal, allowing them greater control and discretion in their jobs (Beer et al., 1984; Hackman and Oldham, 1980). Even at the macro-level, the State and the community at large may benefit from positive workplace relations based on trust, open communications and employee satisfaction (Beer et al., 1984, 1985).

However, the achievement of real, effective participation within organisations remains problematic (Marchington and Parker, 1990; Salamon, 1992). Employer organisations may argue that business confidence and discretion in decision making must be maintained to encourage investment and expansion, while at the same time suggesting that barriers to worker involvement must be removed and employees be given a worthwhile say in decision making. This perspective is commonly used to encourage and facilitate employee involvement in shop-floor issues while legitimising the retention of management prerogative in higher-level business decision making (Gunnigle and Morley, 1993).

Indeed, it might be suggested that the four forms of participation described above may be viewed as options in a participative mix, any combination of which may suit a particular organisational context. The imposition of particular models may often prove problematic and it is important that any legislative measures allow for flexibility in the modes of participation to be adopted. As much as anything, it would appear that effective participation requires a high level of commitment and positive support from both management (at all levels), employees and their representative organisations (particularly trade unions). Trust has been identified as a key factor in facilitating effective communications and information disclosure/exchange (Lawler, 1978, 1982; Whelan, 1982). Indeed, it would appear that the existence of high-trust relations is more important than the actual participative form or mechanism adopted (Beer et al., 1984). Significantly, however, an ESRI report, which suggests that the prospects for success in worker participation depends on a high degree of trust in the worker–management relationship, noted the 'strikingly low levels of trust' which employees had of management in Irish organisations, and concluded that progress in achieving employee participation had been disappointing (Whelan, 1982). The study also suggested that the traditional approaches of trade unions and management in collective bargaining resulted in their adopting adversarial positions which militated against employee participation. This report suggests that effective participation requires a reappraisal of this approach which would involve management and unions reviewing traditional approaches to employee relations and altering these to suit more participative approaches. The previous chapter on management styles in industrial relations has considered some recent management initiatives in the area of employee participation. We have also noted above some evidence of change in trade union approaches, particularly in the light of the recent Irish Congress of Trade Unions' report on new forms of work organisation (ICTU, 1993).

The issue of employee participation is further explored below in the context of developments in management–employee communications.

10.5. MANAGEMENT–EMPLOYEE COMMUNICATIONS

Differences in organisational approaches to communications with employees tend to focus on the nature and content of management–employee communications and the range of mechanisms used to facilitate such communications. The most notable developments arising from the Price Waterhouse Cranfield Project data was the increase in direct verbal and written communications with employees (see table 10.9).

Table 10.9. Communications with employees (in %, N = 267)

Mode of communication	Change in level of utilisation (%)			
	Increased	Decreased	Same	Don't know / missing
Through representative staff bodies, e.g. trade unions	14.2	11.2	44.2	30.3
Verbally, direct to employees	49.8	1.5	38.2	10.5
Written, direct to employees	36.0	3.0	41.9	19.1

Source: Price Waterhouse Cranfield Project (Ireland), 1992.

It appears from the research evidence that methods of communication employed by organisations and the type of information being communicated to employees has changed in recent years. A number of factors may be used to explain this development, notably (1) the increase in quality enhancement initiatives; (2) a move towards flatter organisation structures which facilitate greater and more informative communication at lower levels in the organisation; (3) the presence of a more educated workforce—'a new kind of person', who desires to be involved and informed as much as possible. The impact of contemporary quality initiatives is felt to have a significant impact on the area of management–employee communications and has facilitated the passing-on directly of relevant information on workplace-related issues.

In considering the role of trade unions in the communications process, the PWC Project data presents quite a stable picture with a majority of organisations reporting little change in the union role. An issue of particular interest here is the degree to which direct communications with employees is being used as a means of circumventing and/or marginalising trade unions in management–employee communications. It is likely that many organisations neither can nor wish to suddenly discontinue to use established collective bargaining fora. Rather, it appears that management–employee communications will increasingly occur through parallel mechanisms.

Turning to the actual content of management–employee communications, the PWC Project data suggests that most Irish firms communicate formally on both business strategy and financial performance with managerial and professional/technical employees (see table 10.10). However, the level of communications on these issues falls dramatically for clerical and manual grades. The most dramatic contrast arises in the area of communication on financial performance, where over 90 per cent of organisations claim to communicate formally on this issue with managerial grades but only 33 per cent do so with manual grades.

Table 10.10. Management communications on strategy and financial performance (in %, N = 267)

Grade of employee	Level of communications/briefing on	
	A. strategy	B. financial performance
Management	92.5	90.6
Professional/technical	64.4	57.3
Clerical	41.6	39.0
Manual	36.0	33.0

Source: Price Waterhouse Cranfield Project (Ireland), 1992.

In general it seems that the more sophisticated firms tend to use a range of communication mechanisms with particular emphasis on direct communications with individual employees. Such expansive approaches seem to be quite evident in newer organisations but not nearly as widespread in longer-established organisations. A study of newly established ('greenfield') companies confirms this focus on extensive direct communications with individual employees (Gunnigle, 1992c). This study suggests that the nature and scope of communications fora are more sophisticated in the great majority of US-owned firms, particularly in the computer/high-technology sector. The more sophisticated firms tend to use a range of communications mechanisms with particular emphasis on direct communications with individual employees. The most common approaches focus on 'cascade' mechanisms with briefings for different employee levels augmented by communications through line management, general workforce meetings and other written and oral communications. However, the majority of older, established Irish organisations seem to adopt less sophisticated approaches and rely primarily on collective bargaining, basic written communications and normal line management–employee interactions.

10.6. TECHNOLOGICAL CHANGE

Technology involves the use of any implement, equipment or machinery which assists work. It took on a major significance during the Industrial Revolution of the eighteenth and nineteenth centuries. The harnessing of steam power and the subsequent generation of electricity led to dramatic economic and social change. Over the past twenty-five years the speed and extent of change have increased dramatically. A new industrial revolution, based upon the microprocessor and biotechnology, is being witnessed. In contrast with past experience, where new developments were interspersed between periods of relative stability, change today is continuous. For example, a new generation of computers now hits the market annually, whilst scientific advances allow the ongoing introduction of new processes and materials affecting practically every branch of industry and service. This has massive implications for blue- and white-collar workers, and for the methods of production of goods and services. For the blue-collar worker these developments have created the spectre of robotic factories, maintained by a small number of multi-skilled technicians. Their white-collar colleagues have also seen their jobs deskilled and, as a result, their differential treatment more difficult to defend.

Technological change is of central relevance to the industrial relations process. In terms of its impact, there is no doubt that it exerts a huge influence on the power position of employers and employees, via its impact on the general demand for labour and on specific job types. New technology also both boosts and eliminates the demand for a plethora of skills. The relevance of technological developments to industrial relations is apparent from the fact that one survey discovered that more than two-thirds of trade union officials had been involved in technology-related negotiations in the course of the previous two years (ICTU, 1989).

10.6.1. THE LABOUR MARKET IMPACT

There is no consensus as to what the overall impact of technological advances has been on employment levels. Whilst these advances serve to obliterate and revise some jobs, they have also created both new jobs and industries, and expanded existing jobs. For example, in Ireland, the positive effects are evident from the growth of the electronics sector, which, up to the beginning of the 1990s, had provided about 15,000 new jobs, with another 3,000 or so people employed in the software industry. Against this, however, process technology tends to lead to job losses. The St James Gate Brewery of Guinness, for example, reduced its workforce by half over a five-year period, as a result of technological modernisation. It is apparent that the technological revolution has contributed to the relative decline of employment in the industrial sector, and to its growth in the services sector. This growth is particularly evident in those jobs which involve the generation, processing or transmission of knowledge or information, e.g. the media, data processing, research, education and training.

Reviewing the British scene, Gennard (1992) concludes that:

> There is no doubt that in some industries, such as coal mining, shipbuilding, railways, steel manufacturing, docks and textiles, technology has been a factor in accounting for the long-run decline in their employment levels. However, it has also been a factor in the growth of employment in such industries as air transport, chemicals, financial services and public utilities such as gas, water and electricity.

In terms of the occupational impact, there has been a definite decline in the availability of some job types, e.g. in manual work. Unfortunately, this decline is not being compensated for by the new employment opportunities created by the 'high-tech' industries, which supply the computers, microchips and new technical systems. In addition, technological change has dramatically altered the nature of work in some industries (e.g. communications). It has also significantly reduced the bargaining power and employment opportunities of workers in many instances (e.g. printing, paper and textile manufacture), whilst strengthening the position of others (e.g. computer manufacture and electronic media). Furthermore, the application of new technologies has obliterated many demarcation lines and boundaries between previously separated trades and industries (e.g. between mechanics, electricians and fitters, in newspaper production and in the printing industry).

As to the actual impact on job skill levels, the earlier debates on whether new technology results in deskilling or enskilling remain inconclusive. Whilst instances of both have been detected, Ramsay et al. (1992) argue that 'the evidence on skill is largely indeterminate', as 'jobs are often just different, gaining and losing skill elements in ways that are not readily commensurable'. It is interesting, then, to note the findings of one survey of trade union members, which discovered that sizeable majorities of males and (to a lesser extent) females reported an increase in their skill requirements as a result of technological change (ICTU, 1989). Furthermore, a majority of those surveyed felt that their working conditions remained the same as a result (ICTU, 1989a). However, an overwhelming majority of the respondents reported an increase in stress levels following the introduction of the new technology (ICTU, 1989b).

10.6.2. EMPLOYER AND TRADE UNION PERSPECTIVES

Whilst the speed and applicability of technological change varies somewhat, it is, nevertheless, persistent. Naturally, the faster the pace of change, the more difficult it is for both employers and trade unions to adapt. Employer motives with regard to new technology tend to be driven by the opportunities presented to consolidate or increase product market competitiveness and to improve productivity levels. The trade union position is largely based upon a recognition of market-place reality and tends, therefore, to support the employers' aspirations where they are based upon 'change by agreement' policies. As the ICTU (1989c) puts it: 'To attempt to embargo change puts the unions in a confrontation with management in which they appear to be adopting a Luddite stance.'

Trade union aspirations, then, in regard to new technology, are concerned with ensuring that its introduction is the subject of negotiation. Accordingly, they attempt to influence the form of the new work arrangements and to ensure that the benefits to be derived from such change are reflected in the terms and conditions of its membership, and in the maintenance or expansion of employment levels. The preference for a 'joint regulatory' approach is reflected in their recommendation for the removal of '. . . (all) issues on which a common approach is clearly desirable from the adversarial approach generated by traditional collective bargaining' (ICTU, 1989a). That is, as issues of mutual interest are addressed in a joint working party, demands for employment protection, improved terms and conditions, and a better work environment are pursued in the bargaining arena.

Of course, particular difficulties are posed in this arena where technological advances jeopardise the demand for the skills of particular groups (e.g. dockers, miners). Against this, however, many workers also see the prospect of a better working environment (e.g. via computer-aided manufacture and design), greater job security and enhanced terms and conditions of employment as attractive. Nevertheless, these developments constitute a particular threat to those trade unions that normally organise their recruitment along occupational or skill lines and base their power on exclusive representation of specific occupations (e.g. craft workers' trade unions). Allied to this is the fact that job losses and reduced employee control are most evident amongst semi-skilled manual groups in manufacturing and clerical/administrative work generally—both categories with a traditionally high level of trade union membership. This threat is accentuated by the fact that many of the employment opportunities created by technological advances are in areas characterised by low unionisation levels, e.g. amongst professional categories and in 'high-tech' non-union policy establishments (Bell, 1983).

10.6.3. IMPLEMENTING TECHNOLOGICAL CHANGE

Approaches to the introduction of new technology adopted by employers may be classified into two categories: the joint and the unilateral. The joint approach involves negotiation with the relevant trade union(s), thus enabling workers' insecurities to be allayed and/or compensated. That is, worker co-operation and commitment (as opposed to confrontation), in the implementation of the new technology is sought. This approach is often based upon the premise that change can be brought about more effectively via active staff participation, rather than if management attempts to impose change unilaterally in the face of negative employee reaction. By involving staff in those decisions which impinge upon their working lives, and by drawing upon their knowledge and experience, a direct improvement in working practices and operations, together with a more committed workforce may emerge. Such an approach is supported by research work undertaken by the European Foundation for the Improvement of Living and Working Conditions (1985). According to the Foundation, however, trade unions face real difficulties in making an effective contribution to strategy formulation when entering into such arrangements, due to a lack of expert support and training in the relevant areas. This experience is, in fact, being repeated with the plethora of 'quality' and 'new forms of work organisation' in evidence as 'one of the key issues identified by workplace representatives is their urgent need for greater guidance and support from their unions in responding to the initiatives' (ICTU, 1993).

In contrast to the joint approach, many employers prefer to introduce new technology 'by stealth', or unilaterally (Bell, 1982). This route assumes automatic and/or eventual employee support for the initiative and, it is often, therefore, introduced on a piecemeal basis. It can also take the form of securing the support of a traditionally 'loyal' group of staff and, as their colleagues see the benefit of the initiative, any potential resistance wanes. Of course, in practice, both strategies have, in instances, left employers to deal with industrial sanctions taken by staff who objected to the absence, or size of, compensation on offer.

However, the available evidence indicates that the economic climate of the 1980s and 1990s has favoured employers, and consequently enabled them to implement change peacefully and on terms more favourable to themselves (Gennard, 1992). Trade unions have been left to negotiate from a position of weakness, as they recognise their common interest with the employer—that the enterprise must survive in the longer term, or be replaced by more competitive employers who have adapted to the necessary technical changes. Allied to this is the belief that these revisions render jobs considerably less amenable to employee control and consequently strengthen management's position in the industrial relations context.

10.6.4. TECHNOLOGY AGREEMENTS

In 1991 the EC published a report entitled 'Joint Opinions', agreed by the social partners, on the introduction of new information technologies in firms. In the document the social partners:

> . . . recognized the need to make use of the economic and social potential offered by technological innovation in order to enhance the competitiveness of European firms and strengthen economic growth, thus creating one of the necessary conditions for better employment and, taking particular account of progress in the field of ergonomics, for improved working conditions. (Commission of the European Communities, 1991)

The social dialogue led to a double agreement on new technologies (covering training and motivation, and information and consultation) in European enterprises. However, to date, this has produced limited results, and has contributed to a demand for such 'Joint Opinions' to be made binding on the parties (Gill, 1992). This failure to secure a consequential agreement between employers and trade unions on technological developments is nothing new. For example, during the late 1970s and the early 1980s, trade unions devoted considerable resources to the procurement of technology agreements. Such agreements ought to be differentiated from the productivity agreements more commonly found in the 1960s and 1970s. Productivity agreements usually involved revised working practices, with employees doing the same or similar work, albeit more flexibly and effectively. In contrast, technology agreements are designed to protect workers' interests in the event of significant revisions brought about by technological advances. According to Benson and Lloyds' (1983) review of new technology agreements in Britain, however, 'health and safety is the most strikingly precise of the issues agreed: the others, such as job security, consultation and disclosure, and sharing benefits, are usually either tentative or vague, and all depend heavily on the maintenance of considerable strength and vigilance on the part of the unions'.

This view is accentuated by the findings of James (1980), who concludes that trade unions rarely receive an assurance from management that change will be introduced with prior negotiation and agreement, or that full information on costs will be made available to them. Daniel (1987) agrees, having discovered in Britain that in only 10 to 15 per cent of cases is the introduction of technical change to unionised establishments negotiated. According to Brewster (1992), this failure on the part of trade unions is attributable to the fact that:

> It is frequently difficult to distinguish agreements on new technology from agreements on changing working practices or pay—new technology is a blanket term, and in reality every situation is different, thus rendering general trade union guidelines inappropriate and/or difficult to follow—and economic circumstances, allied to management confidence, have allowed trade unions to be bypassed on the introduction of technical change.

Of course it is difficult to reach a definitive conclusion on whether trade unions have been able to secure financial compensation for their members; as such compensation may well be 'buried' in an overall wage-round award or accommodated in a local bargaining clause under a national agreement. However, given the employer's general reluctance to provide relevant cost-benefit estimate data when introducing new technology, it is somewhat ambitious to talk of a 'distribution of benefits' resulting from such changes. Indeed, even in those instances where trade unions have had recourse to the Labour Relations Commission or Labour Court to secure compensation on behalf of their membership for new technology initiatives, it is striking to observe the preponderance of (arguably) modest once-off lump-sum cash award recommendations.

Related to this is the fact that, in general, interested parties have supported the implementation of technological change at work. In fact, research indicates that there is often little worker resistance to the introduction of new technology (Blennerhasset and Haskins, 1985; Daniel, 1987; Daniel and Hogarth, 1990). For example, a survey of the 'general attitude' of trade union members toward technology revealed a majority in favour (ICTU, 1989). However, where the advent of such technology threatens employment prospects, the resolution of differing group interests is much more likely to be protracted. Yet, in general, one may conclude that the paucity of technology-related conflict stands alongside 'the often low wage settlements, the abortive industrial actions, the often hopeless factory occupations and mass redundancies as evidence of trade union weaknesses' (Benson and Lloyd, 1983).

10.7. NEW WORK ORGANISATION AND QUALITY INITIATIVES

In recent years the term 'Japanisation' is being used to describe many of the organisational changes taking place across Europe and North America. Just as North America itself has influenced the practice and language of 'human resource management', so has the Japanese experience driven the adoption of many 'Total Quality Management' (TQM) techniques. Put simply, 'Japanisation' reflects a coherent and distinctive managerial strategy seeking to enlist employees' ingenuity, initiative and co-operation at the point of production or service provision. That is, employees are now to be encouraged to come to work mentally or intellectually, as well as physically! This also entails a range of human resource management policies designed to promote a high degree of worker commitment, and to minimise the likelihood of industrial action. TQM and 'World-Class Manufacturing' (WCM)-type initiatives involve such practices as 'lean production', cellular manufacturing and teamwork, autonomous work groups and self-inspection, total preventative maintenance, statistical process control and just-in-time (JIT) systems of production and service provision. 'Lean production' is reflected in organisational and work structures which facilitate flexible working arrangements, JIT inventory levels and staff–management collaboration. In contrast with 'Taylorism', and the specialised machinist operating one machine at one particular work station, there is now a generalised, skilled machinist with flexible job boundaries. Under a JIT system waste is minimised in a 'hand-to-mouth' mode of manufacturing, which aims to produce the necessary components, in the required quantities, to quality specifications on demand.

Under a TQM system, responsibility for quality production is assigned to the worker. TQM is concerned with continuously improving customer satisfaction by quality-led company-wide management (Wilkinson, 1992). The genuine TQM company is one which practises TQM without thinking about it, as quality is a way of life which permeates every part and aspect of the organisation. This requires an abandonment of efficiency in favour of effectiveness, with an emphasis on customer satisfaction rather than quality control specifications. Indeed, some would say that the focus with quality initiatives is now on 'customer delight' rather than 'customer satisfaction' (Pearson, 1991). If customers are in fact 'delighted', the implications for an expanding market share are apparent. Accordingly, quality is transformed from being a single aspect of corporate affairs to one of strategic importance. The competitive pressures for the adoption of this orientation come mainly from:

– the need to increase productivity and reduce unit costs;
– the need to guarantee quality to customers; and
– the need to have more flexible and adaptable operations.

Organisations successfully introducing TQM have found that the costs incurred during implementation are outweighed by the eventual cost savings (Hogg, 1990). One would, of course, expect reduced physical costs in terms of lower inventory, reduced recalls and fewer corrections or replacements where quality products or services are being provided. Lower labour costs should also materialise where organisations are discovering ways of increasing production or of improving the service with fewer employees. Certainly, the traditional inspection team would no longer be required and complaints departments could be scaled down. TQM is also attributed with a sizeable motivational impact via the provision of employees with increased control over their own work and greater opportunities to train and experiment. One could also expect greater levels of motivation where a unifying theme—a commitment to total quality—pervades all transactions in the organisation, including those between different levels in the hierarchy.

An initial import from Japan (though the original idea stemmed from the US) was the Quality Circle (QC). It is estimated that there are now over 10 million workers involved in 1 million such quality circles in Japan. The quality circle actively encourages employee involvement in decision making, albeit at task level and within specified boundaries. Their objective is to improve decision making and to iron out problems at the earliest possible opportunity. Additional beneficial by-products of such arrangements are adjudged to be improved organisational morale, the development of a range of employees' skills, and superior quality and company profitability. In many instances the QC has either been replaced by, or incorporated into, a TQM programme. Given a failure rate for QCs of over 20 per cent in the UK and 50 per cent in the US, it is felt that TQM schemes have more chance of success and continuity as they resolve some of the organisational and strategic problems that QCs, by their nature, could not (Cressey, 1991).

The main distinguishing feature of the TQM organisation, then, is that quality is seen as a strategic issue rather than an operational one. It extends to both horizontal and vertical improvements in organisational attitudes and practices (i.e. with regard to outside customers and internal (co-worker) ones). The impetus and drive toward TQM comes from senior management, as reflected by their approach, priorities, attitudes and resource allocations. In fact, the complete corporate culture of the TQM organisation is one of open communication, multidisciplinary team-work, employee involvement, high-trust relations, the internalisation of quality and customer responsiveness. In short, TQM is not something that applies for one hour out of the forty in the working week, rather it is intended to be transformative in its effect on the complete organisation culture (Cressey, 1991).

Interest in this quality orientation is reflected by the fact that, for example, by the end of 1993, over 1,000 companies operative in the Republic of Ireland had been registered to the ISO 9000 (an international quality standard), by the National Standards Authority of Ireland (EOLAS, 1993). In addition, the

Irish Quality Association (IQA) had conducted 1,500 system audits in the same year, for the purpose of assessing the adequacy of companies' quality assurance programmes. This interest is fuelled by national survey findings which reveal that 'people regard quality as the most important feature when buying a product' (IQA, 1994), and is reinforced by separate survey findings across a sample of Irish service companies which reveal that 'quality significantly overshadowed price (86.1 per cent versus 13.9 per cent) in competitive pressures' (IQA, 1994).

10.7.1. WHY DOES TQM FAIL?

Though the interest in the Japanese model is more than a 'passing fad' (Jurgens, 1989), it is nevertheless notable that the overwhelming majority of organisations have cherry-picked from the range of possible TQM and WCM initiatives. That is, there are hardly any organisations in Britain or Ireland that adopt the total approach (Brewster, 1992; Wilkinson, 1992). Furthermore, only 8 per cent of British managers rate their quality initiatives as totally successful—the majority claim only a moderate degree of success, or are neutral about such practices (Wilkinson et al., 1993). The main reasons for this derive from the challenge which TQM poses to existing corporate cultures. According to Wilkinson (1992), this is reflected in a preoccupation with:

– short-termism;
– organisational structure;
– a lack of management support; and
– a lack of employee support.

Short-termism refers to the emphasis on short-term performance indicators rather than on longer-term objectives. For example, the focus remains on current sales quantities as opposed to the quality of sales, and the consequent building of market shares, together with the development and exploitation of more effective new technologies and work methods. The quantity- rather than quality-driven preoccupation is therefore reflected in short-term quantitative controls rather than longer-term qualitative experimentation. This is also evident from the surge in popularity of merit-/performance-related pay systems. In the opinion of Deming, the leading 'guru' in the field, quality is incompatible with 'annual or merit rating and . . . management by objectives' (Brewster, 1992). For the complete TQM package to apply, however, workers must be free to experiment, take risks and make mistakes. They cannot be restrained by pre-established targets. In contrast, however, for merit pay to work it is argued that effective, tight, pre-established targets, against which performance can be evaluated, are required.

The *organisational structure* barrier is rooted in the anti-expert or specialisation orientation of TQM. That is, TQM emphasises that all workers can, and should, contribute to quality. This, however, has implications for power sharing and its delegation to both customers and the workforce. If the customer and the subordinate are to be allowed to influence 'the expert', then 'the expert' surrenders his/her total power. This goes against both human nature and organisational power cultures.

Top management support is also suspect, given that TQM requires new propensities, abilities and attitudes from management. Consequently, the team-work or participative 'language' may be widespread, but the actual practice sparse. Corporate cultures still emphasise compliance over commitment, with low-trust levels (see Whelan, 1982) and inter-departmental rivalry still dominant. Some managers also see the TQM initiative as another costly fad, fashion or flavour of the month. For example, in contrast with the Japanese experience with QCs, UK research suggests that most of their QC initiatives have been 'less than successful because of a lack of commitment from managerial grades' (Atkinson and Naden, 1989). Research also indicates that this experience is being repeated with the other ingredients of the quality package (Wilkinson et al., 1993). According to Deming, many managers see TQM as the application of a range of statistical techniques in order to understand and measure physical processes, whilst neglecting their responsibility in the management and development of people (Bratton and Gold, 1994).

Employee support is lukewarm, given the low employer–employee trust levels, together with the fact that working relationships between 'superiors and subordinates' have traditionally been the battleground for disputes over payment schemes, productivity, demarcation, work practices and staffing levels. Increased employee involvement may also be viewed as greater responsibility and pressure for workers without extra pay. Put bluntly, it is one thing for workers to be encouraged to come up with ideas, it is another that they be expected to do so! Where top management have adopted an elitist approach via prioritised car parking, the segregation of staff facilities and other differential terms and conditions of employment, the implications for participative forms of management along the lines prescribed by TQM are apparent. Related to this is the Volkswagen experience with the 'quality' initiative:

> Resistance is particularly strong where change has been implemented from the top without involving those affected. It is also strong where management takes account of only the quantifiable benefits and excludes issues where no quantifiable advantage is evident. In such cases, the labour force rapidly withdraws its support and stops raising issues, thus bringing about the collapse of the whole project. (Marciniak, 1991)

Consequently, it is hardly surprising that instances of failed initiatives with 'quality' and 'new forms of work organisation' have been identified where 'relationships were characterised by low trust and a traditional adversarial

329

approach' (ICTU, 1993). Indeed, given the 'strikingly low levels of trust' which workers have of management in Irish organisations (Whelan, 1982), the prospects for significant advancement in this important area are less than encouraging.

The industrial relations dimension. Trade unions are also sceptical about, or hostile toward initiatives perceived to compete with or to bypass them. Nevertheless, the pressures created by JIT and TQM, involving lower staff levels and more intensive work systems, demand a more active and co-operative workforce. It is interesting, therefore, in this context, that: 'A mere work-to-rule or overtime ban could be as disastrous for a company operating a JIT system as could a strike for a company not doing so.' (Oliver and Wilkinson, 1989)

For example, given the absence of buffer stocks in the JIT environment and the continuous improvement focus under TQM, there is effectively an acute management dependency on labour co-operation. This dependency was less apparent when (higher) stock levels protected management from short-term production disruptions, or when the same product (or service) could be produced (or supplied) in the same way for years on end, without any real fear of losing market share to higher quality or more effective competitors (Turnbull, 1988; Wilkinson and Oliver, 1990).

Consequently, though such terms as 'worker empowerment' and 'mutual dependency' accompany the quality initiative, some commentators argue that real autonomy for the workforce is largely cosmetic. That is, the production decisions and quality targets are effectively determined by management decree and customer preference. Workers end up experiencing TQM as a 'low-trust' activity (Klein, 1989), and as a system of 'information and control' rather than genuine participation (Sewell and Wilkinson, 1992; Taylor et al., 1991). According to Delbridge and Turnbull (1992):

> Responsibility is devolved to the shop-floor but not control, which remains highly centralized in the hands of management. Employees are only required to participate in incremental improvements to product quality and process efficiency, which simply incorporates workers in the projects of capital without extending any real control or collective autonomy to the workforce.

As with new technology advances, the response of the international trade union movement to these new forms of work organisation is based upon an acceptance of their inevitability. Consequently, they have endeavoured to avail of this opportunity to address many of their traditional concerns about improving the quality of work life. To date, Irish trade unions have had minimal involvement in the formal organisational structures that implement the quality initiatives. However, given that such initiatives are expected to deepen where they are already in place, and to spread to other manufacturing

and service organisations, in 1993 the ICTU categorised three possible responses to the 'quality' developments (ICTU, 1993):
– opposition, on the assumption that such initiatives represent a move toward a non-union environment;
– pragmatic scepticism, which accepts that change is permanent and responds accordingly by advising and guiding its membership on appropriate responses;
– 'shaping the agenda', which accepts that change is permanent and endeavours to actively influence the quality of worker participation in all of the enterprise's affairs.

Reviewing these options, the ICTU discussion document concluded that the 'opposition' route would not meet the needs of its membership and would do little to enhance the movement's own perception and credibility. Accordingly, it was concluded that the most effective trade union response should entail the development of a 'flexible and supportive approach while seeking to optimise the outcome for both their members and the companies they are employed within. Moving from an adversarial role which concentrates on pay and conditions to the new role envisaged will require a new orientation at all levels of union organisation.'

10.8. THE EUROPEAN UNION AND DEVELOPMENTS IN INDUSTRIAL RELATIONS

It would be difficult to dispute that Ireland's membership of the European Union (EU) has had and will continue to have a significant impact on the conduct of industrial relations in this country [2]. The EU has emerged as an important agent in the operating environment of Irish organisations and exerts a growing influence in the Irish industrial relations system. For example, at a macro-level Hourihan (1994) argues that membership of the EU has contributed to a shift in the focus of industrial relations away from an adversarial model of industrial relations inherited from Britain to the adoption of European models of corporatism as evidenced by the current bout of centralised bargaining beginning with the Programme for National Recovery, succeeded by the Programme for Economic and Social Progress (PESP) and the present arrangements in the Programme for Competitiveness and Work.

In many ways the most tangible influence of the EU on Irish industrial relations has been the considerable increase in employment legislation, particularly in the 1970s, in response to EU social policy. Accession to the EU in 1973 committed Ireland to implementing in full the legislative and social policy changes already adopted by the Community since 1958, and equally obliged the State to adopt a programme of European social and legislative initiatives advocated by the Council of Ministers in January 1974. As a result, many pieces of Irish labour legislation considered in chapter 2, for example the Anti-Discrimination (Pay) Act 1974 and the Employment Equality Act

1977, owe their intellectual parentage to this social action programme and to directives emanating from Brussels.

Recent EU developments in social policy, whose immediate origins lie in the signing of the Single European Act in 1987, will equally lead to the alteration of the existing labour law framework. The Single European Act, which aimed to strengthen economic cohesion in the EU by removing all barriers to competition between Member States, had central to it the issue of integration of social policy throughout the EU. In 1989, a Charter of Fundamental Social Rights of Workers, the Social Charter, containing twelve articles (see box 10.1 for a summary of these articles) was signed in Strasbourg by the Member States except the UK. The Social Charter was drafted in response to the objectives set by the Single European Act of harmonising working conditions in the EU, and is a non-binding largely aspirational document. The Social Charter (which was subsequently renamed the Social Chapter) has an attendant Social Action Programme (see Hourihan, 1994) agreed in 1990, which comprises of forty-nine legally binding directives and recommendations designed to realise the aims of the Social Charter. The attainment of the rights set out in the Social Chapter has been agreed by the Irish Government, trade unions and employers as signatories of the PESP, which commits Ireland to 'support Community action geared to promoting social cohesion' (PESP, 1991). Many of the provisions of the Social Chapter, though, already exist under Irish employment law.

The Community has long viewed the social dimension as a crucial part of the single European market. The rationale for this, as Rollinson (1993) explains, lies in the fact that there are considerable differences in prosperity among the different member countries, and unless employment rights and conditions are levelled up, the single market could create a situation which would give some states an unfair competitive advantage over others. This, of course, was central to the UK seeking an opt-out clause from the Social Chapter prior to the ratification of the Maastricht Treaty. To date considerable progress has been made on many of the points contained in the Social Action Programme, with the most important developments occurring in the adoption of directives covering working time, the protection of pregnant workers, the protection of young workers, health and safety, employment contracts and, most recently, on information and consultation.

Setting aside the issue of social policy, the EU may also influence Irish industrial relations in a number of other areas of equal importance. For example, the disciplines imposed on the Irish Government as a result of the Maastricht Treaty, necessary for entry into the third phase of the Economic and Monetary Union, which covers inflation, exchequer debt, convergence of interest rates and debt/GDP ratios, may pose serious budgetary problems for the Government, particularly in relation to the management of the public sector pay bill. This obviously will have implications for ongoing pay determination and for industrial relations generally in the public sector. The completion of the internal market and the removal of technical barriers have exposed organisations in this country to new levels of competition, which has undoubtedly had implications for company-level personnel and industrial relations policies. Similarly, completion of economic and monetary union and a single European currency, although still far from being a *fait accompli*, would have wide-ranging implications for collective bargaining and pay determination within Member States (see Teague, 1993).

Box 10.1. The provisions of the Social Chapter

Article 1: Freedom of Movement
Workers have the right to work in any Member State and are entitled to the same working conditions and social protection as nationals in that country.

Article 2: Employment and Remuneration
The freedom to choose an occupation and the right to be fairly remunerated.

Article 3: Improvements in Living and Working Conditions
Workers have the right to improved working and living conditions.

Article 4: Social Protection
Each worker has the right to social protection.

Article 5: Freedom of Association and Collective Bargaining
Workers have the right to join or not to join trade unions. Workers and employers' organisations have the right to engage in collective bargaining.

Article 6: Vocational Training
Each worker has the right to vocational training.

Article 7: Equal Treatment for Men and Women
Men and women have the right to equal treatment.

Article 8: Information, Consultation and Participation
Workers have the right to information, consultation and participation.

Article 9: Health Protection and Safety at the Workplace
All workers have the right to health protection and safety at work.

Article 10: The Protection of Children and Adolescents
The minimum employment age should not be lower than fifteen years and young persons should receive equitable remuneration in accordance with national practice.

Article 11: Elderly Persons
Elderly persons have the right to a decent standard of living.

Article 12: Disabled Persons
All disabled persons are entitled to measures designed to improve their social and professional integration.

Hourihan (1994) submits that membership of the EU has had a significant impact on the nature of national-level collective bargaining in recent years. He argues that 'we may be seeing a new facet to the decision-making process affecting industrial relations, with the European Commission being afforded a validation role which directly affects the conduct of national-level bargaining'. Hourihan suggests that access to EU funding is being firmly tied to the acceptance or validation of policy decisions achieved at national-level bargaining by the European Commission, and also that the use of EU funds may be linked to the adoption of labour market reforms put forward by Brussels. This, Hourihan (1994) contends, 'implies a new collective bargaining dimension and affords the European Commission an unheralded place in the formation of labour market policies within Member States'.

10.9. CONCLUSIONS

This chapter has attempted to review contemporary developments in Irish industrial relations. In particular, it has focused on areas of change in industrial relations and analysed some research evidence on current developments in the field. It has been argued that developments in the labour market, including the growth of employment in the services sector, the growth of 'atypical' employment and widespread flexibility initiatives, have their attendant implications for the conduct of industrial relations.

Employee participation can take a variety of directions and proceed at different paces in different countries, but what seems certain is that it is likely to appear high on the industrial relations agenda in this country in the coming years, particularly in the light of recent EU initiatives on participation, information and consultation.

From the vast array of research work undertaken across Europe in recent years it is clear that technological change is, and will continue to be, widespread (see Bratton and Gold, 1994). Furthermore, it will present new opportunities for co-operation, together with potential for conflict, between management and staff. In this regard it is interesting to note the British experience, which has revealed that where the personnel specialists were involved in the process of change, they have had a positive impact. That is, 'their involvement was associated with a stronger level of workers' support for change' (Daniel and Millward, 1983). This conclusion has important implications both for the Human Resource/personnel function and the Irish economy. With productivity levels in Irish industry lagging behind most of our industrialised competitors, it would be remiss if employers opted to rely on relatively low wages rather than updated technology (in generally co-operative work environments), in an attempt to remain competitive. Given the afore-mentioned importance of, and scope for improving productivity levels, together with the fact that Ireland has the highest proportionate level of low pay in the European Community (McMahon, 1992), the case for a progressive attitude toward technological change is strong and, fortunately, at least from an industrial relations perspective, apparent (ICTU, 1993).

With TQM we are witnessing a total revolution compared to the era when the craft worker was directly responsible to the consumer. Responsibility for quality has been transferred in turn to the foreman, the inspector, the quality control department and now, eventually, back to the worker! The merit of TQM warrants a fundamental shift in attitudes and values, an investment of time and money, patience—whilst awaiting tangible results—and a degree of strategic thinking that few enterprises have yet fully achieved. The 'quality' initiatives have huge implications, both for organisational survival and growth, and for the management of people at work. Whether the requisite level of maturity can be displayed to give effect to mutually beneficial change in the future is open to question. Despite the fairly progressive attitude being adopted by the trade union hierarchy, it is a moot point as to whether this can be translated to the shop floor. It may be argued that the history of 'technological change' will repeat itself, as unions are bypassed and management proceed to take the 'direct' route with a host of superficial quality initiatives. The economic and social consequences of such a strategy, however, hardly bear thinking about.

It should now be apparent that membership of the European Union has clear implications for both the nature and conduct of collective bargaining and industrial relations in Ireland. These implications not only emanate from on-going developments in European social policy but also from the perhaps less obvious policy issues arising from the completion of the internal market and movement towards an economic and monetary union.

NOTES

1. This section on employee participation draws primarily on material from P. Gunnigle and P. Flood, *Personnel Management in Ireland: Practice, Trends and Developments*, Gill and Macmillan, Dublin, 1990.
2. For a more detailed account of this subject matter see F. Hourihan, 'The European Union and Industrial Relations', in T. Murphy and B. Roche (eds.), *Industrial Relations in Ireland*, Oaktree Press, Dublin, 1994.

Bibliography

Abell, D.F. and Hammond, J.S., *Strategic Market Planning*, Prentice-Hall, Englewood Cliffs, NJ, 1979.

Advisory Conciliation Arbitration Service, *Disciplinary Practices and Procedures in Employment*, Code of Practice No. l: Employment, HMSO, London, 1977.

Advisory Conciliation Arbitration Service, *Discipline at Work: The ACAS Advisory Handbook*, ACAS/HMSO, London, 1987.

Ahern, B., 'The Industrial Relations Act 1990', speech by the Minister for Labour at the Seminar on the Industrial Relations Act 1990, organised by the Irish Society for Labour Law on 13 July 1991, Department of Labour, Dublin, 1991a.

Ahern, B., 'Keynote Address', by the Minister for Labour to the Institute of Personnel Management Annual Conference, Killarney, 1991b.

Allen, V., *The Sociology of Industrial Relations*, Longman, Harlow, 1971.

Anthony, P.D., *The Conduct of Industrial Relations*, Institute of Personnel Management, London, 1980.

Armstrong, M., 'Human Resource Management: A Case of the Emperor's New Clothes', *Personnel Management*, August 1987.

Armstrong, M., *A Handbook of Personnel Management Practice*, Kogan Page, London, 1991.

Armstrong, P., 'The Personnel Profession in the Age of Management Accountancy', *Personnel Review*, Vol. 17, No. 1, 1988.

Atkinson, G., *The Effective Negotiator*, Quest Research Publications, London, 1977.

Atkinson, J., *Flexible Manning: The Way Ahead*, Institute of Manpower Studies, London, 1984a.

Atkinson, J., 'Manpower Strategies for Flexible Organisations', *Personnel Management*, August 1984b.

Atkinson, J. and Meager, N., 'Is Flexibility just a Flash in the Pan?', *Personnel Management*, September 1986.

Atkinson, P. and Naden, J., 'Total Quality Management: Eight Lessons from Japan', *Management Services*, March 1989, pp. 12–20.

Bain, G.S., *The Growth of White-Collar Unionism*, Clarendon Press, Oxford, 1970.

Bain, G.S. and Elias, P., 'Trade Union Membership in Great Britain: An Individual Level Analysis', *British Journal of Industrial Relations*, Vol. 23, 1985, pp. 71–82.

Bain, G.S. and Elsheikh, F., *Union Growth and the Business Cycle*, Blackwell, Oxford, 1979.

Bain, G.S. and Elsheikh, F., 'Unionisation in Britain: An Inter-establishment Analysis Based on Survey Data', *British Journal of Industrial Relations*, Vol. XVIII, 1980.

Bain, G.S. and Price, R., 'Union Growth: Dimensions, Determinants and Destiny', in G.S. Bain (ed.), *Industrial Relations in Britain*, Blackwell, Oxford, 1983.

Bargaining Report, 'Problems with Performance-Related Pay', No. 113, Labour Research Department, London, 1992.

Barret, S., 'A Case of National Misunderstanding', *Business and Finance*, January 1991.

Barret, S., 'Don't Try Another PESP', *Sunday Independent*, 9 May 1993.

Barrington, D., 'Report of the Commission of Inquiry on Safety, Health and Welfare at Work', Government Publications Office, Dublin, 1982.

Batstone, E., *Working Order*, Blackwell, Oxford, 1984.

Bean, R., 'Industrial Reactions', in E. Cohen and G. Studdard, (eds.), *The Bargaining Context*, Arrow, London, 1976.

Beaumont, P., *Change in Industrial Relations: The Organization and the Environment*, Routledge, London, 1990a.

Beaumont, P.D., *Change in Industrial Relations*, Faber and Faber, London, 1990b.

Beaumont, P., 'Trade Unions and HRM', *Industrial Relations Journal*, Vol. 22, No. 4, 1991.

Beaumont, P. and Harris, R., 'The North-South Divide in Britain: The Case of Trade Union Recognition', *Oxford Bulletin of Economics and Statistics*, Vol. 51, No. 4, 1989.

Beaumont, P. and Harris R., 'Trade Union Recognition and Employment Contraction, 1980–1984', *British Journal of Industrial Relations*, Vol. 29, No. 1, 1991.

Beer, M., Spector, B., Lawrence, P.R., Quinn-Mills, D. and Walton, R.E., *Managing Human Assets*, Collier Macmillan, London and New York, 1984.

Beer, M., Spector, B., Lawrence, P.R., Quinn-Mills, D. and Walton, R.E., *Human Resource Management: A General Managers Perspective*, The Free Press, New York, 1985.

Bell, A., 'Computer in the Office: The I.R. Implications', *Industrial Relations News*, 14 January 1982.

Bell, A., 'The Non-Union Company Approach to I.R.: The Computer Industry', *Industrial Relations News*, 4 February 1983.

Bendix, R., *Work and Authority in Industry*, Wiley, Chichester, 1956.

Benson, I. and Lloyd, J., *New Technology and Industrial Change*, Kogan Page, London, 1983.

Berridge, J., 'Human Resource Management in Britain', *Employee Relations*, Vol. 14, No. 5, 1992.

Bew, P., Hazelkorn, E. and Patterson, H., *The Dynamics of Irish Politics*, Lawrence and Wishart, London, 1989.

Blackburn, R.A. and Mann, D., *The Working Class in the Labour Market*, Macmillan, London, 1979.

Blennerhassett, E. and Haskins, J., 'Technological Developments and the Public Service: Impact on the General Public and Employees', Consolidated Report, IPA, Dublin, June 1985.

Blyton, P. and Morris, J., 'HRM and the Limits of Flexibility', in P. Blyton and P. Turnbull (eds.), *Reassessing Human Resource Management*, Sage, London, 1992.

Blyton, P. and Turnbull, P. (eds.), *Reassessing Human Resource Management*, Sage, London, 1992.

Bonner, K., 'Industrial Relations and the Law: What Next?', in *Industrial Relations in Ireland*, 1st edn, University College Dublin, 1987.

Bonner, K., 'Industrial Relations Reform', in *Industrial Relations in Ireland: Contemporary Issues and Developments*, University College Dublin, 1989.

Booth, A., 'Estimating the Probability of Trade Union Membership: A Study of Men and Women in Britain, *Economica*, No. 53, 1986.

Boyd, A., *The Rise of Irish Trade Unions, 1729–1970*, Anvil, Tralee, 1972.

Boyd, A., *Have Trade Unions Failed the North?*, Mercier Press, Cork, 1984.

Brannick, T. and Doyle, L., 'Industrial Conflict', in T.V. Murphy and W.K. Roche (eds.), *Irish Industrial Relations in Practice*, Oak Tree Press, Dublin, 1994.

Bratton, J. and Gold, J., *Human Resource Management: Theory and Practice*, Macmillan, London, 1994.

Breen, R., Haman, D.F., Rottman, D.B. and Whelan, C.T., *Understanding Contemporary Ireland*, Gill and Macmillan, Dublin, 1990.

Brewster, C., *Employee Relations*, Macmillan, London, 1989.

Brewster, C., 'Managing Industrial Relations', in B. Towers (ed.), *A Handbook of Industrial Relations Practice*, 3rd edn, Kogan Page, London, 1992.

Brewster, C. and Hegewich, A. (eds.), *The Price Waterhouse Cranfield Study on International Strategic Human Resource Management*, Cranfield School of Management/Price Waterhouse, Cranfield, 1993.

Brewster, C. and Hegewich, A. (eds.), *Policy and Practice in European Human Resource Management: The Price Waterhouse Cranfield Survey*, Routledge, London, 1994.

Briscoe, T., 'Accident Statistics Make Grim Reading', *Occupational, Health and Safety Newsletter*, Federation of Irish Employers, Dublin, 1992.

Brown, W. (ed.), *The Changing Contours of British Industrial Relations*, Blackwell, Oxford, 1981.

Brown, C. and Medoff, J., 'Trade Unions in the Production Process', *Journal of Political Economy*, Vol. 86, No. 3, June, 1978.

Business and Finance, 'Dilemmas All Round in Tripartite Talks, 30 July 1987.

Butler, J.E., 'HRM as a Driving Force in Business Strategy', *Journal of General Management*, Vol. 13, No. 4, 1988.

Butler, P., 'Employer Organisations: A Study', unpublished BBS project, University of Limerick, 1985.

Buzzell, R.B. and Gale, B.T., *The PIMS Principles: Linking Strategy to Performance*, The Free Press, New York, 1987.

Calmfors, L. and Drilfill, J., 'Bargaining Structure, Corporatism and Macro-Economic Performance', *Economic Policy*, Vol. 6, 1988.

Canning, L., 'Negotiating in Industrial Relations', unpublished, Irish Management Institute, Dublin, 1979.

Cappelli, P. and McKersie, R., 'Management Strategy in the Redesign of Workrules', *Journal of Management Studies*, No. 24, September 1987.

Carroll, C., Building *Ireland's Business: Perspectives from PIMS*, Irish Management Institute, Dublin, 1985.

Carroll, C. and Byrne, R., 'EC Requirements on Safety and Health at Work: An Update', *Industrial Relations News*, 25 June 1992.

Carroll, J., 'Changes in Industrial Disputes Law Unlikely to Benefit Unions', *Liberty News*, (Winter) 9, 1986.

Chamberlain, N.W., *The Union Challenge to Management Control*, Harper, New York, 1948.

Chamberlain, N. and Kuhn, J., *Collective Bargaining*, McGraw-Hill, New York, 1965.

Chandler, A.D., *Strategy and Structure*, MIT Press, Cambridge, MA, 1962.

Clarke, K. and Clarke, K., 'Personnel Management: Defence, Retrenchment, Advance?', *Personnel Review*, Vol. 20, No. 1, 1991.

Clegg, H.A., 'Pluralism in Industrial Relations', *British Journal of Industrial Relations*, London School of Economics, November 1975.

Clegg, H., *Trade Unionism under Collective Bargaining: A Theory Based on Comparisons of Six Countries*, Blackwell, Oxford, 1976.

Coates, K. and Topham, A. (eds.), *Industrial Democracy in Great Britain*, McGibbon and Kee, London, 1968.

Cole, G.A., *Personnel Management: Theory and Practice*, DP Publications, London, 1988.

Cole, R.E., 'Diffusion of Participatory Work Structures in Japan, Sweden and the United States', in P.S. Goodman (ed.), *Change in Organisations*, Jossey Bass, San Francisco, 1982.

Commission of the European Communities, 'Joint Opinions', European Social Dialogue Documentary Series, 1991.

Commission on Industrial Relations, *Employers Organisations and Industrial Relations*, Study No. 1, HMSO, London, 1972.

Conniffe, D. and Kennedy, K.A., *Employment and Unemployment Policy for Ireland*, Economic and Social Research Institute, Dublin, 1984.

Cordova, E., 'From Full-Time Wage Employment to Atypical Employment: A Major Shift in the Evolution of Labour Relations, *International Labour Relations Review*, Vol. 125, No. 6, 1988.

Cox, B. and Hughes, J., 'Industrial Relations in the Public Sector', in *Industrial Relations in Ireland: Contemporary Issues and Developments*, University College Dublin, 1989.

Cradden, T., 'Trade Unionism and HRM: The Incompatibles', *Journal of Irish Business and Administrative Research*, Vol. 13, 1992.

Cressey, P., 'Total Quality Management and Worker Participation', in M. Gold (ed.), *P+: Total Quality Management and Worker Participation*, Vol. 2, European Foundation for the Improvement of Living and Working Conditions, Dublin, 1991.

Crouch, C., *The Politics of Industrial Relations*, 2nd edn, Fontana, London, 1982a.

Crouch, C., *Trade Unions: The Logic of Collective Action*, Fontana, London, 1982b.

Dahrendorf, R., Class and Class *Conflict in Industrial Society*, Routledge, London, 1959.

Dáil Éireann, *Dáil Debates Collections*, The Stationery Office, Dublin, 1963.

Dáil Éireann, *Dáil Debates Collections*, The Stationery Office, Dublin, 1969.

Dáil Éireann, *Dáil Debates Collections*, The Stationery Office, Dublin, 1970.

Dáil Éireann, *Dáil Debates Collections*, The Stationery Office, Dublin, 1977.

Dáil Éireann, *Dáil Debates Collections*, The Stationery Office, Dublin, 1981.

Daly, A., 'Representing Employers: the Irish Business and Employers Confederation', in T.V. Murphy and W.K. Roche, *Irish Industrial Relations in Practice*, Oak Tree Press, Dublin, 1994.

Daniel, W. (ed.), *Workplace Industrial Relations and Technical Change*, DE/ESRC/Policy Studies Institute/ACAS/Heinemann, London, 1987.

Daniel, W. and Hogarth, T., 'Worker Support for Technical Change', *New Technology, Work and Employment*, Vol. 5, No. 2, 1990, pp. 18–24.

Daniel, W. and Millward, N., Workplace Industrial Relations in Britain: The DE/PSI/ESRC Survey, Heinemann, London, 1983.

Dastmalachian, A., Blyton, P. and Adamson, R., *The Climate of Workplace Relations*, Routledge, London, 1991.

Deaton, D., 'Management Style and Large-Scale Survey Evidence', *Industrial Relations Journal*, Vol. 6, No. 2, 1985.

Deaton, D.R. and Beaumont, P.B., 'The Determinants of Bargaining Structure: Some Large-Scale Survey Evidence', *British Journal of Industrial Relations*, Vol. 18, July 1980.

Deery, S. and De Cieri, H., 'Determinants of Trade Union Membership in Australia', *British Journal of Industrial Relations*, Vol. 29, March 1991.

Delbridge, R. and Turnbull, P., 'Human Resource Maximisation: The Management of Labour under Just-In-Time Manufacturing Systems', in P. Blyton and P. Turnbull (eds.), *Reassessing Human Resource Management*, Sage, London, 1992.

Department of Enterprise and Employment, 'Annual Report 1993', The Stationery Office, 1994.

Department of Labour, 'Discussion Document on Industrial Relations Law Reform', Department of Labour, Dublin, 1983.

Department of Labour, 'Discussions on Industrial Relations Reform', Department of Labour, Dublin, 1985.

Department of Labour, 'Employers' Perception of the Effect of Labour Legislation', Department of Labour, Dublin, 1986.

Department of Labour, 'Proposals on Industrial Relations Reform', Department of Labour, Dublin, 1988.

Department of Labour, 'Department of Labour Annual Report', Department of Labour, Dublin, 1991a.

Department of Labour, 'A Guide to the Industrial Relations Act 1990', Department of Labour, Dublin, 1991b.

Department of Public Services, 'Department of Public Services Estimates', The Stationery Office, Dublin, 1987.

Dineen, D.A., 'Atypical Work Patterns in Ireland: Short-Term Adjustments of Fundamental Changes', *Administration*, Vol. 40, No. 3, Autumn 1992.

Dineen, D. and Wallace, J., 'An Overview of Irish Labour Market Issues', paper presented at the Université Catholique de Louvain, October 1991.

Dore, R., *British Factory — Japanese Factory*, Allen and Unwin, London, 1973.

Dubin, R., Kornhauser, A. and Ross, A. (eds.), *Industrial Conflict*, McGraw-Hill, New York, 1954.

Duffy, K., 'Industrial Relations Act 1990 — The Trade Union Experience', paper presented to an ICTU Conference on Industrial Relations, 19 November 1993.

Dunlop, J., *Industrial Relations Systems*, Southern Illinois University Press, Carbondale, 1958.

Dunlop, J., *Industrial Relations Systems*, Harvard Business School Press, Boston, 1993.

Edwardes, P., 'Managing through the Recession: The Plant and the Company', *Employee Relations*, Vol. 7, No. 3, 1985.

Edwardes, P., 'Factory Managers: Their Role in Personnel Management and Their Place in the Company', *Journal of Management Studies*, Vol. 24, No. 5, September 1987.

Elger, T., 'Flexible Futures? New Technology and the Contemporary Transformation of Work', *Work, Employment and Society*, Vol. 1, No. 4, 1991.

Employment Appeals Tribunal, 'Twenty-fifth Annual Report', The Stationery Office, Dublin.

Employment Equality Agency, 'Code of Practice: Equality of Opportunity in Employment', EEA, Dublin, 1983.

Employment Equality Agency, 'Transitions to Equal Opportunities at Work: Problems and Possibilities', EEA, Dublin, 1986.

Employment Equality Agency, 'A Model Equal Opportunities Policy', EEA, Dublin, 1991.

EOLAS, 'Concluding Statement of the Board — 15th December 1993', EOLAS, The Irish Science and Technology Agency, Dublin, 1993.

European Foundation for the Improvement of Living and Working Conditions, *The Role of the Parties Involved in the Introduction of New Technology*, Dublin, 1985.

European Foundation for the Improvement of Living and Working Conditions, *Hygeia: A Newsletter for the European Year of Safety, Hygiene and Health at Work*, No. 3, 1991.

Farnham, D. and Pimlott, J., *Understanding Industrial Relations*, 4th edn, Cassell, London, 1990.

Federated Union of Employers, 'Profit Sharing', *FUE Bulletin*, 1984.

Federated Union of Employers, *FUE Annual Report 1986*, FUE, Dublin, 1987.

Federation of Irish Employers, 'Accident Rate Is Too High Says FIE', *FIE Bulletin*, May 1991.

Feigenbaum, A., *Total Quality Control*, McGraw Hill, London, 1983.

Hackman, J.R. and Oldham, G.R., *Work Redesign*, Addison Wesley, New York, 1980.

Fennell, C. and Lynch, I., *Labour Law in Ireland*, Gill and Macmillan, Dublin, 1993.

Fiorito, J., Lowman, C. and Nelson, F.D., 'The Impact of Human Resource Policies on Union Organising', *Industrial Relations*, Vol. 26, No. 2, Spring 1987.

Fisher, R. and Ury, W., *Getting to Yes*, Hutchinson, London, 1986.

Fitzpatrick, D., *Politics and Irish Life, 1913–21*, Gill and Macmillan, Dublin, 1977.

Flanders, A., *Collective Bargaining: Prescription for Change*, Faber and Faber, London, 1967.

Flanders, A., 'Collective Bargaining — A Theoretical Analysis', *British Journal of Industrial Relations*, March 1968.

Flood, P., 'Human Resource Management: Promise, Possibility and Limitations', Research Paper, University of Limerick, 1989.

Flood, P., 'Atypical Employment: Core–Periphery Manpower Strategies — The Implications for Corporate Culture', *Industrial Relations News*, Nos. 9 and 10, 1990a.

Flood, P., *Trends and Developments Affecting Personnel Management Practice in the 1980s*, University of Limerick, 1990b.

Fogarty, M.P., Egan, D. and Ryan, W.J.L., *Pay Policy for the 1980s*, Federated Union of Employers, Dublin, 1981.

Foley, K. and Gunnigle, P., 'A Review of Organisational Reward Practices', in P. Gunnigle, P. Flood, M. Morley and T. Turner, *Continuity and Change in Irish Employee Relations*, Oak Tree Press, Dublin, 1994.

Fombrun, C., 'Environmental Trends Create New Pressures on Human Resources', in S.L. Rynes and G.T. Milkovich, *Current Issues in Human Resource Management: Commentary and Readings*, Business Publications Inc. Texas, 1986.

Fombrun, C.J., Tichy, N.M. and Devanna, M.A., *Strategic Human Resource Management*, Wiley, Chichester, 1984.

Forde, M., *Employment Law*, Roundhall Press, Dublin, 1992.

Foulkes, F.K., *Effective Personnel Policies: A Study of Larger Non-Union Enterprises*, Prentice-Hall, Englewood Cliffs, NJ, 1980.

Fox, A., 'Industrial Sociology and Industrial Relations', Research Paper No. 3 to the Royal Commission on Trade Unions and Employers' Associations, HMSO, London, 1966.

Fox, A., 'Industrial Relations: A Social Critique of Pluralist Ideology', in J. Child (ed.), *Man and Organisation*, Allen and Unwin, London, 1973.

Fox, A., *Man Management*, Hutchinson, London, 1974a.

Fox, A., *Beyond Contract: Work, Power and Trust Relations*, Faber and Faber, London, 1974b.

Fox, A., 'Collective Bargaining: Flanders and the Webbs', *British Journal of Industrial Relations*, Vol. 13, No. 2, 1975.

Frawley, M., 'Large Increase in Sexual Harassment Cases Reported by EEA', *Industrial Relations News*, 12 September 1991.

Frawley, M., 'Sexual Harassment Enquiries Leap by 350%', *Industrial Relations News*, 5 November 1992.

Friedman, A., *Industry and Labour*, Macmillan, London, 1977.

Friedman, A., 'Management Strategies, Market Conditions and the Labour Process', in R. Stephen (ed.), *Firms, Organisation and Labour*, Macmillan, London, 1984.

Garavan, T., 'Strategic Human Resource Development: Characteristics, Conditions and Benefits', *Journal of European Industrial Training*, August 1990.

Gennard, J., 'Industrial Relations and Technological Change', in B. Towers (ed.), *A Handbook of Industrial Relations Practice*, 3rd edn, Kogan Page, London, 1992.

Gill, C., 'British Industrial Relations and the European Community', in B. Towers (ed.), *A Handbook of Industrial Relations Practice*, 3rd edn, Kogan Page, London, 1992.

Gladstone, A., 'Employers' Associations in Comparative Perspective: Functions and Activities', in J.P. Windmuller and A. Gladstone (eds.), *Employers' Associations and Industrial Relations: A Comparative Study*, Clarendon Press, Oxford, 1984.

Goldthorpe, J., 'Industrial Relations in Great Britain: A Critique of Reformism', *Politics and Society*, Vol. 4, No. 4, 1974.

Goold, M. and Campbell, A., *Strategies and Styles: The Role of the Centre in Managing Diversified Corporations*, Blackwell, Oxford, 1987.

Government Social Survey, *Workplace Industrial Relations*, SS4OZ, HMSO, London, 1968.

Green, G., *Industrial Relations*, Pitman, London, 1991.

Guest, D., 'Human Resource Management and Industrial Relations', *Journal of Management Studies*, Vol. 24, No. 5, 1987.

Guest, D., 'Human Resource Management: A New Opportunity for Psychologists or Another Passing Fad?', *The Occupational Psychologist*, February 1988.

Guest, D., 'Human Resource Management: Its Implications for Industrial Relations and Trade Unions', in J. Storey (ed.), *New Perspectives on Human Resource Management*, Routledge, London, 1989a.

Guest, D., 'Personnel and HRM: Can You Tell the Difference?', *Personnel Management*, January 1989b.

Gunnigle, P., 'Management Approaches to Industrial Relations in the Small Firm', in *Industrial Relations in Ireland: Contemporary Issues and Developments*, University College Dublin, 1989.

Gunnigle, P., 'Determinants and Nature of Personnel Policy Choice: The Context for Human Resource Development', *Journal of European Industrial Training*, Vol. 15, No. 3, 1991, pp. 22–31.

Gunnigle, P., 'Changing Management Approaches to Employee Relations in Ireland', *Employee Relations*, Vol. 14, No. 1, 1992a.

Gunnigle, P., 'Human Resource Management in Ireland', *Employee Relations*, Vol. 14, No. 5, 1992b.

Gunnigle, P., 'Management Approaches to Employee Relations in Greenfield Sites', *Journal of Irish Business and Administrative Research*, Vol. 13, 1992c.

Gunnigle, P., 'Collectivism and the Management of Industrial Relations in Greenfield Sites', paper presented to the International Industrial Relations Association European Congress, Helsinki, August 1994.

Gunnigle, P. and Brady, T., 'The Management of Industrial Relations in the Small Firm, *Employee Relations*, Vol. 6, No. 5, 1984.

Gunnigle, P. and Daly, A., 'Craft Integration and Flexible Work Practices', *Industrial and Commercial Training*, Vol. 24, No. 10, 1992.

Gunnigle, P. and Flood, P., *Personnel Management in Ireland: Practice, Trends and Developments*, Gill and Macmillan, Dublin, 1990.

Gunnigle, P. and Morley, M., 'Something Old, Something New: A Perspective on Industrial Relations in the Republic of Ireland', paper presented to the Labour Relations Agency conference on Northern Ireland and Regional Industrial Relations, Belfast, February 1993.

Gunnigle, P. and Shivanath, G., 'Role and Status of the Personnel Practitioner — A Positive Picture', *Journal of Irish Business and Administrative Research*, Vol. 9, No. 1, 1988, pp. 1–9.

Gunnigle, P., Garavan, T. and Fitzgerald, G., *Employee Relations and Employment Law in Ireland*, The Open Business School — PMTC, University of Limerick, 1992.

Gunnigle, P., Flood, P., Morley, M. and Turner, T., *Continuity and Change in Irish Employee Relations*, Oak Tree Press, Dublin, 1994.

Hakim, C., 'Impact of Changing Employment Patterns on Manpower Policy', paper presented to the Conference on Industrial Relations: Outlook and New Employment Patterns, IPA, Dublin, 1991.

Hannaway, C., 'New Style Collective Agreements: An Irish Approach', *Industrial Relations News*, Vol. 13, 1987.

Hannaway, C., 'Why Irish Eyes Are Smiling', *Personnel Management*, May 1992.

Harbison, F., *Industrial Relations: Challenges and Responses*, University of Toronto Press, Toronto, 1966.

Hardiman, N., Pay, *Politics and Economic Performance in Ireland, 1970–1987*, Clarendon Press, Oxford, 1988.

Hawkins, K., *Conflict and Change: Aspects of Industrial Relations*, Holt, Rinehart and Winston, London, 1972.

Hawkins, K., *A Handbook of Industrial Relations Practice*, Kogan Page, London, 1979.

Hendry, C., Pettigrew, A. and Sparrow, P., 'Changing Patterns of Human Resource Management', *Personnel Management*, November 1988.

Hillery, B., 'Necessary Changes in Irish Industrial Relations', *Journal of the Statistical and Social Inquiry Society of Ireland*, Vol. 24, Part 1, 1979.

Hillery, B., 'An Overview of the Irish Industrial Relations System', in *Industrial Relations in Ireland: Contemporary Issues and Developments*, University College Dublin, 1989.

Hirsch, B.T. and Berger, M., 'Union Membership Determination and Industry Characteristics', *Southern Economic Journal*, Vol. 1, 1984.

Hogg, C. (ed.), 'Total Quality', Factsheet No. 29, Institute of Personnel Management, May 1990.

Horgan, J., 'The Future of Collective Bargaining', paper presented to the Annual Conference of the IPM in Ireland, Galway, 1985.

Horgan, J., 'The Future of Collective Bargaining' in *Industrial Relations in Ireland: Contemporary Issues and Developments*, University College Dublin, 1989.

Horwitz, F.M., 'HRM: An Ideological Perspective', *Personnel Review*, Vol. 19, No. 2, 1990.

Hourihan, F., 'I.R. Bill 1989 — Dail Debate Raises Serious Issues', *Industrial Relations News Report*, 12 April 1990 .

Hourihan, F., 'The European Union and Industrial Relations', in T.V. Murphy and W.K. Roche (eds.), *Irish Industrial Relations in Practice*, Oak Tree Press, Dublin, 1994.

Hyman, R., *Industrial Relations: A Marxist Introduction*, Macmillan, London, 1975.

Hyman, R., *Strikes*, Fontana, London, 1981.

Income Data Services, 'Pay and Benefits', IPM, London, 1992.

Industrial Participation Association/Institute of Personnel Management, 'Employee Involvement and Participation: Principles and Standards of Practice', IPM/IPA, London, 1983.

Industrial Relations News Report, 'Labour Law Society Reviews IR act 1990', No. 28, 18 July 1991.

Institute of Personnel Management, 'Performance-Related Pay', Factsheet No. 30, IPM, London, 1990.

Institute of Personnel Management, *Performance Management in the UK*, IPM, London, 1992.

International Labour Organisation, *Collective Bargaining: A Workers Manual*, ILO, Geneva, 1960.

International Labour Organisation, *Collective Bargaining in Industrialised Market Economies*, ILO, Geneva, 1973.

Irish Business and Employers Confederation, 'IBEC: An Introduction', IBEC, Dublin, 1993.

Irish Business and Employers Confederation, 'Annual Reports', IBEC, Dublin, 1984–1992.

Irish Congress of Trade Unions, 'Annual Report 1975', ICTU, Dublin.

Irish Congress of Trade Unions, 'Technology: Getting Agreements, ICTU, Dublin, 1989a.

Irish Congress of Trade Unions, 'Technology: Who Decides?', ICTU, Dublin, 1989b.

Irish Congress of Trade Unions, 'Technology: New Hazards', ICTU, Dublin, 1989c.

Irish Congress of Trade Unions, 'Technology and Work', ICTU, Dublin, 1989d.

Irish Congress of Trade Unions, 'New Forms of Work Organisation: Implications for Unions', ICTU, Dublin, 1993.

Irish Industrial Relations Review, 'Trade Union Organisation in the Republic', Vol. 2, No. 7, July 1993.

Irish Quality Association, 'The Value of Marked Improvements', IQA, 1994.

Jackson, M., *Industrial Relations: A Textbook*, Kogan Page, London, 1982.

James, B., 'The Trade Union Response to New Technology', Internal Papers in Economics, No. 5, Polytechnic, Middlesex, 1980.

Jensen, V., 'Notes on the Beginnings of Collective Bargaining', *Industrial and Labour Relations Review*, Vol. 9, No. 2, January 1956, pp. 230–32.

Jurgens, U., 'The Transfer of Japanese Management Concepts in the International Automobile Industry', in S. Wood (ed.), *The Transformation of Work?*, Unwin, London, 1989.

Kahn-Freund, O., *Labour and the Law*, Stevens, London, 1977.

Kanter, R., *The Change Masters*, Allen and Unwin, London, 1984.

Kavanagh, R., *Labour from the Beginning — 75 Years*, The Labour Party, Dublin, 1987.

Keating, M., 'Personnel Management in Ireland', in *Industrial Relations in Ireland: Contemporary Issues and Developments*, University College Dublin, 1989.

Keenoy, T., 'HRM: A Case of the Wolf in Sheep's Clothing?', *Personnel Review*, Vol. 19, No. 2, 1990.

Kelly, A., 'Changes in the Occupational Structure and Industrial Relations in Ireland, *Management*, No. 2, 1975.

Kelly, A., 'The Nature of Worker Participation in Ireland: The Incongruity of European and Irish Industrial Relations Structures', paper presented at the National Conference on Industrial Relations, Galway Regional Technical College, 1979.

Kelly, A., 'The Worker Director in Irish Industrial Relations', in *Industrial Relations in Ireland: Contemporary Issues and Developments*, University College Dublin, 1989a.

Kelly, A., 'The Rights Commissioner: Conciliator, Mediator or Arbitrator', in *Industrial Relations in Ireland: Contemporary Issues and Developments*, University College Dublin, 1989b.

Kelly, A. and Bourke, P., *Management, Labour and Consumer*, Gill and Macmillan, Dublin, 1979.

Kelly, A. and Brannick, T., 'The Pattern of Strike Activity in Ireland, 1960–1979: Some Preliminary Observations', *Irish Journal of Administrative and Business Research*, Vol. 5, No. 1, April 1983.

Kelly, A. and Brannick, T., 'Explaining the Strike-Proneness of British Companies in Ireland', *British Journal of Industrial Relations*, Vol. 26, No. 1, 1988a.

Kelly, A. and Brannick, T., 'The Management of Human Resources: New Trends and the Challenge to Trade Unions', *Arena*, August 1988b.

Kelly, A. and Brannick, T., 'The Changing Contours of Irish Industrial Conflict', paper presented to the International Polish/Irish Conference, University of Warsaw, 1989.

Kelly, A. and Roche, W., 'Institutional Reform in Irish Industrial Relations', *Studies*, Autumn 1983.

Kerr, A., 'Trade Unions and the Law', in *Industrial Relations in Ireland: Contemporary Issues and Developments*, University College Dublin, 1989.

Kerr, A., *Irish Current Law Statutes Annotated*, Sweet and Maxwell, London, 1991a.

Kerr, A., 'Irish Industrial Relations Legislation: Consensus, not Compulsion', *Industrial Law Journal*, Vol. 20, No. 4, December 1991b.

Kerr, T., 'Maternity Protection — The Spectre of Legalism', *Industrial Relations News*, 5 March 1987.

Kerr, T. and Whyte, G., *Irish Trade Union Law*, Professional Books, Abington, 1985.

Kinnie, N., 'Patterns of Industrial Relations Management', *Employee Relations*, Vol. 8, No. 2, 1986.

Klein, J., 'The Human Cost of Manufacturing Reform', *Harvard Business Review*, March/April 1989.

Kochan, T., *Collective Bargaining and Industrial Relations*, Irwin, Homewood, IL, 1980.

Kochan, T., McKersie, R. and Capelli, P., 'Strategic Choice and Industrial Relations', *Industrial Relations*, No. 23, 1984.

Kochan, T.A., Katz, H.C. and McKersie, R.B., *The Transformation of American Industrial Relations*, Basic Books, New York, 1986.

Labour Court, 'Explanatory Handout', Labour Court, Dublin.

Labour Court, 'Third Annual Report', The Stationery Office, Dublin.

Labour Court, 'Thirty-first Annual Report', The Stationery Office, Dublin.

Labour Court, 'Forty-second Annual Report', The Stationery Office, Dublin.

Labour Relations Commission, 'Labour Relations Commission Annual Report', The Stationery Office, Dublin, 1993.

Larkin, E., *James Larkin, 1876–1947: Irish Labour Leader*, Routledge and Kegan Paul, London, 1965.

Lash, S. and Ury, J., *The End of Organised Capitalism*, Polity Press, Cambridge, 1988.

Lawler, E.E., 'The New Plant Revolution', *Organisational Dynamics*, Winter 1978.

Lawler, E., 'Increasing Worker Involvement to Enhance Organisational Effectiveness', in P.S. Goodman (ed.), *Change in Organisations*, Jossey Bass, San Francisco, 1982.

Leddin, A. and B. Walsh, *The Macro-Economy of Ireland*, Gill and Macmillan, Dublin, 1990.

Lee, J., 'Worker and Society since 1945', in D. Nevin (ed.), *Trade Unions and Change in Irish Society*, Mercier/RTE, Dublin, 1980.

Legge, K., *Power: Innovation and Problem-solving in Personnel Management*, McGraw-Hill, New York, 1978.

Legge, K., 'Human Resource Management: A Critical Analysis', in J. Storey (ed.), *New Perspectives on Human Resource Management*, Routledge, London, 1988.

Lehmbruch, G., Schmitter, F. and Philippe, C., *Patterns of Corporatist Policy Making*, Sage, London, 1982.

Leiserson, W., 'Constitutional Government in American Industries', *American Economic Review*, Vol. 12, 1922, p. 21.

Lennon, P., 'The Unfair Dismissals Act 1977: A Critical Evaluation', *Industrial Relations News*, No. 21, 1983.

Mackay, L., 'Personnel: Changes Disguising Decline', *Personnel Review*, Vol. 16, No. 5, 1987.

Madden, D. and T. Kerr, *Unfair Dismissal: Cases and Commentary*, Federation of Irish Employers, Dublin, 1990.

Marchington, M., *Managing Industrial Relations*, McGraw-Hill, New York, 1982.

Marchington, M. and Parker, P., *Changing Patterns of Employee Relations*, Harvester Wheatsheaf, Hemel Hempstead, 1990.

Marciniak, F., 'VW Circles as a Component in Total Quality Management', in M. Gold (ed.), *P+ Total Quality Management and Worker Participation*, No. 2, European Foundation for the Improvement of Living and Working Conditions, Dublin, 1991.

Marsh, A.I., *Managers and Shop Stewards: Shop Floor Revolution*, IPM, London, 1973.

McCall, B., 'Labour Law: All Changed', *Management*, Vol. 35, No. 11, 1988.

McCarthy, C., *The Decade of Upheaval*, IPA, Dublin, 1973.

McCarthy, C., *Trade Unions in Ireland, 1894–1960*, IPA, Dublin, 1977.

McCarthy, C., 'Reform: A Strategy for Research', in H. Pollock (ed.) *Reform of Industrial Relations*, O'Brien Press, Dublin, 1982.

McCarthy, C., *Elements in a Theory of Industrial Relations*, Irish Academic Press, Dublin, 1984.

McCarthy, C. and von Prondzynski, F., 'The Reform of Industrial Relations', *Administration*, Vol. 29, No. 3, 1982.

McCarthy, W.E.J., O'Brien, J.F. and Dowd, V.G., 'Wage Inflation and Wage Leadership', Paper No. 79, ESRI, Dublin, 1975.

McGinley, M., 'Pay in the 1980s: The Issue of Control', *Industrial Relations News*, No. 30, August 1989a.

McGinley, M., 'Pay Increases between 1981–1987', in *Personnel and Industrial Relations Directory*, IPA, Dublin, 1989b.

McGinley, M., 'Trade Union Law: Look Back in Anguish', *Industrial Relations News*, No. 16, 26 April 1990.

McGovern, P., 'Increasing Opposition to Unionisation in the 1980s', *Industrial Relations News*, No. 45, 24 November 1988.

McGovern, P., 'Trade Union Recognition: Five Case Studies', *Industrial Relations News*, No. 6, 6 February 1989a.

McGovern, P., 'Union Recognition and Union Avoidance in the 1980s', in *Industrial Relations in Ireland: Contemporary Issues and Developments*, University College Dublin, 1989b.

McMahon, G., 'Selection Interviewing and the Employment Decision: A Recipe for Discrimination', *Industrial Relations News*, 2 July 1987a.

McMahon, G., 'Wage Structure in the Republic of Ireland', *Advances in Business Studies*, Vol. 1, No. 1, 1987b.

McMahon, G., 'Rush the Recruitment, Rue the Results', *Management*, February 1988.

McMahon, G., 'Low Pay and the Joint Labour Committee System', in *Industrial Relations in Ireland: Contemporary Issues and Developments*, University College Dublin, 1989.

McMahon, G., 'Multinationals: The Labour Relations Experience in Ireland', *Advances in Business Studies*, Vol. 2, No. 2, 1990.

McMahon, G., 'Pay Inequality in the 1990s: An Evaluation of Strategic Alternatives', Administration, *Journal of the Institute of Public Administration*, Vol. 40, No. 2, Summer 1992.

McNamara, G., Williams, K. and West, D., *Understanding Trade Unions: Yesterday and Today*, O'Brien Educational Press, Dublin, 1988.

Meenan, F., 'A Survey of Unfair Dismissal Cases 1977–1984', *FUE Bulletin Supplement*, June 1985.

Meenan, F., 'Industrial Relations Act 1990: A Commentary on the Trade Disputes Provisions Part 1 and Part 2', *IR Data Bank*, Vol. 9, Nos. 207 and 208, February 1991.

Miles, R.E. and Snow, C.C., 'Designing Strategic Human Resources Systems', *Organisational Dynamics*, Vol. 6, No. 1 (Spring), 1984, pp. 24–42.

Milner, S. and Richards, E., 'Determinants of Union Recognition and Employee Involvement: Evidence from the London Docklands', *British Journal of Industrial Relations*, Vol. 29, No. 3, 1991.

Monks, K., 'Models of Personnel Management: A Means of Understanding the Diversity of Personnel Practices', *Human Resource Management Journal*, Vol. 2, No. 2, 1992.

Morrissey, T.J., 'Employee Participation at Sub-Board Level', in *Industrial Relations in Ireland: Contemporary Issues and Developments*, University College Dublin, 1989.

Mulligan, H., 'The Unfair Dismissals Act: Day to Day Reality', *Industrial Relations News*, 4 March 1993.

Mulvey, C., 'Industrial Democracy: A Report by the Federated Union of Employers and the Confederation of Irish Industry', FUE/CII Dublin, n.d.

Mulvey, K., 'The Potential Role of the Labour Relations Commission', paper presented to the Irish Association of Industrial Relations, 16 April 1991, The Labour Relations Commission, Dublin, 1991a.

Mulvey, K., 'The Labour Relations Commission', paper presented to the Mid-West Chapter of the IPM, November 1991, The Labour Relations Commission, Dublin, 1991b.

Murphy, T., 'The Dismissal Issue in Industrial Relations: Employers and Trade Unions Show Improved Performances since 1977', *Industrial Relations News*, No. 29, 24 July 1986.

Murphy, T., 'The Impact of the Unfair Dismissals Act, 1977 on Workplace Industrial Relations', in *Industrial Relations in Ireland: Contemporary Issues and Developments*, University College Dublin, 1989.

Murphy, T.V. and Roche, W.K. (eds.), *Irish Industrial Relations in Practice*, Oak Tree Press, Dublin, 1994.

Murray, S., *Employee Relations in Irish Private Sector Manufacturing Industry*, Industrial Development Authority, Dublin, 1984.

Myers, M., *Managing without Unions*, Addison-Wesley, Wokingham, 1976.

National Economic and Social Council, *A Strategy for Development, 1986–1990*, NESC, Dublin, 1986.

Nierenberg, G.I., *The Art of Negotiating*, Cornerstone, New York, 1968.

O'Brien, J.F., *A Study of the National Wage Agreements in Ireland*, Economic and Social Research Institute, Dublin, 1981.

O'Brien, J.F., 'The PNR in Perspective: Another Round?', Eighth Annual Industrial Relations Guest Lecture, University of Limerick, 1989a.

O'Brien, J.F., 'Pay Determination in Ireland', in *Industrial Relations in Ireland: Contemporary Issues and Developments*, University College Dublin, 1989b.

O'Connor, K., 'The Impact of the Unfair Dismissals Act, 1977 on Personnel Management and Industrial Relations', *Journal of Irish Business and Administrative Research*, Vol. 5, No. 2, 1982.

O'Hagan, J., *The Economy of Ireland: Policy and Performance*, 5th edn, Irish Management Institute, Dublin, 1987.

O'Malley, E., 'Late Industrialisation under Outward Looking Policies: The Experience and Prospects of the Republic of Ireland', unpublished Ph.D. thesis, University of Sussex, 1983.

O'Shea, F., 'Neo-Corporatism', mimeo, University of Limerick, 1983.

Oechslin, J.J., 'Employers Organisations', in R. Blanpain (ed.), *Labour Law and Industrial Relations*, Kluwer, Deventer, 1985.

Oliver, N. and Wilkinson, B., 'Japanese Manufacturing Techniques and Personnel and Industrial Relations in Britain: Evidence and Implications', *British Journal of Industrial Relations*, Vol. 27, No. 2, 1989.

Organisation for Economic Co-operation and Development, *Wage Policies and Collective Bargaining Developments in Finland, Ireland and Norway*, OECD, Paris, 1979.

Parker, P.A.L., Hayes, W.R. and Lumb, A.L., *The Reform of Collective Bargaining at Plant and Company Level*, HMSO, London, 1971.

Pearson, R., *The Human Resource*, McGraw-Hill, New York, 1991.

Perlman, S., 'The Principle of Collective Bargaining', *The Journal of the American Academy of Political and Social Science*, March 1936, pp. 154–9.

Peters, T. and Waterman, R.H., *In Search of Excellence*, Harper and Row, New York, 1982.

Phelps-Brown, E.H., *Collective Bargaining Considered*, Athlone Press, London, 1971.

Pollock, H. and O'Dwyer, L., *We Can Work It Out: Relationships in the Workplace*, O'Brien Educational Press, Dublin, 1985.

Poole, M., *Industrial Relations: Origins and Patterns of National Diversity*, Routledge, London, 1986.

Porter, M., *Competitive Advantage: Creating and Sustaining Superior Performance*, The Free Press, New York, 1985.

Porter, M., 'From Competitive Advantage to Corporate Strategy', *Harvard Business Review*, May/June 1987.

Purcell, J., 'Macho Managers and the New Industrial Relations', *Employee Relations*, Vol. 4, No. 1, 1982.

Purcell, J., 'The Management of Industrial Relations in the Modern Corporation: Agenda for Research', *British Journal of Industrial Relations*, No. 21, 1983.

Purcell, J., 'Mapping Management Styles in Employee Relations', *Journal of Management Studies*, Vol. 24, No. 5, 1987.

Purcell, J., 'The Impact of Corporate Strategy on HRM', in J. Storey (ed.), *New Perspectives on Human Resource Management*, Routledge, London, 1989.

Purcell, J. and Gray, A., 'Corporate Personnel Departments and the Management of Industrial Relations: Two Case Studies in Ambiguity', *Journal of Management Studies*, Vol. 23, No. 2, 1986, pp. 205–23.

Purcell, J. and Sisson, K., 'Strategies and Practice in the Management of Industrial Relations', in G. Bain (ed.), *Industrial Relations in Britain*, Blackwell, Oxford, 1983.

Rabbitte, P. and Gilmore, E., *Bertie's Bill*, The Workers Party, Dublin, 1990.

Ramsay, H., Pollert, A. and Rainbird, H., 'A Decade of Transformation? Labour Market Flexibility and Work Organisation in the United Kingdom', in *New Directions in Work Organisation: The Industrial Relations Response*, OECD, Paris, 1992.

Report of the Commission of Inquiry on Industrial Relations, Government Publications Office, Dublin, 1981.

Reynaud, J.P., 'Problems and Prospects for Collective Bargaining in the EEC Member States', Commission of the European Community Document, No. V/394/78-EN, Brussels, 1978.

Ridgely, P., 'How Relevant is the FUE?', *Irish Business*, February 1988.

Roche, W.K., 'State Strategies and the Politics of Industrial Relations in Ireland', in *Industrial Relations in Ireland: Contemporary Issues and Developments*, University College Dublin, 1989.

Roche, W.K., 'Trade Unions in Ireland in the 1980s', *European Industrial Relations Review*, No. 176, 1990a.

Roche, W.K., 'Industrial Relations Research in Ireland and the Trade Union Interest', paper presented to the Irish Congress of Trade Unions Conference on Joint Research between Trade Unions, Universities, Third-Level Colleges and Research Institutes, Dublin, 1990b.

Roche, W.K., 'Modelling Trade Union Growth and Decline in the Republic of Ireland', *Journal of Irish Business and Administrative Research*, Vol. 14, 1992a.

Roche, W.K., 'The Liberal Theory of Industrialism and the Development of Industrial Relations in Ireland', in J. Goldthorpe and C. Whelan (eds.), *The Development of Industrial Society in Ireland*, Oxford University Press, 1992b.

Roche, W.K., 'Human Resource Management and Unionisation in Ireland', paper presented at the Second Annual John Lovett Memorial Lecture, University of Limerick, April 1994.

Roche, W.K. and Larragy, J., 'Pattern of Merger and Dissolution of Trade Unions in Ireland since 1940', *Industrial Relations News*, No. 38, 1986, pp. 15–22.

Roche, W.K. and Larragy, J., 'The Trend of Unionisation in the Irish Republic', in *Industrial Relations in Ireland: Contemporary Issues and Developments*, University College Dublin, 1989a.

Roche, W.K. and Larragy, J., *The Determinants of the Annual Rate of Trade Union Growth and Decline in the Irish Republic: Evidence from the DUES Membership Series*, University College Dublin, 1989b.

Roche, W.K. and Larragy, J., 'Cyclical and Institutional Determinants of Annual Trade Union Growth and Decline in Ireland: Evidence from the DUES Data Series', *European Sociological Review*, No. 6, 1990.

Roche, W.K. and Turner, T., 'Testing Alternative Models of Human Resource Policy Effects of Trade Union Recognition in the Republic of Ireland', mimeo, Graduate School of Business/University College Dublin, 1994.

Rollinson, D., *Understanding Employee Relations: A Behavioural Approach*, Addison Wesley, Wokingham, 1993.

Rothenberg, I.H. and Silverman, S.B., 'Labor Unions: How to Avert them, Beat them, Out-Negotiate them, Live with them, Unload them', *Management Relations*, No. 6, 1973.

Royal Commission on Trade Unions and Employers' Associations, 1965–1968, CMND 3623, HMSO, London, 1968.

Salamon, M., *Industrial Relations: Theory and Practice*, Prentice-Hall, London and New York, 1992.

Schregle, J., 'Labour Relations in Western Europe: Some Topical Issues', *International Labour Review*, January–June 1974.

Schuler, R.S., *Personnel and Human Resource Management*, West Publishing Company, St Paul, MN, 1987a.

Schuler, R., 'Personnel and HRM Choices and Organisational Strategy', *Human Resource Planning*, Vol. 10, No. 1, 1987b.

Schuler, R. and Jackson, S., 'Organisational Strategy and Organisational Level as Determinants of HRM Practices', *Human Resource Planning*, Vol. 10, No. 1, 1987.

Schuler, R.S., Galante, S.P. and Jackson, S.E., 'Matching Effective HR Practices with Competitive Strategy', *Personnel*, September 1987.

Scott, B., *The Skills of Negotiating*, Gower, Aldershot, 1981.

Sewell, G. and Wilkinson, B., 'Employment or Emasculation? Shopfloor Surveillance in a Total Quality Organisation', in P. Blyton and P. Turnbull (eds.), *Reassessing Human Resource Management*, Sage, London, 1992.

Sheehan, B., 'Social Consensus and Incomes Policy: Has Centralised Bargaining Served the Country Well?', *Industrial Relations News*, No. 26, September 1991.

Sheehan, B., 'SIPTU Analysis of National Agreements Shows Real Increases in Take Home Pay', *Industrial Relations News*, No. 36, September 1992.

Sheehan, B., 'Atley Predicts Difficult Pay Bargaining Climate for Trade Unions', *Industrial Relations News*, No. 9, March 1993.

Shivanath, G., 'Personnel Practitioners 1986: Their Role and Status in Irish Industry', unpublished MBS thesis, University of Limerick, 1987.

Silverman, J., *The Theory of Organisations*, Heinemann, London, 1970.

Sisson, K., *Negotiating in Practice*, Institute of Personnel Management, London, 1977.

Sisson, K., 'Employers Organisations', in G. Bain (ed.), *Industrial Relations in Britain*, Blackwell, Oxford, 1983.

Sisson, K., *The Management of Collective Bargaining: An International Comparison*, Blackwell, Oxford, 1987.

Sisson, K. (ed.), *Personnel Management in Britain*, Blackwell, Oxford, 1989.

Sisson, K., 'Industrial Relations: Challenges and Opportunities', *Employee Relations*, Vol. 13, No. 6, 1991.

Smith, A., *The Wealth of Nations*, Pelican, London, 1970.

Sproull, A. and MacInnes, J., 'Patterns of Union Recognition in Scottish Electronics', *British Journal of Industrial Relations*, Vol. 25, No. 3, 1987.

Stevens, C.M., *Strategy and Collective Bargaining Negotiations*, McGraw-Hill, New York, 1963.

Storey, J., *New Perspectives on Human Resource Management*, Routledge, London, 1989.

Storey, J., *Developments in the Management of Human Resources*, Blackwell, Oxford, 1992.

Storey, J. and Sisson, K., 'Limits to Transformation: Human Resource Management in the British Context', *Industrial Relations Journal*, Spring 1990.

Suttle, S., 'Labour Market Flexibility', *Industrial Relations News*, No. 38, 1988.

Tansey, P., 'Pay Deal Scuppers Budget', *The Sunday Tribune*, 13 February 1994.

Taylor, B., Elger, T. and Fairbrother, P., 'Work Relations in Electronics: What Has Become of Japanisation in Britain?', paper presented to the Ninth Annual Labour Process Conference, Institute of Science and Technology, University of Manchester, 1991.

Teague, P., 'Co-ordination or Decentralisation: EC Social Policy and Industrial Relations', in J. Lodge (ed.), *The European Community and the Challenge of the Future*, Pinter Publishers, London, 1993.

Thelan, H.A. and Withall, J., 'Three Frames of Reference: The Description of Climate', *Human Relations*, Vol. 2, No. 2, 1979, pp. 159–76.

Thomason, G., *A Textbook of Industrial Relations Management*, IPM, London, 1984.

Thurley, K. and Wood, S., *Industrial Relations and Management Strategy*, Cambridge University Press, Cambridge, 1983.

Tiernan, F., 'Sexual Harassment in the Workplace', *IPM News*, Institute of Personnel Management (Ireland), February 1993.

Toner, B., 'Union or Non-Union–Employee Relations Strategies in the Republic of Ireland', unpublished Ph.D. thesis, London School of Economics, 1987.

Torrington, D. and Hall, L., *Personnel Management: A New Approach*, Prentice-Hall, Englewood Cliffs, NJ, 1991.

Towers, B., *A Handbook of Industrial Relations Practice*, 3rd edn, Kogan Page, London, 1992.

Turnbull, P., 'The Limits to "Japanisation": Just-In-Time, Labour Relations and the UK Automotive Industry', *New Technology, Work and Employment*, Vol. 3, No. 1, 1988.

Turner, H., *Trade Union Growth, Structure and Policy*, Allen and Unwin, London, 1962.

Turner, T., 'Unionisation and Human Resource Management in Irish Companies', *Industrial Relations Journal*, Vol. 25, No. 1, 1993.

Turner, T., Morley, M. and Gunnigle, P., 'Developments in Industrial Relations and Human Resource Management in the Republic of Ireland', *Journal of Irish Business and Administrative Research*, Vol. 15, 1994.

Tyson, S., 'Is This the Very Model of the Modern Personnel Manager?', *Personnel Management*, May 1985.

Tyson, S., 'The Management of the Personnel Function', *Journal of Management Studies*, September 1987.

Von Prondzynski, F., 'Trade Disputes and the Courts: the Problem of the Labour Injunction', *Irish Jurist*, Vol. 16, Part 2 (winter), 1981.

Von Prondzynski, F., 'Operating a Disciplinary Procedure: The Essential Requirements', *Industrial Relations News*, No. 45, 26 November 1982.

Von Prondzynski, F., 'The Death of the Pay Round', *Industrial Relations News*, No. 43, 16 November 1985.

Von Prondzynski, F., 'Social Partnership in Ireland and Austria', in A. Matthews and A. Sagarri (eds.), *Economic Performance in Two Small European Economies: Ireland and Austria*, Trinity College, Dublin, 1988.

Von Prondzynski, F., 'Collective Labour Law', in *Industrial Relations in Ireland: Contemporary Issues and Developments*, University College Dublin, 1989a.

Von Prondzynski, F., *Employment Law in Ireland*, Sweet and Maxwell, London, 1989b.

Von Prondzynski, F., 'Ireland between Centralism and the Market', in A. Ferner and R. Hyman (eds.), *Industrial Relations in the New Europe*, Blackwell, Oxford, 1992.

Wallace, J., 'Selected Aspects of Employment Legislation', mimeo, University of Limerick, 1987.

Wallace, J., 'Workplace Aspects of Unofficial Strikes', *Industrial Relations News*, No. 9, 3 March 1988a.

Wallace, J., 'A Review of Proposed Reforms of Trade Disputes Legislation in Ireland', *Advances in Business Studies*, Vol. 1, No. 2, 1988b.

Wallace, J., 'Procedure Agreements and their Place in Workplace Industrial Relations', in *Industrial Relations in Ireland: Contemporary Issues and Developments*, University College Dublin, 1989.

Wallace, J., 'The Industrial Relations Act 1990 and Judicial Constructivism: A Threat to Neo-Corporatism in Ireland?', paper presented to the University of Cardiff conference entitled 'The Future of Employment Relations: International Comparisons in an Age of Uncertainty', University of Cardiff, 1991a.

Wallace, J., 'Selected Aspects of Employment Legislation', mimeo, University of Limerick, 1991b.

Wallace, J., 'The Industrial Relations Act 1990 and Other Developments in Labour Law', paper presented to the Mid-West Chapter of the Institute of Personnel Management, University of Limerick, November 1991c.

Wallace, J., 'Industrial Relations: An Economic, Social, Political and Legal Perspective', mimeo, University of Limerick, 1994.

Wallace, J. and O'Shea, F., *A Study of Unofficial Strikes in Ireland*, Government Publications Office, Dublin, 1987.

Walton, R.E., 'From Control to Commitment in the Workplace', *Harvard Business Review*, March/April 1985, pp. 77–84.

Walton, R.E. and McKersie R.B., *A Behavioral Theory of Labor Negotiations*, McGraw-Hill, New York, 1965.

Warr, P., *Psychology and Collective Bargaining*, Hutchinson, London, 1973.

Webb, B. and Webb, S., *Industrial Democracy*, Longman, Harlow, 1897.

Webb, S. and Webb, B., *The History of Trade-Unionism*, 2nd edn, Longman, Harlow, 1920.

Wedderburn, K.W., *The Worker and the Law*, Penguin, Harmondsworth, 1965.

Wedderburn, Lord, *The Worker and the Law*, Penguin, London, 1986.

Wheelan, T.L. and Hunger, J.D., *Stategic Management*, Addison Wesley, London/New York, 1990.

Whelan, C., 'Worker Priorities, Trust in Management and Prospects for Worker Participation', Paper 111, Economic and Social Research Institute, Dublin, 1982.

Wilkinson, A. and Oliver, N., 'Fitness for Use? Barriers to Full TQM in the UK', *Management Decision*, Vol. 29, No. 8, 1992.

Wilkinson, A., Redman, T. and Snape, E., *Quality and the Manager*, Institute of Management, London, 1993.

Wilkinson, B. and Oliver, N., 'Obstacles to Japanization: The Case of Ford UK', *Employee Relations*, Vol. 12, No. 1, 1990.

Windmuller, J.P., 'Employers' Associations in Comparative Perspective: Organisation, Structure and Administration', in J.P. Windmuller and A. Gladstone (eds.), *Employers' Associations and Industrial Relations: A Comparative Study*, Clarendon Press, Oxford, 1984.

Wood, S., 'Ideology in Industrial Relations Theory', *Industrial Relations Journal*, Vol. 9, No. 4, 1978/79.

Wood, S. and Pecci, R., 'Preparing for 1992? Business Led versus Strategic Human Resource Management', *Human Resource Management*, Vol. 1, No. 1, Autumn 1990.

Worsley, P. (ed.), *Introducing Sociology*, Penguin, London, 1977.

Yeates, P., 'Personnel Managers Favour a New PESP', *Irish Times*, 21 December 1993.

Index

Abbott and Whelan v Southern Health Board (1981), 117

Abell, D.F., and Hammond, J.S., 250

absenteeism, 36, 219

accidents. *see* health and safety at work

adversarial collective bargaining, 200, 201, 211, 212, 301

Advisory Conciliation and Arbitration Service (UK)
  code of practice (1977), 229, 230, 232

advisory service, 84-5

AEEU, 104

agriculture
  employment changes, 1961-92, 16

Ahern, Bertie, 57, 59, 196

all-out pickets, 110

Allen, V., 212

Amalgamated Engineering and Electrical Union, 104

Amalgamated Society of Engineers, 103

Amalgamated Society of Railway Servants, 52

Amalgamated Transport and General Workers' Union (ATGWU), 124

amalgamations and mergers. *see* trade union rationalisation

annual delegates' conferences, 109-10

Anthony, P.D., 164-5, 170

Anti-Discrimination (Pay) Act 1974, 89, 331. *see also* equal pay
  determination of disputes under, 75

anti-union organisations, 295

appeals. *see also* Employment Appeals Tribunal
  EAT decisions, from, 79

equality officers' decisions, from, 71, 72, 74

Rights Commissioners' recommendations, from, 71, 74, 76, 88, 89

appraisal, 261

apprenticeship system
  historical background, 8

approaches to industrial relations. *see* State approaches to industrial relations

arbitration, 226-7

Armstrong, M., 238, 260

army representative associations
  membership, 112

Association of Scientific Technical and Managerial Staffs (ASTMS), 105

Association of Secondary Teachers of Ireland (ASTI), 106

ASTMS, 105

Atkinson, G., 211, 236

Atkinson, J., 308

Atkinson, P., and Naden, J., 329

attitude surveys, 315

Attley, Bill, 190, 191

atypical employment, 17-18, 296
  growth of, 306-8

'authorised trade unions', 55, 117

authoritarianism, 25

auxiliary State control, 66, 69

Bain, G.S., 97

Bain, G.S., and Elias, P., 116

Bain, G.S., and Elsheikh, F., 116, 121

Bain, G.S., and Price, R., 115, 116

bargained corporatism, 68, 69
bargaining. *see* collective bargaining;
    individual bargaining
Barret, S., 194
Barrington, D., 42
Batstone, E., 292
BATU, 104
Bean, R., 213
Beaumont, P., 126, 171, 172
Beaumont, P., and Harris, R., 121, 295
Beaumont, P.B., 169
Beer, M., 125, 238, 239, 241, 242, 247,
    261, 263, 269, 272, 279, 284, 285,
    286, 293, 294, 295, 314, 317, 318
Bell, A., 323
Bell, Richard, 52
Bendix, R., 278
Benson, I., and Lloyd, J., 324, 325
Bew, P., 14
Blennerhasset, E., and Haskins, J., 325
Blyton, P., and Morris, J., 247
Blyton, P., and Turnbull, P., 246, 247, 264
Bonner, K., 58, 75, 80
Booth, A., 116
Bowey, A., 220
Boyd, A., 7, 8, 103, 104
Brady, T., 118, 152, 303
branch level trade union structure, 109
Bratton, J., and Gold, J., 329, 334
Breen, R., 178, 179, 184, 302
Brewster, C., 325, 328
Brewster, C., and Hegewich, A., 114
Briscoe, T., 42
British unions, 124
Brown, W., 144, 145, 148, 152, 158
Browne, Edmund, 195
Building and Allied Trades' Union, 104
Business and Finance, 191, 196
business-led human resource
    management, 279
business strategy
industrial relations styles, and, 275-6
personnel/IR policy link, 238, 248, 253-5,
    264-5
    'defenders, prospectors, analysers'
      model, 255

    'life cycle-employee characteristics'
      model, 258-60
    'strategy implementation' model, 260-
      61
business strategy
    product market change and, 262-3
Butler, J.E., 261
Butler, P., 154
Byrne, R., 42

Calmfors, L., and Drilfill, J., 172
Campbell, A., 251, 280
Canning, L., 204
capability
    dismissals pertaining to, 36
Carroll, C., 239, 280
Carroll, C., and Byrne, R., 42
Carroll, John, 58, 190
casual work
    union status and, 130
Central Review Committee, 142
centralised bargaining, 21, 159, 172-3,
    302-3, 331
    European Union, influence of, 333-4
    national understandings (1979-1980),
      184-6, 187. *see also* national
      understandings
    national wage agreements (1970-78),
      179, 180-84, 186-7. *see also* national
      wage agreements
    performance of agreements, 1970-81,
      186-7
    positive benefits, 196
    Programme for Competitiveness and
      Work (PCW, 1994-1997), 195-7
    Programme for Economic and Social
      Progress (PESP, 1990-1993), 193-5
    Programme for National Recovery
      (PNR, 1987-1990), 189-93
    wage rounds, 176-7
Chamberlain, N.W., and Kuhn, J., 165,
    166
Chamberlain, N.W., 311
Chandler, A.D., 254, 261
change in industrial relations, 304
    atypical employment, growth of, 306-8

flexibility debate, 308-10
labour market developments, 304-6
CIE (Coras Iompair Eireann), 55
CIF. *see* Construction Industry Federation
CII. *see* Confederation of Irish Industry
Circuit Court
    appeals from EAT decisions, 79
Civil and Public Services Union (CPSU),
    106
civil conspiracy, 51-2
civil service
    access to adjudication bodies, 93
    Conciliation and Arbitration scheme,
      92
Clarke, K., and Clarke, K., 288
Clegg, H., 23, 161
closed shop arrangements, 91, 117
co-operative bargaining, 201, 211-12
Coates, K., and Topham, A., 311
codes of practice, 85-6
    employee representatives, 107-8
Cole, G.A., 206
collective agreements, 23, 170
collective bargaining, 6, 23, 161-2
    advantages, 170-71
    adversarial model, 200, 201, 211, 212,
      301
    appraisal, 170-72
    bargaining form, 169-70
    bargaining levels, 167-8
    bargaining scope, 170
    bargaining units, 169
    beginnings, 174-5
    centralised bargaining, 159, 172-3. *see*
      also centralised bargaining
      developments, 176-97
    co-operative model, 201, 211-12
    collective agreements, 23, 170
    company level bargaining, 173
    conflict resolution, 220-21
    consensus of agreement, 166
    consent, 171
    corporatist approach, 173
    criticisms of, 171
    decentralised bargaining (1982-87),
      158, 159, 187-9, 302

definitions, 165-6
development in Ireland, 173-97
distributive bargaining, 200, 211
economic efficiency, 171
employer associations, role of, 157-9
enterprise-level collective bargaining,
    158-9, 187-9
European Union, influence of, 333-4
flexibility, 170
'free' collective bargaining, 158, 159,
    187-9
future of, 197-8
governmental theory, 165
industry-wide bargaining, 173
Irish system, 172-3
labour market changes and, 18
local bargaining, 158-9, 193, 196, 199
managerial theory, 165-6
marketing theory, 165
multi-employer bargaining, 158, 167,
    168-9, 199
multi-establishment bargaining, 167,
    169
national-level tripartite bargaining, 20,
    173, 179
national understandings (1979-1980),
    184-6; *see also* national
    understandings
national wage agreements (1970-
    1978), 179-84; *see also* national wage
    agreements
nature of, 162-5
negotiation licences, 102
participation through, 315, 316
practice, 199-200. *see also* discipline
    administration; grievance handling;
    industrial conflict; industrial
    relations negotiations
principal feature, 161
Programme for Competitiveness and
    Work (PCW), 195-7
Programme for Economic and Social
    Progress (PESP), 193-5
Programme for National Recovery
    (PNR), 189-93
single-employer bargaining, 167-8,
    169, 199

collective bargaining *contd*
statutory control, 179
  structure, 167-70
  union recognition. *see* trade union
    recognition
  voluntaristic system, 172
  wage rounds, 175-9
  workplace bargaining, 167-8, 199-200
collective labour law, 49-50, 91
  categories of, 49-50
  evolution of, 50-55
  reform of, 55-8. *see also* Industrial
    Relations Act 1990; trade disputes
    law; trade union law
  summary of legislation enacted by
    Oireachtas, 54
collective redundancies, 49
collectivism, 281-3
colonial exploitation, 11
combinations, 7-8
commercial State bodies
  access to adjudication bodies, 93
Commission of Inquiry on Industrial
  Relations. *see* Report of the
  Commission of Inquiry on Industrial
  Relations (1981)
Commission on Industrial Relations 1972
  (UK), 154
Committee on Industrial Organisation, 20
communications. *see* management-
  employee communications
Communications Workers' Union
  (CWU), 106
compensation for unfair dismissal, 38
competence
  dismissals pertaining to, 36
competitive advantage, 238-9, 253
competitive strategy, 252-3. *see also*
  business strategy
  cost leadership, 253
  focus, 253
  product differentiation, 253
competitiveness
  unionisation, and, 116
conciliation and arbitration schemes
  public sector, 92

conciliation service, 71, 82-4
  increase in referrals, 83-4
  origins of, 82
  referrals, 1971-92, 83
  transfer of functions to Labour
    Relations Commission, 81-2, 83
Confederation of British Industry (CBI),
  143
Confederation of Irish Industry (CII), 9,
  136, 155
conflict. *see* industrial conflict
conflict resolution, 220-21
Conniffe, D., and Kennedy, K.A., 187
Connolly, James, 19
conspiracy
  civil, 51-2
  criminal, 50, 51
Conspiracy and Protection of Property
  Act 1875, 51, 52
Constitution of Ireland 1937, 50, 71
  freedom of association, 91, 117, 175,
    303
  personal rights, 91
Construction Industry Federation (CIF),
  138, 139, 156
Construction Industry Joint Industrial
  Council, 86
constructive dismissal, 34, 37
contemporary developments in industrial
  relations, 301
  atypical employment, 306-8
  centralised agreements, 302-3
  change in industrial relations, 304-10
  employee participation, 310-18
  European Union and, 331-4
  flexibility debate, 308-10
  freedom of association, 303
  industrial development, 303
  labour market developments, 304-6
  management-employee
    communications, 318-20
  new work organisation and quality
    initiatives, 326-31; *see also* total
    quality management public policy,
    302-4
  technological change, 320-25

contextual setting of industrial relations, 6-7
  economics, 10-14
  historical factors, 7-10
  labour market, 14-18
  political factors, 18-22
contract for service
  contract of service distinguished, 32-3
contract of employment, 32, 91-2
  contracts of service and contracts for service, 32-3
Coras Iompair Eireann (CIE), 55
Cordova, E., 306
Cork City, 7-8
Cork Employers' Organisation, 174
corporate culture, 253-4, 294
corporate strategy, 249, 250-51, 252
corporatism, 66-7, 272
  bargained corporatism, 68, 69
  State corporatism, 67, 68
cost leadership strategy, 253
Cox, B., and Hughes, J., 92
CPSU (Civil and Public Services Union), 106
Cradden, T., 246
craft unions, 8, 103-4
  engineering unions, 104
  ICTU membership, share of, 104
Cressey, P., 327
criminal conspiracy, doctrine of, 50, 51
Crouch, C., 63, 65, 67, 236
culture, 253-4, 294
currency crisis (1993), 196
CWU (Communications Workers' Union), 106

Dahrendorf, R., 24
Dairy Executives' Association (DEA), 111
Daniel, W., 17, 325
Daniel, W., and Hogarth, T., 325
Daniel, W., and Millward, N., 148, 152, 334
Dastmalachian, A., 304
data protection, 48
Data Protection Commissioner, 48
De Cieri, H., 116

Deaton, D.R., 291-2
Deaton, D.R., and Beaumont, P.B., 169
decentralised bargaining, 69, 187-9, 302
  private sector pay increases, 1981-87, 188
Deery, S., and De Cieri, H., 116
Delbridge, R., and Turnbull, P., 330
Deming, W.E., 328
Department of Enterprise and Employment, 112, 214
Department of Finance, 144
  public sector industrial relations, role in, 94
Department of Labour, 33, 56, 57, 58, 59
differentiation strategy, 253
Digital, 147
Dineen, D., and Wallace, J., 191
Dineen, D.A., 17, 304, 305, 306
direct discrimination, 40
disciplinary procedures, 35, 228, 229-30
  ACAS (UK) code of practice, 229, 232
  interviews, 233-4
  objectives, 229
  record keeping, 232-3
  representation, 232
  right of appeal, 233
  rules and standards, 229-30
  sample procedure (manufacturing company), 231
  warnings, 230, 232
discipline administration, 227-8. see also disciplinary procedures
  disciplinary rules, 228
  legal context, 228-9
  management approaches, 233-4
  natural justice, principles of, 228
  procedures, 228, 229-35
discrimination. see also employment equality; equal pay
  direct discrimination, 40
  indirect discrimination, 40
dismissals. see also unfair dismissals
  minimum notice legislation, 46
  summary dismissal, 229, 236
dispute resolution facilities, 69-71
  advisory service, 84-5

dispute resolution facilities *contd*
    codes of practice, 85-6
    conciliation service, 82-4
    Employment Appeals Tribunal, 76-9
    Employment Equality Agency, 90-91
    Equality Officers, 89-90
    Joint Industrial Councils, 86
    Joint Labour Committees, 86, 87
    Labour Court, 71-6
    Labour Relations Commission, 80-82
    Rights Commissioners, 87-9
disputes investigation. *see* dispute
    resolution facilities
disputes procedures, 75, 222-5
    arbitration, 226-7
    documentation, 226
    employer associations, role of, 159
    grievance interview, 225-6
Disraeli, Benjamin, 51
distributive bargaining, 200, 211
Donnelly Mirrors, 314
Donovan Commission, 1968 (UK), 75,
    142, 157, 162
Dore, R., 278
Doyle, Maurice, 194
Drilfill, J., 172
Dubin, R., 23
Dublin Employers' Federation, 9
Dublin lock-out (1913), 9-10, 96, 104, 175
Dublin Wholesale Fruit and Vegetable
    Trade JIC, 86
DUES data series, 112
Duffy, K., 56, 62, 81, 84, 86
Dunlop, John, 28
Dunnes Stores, 278

EAT. *see* Employment Appeals Tribunal
Economic and Monetary Union
    disciplines imposed by Maastricht
    Treaty, 332-3
Economic and Social Research Institute
    (ESRI), 318
economic performance
    managerial styles in industrial
    relations, and, 272
economics, and industrial relations, 10-14

foreign debt, 13
labour market, 14-18
'new realism', 14
trade union membership levels, 11-14
*Educational Company of Ireland v Fitzpatrick
    and Others* (1961), 117
Edwardes, P., 292
EEA. *see* Employment Equality Agency
ELC. *see* Employer-Labour Conference
Elias, P., 116
Elsheikh, F., 116, 121
Emergency Powers Act 1939, 175
emigration, 305
employee communications. *see*
    management-employee
    communications
employee development, 127, 261
employee grievances. *see* grievance
    handling
employee involvement, 242
    quality circles (QC), 327
employee participation, 310-18, 334
    achieving participation, 317-18
    attitude surveys, 315
    collective bargaining, 315, 316
    equity participation, 313, 316
    European Union measures, 312
    IPM/IDA code of practice, 311
    job/work participation, 314-15
    options, 312-13
    representative participation, 313, 316
    smaller-scale initiatives, 315
    suggestion schemes, 315
    trade unions and, 315-17
    trust, 317-18
    Vredeling Directive, 312
Employee Relations Services Ltd (ERS),
    147, 148
employee representatives. *see also* shop
    stewards
    code of practice, 107-8
employer association membership, 143-5
    advantages and disadvantages of
    membership, 145-8
    corporate personnel philosophy and,
    147

costs, 148, 150
figures, 1993, 136
foreign-owned companies, 144, 152
greenfield companies, 147, 152, 153
management approaches in industrial
    relations, and, 152-3
public sector organisations, 144
size of organisation and, 144-5
trade union recognition, and, 152
US-owned companies, 144, 147
employer association services, 143, 153-4
collective bargaining, 157-9
disputes procedures and adjustment,
    159
education and training, 157
representation, 155-7
research and advisory services, 154-5
employer associations, 133-4. *see also*
    employer association membership;
    employer association services
authority and control over member
    firms, 150-51
categories, 135-6
Construction Industry Federation
    (CIF), 138
costs of membership, 148, 150
definition, 134
early employer associations, 174-5
governing structure, 148-51
historical development, 9, 135
IBEC, 136-8, 151. *see also* Irish Business
    and Employers' Confederation
industrial relations role, 141-2
informal groupings, 139-40
Irish Employers' Confederation (IEC),
    139
Irish Hotels Federation, 138
Licensed Vintners' Association, 138
Limerick Employers' Association, 138
membership. *see* employer association
    membership
objectives of, 140-43
political role, 140-41, 142-3
services to members. *see* employer
    association services

Society of the Irish Motor Industry
    (SIMI), 138
sources of revenue, 150
trade associations distinguished, 134,
    136
Employer-Labour Conference (ELC), 69,
    142, 178
national wage agreements, role in,
    180-81, 182
reconstitution, 179
State representation, 94
employers. *see also* employer associations;
    employer's liability
industrial relations objectives, 133-4
insolvency, 49
State as employer, 92-4; *see also* public
    sector
technological change, and, 322-3
Employers' Executive Committee, 174
employer's liability, 42-3
employer's duty of care, 43
safe place of work, 43
safe system of work, 43
vicarious liability, 43
employment
labour market developments, 14-18,
    304-6
Employment Appeals Tribunal, 24, 76-9,
    235
appeals from determinations, 79
applications to, 78
composition, 78
decisions, 78-9
employer representation, 143, 156
evidence to, 78
functions, 76
hearings, 78
jurisdiction, 76
minimum notice cases, 46
natural justice, requirements of, 78
number of referrals, 1978-93, 79
outcome of appeals, 77
procedures, 78
representation, 78
unfair dismissals cases, 33, 35
workload, 77

employment equality, 38-40
  claims procedure, 40-41
  direct discrimination, 40
  disputes determination, 75-6
  disputes investigation, 89-90; see also
    Equality Officers
  indirect discrimination, 40
  remedy routes, 40-41
  sexual harassment, 41
Employment Equality Act 1977, 39-40, 75,
  89, 331-2
Employment Equality Agency (EEA), 40,
  75, 90-91, 142
  Code of Practice, 40
  Model Equal Opportunities Policy, 40
employment law. see labour law
Employment Regulation Orders, 87
Enderwick, P., 98
engineering craft unions
  percentage share of ICTU
    membership, 104
enterprise-level collective bargaining, 159
EOLAS, 327
equal pay, 39, 89
  arrears, 39
  claims procedure, 40
  disputes determination, 75-6
  disputes investigation, 89-90; see also
    Equality Officers
  remedy routes, 40
equality legislation. see employment
  equality; equal pay
Equality Officers, 89-90
  appeals from recommendations, 71,
    72, 74
  functions, 89
  investigation of disputes, 90-91
  number of recommendations, 1978-
    92, 90
equity participation, 313-14, 316
EROs. see Employment Regulation Orders
ERS. see Employee Relations Services Ltd
ESRI (Economic and Social Research
  Institute), 318
EU. see European Union
European Community, 21, 22. see also
  European Union

Joint Opinions (1991), 324
European Foundation for the
  Improvement of Living and Working
  Conditions, 42, 323
European-owned companies
  trade union recognition, 119
European Parliament, 22
European Union
  developments in industrial relations,
    331-4, 335
  employee participation, 312
  labour law, influences on, 331-2
  national bargaining, influence on,
    333-4
  Social Action Programme, 332
  Social Chapter, 332, 333
  social policy developments, 332
'excellence' literature, 239

Farnham, D., and Pimlott, J., 70, 163
FAS (Foras Aiseanna Saothair), 142
Federated Union of Employers (FUE), 9,
  136, 139, 155, 176
  decentralised bargaining (1982-87),
    188
  maintenance craftsmens' dispute, 178-
    9
  national understandings, 185, 186
Federated Workers' Union of Ireland
  merger with ITGWU, 99, 105. see also
  Services Industrial Professional and
  Technical Union
Federation of Builders, Contractors and
  Allied Employers, 139
Federation of Irish Employers (FIE), 57,
  136, 138, 153, 155
Feigenbaum, A., 239
female employment, 15, 16, 17, 305, 307
Fennell, C., and Lynch, I., 33, 35, 38, 39,
  45, 49, 75, 78, 79, 236
Fianna Fail, 20, 21, 184, 190, 302-3
FIE. see Federation of Irish Employers
financial control organisations, 251, 252
financial flexibility, 309
financial services sector
  trade unions, 105, 106
Fine Gael, 55

Fine Gael-Labour Coalition (1982), 20-21, 186

Fiorito, J., 125, 126

Fisher, R., and Ury, W., 203, 211, 212, 236

Fitzpatrick, D., 19

Flanders, A., 163-5, 166, 171

flexibility, 6, 246-7, 308-10
  financial, 309
  functional, 309-10
  trade union status and, 128-30

Flood, P., 87, 108, 125, 161, 168, 238, 243, 246, 263, 280, 293, 299, 302, 304, 308, 312

focus strategy, 253

Fogarty, M.P., 186, 187

Foley, K., 287

Foley, K., and Gunnigle, P., 188, 189

Fombrun, C., 238, 248, 254, 260, 261, 264, 293

Foras Aiseanna Saothair. see FAS

Forde, M., 70, 71, 78, 87

foreign debt, 13

foreign investment, 303

foreign-owned companies. see also US-owned companies
  employer association membership, 144, 152
  union recognition, 119-20
  unionisation in, 116

Foulkes, F.K., 225, 278, 292, 295, 296

Fox, A., 23, 25, 29, 64, 164, 165, 171, 212, 213, 267, 289, 291

freedom of association, 91, 117, 175, 303

freedom of expression, 91

Friedman, A., 277, 295

FUE. see Federated Union of Employers

functional flexibility, 309-10

functional strategy, 249

FWUI. see Federated Workers' Union of Ireland

Galvin, D., 313

Garavan, T., 302

Garda Siochana
  access to adjudication bodies, 93

representative association membership, 112

General Strike 1926 (Britain), 96

general unions, 9, 104-5

Gennard, J., 321, 324

Gladstone, A., 154

Gold, J., 329, 334

Goldthorpe, J., 29

Goold, M., and Campbell, A., 251, 280

Government expenditure, 12-13

Gray, A., 267, 281

Green, G., 121, 166

greenfield companies
  employer association membership, 152, 153
  management-employee communications, 320
  trade union influence, 122-3
  trade union recognition, 119, 120

grievance handling, 221-2
  arbitration, 226-7
  definition of grievance, 221
  documentation, 226
  external referral, 226-7
  grievance and disputes procedures, 222-6
  grievance interview, 225-6
  management checklist, 221-2
  responses to, 225-6

Guest, D., 125, 127, 238, 243, 244-5, 246, 247, 248, 251, 263, 264, 269, 272, 277, 281, 282, 286, 293, 294, 295

Guinness' Brewery (Dublin), 321

Guinness Peat Aviation, 278

Gunnigle, P., 32, 43, 45, 46, 47, 49, 99, 114, 115, 116, 118, 119, 122, 123, 127, 128, 131, 144, 145, 152, 167, 188, 189, 209, 212, 213, 240, 247, 275, 293, 299, 304, 315, 320

Gunnigle, P., and Brady, T., 118, 152, 303

Gunnigle, P., and Flood, P., 87, 161, 168, 238, 299, 312

Gunnigle, P., and Kerr, A., 86

Gunnigle, P., and Morley, M., 16, 212, 317

Gunnigle, P., and Shivanath, G., 199

Hackman, J.R., and Oldham, G.R., 276, 317

Hakim, C., 308

Hammond, J.S., 250

Hannaway, C., 264, 299, 302, 304

Harbison, F., 164

'hard' human resource management, 242, 264, 296

Hardiman, N., 176, 178, 183, 184, 189

Harris, R., 121, 295, 296

Harvard Business School (HBS)
HRM model, 238, 241, 242, 246, 247, 263-4

Haskins, J., 325

Hawkins, K., 166, 200, 202, 205, 222, 232, 236

HBS. see Harvard Business School

health and safety at work, 42-5
employer's liability, 42-3
inspectorate system, 43-4
safe place of work, 43, 44
safe system of work, 43
Safety, Health and Welfare at Work Act 1989, 43-5
safety representatives, 45
safety statements, 44
vicarious liability, 43

Health and Safety Authority, 42

health boards
Conciliation and Arbitration scheme, 93

Hendry, C., 293

Hewlett-Packard, 252, 256, 278

high-technology sector. see also US-owned companies
HRM approaches, 240

Hillery, B., 80, 81, 177, 302

Hirsch, B.T., and Berger, M., 115

historical background, 7-10
Dublin lock-out (1913), 9-10
employer associations, 9, 135
trade unions, 7-10, 95-9

Hogarth, T., 325

Hogg, C., 327

holiday legislation, 46, 47

Horgan, John, 75, 187, 227

Horwitz, F.M., 299

Hotel Joint Labour Committee, 138

Hourihan, F., 81, 331, 332, 333, 334

HRM. see human resource management

Hughes, J., 92

human resource flow, 242, 261

human resource management (HRM), 6, 123, 237-40, 293-4
business-led, 279
business strategy and personnel policy choice, 248-9, 253-5. see also business strategy models, 255-62
compensation practices, 127
competitive advantage, quest for, 238-9
competitive strategy, importance of, 252-3
contradictions and inconsistencies, 245-8
definitions, 242
emergence in Ireland, 240
employee communication, 130-32
employee development, 127
'excellence' literature, 239
explicit strategy, 126
flexibility, 128-30, 246-7
Guest's theory (1987), 243-4, 247
'hard' approach, 242, 264, 296
Harvard Business School (HBS) model, 241, 242, 246, 247, 263-4
individualism, 247-8
job security, 247
levels of strategic decision-making, 249-52
nature of, 241-4
non-union phenomenon, 240-41
performance related pay, 127-8
profit-sharing schemes, 127-8
'soft' approaches, 238, 245-6, 263-4, 285, 295-6, 299
strategic, 279
trade unions and, 125-32, 240-41
PWC Project findings, 126-31
traditional personnel management and, 244-5
union recognition, effect on, 125-7
unitarist perspective, 247-8

Hunger, J.D., 249
Hyman, R., 27, 64, 164, 171, 212

Iarnrod Eireann v Darby and O'Connor (1991), 61
IBEC. *see* Irish Business and Employers' Confederation
IBEC/ERSI Monthly Industrial Survey, 154
IBM, 252
IBOA (Irish Bank Officials' Association), 106
ICTU. *see* Irish Congress of Trade Unions
IDATU. *see* Irish Distributive and Administrative Trade Union
IEC. *see* Irish Employers' Confederation
ILO. *see* International Labour Organisation
immunities, 52-3, 57, 58, 60
IMPACT (Irish Municipal Public and Civil Trade Union), 106
Income Data Services, 172, 189
report, 1992, 196
income levy, 194, 195
indirect discrimination, 40
individual bargaining, 99, 162, 164, 165
individual employment law, 31-49, 91
summary of legislation, 45
individualism, 280-81
industrial conflict, 6, 212-13
absenteeism, 219
conflict resolution, 220-21
forms of, 213-14, 219
implicit forms, 213, 219
industrial sabotage, 219
labour wastage/turnover, 219-20
lock-out, 219
managerial attitudes, 290
strikes, 213-18. *see also* strikes
industrial development
approaches to, 303
Industrial Development Authority (IDA), 56
industrial employment
changes, 1961-92, 16, 17
industrial relations, 1-6

contextual setting, 6-7
economics and, 10-14
historical background, 7-10
Irish system of industrial relations, 4-5
labour market and, 14-18
politics and, 18-22
theoretical perspectives, 22-30
Industrial Relations Act 1946, 71, 82
Labour Court, 97
Industrial Relations Act 1969, 72, 73, 74, 82
Rights Commissioners, 87
Industrial Relations Act 1990, 50, 58-9, 91
advisory service, 84
background, 55-9
codes of practice, 85
industrial relations legislation, 60
injunctions, 60, 61, 62
Labour Court provisions, 71-2
Labour Relations Commission, 80, 84
Rights Commissioners' service, 87, 88
secret ballots, 60, 61, 62
trade disputes provisions, 59-60, 61-2, 102
trade unions, 60, 102, 112
industrial relations advisory service, 84-5
industrial relations management
HRM. *see* human resource management
industrial relations negotiations, 200-201
administrative arrangements, 203
adversarial model, 200, 201, 211, 212
alternative approach, 212
bargaining phase, 206-11
bargaining power, 206
bargaining range, 205
co-operative model, 201, 211-12
critical evaluation, 211-12
definition, 200
distributive bargaining, 211
key skills, 204
negotiating process, 201-8
negotiating team, 203-4
objectives, 204-5
'positional' bargaining, 212

industrial relations negotiations *contd*
post-negotiations phase, 211
pre-negotiations issues, 202-6
priorities, 204
research, 203
stages in bargaining, 208-11
strategy and tactics, 206-8
towards effective negotiation, 211-12
Industrial Relations News (IRN), 62
Industrial Relations Officers, 82, 83, 86
industrial relations styles. *see* managerial
styles in industrial relations
Industrial Revolution, 11, 23, 311
industrial sabotage, 219
inflation, 8
information disclosure
union status and, 130-32
Vredeling Directive, 312
injunctions
Industrial Relations Act 1990
provisions, 60, 61, 62
INO (Irish Nurses' Organisation), 106
insolvency of employer, 49
Institute of Personnel and Development
(IPD), 140
Institute of Personnel Management
(IPM), 41, 196, 313
institutions, 2, 5
dispute resolution, for. *see* dispute
resolution facilities
International Labour Organisation
(ILO), 137, 144-5, 163, 174, 175
collective bargaining, 166, 170
International Organisation of Employers
(IOE), 137
INTO (Irish National Teachers'
Organisation), 106
INUVGATA, 106, 138
IPC. *see* Irish Productivity Centre
IPM. *see* Institute of Personnel
Management
IPU (Irish Print Union)
merger with NUJ, 124
Irish Bank Officials' Association (IBOA),
106

Irish Business and Employers'
Confederation (IBEC), 9, 24, 136-8,
139
absenteeism, definition of, 219
collective bargaining, 158
Distribution and Services Division, 137
dual role, 143
Employee Relations Services Ltd
(ERS), 147, 153
governing structure, 151
individual client relationships, 147
Industrial Division, 137
industrial relations role, 142, 144, 156-7
membership subscriptions, 148
mission statement, 137
representational role, 143, 155-6
Research and Information Service, 154
role of, 137
Irish Citizens' Army, 10
Irish Congress of Trade Unions (ICTU),
10, 24, 55, 57, 58, 110-11, 176, 322
all-out pickets, 110
annual delegates conference, 110
craft union membership, 104
Demarcation Tribunal, 110
Disputes Committee, 110
establishment of, 19
Industrial Relations Act 1990, and, 62
Industrial Relations Committee, 110
national understandings, 185, 186
national wage agreements, 179, 182,
183, 184, 185
new forms of work organisation -
report (1993), 316-17, 318
Programme for Competitiveness and
Work, 195-6
Programme for National Recovery,
190-91, 193
public-sector unions, 105-6
quality developments, responses to,
331
role of, 110
unions not affiliated to, 111
Irish Distributive and Administrative
Trade Union (IDATU), 62, 106
Irish Employers' Confederation (IEC), 139

Irish Hotels Federation, 138
Irish Labour Party. *see* Labour Party
Irish Management Institute, 219
Irish Municipal Public and Civil Trade
    Union (IMPACT), 106
Irish National Teachers' Organisation
    (INTO), 106
Irish National Union of Vintners, Grocers
    and Allied Trades Assistants
    (INUVGATA), 106, 138
Irish Nurses' Organisation (INO), 106
Irish Print Union (IPU)
    merger with NUJ, 124
Irish Productivity Centre (IPC), 313
    employer representatives, 143
Irish Quality Association, 328
Irish Trades Union Congress (ITUC), 9,
    10, 19
Irish Transport and General Workers'
    Union (ITGWU), 10, 55, 96, 174
    establishment, 9, 104
    merger with FWUI, 99, 105. *see also*
        Services Industrial Professional and
        Technical Union
    white-collar section, 105
IRO. *see* Industrial Relations Officers
ISO 9000, 327
ITGWU. *see* Irish Transport and General
    Workers' Union
ITUC. *see* Irish Trades Union Congress

Jackson, M., 27, 220
Jackson, S., 258, 259, 260
James, B., 325
Japan
    enterprise unions, 103
    quality circles (QC), 327, 329
Japanese-owned companies
    trade union recognition, 119
Japanese system of industrial relations
    'benevolent paternalism', 278
'Japanisation', 326
Jensen, V., 163
JIC. *see* Joint Industrial Councils
JIT system. *see* just-in-time systems
JLCs. *see* Joint Labour Committees

job enrichment, 276
job security, 247
job/work participation, 314-15
John Lewis Partnership (UK), 314
Joint Board of Conciliation and
    Arbitration for the Footwear
    Industry, 86
Joint Industrial Councils, 71, 86
Joint Labour Committees, 60, 86, 87, 132
    functions, 87
joint problem-solving
    co-operative model of collective
        bargaining, 201, 211-12
joint shop stewards' committee, 109
Journeymen Hatters' Trade Union of
    Great Britain and Ireland, 7
Jurgens, U., 328
just-in-time systems (JIT), 326
    labour co-operation, 330

Kahn-Freund, O., 31
Kanter, R., 239
Kavanagh, R., 19
Keating, M., 199
Keenoy, T., 246, 264, 293, 295
Kelly, A., 87, 88, 97, 105, 226, 313
Kelly, A., and Bourke, P., 102
Kelly, A., and Brannick, T., 125, 214, 216-
    17, 218, 236, 280, 299, 304
Kelly, A., and Roche, W., 57
Kennedy, K.A., 187
Kerr, A., 36, 38, 42, 49, 50, 56, 57, 59, 61,
    101
Kerr, A., and Whyte, G., 53, 73, 82, 86,
    101, 102
Kinnie, N., 169
Klein, J., 330
Kochan, T., 262, 267, 271-2, 273, 275,
    277, 278, 279, 285, 295, 296, 297, 298
Kuhn, J., 165, 166

Labour Court, 55, 71-6
    appeals from equality officers or
        Rights Commissioners, 71, 74
    composition, 72
    conciliation service

Labour Court *contd*
transfer to Labour Relations
Commission, 81-2, 83
'court of last resort', 81
divisions, 72
employer representatives, 143, 156
equality determinations, 75-6
establishment, 97, 175
functions, 71, 81
hearings, 72-3
increase in caseload, 74-5
Industrial Relations Act 1990
provisions, 60
investigation of disputes, 71-3
membership, 72
oral submissions, 73
recommendations, 73-4
referral procedure, 71-2
witnesses, 73
written submissions, 73
labour law, 31. *see also* Industrial Relations
Act 1990; trade disputes law; trade
union law
collective law, 49-62, 91; *see also*
collective labour law
contract of employment, 32-3
data protection, 48
dismissals, 33-8; *see also* unfair
dismissals
employment equality, 38-42
European Union influences, 331-2
health, safety and welfare at work, 42-5
holidays, 46
individual employment law, 31-49, 91-2
minimum notice, 46
part-time workers, 47
payment of wages, 47
pensions, 47
redundancy and ownership changes,
48-9
summary of enactments, 45, 54
young workers, 46
labour market
developments, 14-18, 304-6
employment changes by sector, 1961-
92, 16

labour force classification, 1977-92, 16
managerial styles in industrial
relations, and, 273
technological change, impact of, 17,
321-2
Labour Party, 19
Fine Gael-Labour Coalition (1982), 20-
21, 186
Labour Relations Commission, 24, 57, 60,
71, 80-82
advisory service, 84-5
codes of practice, 85-6
conciliation service, 71, 82-4
employer representatives, 143, 156
Equality Officers. *see* Equality Officers
establishment of, 80-81
functions, 80-81
JICs and JLCs, functions in relation to,
86-7
Rights Commissioners, 87. *see also*
Rights Commissioners' service
labour wastage/turnover, 219-20
laissez-faire economics, 7, 8, 18, 65-6
resurgence of, 22
Land League, 9
Larkin, James, 9, 19, 96, 104
Larragy, J., 11, 99, 105, 112, 114, 123, 124,
302
law. *see* labour law
Lawler, E.E., 314, 317
'lean production', 326
Leddin, A., and Walsh, B., 15
Lee, J., 11, 12, 19
Legge, K., 239, 246
Lehmbruch, G., 67
Leiserson, W., 165
Lemass, Sean, 21, 56, 178
Lennon, P., 235
LGSNB. *see* Local Government and Staff
Negotiations Board
liberal capitalism, 66
liberal collectivism, 66, 69
liberal corporatism, 68
Licensed Vintners' Association, 138
like work
equal pay for, 39

Limerick Employers' Association, 138, 139
Limerick/Shannon Personnel Managers Group, 140
Lincoln Electric, 256
Lloyd, J., 324, 325
local authorities
Conciliation and Arbitration scheme, 93
local bargaining, 158-9, 193, 196
Local Government Staff Negotiations Board (LGSNB), 94, 144
lock-outs, 219
Dublin lock-out (1913), 9-10, 96, 104, 175
low pay, 334
Lynch, I., 33, 35, 38, 39, 45, 49, 75, 78, 79, 236

Maastricht Treaty, 332
McCall, B., 56
McCarthy, C., 12, 13, 57, 73, 80, 98, 175, 177
McGinley, M., 181, 185, 187, 188
McGovern, P., 18, 99, 112, 116, 118, 123, 299, 303, 304
MacInnes, J., 121
McKersie, R.B., 200, 236
McMahon, G., 21, 39, 40, 41, 132, 334
McNamara, G., 96, 104
Madden, D., and Kerr, A., 36, 38
maintenance craftsmen
agreement (1966), 178
dispute with FUE, 178-9
management
by objectives, 314
TQM. *see* total quality management
management-employee communications, 285, 318-20
greenfield companies, 320
Price Waterhouse Cranfield Project, 318-19
trade unions, role of, 319
union status and, 130-32
management values and ideology
industrial relations styles, influence

on, 276-8
managerial prerogative, 290
managerial styles in industrial relations, 267
alternative typologies, 289
frames of reference, 289-91
'ideal-typical' style typologies, 291
analysing styles, 298
changing patterns of industrial relations, 293-9
collectivism, 281-3
dimensions of, 279-83
emergent styles, 298-9
external influences, 272-5
'hard' human resource management, 296
HRM approaches and styles, 293-4
impact of strategic choice on, 270-71
individualism, 280-81
influences on, 271-8
internal influences, 275-6
managerial values and ideology and, 276-8
meaning of management style, 267
neo-pluralism, 296-7, 298, 299
paternalist, 295, 298
personnel policy choice and, 283-8
'soft' human resource management, 295-6, 299
strategic decision making and industrial relations, 268-70
strategic integration, 279-80
traditional anti-union, 295, 298
traditional unionised, 297-8
typology of styles in Irish context, 294-8
manufacturing industry
strike activity, 217
Manufacturing Services and Finance Union (MSF), 106, 124
Marchington, M., 125, 213, 272, 289
Marchington, M., and Parker, P., 267, 268, 271, 273-4, 281, 282, 283, 317
Marciniak, E., 329
Marine Port and General Workers' Union (MPGWU), 105

marital status
  discrimination on grounds of. *see*
    employment equality; equal pay
market individualism, 65-6, 69
Marks & Spencer, 252, 278
Marsh, A.I., 97, 108
Marx, Karl, 64
Marxist analysis, 23, 24, 26-7, 29, 311
  industrial conflict, 212
  State's role in industrial relations, 64
maternity leave, 41-2
Meenan, F., 62, 235
mergers of unions. *see* trade union
  rationalisation
merit pay. *see* performance-related pay
Microsoft, 147
Miles, R.E., and Snow, C.C., 239, 255-6
Millward, N., 148, 152, 334
Milner, S., and Richards, E., 121, 126
minimum notice legislation, 46, 76
minimum wages
  JLC functions, 87
misconduct
  dismissal for, 35-6
MNCs. *see* multinational companies
Monks, K., 199
Morley, M., 16, 212, 317
Morris, J., 247
Morrissey, T.J., 313, 315
Mortished, R.J.P., 73
Motorola, 147
MPGWU, 105
MSF. *see* Manufacturing Services and
  Finance Union
Mulligan, H., 33, 38
multi-employer bargaining, 167, 168-9,
  199
multi-skilling, 6, 246
multinational companies, 98, 303-4
  Vredeling Directive on information
    disclosure, 312
Mulvey, C., 311
Mulvey, K., 81, 82, 84
Mundella, A.J., 82
Munns, V.G., 142
Murphy, T., 33, 235

Murphy, T.V., and Roche, W.K., 235
Murphy, William Martin, 9
Murray, S., 98, 264, 302
Myers, M., 278

Naden, J., 329
national agreements, 173
National Authority for Occupational
  Safety and Health, 43, 44, 142
National Bus and Rail Workers' Union
  (NBRWU), 111
National Economic and Social Council
  (NESC), 142
  A Strategy for Development 1986-1990,
    190
*National Engineering and Electrical Trade
  Union v McConnell* (1983), 236
national executive council, 109-10
National Industrial and Economic
  Council, 20, 69, 179
national level trade union structure, 109-
  11
National Standards Authority of Ireland,
  327
national understandings, 20, 21, 69, 75,
  180, 184-6
  1979 understanding, 185-6
  1980 understanding, 186
  performance of, 187
  terms and conditions, summary of, 185
National Union of Dock Labourers
  (NUDL), 104
National Union of Journalists (NUJ)
  merger with IPU, 124
National Union of Railwaymen (NUR),
  55
National Union of Sheet Metal Workers
  of Ireland, 104
national wage agreements (NWA), 21, 69,
  75, 97-8, 180-84, 302
  1970 agreement, 180, 181
  1972 agreement, 182
  1974 agreement, 182
  1975 agreement, 182-3
  1976 agreement, 183
  1977 agreement, 183-4

1978 agreement, 184
disputes arising from, 181
emergence of, 179
Employer Labour Conference, role of, 180-81, 182
evolution of, 181-4
features, 180
Government involvement, 180, 182, 183
performance of, 186-7
terms and conditions, summary of, 181
National Wage Recommendation, 1964 (NWR), 178
natural justice, principles of, 228
negotiating licences, 54-5, 60, 102, 117
exempted bodies, 102
negotiating process, 201-8
negotiations. *see* industrial relations negotiations
neo-laissez-faire, 14
neo-pluralism, 296-97
NESC. *see* National Economic and Social Council
new technology. *see* technological change
Nierenberg, G.I., 202, 204, 211
1913 Dublin lock-out, 9-10, 96, 104, 175
1918 General Election, 19
non-commercial State bodies
access to adjudication bodies, 93
non-union companies, 18, 21
HRM approaches, 240-41
NUSMWI, 104
NWA. *see* national wage agreements

O'Brien, J.F., 98, 175, 176, 177, 178, 184, 188, 189, 192, 197
O'Connor, K., 235
O'Dwyer, L., 138
OECD, 177, 182
Oechslin, J.J., 134, 135, 142, 144
O'Hagan, J., 11
Oldham, G.R., 276, 317
Oliver, N., and Wilkinson, B., 330
O'Malley, E., 98
'one per cent' income levy, 194, 195
Operative Plasterers' and Allied Trades'

Society of Ireland (OPATSI), 104
Ordnance of Labourers 1349, 31
O'Reilly, Michael (ATGWU), 195-6
organisation structure and style, 254
industrial relations style, and, 275
organisational power cultures
TQM and, 328-9
Osborne v Amalgamated Society of Railway Servants, 53
O'Shea, F., 57, 68, 214, 218, 235
overtime
union status and use of, 130
ownership changes, 49

Parker, P.A.L., 167, 267, 268, 271, 273-4, 281, 282, 283, 317
part-time employment, 6, 15, 306
protective legislation, 47
unfair dismissals, 34
union status and, 130
participative forms of management. *see* total quality management
paternalism, 25, 295
pay determination. *see* collective bargaining
pay practices
unionisation, and, 127-8
payment of wages, 47
PCW. *see* Programme for Competitiveness and Work
Pearson, R., 326
Pecci, R., 279
pensions
legislative provisions, 47
Pensions Board, 47
performance-related pay
TQM and, 328
union status and utilisation of, 127-8
Perlman, S., 164
personal injuries. *see* health and safety at work
personnel management
HRM and, 244-5. *see also* human resource management
personnel policy choice
business strategy link, 238, 248, 253-5, 264-5

personnel policy choice *contd*
    models, 255-62
  communications, 285
  industrial relations style, and, 283-8
  key areas of, 283-8
  recruitment, 286
  reward system, 285
  specialist personnel function, role of, 286
  work system, 284-5
personnel practices
  industrial relations styles, and, 276
PESP. *see* Programme for Economic and Social Progress
Peters, T., and Waterman, R.H., 239, 261, 294
Phelps-Brown, E.H., 171-2
picketing
  all-out pickets, 110
  Industrial Relations Act 1990 provisions, 60, 61
Pimlott, J., 70, 163, 168
pluralism, 66
pluralist analysis, 23-4, 29, 237, 244, 289, 290
  industrial conflict, 212
PNR. *see* Programme for National Recovery (1987)
politics, and industrial relations, 18-22
Pollock, H., and O'Dwyer, L., 138
Poole, M., 63, 67, 267, 271, 272, 273, 275, 277, 278, 292
Porter, M., 238, 252, 253, 254, 261, 275, 293
post-capitalist perspective, 23-4
pre-production agreements, 21
pregnancy
  dismissal on grounds of, 34
  maternity leave, 41-2
Price, R., 115, 116
Price Waterhouse Cranfield Project (PWC), 114, 115, 318-19
  HRM practices and union status, 126-31
  trade union influence, 122
  trade union recognition, 118, 119, 121

private sector
  strike activity, 1960-92, 217
product market
  business strategy, and, 262-3, 273
  managerial styles, influence on, 273-4
professional staff. *see* white-collar unions
profit-sharing schemes
  union status and utilisation of, 127-8
Programme for Competitiveness and Work (PCW, 1994-1997), 69, 142, 173, 195-7, 303
  pay terms, 197
Programme for Economic and Social Progress (PESP, 1990-1993), 69, 158, 173, 193-5, 303
  criticisms, 194, 196
  industrial harmony, commitment to, 194
  local bargaining, 193, 196
  objectives, 193
  pay terms, 193
  performance, 194-5
  public sector protest, 194
  Social Chapter commitment, 332
Programme for National Recovery (PNR, 1987-1990), 21, 58, 59, 69, 158, 173, 189-93, 303
  criticisms, 193, 196
  pay terms, 192
  provisions, 191-2
protectionist economic policies, 11
Psychiatric Nurses' Association (PNA), 111
public policy, 272, 302-4
public sector
  access to adjudication bodies, 93
  Conciliation and Arbitration schemes, 92
  employer association membership, 144
  employment, 307
  industrial relations, 5, 92-4
  strike activity, 1960-92, 217
  trade unions, 105-6
Public Services Executive Union (PSEU), 106
Purcell, J., 250, 251-2, 260, 261, 267-8,

269, 270, 271, 273, 275, 279, 281, 282-3, 298

Purcell, J., and Gray, A., 267, 281

Purcell, J., and Sisson, K., 144, 267, 275, 277, 291, 292, 296, 297

PWC. *see* Price Waterhouse Cranfield Project

quality assurance, 327-8

quality initiatives

quality circles (QC), 327, 329

TQM, 326-31, 334-5; *see also* total quality management

Quality of Working Life movement, 314

Quinn v Leathem (1901), 51-2

Rabbitte, P., 105

Rabbitte, P., and Gilmore, E., 58

Ramsay, H., 322

re-engagement, 37-8

recognition. *see* trade union recognition

recruitment, 286

redundancy

collective redundancies, 49

dismissal on grounds of, 36-7

employer's insolvency, 49

legislative provisions, 48-9

payments, 48

unfair selection for, 36

Redundancy and Employers' Insolvency Fund, 49

Redundancy Appeals Tribunal, 76

redundancy payments, 48

Registrar of Friendly Societies, 50

registration of trade unions, 102

Regular Carpenters of Dublin, 7

reinstatement, 37

remedies for unfair dismissal, 37-8

Report of the Commission of Inquiry on Industrial Relations (1981), 56-7, 58, 85, 92, 117

collective bargaining system, 172

representative participation, 313, 316

Republican politics, 19

reward system, 242, 261, 285-6

Reynaud, J.P., 148

Ribbonmen, 8

Richards, E., 121, 126

Ridgely, P., 148

right to strike, 58

Rights Commissioners' service, 33, 55, 87-9

appeals from decisions, 71, 74, 76, 88, 89

caseload, 88

disputes investigation functions, 87-8, 89

recommendations, 88, 89

Roche, W.K., 18, 66, 68, 69, 112, 114, 118, 123, 180, 185, 186, 212, 235, 237, 245, 294, 298, 299, 301, 302

Roche, W.K., and Larragy, J., 11, 99, 105, 112, 114, 123, 124, 302

Roche, W.K., and Turner, T., 126, 127

Rollinson, D., 65, 277, 332

Rothenberg, I.H., and Silverman, S.B., 278

Royal Commission on Trade Unions and Employers' Associations, 1968. *see* Donovan Commission

safety at work. *see* health and safety at work

safety statements, 44

Salamon, M., 63, 66, 101, 106, 108, 267, 277, 294, 296, 297, 298, 317

Schregle, J., 311

Schuler, R., 258, 261, 314

Schuler, R., and Jackson, S., 258, 259, 260

Scott, B., 202, 211, 236

Second World War, 11, 12, 175

secondary action

Industrial Relations Act 1990 provisions, 60, 61-2

secret ballots

Industrial Relations Act 1990 provisions, 60, 61, 62, 102

selection/promotion/placement, 261

self-employment, 307

semi-skilled workers. *see* general unions

Services Industrial Professional and Technical Union (SIPTU), 123, 195

formation, 99, 105

(SIPTU) *contd*
  membership figures, 105
  percentage share of union
    membership, 124
services sector
  employment changes, 1961-92, 16-17
Sewell, G., and Wilkinson, B., 330
sex discrimination. *see* employment
  equality; equal pay
sexual harassment, 41
Sheehan, B., 195
Shivanath, G., 199, 240
shop stewards, 97, 106-8
  committees, 108-9
  time off for union duties, 107-8
short-term performance indicators, 328
Silverman, J., 28, 214
single-employer bargaining, 159, 167-8,
  169
Single European Act 1987, 22, 332
single independent establishments
  unionisation in, 116
Sinn Fein, 19
SIPTU. *see* Services Industrial Professional
  and Technical Union
Sisson, K., 144, 147, 154, 168, 236, 267,
  275, 277, 280, 291, 292, 293, 294,
  296, 297
Smith, Adam, 133, 135
Snow, C.C., 239, 255-6
social action analysis, 27-8, 30
Social Action Programme (EU), 332
Social Chapter (formerly 'Social
  Charter'), 22, 332
  provisions, 333
  Social Action Programme, 332
social partnership, 21
societal corporatism, 68
Society of the Irish Motor Industry
  (SIMI), 138
'soft' human resource management, 238,
  245-6, 263-4, 285, 295-6, 299
specialist personnel function, 237-8, 286-8
Sproull, A., and MacInnes, J., 121
staff associations, 99-100
  trade unions contrasted, 100

State, 63-4
  corporatism, 67, 68
  dispute resolution institutions. *see*
    dispute resolution facilities, and
    individual institutions
  employer, as, 92-4
  legislative role, 91-2; *see also* labour
    law
  national-level tripartite bargaining, 20,
    173, 179-97. *see also* collective
    bargaining
  public sector industrial relations, 92-4;
    see also public sector
  role in industrial relations, 5, 18-22,
    63-94. *see also* dispute resolution
    facilities; state approaches to
    industrial relations
State approaches to industrial relations,
  65
  auxiliary State control, 66, 69
  bargained corporatism, 68, 69
  changing nature of Irish State
    strategies, 69
  corporatism, 66-7
  liberal collectivism, 66
  market individualism, 65-6, 69
  State corporatism, 67, 68
  State-sponsored bodies
  access to adjudication bodies, 93, 94
Stern, R., 236
Stevens, C.M., 164
Storey, J., 264, 279, 287, 293, 296
Storey, J., and Sisson, K., 280, 294
strategic choice
  impact on industrial relations style,
    270-71
strategic control organisations, 251
strategic decisions, 248-9
  business strategy and personnel policy
    choice, 248-62. *see also* business
    strategy
  corporate strategy, 249, 250-51
  first-order (upstream) decisions, 250,
    251, 252
  functional strategy, 249
  industrial relations, and, 268-9
  levels of strategic decision making,

249-52
personnel/IR policy choices, 248, 250
second-order (downstream) decisions, 250, 251, 252
third-order decisions, 250, 252
strategic HRM, 242, 248, 279; *see also* human resource management
strategic integration, 279-80
strategic management, 248, 254
strategic planning organisations, 251, 252
strikes, 213
    decisions on strike action, 214
    frequency, 1922-91, 214, 215
    influences on strike activity, 218
    Irish strike patterns, 214-18
    official, 213-14, 218
        frequency and working days lost, 1980-91, 218
    private sector, 1960-92, 217
    public sector, 1960-92, 217
    unofficial, 214
        frequency and working days lost, 1980-91, 218
    workers involved, 1922-91, 215
    working days lost
        1922-91, 216
        1946-92, 217
suggestion schemes, 315
summary dismissal, 229, 236
SuperQuinn, 278
Suttle, S., 308
systems analysis, 28-9, 30

Taff Vale Railway Company v Amalgamated Society of Railway Servants (1901), 52, 53
taxation
    'one per cent' income levy, 194, 195
    PESP terms, 194
Taylor, B., 330
teachers
    access to adjudication bodies, 93
    trade unions, 106
Teachers' Union of Ireland (TUI), 106
Teague, P., 333
Technical, Electrical and Engineering

Union (TEEU), 104
technological change, 320-25, 334
    employer and trade union perspectives, 322-3
    implementation, 323-4
    labour market impact, 17, 321-2
    managerial styles in industrial relations, and, 272-3
    technology agreements, 324-5
technology agreements, 324-5
TEEU, 104
temporary employment, 15, 306
    union status and, 130
Texas Instruments, 256
Thelen, H.A., and Withall, J., 289
theoretical perspectives, 22-3
    Marxist analysis, 26-7, 29
    pluralist analysis, 23-4, 29
    post-capitalist society, 23
    social action analysis, 27-8, 30
    systems analysis, 28-9, 30
    unitary analysis, 24-6, 29
third-party dispute resolution institutions. *see* dispute resolution facilities
Thomason, G., 19, 134, 144, 311
Thurley, K., and Wood, S., 262, 263
Tiernan, F., 41
Toner, B., 225, 240, 241, 280
Topham, A., 311
total quality management (TQM), 326-8, 334
    barriers to success of, 328-31
    employee support, 329-30
    features, 327
    industrial relations dimension, 330
    labour co-operation, dependency on, 330
    merits of, 334-5
    organisational structure and, 328-9
    quality circles (QC), 327
    short-termism and, 328
    top management support, 329
totalitarianism, 66
TQM system. *see* total quality management
trade associations, 134, 135-6

trade disputes. *see also* disputes
  procedures; picketing
trade union funds, 102
trade union influence, 122-3
trade union law, 50-55, 59, 91, 101-2
  Industrial Relations Act 1990, 60, 102,
  112
  Trade Union Act 1871, 50-51
  Trade Union Act 1913, 53
  Trade Union Act 1935, 53
  Trade Union Act 1941, 53-5, 59, 117
  Trade Union Act 1971, 55, 59, 117
  Trade Union Act 1975, 59, 60
  Trade Union Amendment Act 1876,
  51
trade union membership, 111-13
  British unions, 124
  decline since 1980, 123
  density. *see* trade union density
  dismissal on grounds of, 91
  distribution, 112
  figures, 1945-90, 111
  freedom of association, 91
  historical background, 11-12
  historical development, 97, 99
  largest unions, 112-13
  organisation level, at, 114-15
  total membership, 111
trade union mergers and amalgamations.
  see trade union rationalisation
trade union rationalisation, 59, 112, 123-4
  Industrial Relations Act 1990
  provisions, 60
  mergers, 123-4
trade union recognition, 117-18, 175, 303
  company of origin, by, 119, 120
  employer association membership
  and, 152
  established companies, 120
  factors affecting, 120-22
  foreign-owned companies, 119-20
  greenfield companies, 119, 120
  human resource management, effect
  of, 125-7
  increased opposition to, in 1980s, 123
  organisation level, 118-20

single-union recognition, 119
  size of company and, 121
  training, and, 127
  workforce characteristics and, 121-2
trade union structure and government,
  106
  annual delegates' conference (ADC),
  109-10
  branch level, 109
  British and Irish unions, 124
  general officers, 110
  Irish Congress of Trade Unions
  (ICTU), 110-11
  national executive council, 109-10
  national level, 109-10
  rationalisation, 123-4
  shop stewards, 106-9
  trades councils, 111
  workplace level, 106-9
trade unions, 95
  alternatives to trade union
  organisation, 99-100
  'authorised' trade unions, 101-2, 117
  British unions, 124
  corporate personality, 52
  craft unions, 103-4
  current issues facing Irish unions, 123-
  32
  declining membership, 123
  democracy, 125
  discipline, 125
  employee participation, and, 315-17
  general unions, 104-5
  government of. *see* trade union
  structure and government
  historical development, 7-10, 95-9
  human resource management
  practices, and, 125-32
  immunities, 52-3, 57, 58, 60
  influence, 122-3
  legal definition, 101
  legal position, 101-2
  legislation. *see* trade union law
  membership. *see* trade union
  membership
  mergers and amalgamations. *see* trade

union rationalisation
negotiating licences, 54-5, 60, 102, 117
non-union companies, 18, 21, 240-41
number, 1980-1990, 124
objectives of, 101
'quality' developments, responses to, 330-31
rationalisation. *see* trade union rationalisation
recognition. *see* trade union recognition
role of, 100-101
shop stewards, 97, 106-9
staff associations contrasted, 100
structure. *see* trade union structure and government
technological change, and, 322-3
types of, 102-6
white-collar unions, 105-6
trades councils, 9, 111, 313
traditional unionised companies
managerial styles, 297-8
training, 127
employer association services, 157
union recognition, and, 127
transfers of undertakings, 49
Turnbull, P., 246, 247, 264, 330
Turner, H., 103
Turner, T., 116, 118, 120, 121, 125, 126, 127, 129, 131, 132, 172, 212, 214
Tyson, S., 287

UCATT, 104
UK
British unions in Ireland, 124
public policy, 302
unemployment, 11, 13-14, 15, 17, 305
unfair dismissals. *see also* unfair dismissals legislation
appeals to Circuit Court, 34
burden of proof, 34-5
constructive dismissal, 34, 37
disciplinary procedures, 35
dismissals deemed unfair, 34
exclusions from scope, 34
fair dismissal, 35-7, 229

capability, 36
conduct, 35-6
redundancy, 36-7
fair procedures, 35
part-time workers, 34
procedure, 33
remedies, 37-8
compensation, 38
re-engagement, 37-8
reinstatement, 37
statutory provisions, 33-5
time limit for claims, 33
unfair selection for redundancy, 36
unfair dismissals legislation
disciplinary procedures, 228-9
Unfair Dismissals Act 1977, 33-5, 76
Unfair Dismissals (Amendment) Act 1993, 33, 34
UNICE, 137
Union of Construction and Allied Trades and Technicians (UCATT), 104
unitarist analysis, 24-6, 29, 289, 290
HRM, 244, 247-8
industrial conflict, 213
University College Dublin, 214
unofficial strikes, 214
unskilled workers. *see* general unions
US-owned companies, 303
employer association membership, 144, 147
strike activity, 218
trade union influence, 122-3
trade union recognition, 119-20
unionisation in, 116, 118

value added tax, 183
vicarious liability, 43
voluntarism, 64, 66
voluntarist tradition, 302
voluntary hospitals
access to adjudication bodies, 93
voluntary wage controls, 68
Von Prondzynski, F., 21, 37, 45, 46, 49, 53, 54, 57, 62, 72, 75, 78, 88, 184, 187, 188, 194, 228, 236
Vredeling Directive, 312

wage payment methods, 47
wage rounds (1946-1970), 158, 175-7
  bargaining level, 176
  evolution of wage rounds, 177-9
  fixed terms, introduction of, 178
Wages Standstill Order (No. 83), 1941, 175
Wallace, J., 52, 56, 57, 58, 61, 62, 70, 75, 81, 85, 191, 202, 214, 221, 222, 227
Wallace, J., and O'Shea, F., 57, 214, 218, 235
Walton, R.E., 244, 246, 247, 292, 298, 314
Walton, R.E., and McKersie, R.B., 200, 236
Wang, 278
warnings, 230, 232
  ACAS (UK) code of practice, 232
Warr, P., 236
Waterman, R.H., 239, 261, 294
Webb, B., and S., 7, 101, 162, 165
  Industrial Democracy, 163
Wedderburn, Lord, 33, 53
welfare state, 12
Westman Holdings v McCormack and Others, 61
Wheelen, T.L., and Hunger, J.D., 249
Whelan, C., 247, 317, 318, 329, 330
white-collar unions, 97, 105-6
Whiteboys, 8
Whitley procedures, 19
Whitley Reports, 1917-18 (UK), 175
Whyte, G., 53, 73, 82, 86, 101, 102
Wilkinson, A., 326, 328, 329
Wilkinson, B., 330
Windmuller, J.P., 140, 148-9
women in employment, 15, 16, 17, 305, 307

Wood, S., 30, 262, 263
Wood, S., and Pecci, R., 279
work-based associations, 99-100
work system, 242
  redesign, 284-5
worker directors, 313, 316
worker participation. see employee participation
Worker Participation (State Enterprises) Act 1977, 312
Worker Protection (Regular Part-Time Employees) Act 1991, 34
Workers' Party, 58
Workers' Union of Ireland, 104
workforce characteristics
  industrial relations styles, and, 276
workforce management, 240. see also human resource management
workplace bargaining, 167-8, 199, 315
workplace industrial relations, 199-200. see also discipline administration; grievance handling; industrial conflict; industrial relations negotiations
Workplace Industrial Relations Survey 1980 (UK), 291
workplace trade union structure, 106-9
  section committee, 108-9
  shop stewards, 106-8
works councils, 316
world-class manufacturing (WCM), 326
Worsley, P., 236
wrongful dismissal, 34

Yeates, P., 196
young persons
  legislative protection, 46